The Management of Service for the Restaurant Manager

SECOND EDITION

Raymond J. Goodman, Jr.

Department of Hospitality Management
The Whittemore School of Business and Economics
University of New Hampshire

IRWIN

Chicago • Bogotá • Boston • Buenos Aires • Caracas
London • Madrid • Mexico City • Sydney • Toronto

© Richard D. Irwin, a Times Mirror Higher Education Group, Inc. company, 1979 and 1996

Irwin Book Team

Executive editor: *Kurt L. Strand*
Editorial assistant: *Kimberly Kanakes*
Marketing manager: *Heather L. Woods*
Project editor: *Amy E. Lund*
Production supervisor: *Pat Frederickson*
Designer: *Matthew Baldwin*
Compositor: *Douglas & Gayle Limited*
Typeface: *10/12 Century School Book*
Printer: *R. R. Donnelley & Sons*

Times Mirror
Higher Education Group

Library of Congress Cataloging-in-Publication Data

Goodman, Raymond J.
    The management of service for the restaurant manager / Raymond J. Goodman, Jr.—[2nd ed.]
        p.   cm.
    Includes bibliographical references.
    ISBN 0-256-18737-1
    1. Food service—Customer services.   2. Restaurant Manager.
I. Title.
TX911.3.C8G66   1996
647.95′ 068—dc20   95-36931

The Management of Service for the Restaurant Manager

As only time distances me from my departed parents, I continue to reflect fondly on my father and my mother and how they contributed to me.

To Rosalie and Chivo—I love you, and I dedicate this second edition to you.

To Louis who always knew.

To Carroll who would have been so proud.

To Helen, Raymond, and David who had to wait.

We may live without poetry,
music, and art;
We may live without conscience and
live without heart;
We may live without friends, we may live
without books;
But civilized man cannot live without
cooks.
He may live without books—what is
knowledge but grieving?
He may live without hope—what is
hope but deceiving?
He may live without love—what is
passion but pining?
But where is the man that can live
without dining?

Anonymous

Preface to the Second Edition

Since the publication of the first edition of *The Management of Service for the Restaurant Manager* in 1979, service and the service industries have hit the big time. Everyone is talking about, writing about, and theorizing and philosophizing about service. Service is on the front cover of *Business Week*, *Newsweek*, and many other popular publications. And, this attention to and focus on service now is 180° out of phase with the feelings on the subject when I first began researching the topic of managing service in the mid 1970s. Indeed, a well-regarded academician back then when presented with a research proposal remarked, "What good will this ever be?" The rest is history.

In 1985, Karl Albrecht and Ron Zemke in *Service America* suggested that their treatise on the subject introduced service management as a concept. Earl Sasser, at the Harvard Business School, published *The Management of Services* in 1979 (the same year that the first edition of this text was published) and certainly knew about the management of the service function long before the book was published. And, the hospitality industry knew about and developed systems to manage service long before that. The Maitre D'Hotel and the Concierge were specifically tasked with managing service. Before 1928, E. M. Statler invoked, "The one who gives a little more, a little more service, is the one who succeeds."

Service *IS* the competitive advantage, and excellent service cannot be copied as easily as the menu or the food presentation, and even, with a little more time, the design and decor. Excellent service speaks to the culture of the organization and fundamentally defines the "total experience service."

Service does need to managed. Yet, service must be managed as unobtrusively as we would wish our servers to serve their guests. As Peter

Drucker said, "Most of what we call management consists of making it difficult for people to get their work done." Witness the hospitality operator who closes her business because, although she offered superb food, she neglected service and, thereby, relegated it to mediocrity at best. Or, the restaurant operator so enamored with technology that he calls his servers *waitrons* and overloads them with point-of-sale devices, hand-held order computers, vibrating or ringing pagers, and the like and forgets that he is in business to give service. Domino's Pizza operations motto is: "If you don't make it, bake it, or take it, then you're the support for those who do." J. Willard Marriott, Jr., feels that his job as CEO of Marriott Corporation (and indeed that of his managers) is to motivate, teach, help, and care about his employees. The employees will then deliver the style of service that the Marriott guests want to receive.

The second edition of *The Management of Service for the Restaurant Manager* is specifically designed to reinforce the collective knowledge historically offered by the hospitality industry. It has also been prepared to address changes that have occurred in the mindset of the guests we serve and who demand even better service. Management techniques and attitudes about giving service have changed significantly, since the first edition, while the technical aspects of dining room service have changed little. Readers will note the inclusion of techniques and service behaviors that acknowledge the trend toward informal dining when compared to a traditional formal dining environment.

The organization of this second edition differs from the first edition with the inclusion of chapter segments, learning objectives, and key words and phrases as each chapter's front matter. The key words and phrases are also in boldface throughout the chapter text to facilitate student understanding. The first seven chapters are managerially focused, and Chapters 8 through 10 are procedurally directed.

Chapter 1 remains structurally the same with substantial updates to the psychology of service that incorporate recent thoughts on service theory. Chapter 2 continues with the historical underpinnings of management and human relations theory with the inclusion of a quality management treatise. Chapter 3 has an expanded discussion of interviewing techniques with an emphasis on behavioral interviewing techniques and a more cautious approach regarding questions that can and cannot be asked during the interview. Chapter 4, "The Types of Service," remains substantially unchanged except for the combination of Chapter 10 from the first edition regarding the modern approach to tableside service. The managerial principles have stood the test of time, yet examples reflect today's current issues. Chapter 5 discusses equipment in general and the new equipment that makes life in the dining room a little easier. An important psychological inclusion in this edition is the discussion of equipment as a design feature. Emphasis on the overall restaurant experience moves the importance of the discussion from the more mundane to equipment's contribution beyond the functional. Chapter 5 now includes the discussion of tableside cookery equipment that previously existed in a separate chapter on tableside cookery. Chapter 6 expands on the importance of sanitation and safety in the service realm by highlighting very recent events that have cast restaurants and their suppliers in a negative light. Indeed, the news media has popularized a fear of communicable diseases such as AIDS, E. coli, Ebola virus, and hepatitis. The front-of-the-house responsibility for sanitation and safety is now more real than ever before when they were only back-of-the-house concerns. Chapter 7 on sales illustrates techniques for improving the top line, but with a caveat: know your market segment and do not overshoot the targeted price points established during the concept and feasibility stages. Chapter 8 has been updated to include the advent of technology as well as considerations for casual dining in addition to fine or more formal dining procedures. As discussed at the beginning of this preface, Chapter 9 remains mostly without modification; the technical aspects of dining room service have seen few changes. Chapter 10 reflects updates on the regions of the world that now produce wines appropriate for restaurant service. And, the popular beer-pub (microbrewery) phenomenon is addressed.

I would like to acknowledge several individuals who helped me with the preparation of this edition. First, Sylvia Marple, my colleague here at the University of New Hampshire, prepared the chapter front matter and revised and updated the questions at the end of each chapter. Thank you, Sylvia. Several industry professionals lent an invaluable hand in the casual theme restaurant procedures addition: Burton "Skip" Sack and Matt Carpenter of Applebee's, Tom Gathers of Uno Restaurant Corporation, and Julie Thompson of California Pizza Kitchen. John Tinios, owner of the Gallery Hatch Restaurant in Hampton, New Hampshire, provided a new-age organization chart and over the several years shared his operational highlights with me. My friends and associates in the Council of Hotel and Restaurant Trainers (CHART) gave me numerous suggestions even when they may not have even known they were doing so. The production crew at Irwin, Kurt Strand, Kim Kanakes, and Amy Lund, were most supportive and helpful. Lastly, the legion of administrative assistants at the Whittemore School, led by Ann Badger of the Department of Hospitality Management, all jumped in to help me when the deadline approached and many details needed to be tied together. Sinthy Kounlasa, Nancy Palmer, and Carol True—thank you. Lastly, I would like to acknowledge the following individuals who reviewed this book: Bharath M. Josiam; University of Wisconsin-Stout, Charles Martin, Spokane Community College; Tannis Reinhertz, City College of San Francisco; Johnny Sue Reynolds, University of North Texas.

Raymond J. Goodman, Jr.

Preface to the First Edition

Service in the United States has traditionally been delegated to European-trained maitres d'hotel who were trained through a long apprentice training program. Trained servers are no longer immigrating to the United States, and the few persons that do immigrate are not trained as waiters. Many are employed for their accents rather than their expertise.

Professor Vance A. Christian at the School of Hotel Administration at Cornell University recognized this fact as well as the fact that even when a food service operator could find skilled servers, he or she did not have the managerial skills to direct the service staffs' efforts. As a result, he asked me to write on and teach a course in service. Certainly there has been instruction in service techniques, yet none was tailored to train future food service, hotel, or hospitality industry executives.

This book is an expansion of the original work which began as a course outline in 1974. Since that time, 230 students per year have studied the Management of Service at Cornell University.

This book will serve three purposes: first, as a *textbook for technical schools, colleges,* and *universities* offering courses in hotel and restaurant administration; second, as a *managerial guide for executives involved in food service;* and third, as a *reference for teachers in food service education* who may not have had the opportunity to study service as a separate discipline.

Much of the service-related literature, although mentioning some management topics, deals mainly in generalities. There are few step-by-step procedures for accomplishing the various tasks necessary to the service function. *There are few specific guidelines* for how one should deal with people—customers or employees. The procedures presented in this text can be used in most service systems.

Research for the book began with an extensive review of any literature that pertained to restaurant service. It was also necessary to interview individuals who had considerable experience in service and to in corporate this information in the text. I held seminars and had personal interviews with these experienced individuals in order to clarify particular shortcomings in the available literature.

The book is divided into two major sections: Part I, "Management," and Part II, "Techniques and Procedures." Chapter 1 discusses the true essence of the hospitality industry—"The Psycology of Service." Chapter 2, "Concepts in Human Relations in Service," is in effect a continuation of Chapter 1; however specific references are directed towards the management of service employees as opposed to guest relations. Chapter 2 incorporates a very brief discussion on the historical development of the human relations movement before launching into the practical aspects of human relations in the dining room. "The Personnel Function in Service," Chapter 3, addresses itself to the manager's duties of organizing, interviewing, selecting, and training service employees. Additional material in Chapter 3 covers the subjects of wages and salaries, tips, performance appraisal, and discipline procedures.

In Chapter 4, a discussion on the types of service—plate, platter, cart, etc.—includes managerial advantages and disadvantages of the types of service. The student will be able to determine which type of service should be instituted when given a series of guidelines. "Equipment used in Service," Chapter 5, is a description of silverware, china, glassware, and other equipment used in the front-of-the-house in a restaurant. In this way the student, the manager, or the teacher may choose the equipment he or she prefers. Chapter 6 on sanitation and safety in service makes no attempt to duplicate the courses presented by NIFI, NRA, and other state and local agencies, but rather proposes to sensitize the student, from yet another perspective, as to how important the subjects of both safety and sanitation are. I honestly feel that we *cannot teach too much* about safety or sanitation.

Part II, "Techniques and Procedures," departs from a general discussion of managerial topics and plunges directly into the how-to approach. Chapter 7, "Sales as a Service Function," however, bridges the gap between a general discussion and teaching service personnel how to sell. The chapter is very short, and it is to the the point. If all servers were knowledgeable in the areas covered in this chapter, management *as well as service personnel* would certainly profit.

"The Director of Service," Chapter 8, was included because a student once came and asked where he could read about how to be maitre d'hotel. In order to fill the need that exists for such information, this chapter begins with a job description, offers a checklist for opening duties and dining room organization, describes a workable reservation system, and literally teaches one how to be a host—from greeting the guests, to seating the guests, to scheduling service personnel. The specific intent is to describe a system that allows one to manage proactively as opposed to reactively. Chapter 9, "The Service Staff: Responsibilities, Procedure, and Techniques," completes the discussion of the system. The chapter begins with job descriptions for all positions in the dining room and subsequently breaks down important standard tasks into step-by-step procedures. A framework is thus established that allows one to complete the breakdown analysis for tasks that may be peculiar to one's operation. This chapter is replete with illustrations that are used to teach proper service procedures.

Chapter 10, "Tableside Service," is a modern departure from the classical approach to Cart Service discussed in Chapter 4. This chapter emphasizes the point that tableside service is not as difficult as the classical approach leads us to believe. Additionally, the advantages and disadvantages of the various pieces of equipment used in tableside cookery are discussed. Chapter 11, "Wine and Beverage Service," not only discusses proper service techniques for serving wine and cocktails, but also provides a short background on wines, spirits, beers, and cocktails. This chapter is also replete with illustrations on proper service techniques.

The appendixes include several interesting sections. The purpose of the glossary and pronunciation guide, Appendix A, is to familiarize the student with both the terminology and the correct pronunciation of menu terms and wines. The presentation in this section is brief. Also included is a myriad of table arrangements, Appendix B, that can be used for banquets, buffets, meetings or conferences, etc. The napkin folding section, Appendix C, includes an *easy-to-understand* guide for folding napkins. Several of the folds are not in any other publication. Appendix D includes a metric conversion table as well as a guide for how to convert to metric.

This book is the culmination of many years of practical experience, research, writing, rewriting and editing, and rewriting. There is no way that I could have done it alone.

I wish first to thank Professor Vance A. Christian for the idea and the opportunity to approach this subject—the management of service. I would be remiss if I did not thank Mrs. Eva Melton for guiding me through the first application of this new approach, and yet I could not have gotten off the ground had it not been for the students and the Cornell Hotel School. My teaching assistants, who have been so close to me and to the course, have given me infinite amounts of feedback—I thank all of you!

I thank Professor James C. White who read the chapter on safety and sanitation and made many helpful suggestions.

I would also like to thank Carol Silvernail, Penny Newland, and Jean Savichky for typing and typing. Jean Pascual, my first editor, was invaluable in giving me encouragement during the early phases; and Janice Lang, my second editor, had to do all the dirty work. Thank you both ever so much.

Joe Durocher has been a sounding board for four years. Sometimes I don't know how he stood it. Thank you, Joe.

I wish to acknowledge my parents, Raymond and Rosalie, who could not be close because they live 1,800 miles away, but who have been an inspiration in my life.

To my two boys Raymond and David, I hope you do not remember when I had to say "Not now honey, Daddy has to work," and to my precious Helen who has lived through an interminable period of writing, writing, writing.

Raymond J. Goodman, Jr.

Contents

The Management of Service for the Restaurant Manager

The Psychology of Service

Chapter Outline

Esteem Needs Related to the
  Restaurant Industry
The Psychology of Service
Remembering Names and Faces
Satisfying the Need for Esteem
Giving Good Service
Special Service Situations

Key Words/Phrases

Procedural dimension
Convivial dimension
Day-part
Attitude
Behavior
Empowerment
Dining experience
Restaurant concept
Maslow's hierarchy of needs
Self-esteem
Return guests
National Restaurant Association
  (NRA)
Order of service
Systems approach
VIPs

Learning Objectives

After studying this chapter, the
student will be able to . . .
1. Define the dimensions of
   quality service.
2. Describe the concept of
   empowering employees to
   satisfy guests' wants, needs,
   desires, and expectations.
3. Explain how the delivery of
   quality service relates to
   Maslow's hierarchy of needs.
4. List the techniques for
   remembering names and faces.
5. Provide examples of three
   situations for anticipating the
   guest's need.
6. Formulate appropriate
   procedures for handling special
   service situations.

The degree to which a restaurant operation meets or exceeds a guest's expectations can establish the reputation of the restaurant. And the restaurant's ability to continue to meet or exceed the expectations of the guests positively strengthens that reputation. Any guest who enters a restaurant has needs, wants, desires, and expectations. If we have marketed to a specific market segment and someone from the targeted market enters the restaurant, we have a match, and the guest's expectations may be met, exceeded, or unmet. If the needs, wants, and desires of a particular guest are mismatched with the restaurant's concept, the restaurant may still be able to meet or even exceed the guest's expectations. When this happens, the guests feel that they have really won! The restaurant wins too.

In a survey, individual customers were asked what single factor best describes service. The top four answers were personal attention, dependability, promptness, and employee competence in that order. William B. Martin condensed quality service to two dimensions supported by categories of actions that define his two dimensions[1]:

Procedural Dimension	**Convivial Dimension**
Accommodation	Attitude
Anticipation	Attentiveness
Timeliness	Tone of voice
Organized flow	Body language
Communication	Tact
Customer feedback	Naming names
Supervision	Guidance
	Suggestive selling
	Problem solving

The manager's task is to identify the behavior and action that the restaurant's market demands. One restaurant may appeal to a different market than another restaurant, and any one restaurant may appeal to different market segments at different times during the day, meal, or week (sometimes referred to as **day-part**). The successful manager is one who has been able to determine what her guests want, whether through sophisticated research or by intuition. The successful manager has also been able to hire and communicate these service standards to the restaurant's service staff.

A server's ability to deliver excellent service depends upon a service orientation that begins with **attitude**. The attitude can be seen or evidenced only by the server's **behavior**, which is a result of the attitude that drives that behavior. A manager will find it difficult, if not impossible, to change a server's attitude. However, the manager can prescribe certain behavior sets through training and can reinforce the desired behavior by rewarding appropriate server behaviors. Nonetheless, the thousands of individual behaviors and interactions with guests that a server engages in during a day can hardly be specifically directed or managed. This lack of control over these behaviors leads to employee **empowerment**. Empowering employees means allowing the employee, at the very moment that a decision needs to be made to satisfy a guest's need, want, or desire, to exercise his or her own judgment in satisfying the guest's need.

A proprietary study I conducted in three urban markets for a family restaurant chain revealed the top service behaviors as rated by frequent guests of the chain and the restaurants' service staffs. Using the critical incident technique (CIT), the service staff should perform following behaviors and be appropriately rewarded by management. These behaviors are time sensitive, specific to family restaurants, and specific to the three geographical markets in which the surveys were taken. While generalizations can be made, the author feels that consumer research should be done frequently and that it is situation specific.

By comparing the ratings of guests to those of the chain's management and service staff, the significant differences in what staff think is important and what guests think is important, we can determine how well we are meeting or not meeting the guests' needs. As you can see, professionals do not feel as strongly about the importance of certain service behaviors as the guests do. The important fact is that, in the eyes of our guests, we may not be training our service staff to be as effective in their

---

The 10 Most Important Behaviors for Servers as Scored by Guests

1. A server is clean (no body odor, bad breath, dirty hands, or is not clean shaven).

2. A server covers his nose and mouth when he needs to cough or sneeze around food.

3. A server responds and renders aid when she sees a guest choking on food or fainting in the dining room.

4. A server gets exactly what the guest orders from the kitchen (that is, she gets the order right).

5. A server asks how guests would like their meat prepared (rare, medium, or well done).

6. A server tries to cover up a mistake in adding the check, and the guest notices the mistake.

7. Items on the buffet are refilled often to avoid customers having "the bottom of the barrel."

8. A server selects a clean glass to serve a beverage in.

9. A server handles flatware by the handle rather than the food contact surface.

10. A server quickly cleans a table when guests are seated at a dirty table in her station.

The 10 Most Important Behaviors for Servers as Scored by Restaurant Professionals

1. A server gets exactly what the guest orders from the kitchen (that is, she gets the order right).

2. A server is clean (no body odor, bad breath, dirty hands, or is not clean shaven).

3. A server tries to cover up a mistake in adding the check, and the guest notices the mistake.

4. A server covers his nose and mouth when he needs to cough or sneeze around food.

5. A server handles flatware by the handle versus the food contact surface.

6. A server comes to work in the proper uniform.

7. A server knows which tables are in his station.

8. When closing at night, servers clean all soiled areas and stock adequately for the morning shift.

9. A server smiles when approaching the table for the first time.

10. A server is well organized.

jobs as they might otherwise be. Managers should modify their standards and training programs to empower the service staff to please the customers and satisfy the guests' wants, needs, desires, and expectations.

When someone comes into your restaurant, she is looking for something more than satisfying the basic hunger or thirst need. Today's sophisticated restaurant guests are looking for far more than gustatory satisfaction when they choose a place to dine. "They are seeking an **experience**—a sensory envelope of sight, sound, taste, smell, and touch that matches a mood or reinforces an image of self. As the mood and the image vary, so does the restaurant experience: It can be funky or formal, casual or opulent, low key or charged with drama."[2]

After the professional restaurateur (who develops the concept) and the architect, interior designer, and contractor have created the intended experience, the direct responsibility of satisfying that "something else" rests with the service personnel (servers) and the manager. It is incumbent upon the manager (for his survival, as well as that of his staff) to satisfy the guest so that she has a positive experience by having her expectations met or exceeded so that she chooses to return to the establishment. Indeed, she may tell many others of her experience.

A discussion of the psychology of service includes an understanding of basic human needs. Several well-known psychologists and psychiatrists have theories about what makes us tick. Most college students are aware of A. H. **Maslow's hierarchy of needs**, and management literature almost always includes descriptions of Maslow's hierarchy of needs when discussing motivation. Certainly, Maslow summarizes what many of the other theorists have postulated, while many others have used Maslow's hierarchy of needs as a framework for their ideas (see Figure 1–1). Few argue with his five basic human needs: physiological, safety, love, esteem, and self-actualization.

1. *Physiological* needs include hunger, thirst, sleep, and sex.
2. *Safety* needs are for protection from danger, threat, or deprivation.
3. *Love* needs are for satisfactory associations with others, for belonging to groups, receiving affection, and friendship.
4. *Esteem* needs for self-respect and respect of others could be labeled ego or status needs.
5. *Self-actualization* (self-fulfillment) needs are to achieve what the individual feels is his maximum potential, development, creativity, and expression.

Figure 1–1

Maslow's hierarchy of needs.

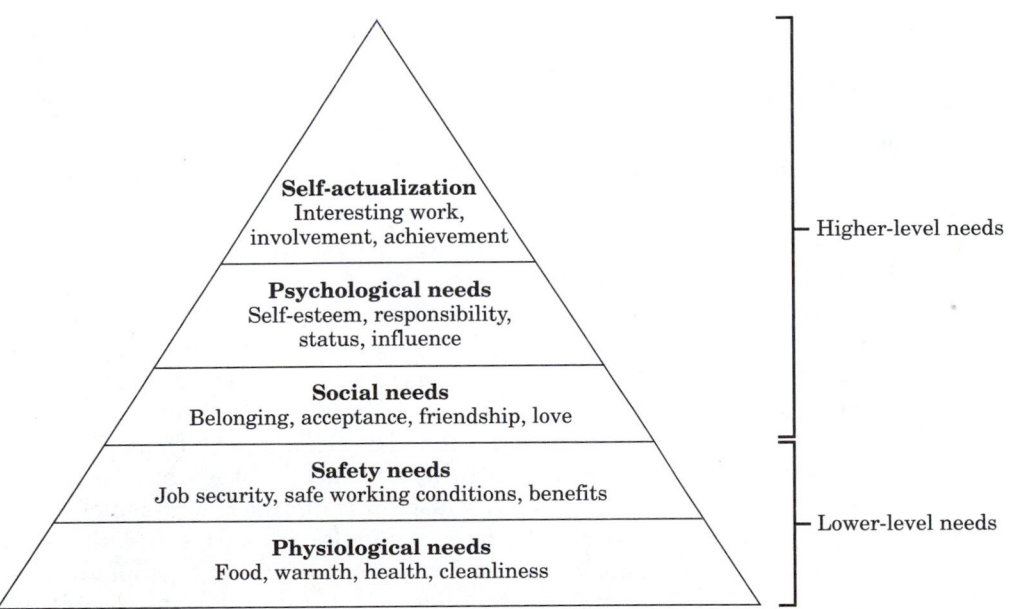

Maslow believed that the basic needs must be significantly satisfied before needs at the next level can be satisfied. However, a person may be satisfying portions of two need levels simultaneously. The need exerting more influence will elicit behavior in response to that need. None of the needs are ever completely satisfied as they tend to recur, but a satisfied (albeit temporarily) need does not motivate behavior. Esteem and self-actualization are rarely satisfied; yet, they cause people to strive for more satisfaction from esteem and self-actualization once they become important.

Self-esteem, status, and success are needs that a service individual can help satisfy for the guest. People need to feel recognized, respected, and approved by friends, and even by enemies. In short, one needs to be recognized by all of those with whom he comes in contact. When these needs are not satisfied, he feels inferior, rejected, isolated, worthless, and resentful. Incidentally, the quest for power, wealth, prestige, and other symbols of status are universal in all societies, but the means of attaining them differ from society to society.

Maslow's notion of self-esteem is related to Hamachek's ideas regarding the self. People tend to relate to others with whom they agree. This fact is one of the most consistent findings in mass communications research. Communications about ourselves are thus either biased in a generally favorable direction or are so ambiguous that our own biases are free to operate. Such is the case suggested by the responses of some adolescent subjects to the question: "What do most people think of you?" Nearly 97 percent said that most people thought well or fairly well of them, and only 3 percent said poorly or very poorly. Even two-thirds of those with low self-esteem attributed such benevolent attitudes towards others. They may, of course, be right. It is possible that a vast wave of mutual love and good engulfs the world. One cannot, however, evade the suspicion that, with the ambiguity inherent in determining another's attitudes, a great many people are giving themselves the benefit of the doubt.

> Groucho Marx once stated that he would never join a club that would accept him as a member.

People find friends and acquaintances and tend to associate with people who think well of them and support their self-concept. They also tend to not make friends or to associate with people whom they dislike or who dislike them. Typically, people like others because they feel liked by that person or persons. Research on groups and on individuals relating to groups corroborates the research findings mentioned above. People cannot always create their own environments, but they can select them. They choose experiences and environments in which they feel they have a fair chance of success—those that match the need or reinforce the image of self. Many select occupations in which their particular interests and skills will be used and appreciated. The need for support influences people in choosing careers, courses or majors in college, lectures, religions, social gatherings, and even places to take their business.

Esteem Needs Related to the Restaurant Industry

The lifeline of the restaurant business is **return guests**. Even a restaurant along a toll road depends on repeat customers. Certainly different tourists travel the roads, but the majority of the people who travel the toll roads travel the same road frequently. A recent study for the **National Restaurant Association (NRA)**, discovered that 78.6 percent of restaurant guests are repeat guests. The few restaurants that do not depend on repeat business include restaurants in a theme park (e.g., Walt Disney World, Great Adventure, Disneyland, Six Flags, Astro World). Any one guest usually goes to a theme park infrequently, spends enough time to see the attractions, and probably eats in different food establishments during the stay. But, the comments made about food and service in general will reflect most positively on the entire experience if the food and service are outstanding and most negatively if the food and service are poor. While most ski resorts are known for greasy food (usually served in a dirty dining room by surly servers), Deer Valley Resort in Park City, Utah, created a distinct competitive advantage with its exquisite gourmet food and impeccable service.

To develop return guests, certain techniques may be used to satisfy the guests by supporting their self-concept, self-esteem, self-image, and so on. In *How to Win Friends and Influence People*, Dale Carnegie outlined techniques for getting people to like you, and these techniques can be modified and used by restaurant managers and staff in the dining room setting.

The Psychology of Service

The restaurant industry is a people business, and those working in the front of the house must be interested—sincerely interested—in serving people. Mike Hurst, of 15th Street Fisheries in Ft. Lauderdale, Florida, and former president of NRA, asks prospective staff members what the funniest thing was that happened to them. Mr. Hurst does not care what happened, he is interested in the person's response. If they can laugh at themselves, he considers them further for employment. Otherwise, the prospective employee will probably not be made a job offer. One of the most important, and emphasized, techniques for demonstrating interest and concern is a smile.

It is easy enough to be pleasant
When life flows along like a song,
But the man worth while
Is the man who can smile
When everything goes dead wrong.

Anonymous

Remembering Names and Faces

Management should train service personnel to remember names and faces.

1. *Get the person's name clearly and distinctly.* Many times when one is introduced to a person, the person mumbles her name. You can't remember a name you have not heard correctly and therefore do not know. Look at the person's face while repeating her name when introduced.

2. *Repeat the name as often as possible in conversation.* This does not mean to conspicuously repeat the name several times, but to use the person's name in conversation as much as possible. "That is really a good idea, Helen." "Where did you say you were from, David?" Each time you repeat a person's name, look at his or her face and make a positive association. In other words, make a concerted, overt effort to record the person's name and face in your mind.

3. *Attach a meaning to the person's name.* The meaning one attaches to the name could be a city, Pat Jackson (Jackson Hole, Wyoming); an object, Marty Caine, Byron Moore (imagine a mooring); an animal, Jaime Lyons; or a nationality/religion, Ken Chew, Don Corleone, Bill Pope, Julie Bishop, and so on.

4. *Write the person's name down, but not in front of her.* This is of great assistance in remembering someone's name. After you get the person's name clearly and distinctly, looking at the written name will reinforce the association.

Satisfying the Need for Esteem

Be a good listener. When handling guest complaints or just conversing, a good service manager should listen attentively and let the other person talk about himself. Two things will result: The person will enjoy listening to himself, and the manager will take less chance of saying the wrong thing. The manager may practice active listening by encouraging the other person to talk more about himself. "That is very interesting, could you tell me more?" Sometimes the manager should remain silent, simply give an affirmative nod or some other encouraging gesture. Do not interrupt; let other people finish their thoughts completely. When you speak, talk about the other person's interest. Find something significant about the person and explore it; even if you have limited experience in the other person's interest, relate your experiences to it as best you can.

Make the other person feel important. This is as easily said as done! Remembering a person's name makes her feel important. Praise also makes people feel important; people love to hear about themselves. There are three types of praise one can use and use sincerely:

- *Physical praise.*   Find something on or about the other person that you like. It could be a piece of jewelry, a tie, a scarf, a hat, a fragrance, and so on. The important thing is to find something that you do, in fact, like so that you can be sincere.
- *Familial praise.*   If a family comes into your establishment, comment to the parents about their children. In a recent informal survey, many servers mentioned how important and how effective it was for them to cater to the children in a family. Parents are certainly flattered by attention given to their child or children and thankful that you have entertained them. One caution here: praise another's spouse or companion only if it is obvious that you will not be misunderstood. There is no need to make a guest feel that you are ogling his or her companion.
- *Praise by inference.*   This form of praise is perhaps the best to use in a restaurant setting because it is subtle. If you recognize a person from a picture in a magazine, newpaper, on television, or any other way, make a favorable remark to the person about having seen the news about them. If someone's relative comes in, you need not compliment him, but you may mention how favorably his grandfather spoke of him. This is seldom recognized as praise by the person, but it makes him or her feel good.

Giving Good Service

Managers must create a positive environment so that servers will perform side duties as required by the procedures established by the individual operation. An **order of service** should be specified, and servers should follow that order whenever possible. However, they should not follow any order or procedure if it inconveniences the guest. Service procedures have been established either to increase productivity or safety or to improve the aesthetics of guest service. Many guests, however, are unaware of service etiquette, and servers should be concerned first with the guests' comfort before rigidly following service etiquette or the restaurant's service procedures.

The guest(s) should be assisted when ordering whenever necessary. This is perceived as caring as long as the server does not engage in high-pressure sales (see Chapter 7). Continue to follow up with service. Food should be served the way *each* guest ordered it, and management must establish a system to ensure that each guest, in fact, gets what he ordered. This may necessitate numbering tables as well as individual seats at the numbered tables to ensure that the correct item is served to the guest who ordered it. A **systems approach** is particularly important when the runner system is used. When a guest's cocktail glass (or wine when served by the glass) is nearing empty, the server should ask if the guest would like another cocktail, and when a wine glass needs refilling (when served from a bottle), the server should promptly fill the glass . . . but do not overfill a wine glass when the guest has a bottle from which to pour.

Servers should be trained to recognize behavior that may indicate a guest needs service. For example, when a guest raises her head apparently looking for someone or something, she should be approached by her server to ask if she needs anything. Whenever possible, servers should be trained to predict what a guest may need: extra flatware, bread and butter, condiments to accompany items, and water and other beverages filled when below half-empty and kept two-thirds to seven-eighths full (wine glasses should be only half-filled to allow for proper gustation of the wine). Likewise, unnecessary flatware, glassware, and china/dishes should be cleared quickly from a guest's table when they will no longer be needed with that course or a subsequent course.

Trays with soiled dishes should be cleared frequently, and when in the guest's view, soiled dishes should be covered with a napkin whenever possible. The buffet table or salad bar should be checked regularly for food quantity, appearance, and proper temperature.

Special Service Situations

After training employees to respond to a standard set of guest requests through the server's behavior, each server must be empowered or trusted to handle situations as each deems necessary. It is impossible to comment about all special service situations, yet a few words in several categories might be helpful. This generalized information should not be taken as absolutely the best way always to handle these special situations. The server must respond directly to the guest's needs, wants, and desires.

Children require some additional or special service. The children's ages will dictate how much special attention they require, but children generally enjoy being treated as adults, and the server should try as much as possible to do this. Do not ignore a child, and do not resort to baby talk. Offer a high chair or booster chair if required. Suggest a child's portion of a popular dish: spaghetti, hamburger, hot dog, or peanut-butter-and-jelly sandwich, and bring it to the table as quickly as possible. Food may help to quiet an irritable child. The server should never reprimand a misbehaving child. Servers who handle children effectively usually fare better with their gratuities.

Teenagers may actually have more disposable income than their parents and will be inclined to order what is popular with their age group. Treating young adults with the same respect with which middle-aged and mature adults are treated can result in several desirable outcomes. They may

A Server's Tips for Good Service

- Never stand around in groups of more than two; stay at your station.
- Always greet your guests; make eye contact with guests, greet them cordially, and smile.
- Avoid conversations with other employees, especially in the presence of guests.
- Do not give loud orders.
- Never argue with anyone, especially a guest.
- Do not mop your face with the side-towel, and never carry a side-towel under your arm or on your shoulder.
- Take a clean towel once in a while.
- Never wipe flatware or glassware with a towel in front of guests. Use a clean, sanitary towel to polish flatware or glassware only before opening the restaurant or when out of the guest's view.
- Do not lean on chairs or put your foot on a chair rung. Stand erect or bend from the waist to listen clearly. Do not crouch down or bend at the knees.
- If the guest spills something or you spill something on a guest, apologize, clean it up, and advise your supervisor.
- If a guest drops a napkin or flatware, replace with a clean one.
- Talk only as necessary for politeness (formal environments).
- Do not smoke in areas where not allowed and never during the serving period or in a guest's view.
- Do not yell in the kitchen.
- Never use profanity.

- Take guest complaints to your supervisor or solve them yourself if within the restaurant's empowerment guidelines.
- Say "thank you" when tipped, regardless of the amount.
- Do not count money or jingle coins in pockets.
- Never hurry your guests.
- Never eat during service or in the kitchen.
- Do not carry pencils, books, and so on, where visible (i.e., in pockets, in your hair, behind ears, etc.).
- Carry menus in your hands—not under arms or in a shirt, blouse, apron, jacket, or inside your pants or skirt.
- Do not lean on walls or sidestands. Do not rest anything on the guest's table. Do not perform any functions on the guest's table such as stacking dishes, placing soiled flatware on plates, writing the guest's order, and so forth.
- Do not put hands in pockets or on hips.
- Do not cross arms in front of chest.
- Cross arms behind you or grasp hands in front or behind you.
- Do not add checks in view of any guests.
- Do not complain about food to kitchen personnel—tell your supervisor.
- Do not point in the dining room or gesture at a table.
- Always be courteous.
- Walk briskly, but never run.
- Do not walk briskly when leading guests to their seats.

order several different items that increase their check; they may tip well (since many teens have worked in food service themselves); and they may behave as adults if treated as such.

Ill guests should be offered any assistance necessary to comfort them, but do not move an ill guest. The manager should summon professional assistance quietly, and servers should try not to embarrass the person or arouse commotion in his area. Any accidents should be quickly wiped clean as this may ruin the appetite of other guests. A restaurant could be held liable and required to pay damages if restaurant staff improperly handle an ill guest or assume that he is inebriated. Recently, a restaurant had to pay damages to a widow whose husband became ill in the restaurant. All the staff as well as the managers assumed that the man was drunk. They treated him accordingly—quietly escorted him out of the restaurant, propped him against a wall outside, and left him unattended. The man died of exposure, an autopsy revealed. This could have been avoided had the restaurant exercised reasonable care in handling this situation.

Mature guests tend to know exactly what they want and how they want it. They are value conscious (many were reared during the Depression); while they may have money, they may be frugal, and they are less easily influenced. Indeed, they have been consumers for a longer time than most. This consumer behavior may be perceived by the staff as demanding. To better cater to the mature guest, menus should have large, easily read typeface (e.g., avoid using old English typeface), should have significant contrast between the typeface and the background paper, and should have a surface that produces no glare. Lighting should be bright, but diffused rather than spots or pools of light (bare bulbs in chandeliers should be shaded). Chairs should be of normal height (avoiding low, banquette-type seats), have firm padding, and have arms to assist in seating and rising. Acoustics should be designed to attenuate sound (background noise is very disturbing if one has hearing difficulties), and servers should address themselves directly to the guest from whom the order is being taken by looking straight at the person. Mature guests tend to be very loyal when well treated, and while they may not tip high, their frequency of visiting the restaurant easily overcomes the lower per-visit tip.

Visually-impaired guests should be treated with as little extra fanfare as possible. If unescorted, they should be led to their seats by the host or their server. Most visually impaired guests will follow by grasping the lead's elbow. A visually impaired guest may ask to have the menu read and should be verbally notified when being served. The server should assist as necessary, and it may be necessary to cut or portion larger items for the blind guest. When tendering change or processing a credit card charge, the guest should dictate the payment procedure so that he is comfortable with the method of payment.

Should a *deaf or hearing-impaired* guest ask for a menu explanation, the server should explain the menu while directly facing the guest. Many deaf persons can read lips, but they need to see the lips to do so. A gentle nudge or a visible approach to the table should be used so that the deaf guest realizes that she is going to be served. Some deaf guests may be able to speak (sometimes in monotone), and others may need to point to specific menu items to place an order. The newly passed Americans with Disabilities Act requires that restaurants have a TDD phone available for use by deaf guests.

International guests may need special assistance if they do not speak or understand the language. The helpful guidelines as listed above can be used for international guests.

VIPs *(very important persons)* deserve special service considerations, but they should not be observed being treated differently by other guests, who thus might feel like second-class citizens. VIPs should be served in private dining rooms as much as possible or in areas of the restaurant that are not readily visible to other guests. VIP guests may not be generous in giving gratuities but, nonetheless, should be given the best available server.

Late-arriving guests who arrive near closing time deserve the same, high-level service as guests arriving at the opening, and management should plan for late customers. A server could be brought in later than the regular shift (staggered shifts) in order to service late guests. However, if a party lingers unnecessarily, it would be more appropriate for the manager to approach the guests and offer a suitable substitute such as a cup of coffee or complimentary cocktail served in the lounge. Closing-time procedures should be explained in an open manner, rather than having the service staff make obvious indirect gestures, such as dimming or increasing illumination of the lights, stacking chairs on unoccupied tables, increasing the volume or turning the sound system off, and so forth. These are inexcusable service behaviors.

If a party arrives near closing time, the hostess or server may do several things. (1) Politely inform the guests that you have closed, but you will make every effort to service them. (2) Politely inform guests that you must check with the manager or the chef to see if they can be seated. The hostess or server may delay briefly in the kitchen and then inform the guests that she will serve them. This sets the stage for politely asking them to leave as soon as they have finished their meals. (3) Inform the guests that you are closing and that you will have something prepared quickly; serve promptly and present check. (4) Ignore the fact that the restaurant is near closing, seat the guests, and do not ask them to leave either early or before seating the late party. Ensure that the service personnel do not serve in haste and make a dissatisfied patron.

The manager and the server should be aware of certain precautions in practicing the techniques presented. Praising people to make them feel good and, in turn, like you must be done subtly. If the guest feels that the praises are not sincere, the technique can backfire. Moreover, persons who have low self-esteem may overrespond to praise and flattery, and other guests may feel discriminated against.

In a real case, a waitress brought some of her homemade strawberry jelly to one of her regular guests who had asked for fresh strawberries, which were out of season. This incident caused many problems in the dining room as other guests requested strawberry jelly, and there was none to be had. One guest was quite happy, but many of the other regulars were upset. Perhaps in this instance, the waitress should have cleared this with her supervisor before serving the guest, and the manager should have disapproved. The manager could explain that the restaurant can be liable for damages should the guest become ill as a result of unwholesome, uninspected food or food from an unapproved source. This anecdote highlights how other guests feel when someone gets special treatment.

Inebriated guests should not be seated if this can be accomplished legally and without offending the guest. Remember that the other guests in the restaurant deserve a quiet meal, and a drunken guest can ruin their evening as well as yours. Intoxicated VIPs pose an additional problem, as they are more difficult to turn away. If a private area is available, it would be an excellent alternative.

While some people are embarrassed when another person praises or flatters them, a restaurant can also demonstrate too much service. A family-type restaurant typically offers friendly service, but the waiter is not expected to fill water glasses after each sip or empty the ashtray after each flick of an ash. Correspondingly, if one were eating at a very elegant, expensive restaurant, the guest would expect, and perhaps demand, this highly attentive service. Another caution for a manager or service person is to not be overly familiar. Frequently, friends of employees may come into an establishment, and although the host/hostess or server should greet their friends warmly, they should not be too loud or overly demonstrative. Selection of words and tone of voice go hand in hand, but are also important separately. For example, "What do you want?" even if uttered in a nice way is not a proper selection of words. However, "May I take your order?" may be uttered in an impolite manner and, therefore, be unacceptable. Service personnel should always remain low key and should be courteous at all times. Giving compliments, praise, and flattery is very helpful, but accepting compliments properly is equally important. A celebrity once gave a waiter quite a compliment on his service technique, manner, and style. The waiter jumped at this opportunity, monopolized the celebrity and his guests for five minutes, talked very loudly, and ignored his other guests. Certainly this behavior did considerable damage to this establishment. Service persons should not belittle themselves, the establishment, or the chef; nor should they be boisterous. They should say, "Thank you very much," and quietly back away.

Questions

1. What are the differences between the procedural and convivial dimensions of quality service? Review the categories of actions in these dimensions. Discuss how a manager might plan for and/or train for service staff to perform well in each of these areas.

2. What is "an attitude of service"? Why is this attitude a critical characteristic in the delivery of quality service?

3. Review the food server behaviors as scored by guests and as scored by restaurant professionals. Where are there crossovers in these behaviors? How can this information be used to empower the server to meet the guests' needs?

4. Examine the hierarchy of basic human needs as outlined by A. H. Maslow. Discuss how each of these needs can be met in a restaurant service encounter.

5. List three examples of how guest behavior reflects the need for service. In each situation, describe how the server would meet that need.

6. Review the section entitled "Special Service Situations." For each of the guest groups or types listed below, describe a brief dining scenario and include a situation requiring attention from the service staff. How would you deal with each situation described? Children, teenagers, ill guests, mature guests, blind or sight-impaired guests, deaf or hearing-impaired guests, international guests, VIPs, late-arriving guests, inebriated guests.

Endnotes

1. William B. Martin, *Quality Service: The Restaurant Manager's Bible*. Ithaca, New York: Cornell University, 1986.

2. *Cambridge Reports* (1987, November 2). Customer service. Quoted in *The Wall Street Journal*, pp. 68, 31.

3. S. Colgan, *Restaurant Design*, New York: Restaurant and Hotel Design International Magazine, 1987. Quote by M.J. Madigan. p. 8.

Additional Readings

Carnegie, Dale. *How to Win Friends and Influence People*. New York: Pocket Books, 1972.

Goodman, R. J., Jr., and Douglas G. Smith. *Retirement Facilities: Planning, Design and Marketing*. New York: Whitney Library of Design, 1992.

Hamachek, D. E. *Encounters with the Self*. New York: Holt, Rinehart, and Winston, 1971.

Jourard, S. *Personal Adjustment*. New York: Macmillan Co., 1963.

The Transparent Self. New York: Van Nostrand, 1964.

McClelland, D. *The Achieving Society*. New York: Van Nostrand, 1961.

Rosenberg, M. "Psychological Selectivity in Self-Esteem Formation," in *Attitudes, Ego Involvement and Change*. Edited by C. W. Sherif and M. Sherif. New York: John Wiley, 1967.

Taylor, F. W. "The Principles of Scientific Management," in *Scientific Management*. New York: Harper & Row, 1947.

Human Relations and Management in Service: A Historical Perspective

Chapter Outline

Introduction
A Historical Background
    of Human Relations
    and Management
Quality Management (QM)
The Food Service Industry
Training as a Means of Promoting
    Effective Human Relations
Participative Management and
    Staff Empowerment
Major Causes of Restaurant
    Failure
Strains on the Service Staff
Characteristics of the Successful
    Service Manager
Conclusion

Learning Objectives

After studying this chapter, the
student will be able to . . .
1. Illustrate how service delivery
   provides a competitive
   advantage to the food service
   operator.
2. Identify and discuss the
   contribution of the early
   contributors to the development
   of management theory.
3. Explain the Theory X and
   Theory Y concept relative to
   human resources within an
   organization.
4. Outline the quality
   management concept and its
   implementation within an
   organization.
5. Describe on-the-job training
   and its implementation in a
   food service organization.
6. Discuss the causes for
   restaurant failure.
7. List the characteristics of a
   new leadership paradigm used
   in a quality management (QM)
   approach.

Key Words/Phrases

Human relations
Intangible products
Competitive advantage
Frederick Taylor
Henry Fayol
Mary Parker Follet

Management theorists
Management behaviorists
Max Weber
Elton Mayo
A. H. Maslow
Douglas M. McGregor
Peter Drucker
Frederick Herzberg
Theory X and Theory Y
Management by objectives (MBO)
Hygiene factors and motivators

W. Edwards Deming
QM, TQM, TQI, CQI
Mom-and-pop restaurants
On-the-job training (OJT)
Participative management
Staff empowerment
Performance standards
Operational environment
Mentoring
Undercapitalization
Paradigm

Introduction

With respect to management literature, the term **human relations** applies to the interaction of management and labor. The early human relationists had two primary concerns: concern for an individual in an organization and concern for the use of knowledge gained in studying organizational behavior. The objective of a business is to realize a fair return on an investment. For a business to succeed in the long run, many subgoals must be specified and accomplished: good working conditions for staff, community involvement, satisfied customers, and fulfilled government requirements. The hospitality industry is no different, except that we offer an **intangible product**. We sell service.

Our products are excellent food; enhanced visual appeal of the restaurant's exterior and interior; the meeting of strict fire and sanitation codes; efficient layout for workflow and maintenance; productive yet durable design; comfortable surroundings and fair price or perceived value. All contribute to the success of a restaurant operation, but we are still selling service. *Service is the **competitive advantage**!*

A Historical Background of Human Relations and Management

A discussion of human relations would lose impact unless a historical perspective of management is developed. During the early twentieth century, **Frederick Taylor** (1856–1915) began writing about management and developed the scientific management movement. Taylor was influenced by the Protestant work ethic of the time and emphasized hard work, economic rationality, individualism, and the view that each person has a particular role in society. He did not develop a general theory of management, but rather emphasized an engineering or mechanistic approach to increase a worker's productivity. Taylor felt that by increasing productivity both the employer and the employee would benefit. By maximizing the productive efficiency of each worker, scientific management would also maximize the earnings (piece rate) of workers and employers. Hence all conflict between capital and labor would be resolved by the findings of science[1].

Taylor sought to:

1. Develop a science for each element of a person's work.
2. Scientifically select, train, teach, and develop the worker.
3. Cooperate with workers so all work would be done on scientific principles.
4. Divide responsibility between workers and managers.

There was some opposition to Taylor's approach at that time. Managers felt their knowledge was being usurped, and the unions felt that its objectives threatened their existence. Nonetheless, Frederick Taylor is considered the father of management.

At the same time that Frederick Taylor was recording his ideas on management in the United States, **Henry Fayol**, a leading French industrialist, was developing his general management theory. In fact, he has been described as the father of management *theory*. Fayol published *Administration Industrielle et Generale* in 1916 in which he defined administration in terms of five primary elements: planning, organization, command, coordination, and control. These elements have come to be seen as the functions of management. Fayol advanced 14 principles providing the basic foundation for his school of thought. Some of his principles include:

1. Division of work.
2. Authority commensurate with responsibility.
3. Unity of command.
4. Unity of direction.
5. The scalar principle (i.e., the organizational hierarchy).

Although both Taylor and Fayol began developing basic management theory, **Mary Parker Follet** emphasized the psychological and sociological aspects of management. Management to Follet was a social process, and the organization was the social system. She emphasized the acceptance of authority, importance of lateral coordination, and the integration of organizational participants. Mary Parker Follet, perhaps more than anyone else, can be viewed as the link between classical administrative **management theorists** and the **management behaviorists**.

Max Weber's bureaucratic model was a significant contribution to economic, social, and administrative thought. He traced the changes in political views, discussed their impact upon the growth of capitalism, and examined the effect of industrialization on organizational structure.

The behavioral model emphasized the psychosocial system and the human aspects of administration. Several forces contributed to the development of this model: (1) heterogeneous operations, (2) diversity of products and objectives, and (3) technological change. At this point the movement shifted from scientific management to behavioral science, which included psychology, sociology, and anthropology. Behavioral scientists approached management from yet a different perspective. They dealt with human behavior and used a scientific method[2].

Elton Mayo was one of the first behavioral science researchers in industry. Prior to his work, employees had been considered mechanistic elements in the production system. Mayo and his associates began a study in 1927 in the Hawthorne Plant of the Western Electric Company to determine the effects on output of working conditions, length of working day, frequency and length of rest periods, and other factors relating to the physical environment. The researchers were astounded when production continued to increase regardless of conditions. Mayo felt that the increased production was a result of the changed social situation of the workers and the different pattern of supervision. Others felt that the recognition given the experimental group (test group) was the main cause of increased productivity. Social and psychological factors were now seen to be important factors in determining productivity. These early human relationists are responsible for developing the basic concern for employees in an organization and the use of the scientific method in studying organizations. In spite of these contributions, the human relations movement has been criticized as being basically a closed-loop, sociocultural system because it does not address economic, political-legal, technological, or environmental factors.

Following these management theories, management thought centered on the theories of **A. H. Maslow**, **Douglas M. McGregor**, **Peter Drucker**, and **Frederick Herzberg**. Maslow's theory of motivation has strongly influenced concepts in organizational behavior. "His hierarchy of needs directed the emphasis away from the satisfaction of basic economic and survival needs toward higher level needs of status, social satisfaction, and self-actualization."[3]

McGregor's **Theory X and Theory Y** advanced two views of personnel within an organization: *Theory X*: (1) Management is responsible for organizing elements of productive enterprise in the interest of economic trends. (2) Management is the process of directing people's efforts, motivating, controlling, and modifying behavior. (3) People are passive and therefore must be persuaded and coerced; management must get things done through other people. *Theory Y*: (1) Management is responsible for organizing elements of productive enterprise in the interest of economic trends. (2) People are not passive but have become so because of organizations. (3) Motivation is present; management's task is to develop motivation by recognizing human characteristics. (4) Management must arrange organizational conditions so that people can achieve their own goals best by directing their own efforts toward organizational objectives.[4]

Drucker popularized several management directions including the Japanese management approach and particularly **management by objectives (MBO)**. MBO is a technique by which managers and their employees sit down and jointly set specific objectives to be accomplished within a certain time frame.[5] Having led management thought for decades, Drucker is a true management philosopher. When he prophesies now, management practice follows his prophesy because he has been omniscient for many years.

Herzberg advances a two factor theory: **hygiene factors** (maintenance) **and motivators**. He includes pay, vacations, and working conditions as hygiene factors, and as true motivators he includes achievement, responsibility, job satisfaction, and advancement.[6] A more recent organizational theory, organization development (OD), is a collaborative effort on the part of management and labor to direct the culture of the organization so that individual, group, and organizational goals are accomplished simultaneously. OD utilizes and applies behavioral science principles and practices within an organization to effect change. OD is planned, directed change, and functions as a self-renewal process for the organization.

Quality Management (QM)

Perhaps the newest management thrust in the United States is an acceptance of an American approach to management, widely used in Japan, offered by **W. Edwards Deming**, J. M. Juran, and Phillip Crosby, leaders in the quality management movement. Since the scientific management movement pioneered by Taylor in the early 1900s, no management issue today has had the impact that the QM phenomenon has. The **QM** movement is referred to by several phrases coupled with an appropriate acronym (**TQM**—total quality management; **TQI**—total quality improvement; **CQI**—continuous quality improvement, etc.) An American Society of Training and Development (ASTD) study revealed that 57 percent of the companies responding to a survey have QM as a strategic goal or policy and the remaining 43 percent intend to adopt QM within three years. The American Management Association reported that 78 percent of 3,000 international respondents to a competitiveness survey declared that improving quality and giving good service to customers *is* the key to competitive success. Ninety-two percent indicated that providing superior service is one of their key responsibilities.[7]

Deming introduced QM in the United States in the early 1950s just after World War II; yet for American managers his concepts fell on deaf ears. In rebuilding Japan after WWII, Japanese managers invited Deming to Japan to introduce his system into Japanese industry. The Japanese Union for Science and Engineering (JUSE) listened, learned, implemented, and . . . the rest is history.

Beginning with a mission and vision statement, QM is a systems approach that guarantees that activities are organized and happen according to a plan, and QM can only be implemented by top management. One can see the progression from scientific management to the human relations school to OD to QM. QM is a cooperative form of doing business where management and labor continually *improve product and service quality and productivity*. QM uses a team approach, is participative, and seeks continuous process improvement. Quality management is absolute:

- Quality is conformance to a standard, not elegance.
- There is no such thing as a quality problem.
- There is no such thing as the economics of quality . . . it is always cheaper to do it right the first time.
- The only performance measurement is the cost of quality.
- The only performance standard is zero defects.

The Food Service Industry

The birth of any business venture begins with an idea that is transformed into reality. Food service dates back to the days of primitive society when individuals first traveled from their dwellings. The food service industry has always been associated with travel, and the increase in travel during the last 30 to 40 years has brought the food service industry into the top ranks in the national census on industry sales volume. Restaurants that were not connected to lodging facilities emerged in the latter half of the 1800s, and with rapid urbanization, those who could afford to leave their lunch pails at home began eating in clubs and eating houses (or restaurants). As the workday extended into the evening, food service establishments began serving dinner. Faster service requirements led to the American diner which then led to the fast-food industry (know in the trade as quick service).

Historically, restaurants were started as a **mom-and-pop restaurant**. One ran the kitchen and the other waited tables. As the business grew, mom and pop had to hire employees to perform some of the required functions. As the business grew even larger, mom and pop no longer cooked, washed dishes, and waited tables, but found themselves planning, organizing, commanding, coordinating, and controlling the business. The historical perspective presented earlier in this chapter suggests some of the stages of management that mom and pop experienced. Key management factors that novice managers lack include an understanding of their target market segment(s) and how to reach that segment(s), how to control costs, and how to deal with employees both from a performance perspective (tasks and competencies) and a legal perspective. Perhaps their lack of knowledge and training in the above-listed key factors and the functions of management accounts somewhat for the high rate of failure of restaurants.

The need for professional management in the industry is vital. The food service industry can no longer operate as it did in the past: the art of managing a food service operation requires professional management with professional skills and professional abilities. The study of human relations in theory and the practice of good human relations and management are necessary for the success of a professional manager. This is true for all industries, but in the food service industry it is vital to the immediate success of the operation, for in no other industry is the philosophy of management and the attitude of the employees displayed in the staff's behavior so vividly communicated to the consumer, our guest.

This level of professionalism involves more than just proper training. The desire to please the customer must come from top and middle management, and must permeate each department, including the back of the house as well as the dining rooms. Any lack of integrity or sincerity on management's part will be felt by the customers, but first noted by the staff. The preparation of food, especially fine food, is regarded by the chef as a work of art; by the nutritionist as therapy; and by the menu planner and the menu designer as an outlet for creative imagination. The industry permits direct contact with people, which intrigues many food-service employees. The food service industry has had difficulty in attracting and retaining employees because of the many strains imposed on the staff during busy periods. The food service employee may be among those of a lower socioeconomic background; therefore, pay and fringe benefits may be of greater importance to satisfy basic needs.

Training as a Means of Promoting Effective Human Relations

Training can provide needed job security. A new employee on the job should be introduced to his immediate supervisor, and his supervisor should introduce him to the job. Care should be taken to instruct supervisors in how to introduce the job to the new staff member, since first impressions are very important. The supervisor should renew the new employee's job description at this time. Job descriptions must be an accurate list of job-related tasks and required competencies, as they can be as binding on management as on the employee. The training of a food service employee should be done systematically by the most qualified individuals in the operation.

On-the-job training or OJT (sometimes referred to as job instruction training or JIT) is a preferred industry training technique, and can best be achieved during slack periods. This does not mean that only slack periods should be used for OJT, since training during a busy period enables the trainee to experience reality. Proper steps must be followed in OJT of all personnel.

1. Prepare the trainee to learn, make her feel at ease, and prepare the learning environment.
2. Make the presentation as clear and as brief as possible.
3. Allow the trainee to perform under careful supervision.
4. Once these three processes are accomplished, a follow-up should be planned.

During the follow-up phase, emphasis should be placed on the proper method to ensure that the trainee has not picked up any bad habits. Only *perfect practice* makes perfect.

A complete listing of tasks and competencies is essential before beginning an OJT training session. These lists should be developed by the management and staff with the assistance of reference sources such as *Tasks to Jobs*, and the National Restaurant Association and the National Skills Training Board (NSTB) research. The OJT method can be used very effectively for dining room staff members for skill training elements. Role-playing, situation analysis, case studies, or case vignettes in group discussion are effective training methods for people-interaction (humanistic or affective) training.

In training the dining room staff, the trainer has an enviable position. Not only will prompt and personal service make the restaurant look good, but an effective server will also earn more in tips. Proper training in sales techniques (i.e., selling wines, desserts, and beverages) increases the check average as well as the server's tips. It behooves both management and staff to increase sales so long as the increase in sales does not exceed the targeted guest average. (See Chapter 7.)

There are several objectives to training: (1) to broaden an individual's knowledge, (2) to improve his skill, and (3) to change his behavior/attitude. A change in attitude usually follows when one is more knowledgeable and proficient in one's job. Yet it is most important for the manager or trainer to know what is the goal to be accomplished before setting up elaborate training programs. A positive method of approaching employee relations is for the manager to consciously determine her goals and objectives. Objectives should include the importance of staff involvement and understanding what will make the business a success.

Participative Management and Staff Empowerment

Although participative management and empowerment should be practiced to the greatest extent possible, **performance standards** must be set. An effort should be made to clearly define functional and behavioral standards. Dr. Fritz Redl uses an analogy in children's psychology that states:

> Behavior falls into three color zones: green, yellow, and red. The green area consists of behavior that is wanted and sanctioned, the area where "yes" is given freely and graciously. The yellow zone includes behavior that is not sanctioned but tolerated for specific reasons. The red zone covers conduct that cannot be tolerated at all and must be stopped.[8]

Richard Wienmann says that in a thousand arbitration cases, many disciplinary action cases are lost by management because of the failure to communicate management's policies and intentions to its employees with sufficient clarity, or because management has been inconsistent in its application with regard to lateness, absence, smoking, drinking, or the like. People working in restaurants form social organizations, and existing relationships and the standing of individuals in the organization have a very important bearing on customer service and efficiency, on satisfaction, and on the morale of both workers and supervisors. Conflict can result when lower status employees (dining room attendants, for example) ask higher status employees (cooks) to perform certain functions.

So far this discussion has centered around the improvement of employee relations at the functional level. At this point something must be said about the managerial level. To ensure an orderly succession of management, the modern business enterprise needs to recruit the ablest, best-educated, and most dedicated people. Some companies feel that extensive management training may invite raids from other companies and, therefore, that they cannot afford investment for executive development. But the industry can no longer tolerate this feeling; progressive companies must build an adequate base for replacement as vacancies are created by retirement, promotion, and expansion. To delay creates instability in the organization and the possible demise of the business.

The college graduate in modern food service is being sought more and more. Historically, very few formally educated people have gone into food service, but the last 15 years have shown a tremendous growth in hotel and restaurant schools. The industry is also in search of professional managers, and this places the college graduate in food service in great demand. Many companies feel the pressure of hiring college men and women for their company. Indeed, many quick-service restaurant chains are seeking hospitality graduates for their management training programs. In understanding employee empowerment, corporations have recognized the need to have individuals with a global, strategic, and more informed perspective than the traditional task or functional approach to management and supervision. College graduates anticipate a participative environment in the work world, and they bring in fresh approaches to handling problems.

The now well-known management practice conducted by several corporations in search of professional food service personnel of placing college juniors and seniors in supervisory positions (sometimes referred to as internships or externships) gives the corporation an opportunity to see how these individuals fare in an **operational environment**. It also gives the students an opportunity to see the corporation and the industry close up while giving them time to decide whether they, in turn, want to work there.

Some corporations have students meet with corporate executives, and the students are allowed to brainstorm, solving problems that they have experienced during their internship. These brainstorming sessions give top management the opportunity to get a composite, firsthand view of the workings of operations and to gather valuable information. The students obviously spout ideas they have learned in the classroom or from their textbooks, and they play on the knowledge obtained from a host of industry speakers in their classes as well as their instructors.

Loyalty must be earned by the company. The company cannot demand it. If top management uses participative management, especially with the college graduate, both the company and the new manager will gain from this experience. The college graduate will then empathize with top management and the organization, and with empathy comes company loyalty. This **mentoring** relationship allows the recent graduate to accumulate the necessary work experience, adding it to his textbook knowledge. The college graduate has an intense desire to succeed, since he has been in an academic environment for four or more years and is anxious to try his wares in the real world. Dr. William P. Fisher, executive vice president of the National Restaurant Association (NRA), in discussing the industry's recruiting problem, said, "The industry is paying more attention to making entry jobs part of a career progression to improve position and pay better wages."

Major Causes of Restaurant Failure

The major cause of restaurant failure is **undercapitalization**—that is, the *lack of capital*. With endless capital, the restaurant could stay in business *ad infinitum*. The *insidious causes* of restaurant failure center on:

No target market identified.

Unfriendly personnel as a result of poor selection and training.

Poor service/disorganization as a result of an absence of standards, tasks, and competencies.

Poor food.

Excessive prices resulting in poor value (with decreasing value to the guest and profits to the owner).

Poor cost control.

Unfriendly personnel reflect management's attitude generally. Friendly personnel are not overfamiliar with guests, but they are courteous. If one has a staff member in the kitchen who is upset with the manager but continues to put out a good product, the job may continue to be accomplished without the guest recognizing that there is or was a personnel problem. But what happens if the service person on the floor is upset with management? He is management's contact with the guest. If he is upset, his attitude affects his behavior, which is directly conveyed to the guest. Additionally, if management is not responsive to guest needs, this attitude can also be conveyed directly to the guest through the server.

Managers must maintain a good relationship with the service staff, but this should not be confused with lax or poor discipline or lack of adherence to the restaurant's standards. Good discipline and the maintenance of stated standards create a smooth-running operation. Management's attitude in the service industries directly affects the success or failure of the business.

Strains on the Service Staff

It may appear that service is an easy job. The cook thinks the waiter has nice working conditions, while she sweats over a hot range or broiler. The dishwashers think the server has a "fat" job. The bartender cannot understand why the server cannot remember the drinks. The cashier or the checker needs the "dupe" before the food goes out the door. The dining room attendant has enough to do, so the server cannot depend on him for help. Management thinks the server should be able to handle 50 guests because "they are only having sandwiches." The host is yelling for tables to be set because guests are breaking down the door, and the manager wonders why Susie or Harry is not smiling at the guests.

The difficulty in service is not in the particular tasks that must be performed (although some of the tasks are not simple). The difficulty is in the number of people that the server must satisfy. Each person places a different demand on the server, which pulls the server in different directions. In the face of it all, the server is supposed to smile! (See Figure 2–1.)

Characteristics of the Successful Service Manager

How can the manager establish good rapport with the service staff? Managers must respect the position of server. In the United States a restaurant waiter ranks approximately in the lowest 10 percent of occupations rated for prestige. Although the restaurant manager cannot change

FIGURE 2–1

Strains on the service staff.

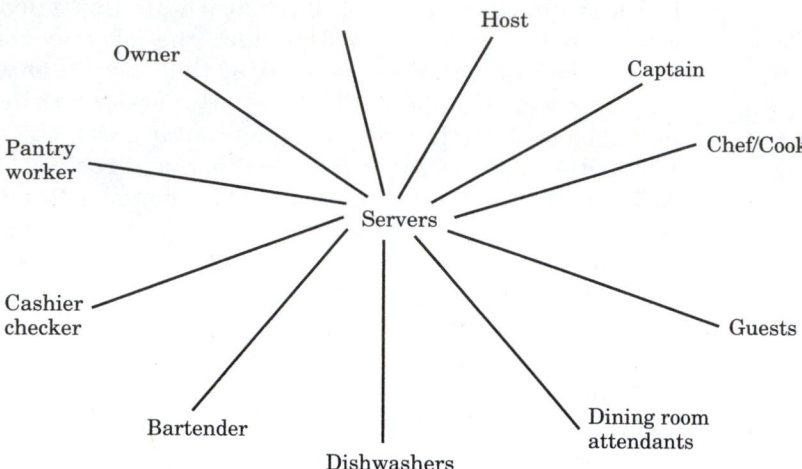

the prestige ratings of the entire population of the United States, he must understand and empathize with the position of his service staff. This prestige rating is quite different in Mexico, Europe, and Asia. A waiter in a fine establishment is respected, and the job is prestigious.

In a group of distinctions between the old management **paradigm** and the new leadership paradigm and using the QM approach, the following are offered:

Old	**New**
Authoritarian	Participative
Position authority	Knowledge authority
Fear of job loss	Job security
Fear of reprisal	Open atmosphere
Close enough for government work	Continuous quality improvement
Systems, policies and procedures for control	Systems, policies and procedures for support
Continuously challenge suppliers	Create supplier partnerships
Quality and standards set by management	Quality and standards set by the customer

The guidelines that follow may be used when dealing with people in general. However, the references made here are specifically intended to help the manager in her relations with her service staff. When beginning a conversation with a server, begin in a friendly manner. This sets the mood of the conversation, and even if corrective words follow, they will be taken better if the individual feels that you are sincere. Avoid a demeaning tone, and say things that will be agreeable to the person (as much as possible). This is not to imply that one should use ridiculous questions, such as "Well, Jaime, wouldn't you like to make more tips?" This in itself belittles and demeans the individual. Empower your staff and allow them to use their own ideas to implement service within the established service standards for the restaurant. Remember that you, as manager, cannot be present for every interaction your servers have with your guests.

A feeling of trust results when certain assignments are controlled by the service group. Station rotation and side duties, as well as scheduling, could be accomplished by the service staff. This would take some of the responsibility away from management without affecting the flow or efficiency of the operation. Be sympathetic to others' problems and ideas and try to see things from their perspective. A manager should never belittle a server or embarrass him, especially in the presence of guests. Management should defend service staff whenever possible, but not necessarily in front of the guest. The manager should make his support clear in private to the server as well as in general (e.g., in staff meetings) and reinforce this idea after any specific incident. Remember that whatever an individual's feelings are, they are his and he is proud of them. Listen, and attempt to see his point of view.

Above all, if someone has an idea, do not tell him that he is wrong—never say the words, "You are wrong!" This immediately places the individual on the defensive, and the remainder of the discussion is apt to be negative. Consider the idea, weigh its relative merits; if you disagree, do not tell the person straight away. Present your idea by picking up on one of his ideas that you find agreeable and adding to it. If you find that you are wrong during a discussion, admit it and admit it quickly. Your staff will respect you for it and know that you are sincere. Do not pretend to know everything.

Conclusion

Management's task is to get the job done with and through other people. Hopefully, management can get the job done through others because the others enjoy doing their work. Management's job is to help people enjoy their work and to provide leadership and guidance. To best accomplish this, a manager must know his staff personally and realize the difficulty of the job. She must know where these individuals are in society and must possess the personal leadership characteristics to motivate the service staff in a positive way. Doing so will cure one, and perhaps two, of the major causes of restaurant failure: unfriendly personnel and poor service. It will directly effect the success of the business.

Questions

1. What were the two primary ideas that the early human relationists had, and how do they apply to the hospitality (service) industry?

2. What are the major causes of restaurant failure?

3. What is meant by "strains on the service staff"?

4. List five personal characteristics the successful service manager should possess and discuss each one.

5. Explain how a high quality level of service can provide a competitive advantage for a food service operator.

6. Discuss how Frederick Taylor's ideas about management and human relations earned him recognition as "the father of management."

7. Review McGregor's Theory X and Theory Y. Give situational examples of how these two theories would play out in food service operation.

8. Prepare a mission statement for a food service operation that would reflect the principles of Deming's quality management concepts.

9. Give three concrete examples of how training food servers can directly affect the operation's bottom line.

10. Discuss how training can directly benefit the server's financial well-being at the end of a shift.

11. List five ways in which servers can become involved in participative management activities.

Endnotes

1. F. W. Taylor, "The Principles of Scientific Management," *Scientific Management,* 1947, p. 140.

2. "Scientific Method principles and procedures for the systematic pursuit of knowledge involving the recognition and formulation of a problem, the collection of data through observation and experiment, and the formulation and testing of hypotheses." By permission from *Webster's New Collegiate Dictionary* (1977 by G & C. Merriam Co., Publishers of the Merriam-Webster Dictionaries).

3. F. E. Kast and J. E. Rosenzweig, *Organization and Management: A Systems Approach* (New York: McGraw-Hill 1970), p. 92.

4. D. McGregor, *The Human Side of Enterprise* (New York: McGraw Hill, 1960), pp. 33–57.

5. P. F. Drucker, *The Practice of Management* (New York: Harper & Row, 1954), pp. 121–136.

6. F. Herzberg, *Work and the Nature of Man* (Cleveland, OH: World Publishing Co., 1966), pp. 72–75.

7. E. Greenberg, "Customer Service: the Key to Competitiveness," *Management Review*, December 1990, p. 29. Reported fully in AMA Research Report, *The New Competitive Edge*, New York: American Management Association, 1991.

8. H. G Ginott, *Between Parent and Child* (New York: Avon Books, 1969), p. 114.

Additional Readings

Farber, B. and F. Berger. *Training in the Hospitality Industry*.

L. C. Forrest, Jr. *Training for the Hospitality Industry*. East Lansing, MI: The Educational Institute of the American Hotel and Motel Association, 1983.

The Personnel Function in Service Management

Chapter Outline

Dining Room Organization
American and European
    Terminology
Recruiting and Selecting Service
    Employees
Interview Techniques
Tips on Interviewing
Conducting Reference Checks
Wages and Salaries
Pooling Tips
Performance Appraisal (Rating
    Systems)
Rating Errors
Promotion
Discipline
Terminations
Training
A Systems Approach to Training
Conducting Meetings with the
    Service Staff
Role-Play Exercises
Conclusion

Learning Objectives

After studying this chapter, the
student will be able to . . .
1. Compare the classical approach
   to organizational structure
   with the service society concept
   of organizational structure.
2. List the traditional dining room
   staff positions in both American
   and French terminology.
3. Identify labor market sources
   for recruiting potential service
   employees.
4. Outline the basic components
   of any job specification
5. Discuss tips for interviewing
   potential employees

Key Words/Phrases

Frederick Taylor
Luther Gulick
Lyndall Urwick
Classical organizational theory
Functional supervisor
Service society conceptual
  framework
Chief executive officer (CEO)

Inverted equilateral triangle
Internal customers
Food and beverage manager
Director of service
Wine steward
Headwaiter
Captain

Waiter
Busperson
Maître d'hôtel
Sommelier
Equal Employment Opportunity
   Commission (EEOC)
Americans with Disabilities Act (ADA)

Dining Room Organization

A food service establishment depends on the performance of the employees for the organization to function effectively. The formal and informal organizations that are formed in the work environment to best accomplish the organization's goals and objectives strongly influence this effectiveness. These organizations form the psychosocial makeup, which directs the establishment or the larger organization toward specific goal accomplishment. A well-designed, formal organization will take into account the informal organization and channel these two organizations, as well as individual goals, to maximize productivity. The organizational structure is a depiction of the lines of communication within the establishment. In other words, in viewing the organizational chart, one should be able to locate himself and trace the hierarchy up the chart to the top manager and down the chart to the lowest level within the organization. These lines also indicate that responsibility commensurate with authority should flow down the chart to the lowest competent level, and, correspondingly, information about job or task accomplishment should flow up the chart. The objective of the organization is to establish the structure required to implement the goals of the organization and to facilitate communications. Two lines of development exist in classical organization thought:

1. **Frederick Taylor**—scientific management.
2. **Luther Gulick** and **Lyndall Urwick**—administrative management.

Taylor's idea is functional (i.e., he divides the organization into functions) and fits the person to the machines (i.e., people are seen as adjuncts to the machines in the performance of routine tasks). He analyzed the interaction between the characteristics of humans and the social and task environments created by the organization. Among other things, he proposed that, for efficient work, management must: (1) find the best way, (2) provide monetary incentive, and (3) use functional foremen.

Gulick and Urwick thought along the lines of giving the organization a purpose and identifying the unit tasks necessary for that purpose. They felt that: (1) tasks should be grouped into jobs (productive, service, coordinative, and supervisory); (2) jobs should then be grouped into administrative units; (3) units should be grouped into larger units; and (4) top-level departments should be established. Gulick and Urwick also disregarded human behavior in the organization and viewed members as inert instruments performing assigned tasks and as givens rather than variables. Both **classical organizational theories**, however, dissolve when placed in practice.

So where does this leave the restaurant operator, or dining room supervisor, who is trying to organize his department for effective goal accomplishment? A combination of the two classical thoughts can serve as a framework from which one can begin to organize personnel in a dining room.

1. Find the best possible way (most efficient and most effective) to accomplish each task.
2. Group tasks into jobs so that the individuals accomplishing these tasks (i.e., the particular job description) can perform them efficiently and effectively.
3. Place someone (**functional supervisor**) in charge of the various jobs.

The classical approach to organizational structure has given way, somewhat, to the **service society conceptual framework**, in which the guest (or customer) is at the top of the organizational chart, the immediate service provider (the server in a restaurant setting) next, the first-level supervisor below the server, and the restaurant owner (or **chief executive officer (CEO)** in any larger organization) on the bottom. In this **inverted equilateral triangle**, we see the head of the organization on the point but at the bottom not the top. And the guest and servers are on the long horizontal line at the top of the organization. This visualization strongly suggests that all positions under those positions on top of the inverted triangle are subservient to those at the top with the guest as the person in charge. The server attends to the guests' needs, wants, and desires while the first level supervisor supports the server in attending to the guests' needs. Each person in the triangle services and supports the person above him (see Figure 3–1). In the TQM model, employees serve other employees (termed the **internal customers**) who serve the guest.

American and European Terminology

In order to sketch the organization of a formal dining room, some definitions must be clarified. A comparison of American and European terminology must also be made because of the latter's historical significance.

FIGURE 3–1
Service society conceptual framework

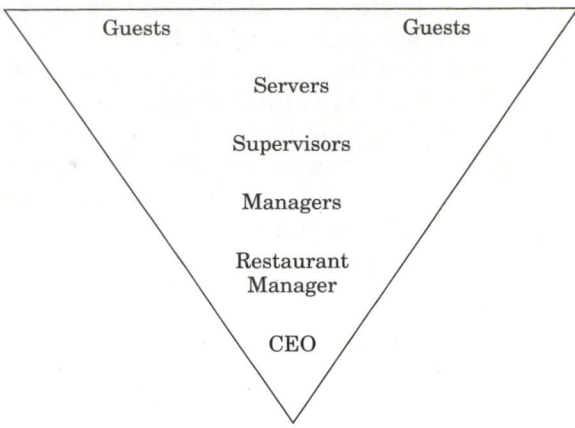

American Terminology	French Terminology
Food and beverage manager	Maître d'hôtel
Director of service	Chef de service
Wine steward	Chef de vin/chef sommelier
Headwaiter	Chef de salle
Captain	Chef d' etage
Waiter	Chef de rang/demi chef de rang
Dining room attendant (busperson)	Commis de rang/apprentice

The comparison of dining room terminologies is confused by modern meanings of the same terms. With the exception of **maître d'hôtel**, **sommelier**, chef de rang, and commis de rang, the other terms are rarely used; and the term maître d'hôtel or maitre d' is used synonomously with director of service, headwaiter/waitress, or host/ess, depending upon the tasks or duties. A chef de rang is synonymous with captain, and a commis de rang may be a server or a dining room attendant.

In a discussion of the classical dining room staff emanating from its European roots, all reference is made to males. This is very antiquated, and in this text the term *director* will be substituted for *host* or *hostess*. This title and position reflect the traditional supervisory duties of a person responsible for service (e.g., scheduling the staff, assigning side duties and service stations, etc.) in the dining room (see job description for director of service in Chapter 8). The director may report to, or could be synonymous with, a *dining room manager*, *service director*, or *assistant restaurant manager*, all of whom, in turn, report to the *restaurant manager* (depending upon the size of the establishment).

Captain is a suitable title for both males and females, and this person may be responsible for a section of the dining room or responsible for two servers. While *waiter* or *waitress* will be used occasionally, the term *server* is the preferred terminology here. *Dining room attendant* is the standard United States government terminology for what was known previously as a *busboy*.

Some establishments use young, inexperienced, perhaps nice-looking individuals to serve as hosts or hostesses to seat guests without the requisite responsibility of managing the dining room or assigning staff duties. This arrangement can work well, but it is important to realize that someone else in authority must be at the entrance, greeting guests, assigning tables, and handling guest complaints. This is a most demanding and difficult task, and it should not be left to one who is not capable of shouldering this responsibility. Indeed, the entire production flow and the entire operation's productivity is established by timing the seating function for the whole dining room and specifically by/for each server's station. It would be difficult to imagine a manufacturing organization allowing an inexperienced, although nice-looking, person to schedule the production workflow!

It is important to emphasize that these titles are standard terminology referring to a job, and a job is a cluster of tasks that define the job. Although there are tasks that are used to define jobs, the independent operator should not feel bound by terminology or the traditional groupings of tasks that constitute traditional jobs. However, union contracts and some government regulations may require more specific information for classifying the jobs; and under these jurisdictions, the operator must comply.

As can be seen in the chart on page 62, lines of authority commensurate with responsibility flow down the chart, while formal channels of communication follow the lines up and down the chart. A dining room attendant may be able to support up to four servers, and, therefore, four lines are drawn to the dining room attendant. However, one captain can support only two, or at best three, servers efficiently. For this reason, the third server from the captain is depicted with a dotted line. When captains are not used in the dining room organizational hierarchy, then servers report to only one dining room manager/supervisor, and dining room attendants (busboys) report to a maximum of four servers. If classical management principles are adhered to, eight to ten persons at maximum are the span of control for one person to supervise at this skill level. In a very large dining room operation, the servers' immediate supervisor could be responsible for a section or a room where upward of eight servers are working. Also each person on the chart should report to and is responsible to only one supervisor. This principle is termed *unity of command*. Ideally, the host could pass instructions only to the section supervisors or captains (classically speaking) and they, in turn, down the

FIGURE 3–2

A typical banquet organization chart

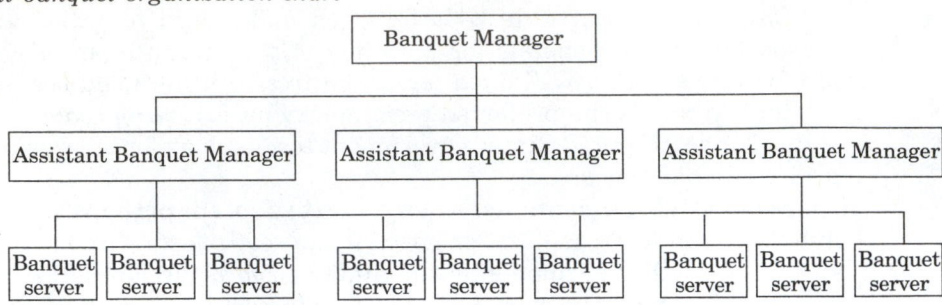

line of formal organizational communication. This is most difficult if not impossible to accomplish in an à la carte dining room, as each person takes direct instruction from the director. Above or beyond the principles of unity of command, span of control, authority commensurate with responsibility, and so forth, a manager must realize that the organization comprises many different elements. For one to assume that the organization chart gives her license to dictate to the staff is a false assumption.

Some casual-theme restaurant chains minimize the channels of communication at the unit level. Uno Restaurants, for example, have one general manager (GM), two assistant general managers (AGM), and the staff. Irrespective of position, each staff member reports directly to the AGMs, and the AGMs, in turn, report to the GM. Dining room attendants (DRAs or bussers) by-pass the servers and report directly to the AGMs. Nonetheless, DRAs follow the traditional duties or tasks of bussers, who, in other restaurants or restaurant chains, may report to the servers although functioning identically to the Uno busser. The Galley Hatch Restaurant in Hampton, N. H., illustrates a unique organizational chart (Figure 3–3) that attempts to minimize the hierarchical structure of most organizations. Viewed from the side (elevation view), the Galley Hatch chart would appear as a series of larger and larger concentric circles cascading down and attached much like an infant's mobile.

It is important that a dining room manager work with her employees and provide leadership so that the group accomplishes the organization's goals, the group's goals, and the individual's goals. Managing people can be compared to trying to move a rope or a chain: pushing a rope or chain will net you little, if any, results, while pulling the rope or chain will be much more effective. Another comparison can be used to illustrate effectiveness: if the tension on a guitar string is too great, the string breaks, and if there is no tension, the string makes no sound and one cannot play the guitar.

FIGURE 3–3
Galley Hatch Restaurant: Organizational Chart

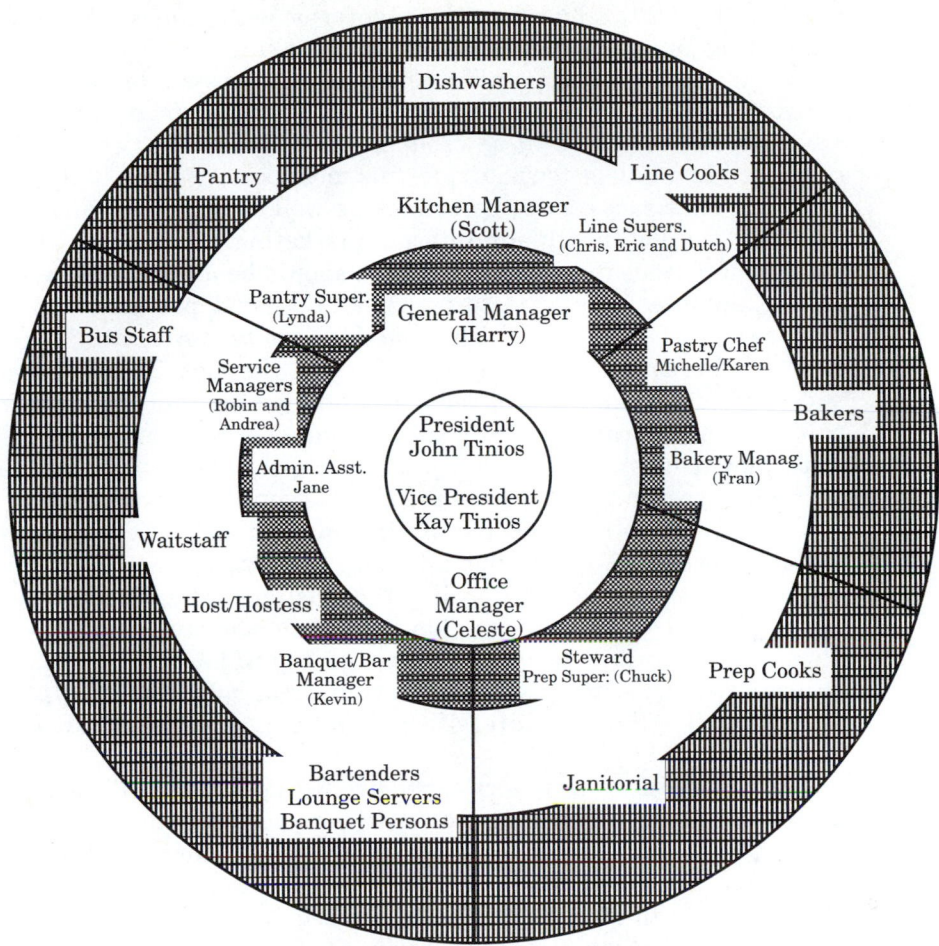

The never-ending circles of service in a casual theme restaurant

Recruiting and Selecting Service Employees

The recruiting and selection process is critical to the on-going effectiveness of the organization. Indeed, the job candidate and future employee, current staff members, and guests all benefit from choosing the right staff members. In some labor markets it is most difficult to recruit servers, while in other labor markets it is quite easy. For example, it is difficult to find qualified service staff in certain urban centers or in rural settings, while in a small town with a large university, finding service personnel may be very simple. In the absence of labor unions that supply service personnel, many reference sources suggest that by placing notices in local newspapers, an operator would attract inquiries for the jobs advertised. Sometimes the number of inquiries inundate the supervisor with requests for interviews, completing job applications, and the like, making it difficult to screen and then select the type of persons being sought. Low-skilled employees (all service personnel do not fit into this category) seldom read newspapers, and advertisements placed in newspapers in a commercial environment, as compared to a college town, are, for the most part, useless. In any case, the best way to attract service personnel, as well as other restaurant personnel, is by word-of-mouth and internal marketing.

All employees in the establishment should be made aware of job openings. Employees may want to transfer to other departments to increase their career possibilities (which could decrease turnover rate); or they may have friends or relatives well qualified for the jobs. This approach also may help the workers accept the new staff member into the organization's culture. One operator actually sets up shop on a street corner in a high unemployment area to attract prospective employees; and perhaps the best employees (and sometimes the greatest number of applicants) simply come to the establishment as walk-ins and ask for a job. No one expressing an interest in working should be turned away. The more applications that are accepted and kept on file, the greater is the probability of finding a qualified or motivated worker. The establishment should have a standard procedure for accepting and encouraging job applicants, and this procedure must comply with Affirmative Action, **Equal Employment Opportunity Commission (EEOC)**, and the **Americans with Disabilities Act (ADA).**

Employee turnover is very expensive. While it may be difficult to detail all costs related to replacing staff members, lower productivity measured in quantity and quality of a person's performance, lower staff morale, loss of business, accidents, litigation, unemployment compensation, and so forth all contribute to increases in costs related to turnover. When employee turnover in general is as high as it is in the food service industry, and when good employees are so hard to find for the hospitality industry, it pays to have a pool of applicants who are waiting to be hired, lest individuals be hired hastily off the streets. In most operations, a small, unobtrusive sign may be posted inviting applications from the general public, as guests may also be a good labor source. "The Management of 'Dale's Restaurant' welcomes anyone interested in applying for employment." However, an elite restaurant should not expect to attract employees from its clientele. The obtrusive and obnoxious "Help Wanted" sign posted (usually permanently and covered with old dirt) in an establishment's window hardly attracts quality applicants, and can serve as a deterrent for guests. "I'll probably get poor food or poor service if they are short of help."

Additional sources include radio and television, which are ideal for locating part-time employees, although expensive for stand-alone operations.

A person whose children are in school during the daytime may be looking for additional income or a change in lifestyle. It would be wise to advertise over radio and TV at the exact time you need the part-time help. Employment agencies, both public and private, are also sources; however, these applicants may need to be screened, depending on the reputation of the employment agency. Organizations for the handicapped, military organizations, and schools and colleges are also sources for job applicants. Also, religious organization leaders in churches, temples, synagogues, and mosques may relish the opportunity to serve as a job referral source for their members. This job source is particularly important in lower-middle socioeconomic geographic areas.

There are advantages to hiring inexperienced or untrained servers. They arrive with no preconceived notions about the nature of the work, and their behavior can be shaped more easily. However, an effective training program is required, which has many benefits over letting the operation run on autopilot. With the advent and increase of vocational-technical schools and community colleges teaching hospitality management, many operators take advantage of these quality resources, which support the industry's efforts by providing well-motivated and well-trained employees. Minimum requirements for the job in the form of job specifications must be established (see Chapter 8), but desirable qualifications should also be specified. Precaution must be taken with those who are too well qualified for the job; they may take the job only temporarily and move on to better things when openings occur. This is particularly important to recognize during economic downturn when potential high quality staff members are readily available.[1]

Dr. Ward Jenssen, a psychologist and management consultant, designed a test for waitress applicants and found four key factors for successful job performance: (1) attention to detail, (2) speed of work, (3) effect on co-workers, and (4) customer service.

The recruiting effort should be evaluated continuously to determine which sources yield the best employees and which sources do not. The following factors, among other things, can be used to measure employee effectiveness: test and interview scores, training program performance, pay, performance appraisal (on-the-job), promotion, turnover, absenteeism, and accident rates. In reviewing a résumé or job application, look for matches in your job specification and the candidate's experience, consistency in career goals of the applicant and what you have to offer, indicators of a cycle of successes rather than cycles of failure, evidence of stability and the profit motive. Be aware of miscues such as gaps in employment, too much discussion of personal issues or overemphasis on formal educational background, messy writing or résumé presentation, and negative comments about reasons for leaving a former employer. After the résumé or job application has been analyzed, the applicant should be given an interview.

Outline for a Job Specification

Job Title:

A. Education:

B. Job knowledge:

C. Character:

D. Judgment:

E. Ingenuity and initiative:

F. Mental ability:

G. Physical requirements:

H. Skill:

I. Training and/or experience:

    Minimum required:

    Desired:

J. Personality traits:

K. Personal appearance:

L. Motivation:

Key Personal Characteristics

1. Good health and physical stamina; the ability to work long hours on one's feet under conditions that call for a high energy level.

2. Higher than average drive; dining room service is not for the lazy or lethargic.

3. Pleasant physical appearance; neatness and freedom from obvious lesions are especially important.

4. Inherent friendliness and courtesy; these traits are the product of a lifetime of personality development, contributed to by family relations, past successes and failures, and physical condition.

5. A need for money; a server who must support a family or pay off debts will be motivated to work hard.

6. Self-confidence and self-reliance; a server must project a competent exterior and impress both the customer and other staff members as capable of taking full responsibility in most situations.

7. Relative freedom from poor habits, such as overdrinking, causing friction with customers, being chronically late, or avoiding side work.

Key Job Requirements

1. Willingness to work the hours and under the conditions required by the job.

2. Acceptability of wages and benefits to the candidate.

3. Willingness to take a physical exam.

4. Time required getting to and from work (some surveys show anyone living more than an hour from the place of work is unsuitable).

5. Length of time in the community (to determine whether or not the candidate is a wanderer).

6. Number of preschool children (more than one makes it almost impossible for success on the job without unusual arrangements; however, you may not use this factor to exclude someone from working).

7. Vocational stability (number of jobs held in the last year).

The professionalism required for recruiting, selecting, and training the labor force, especially of the casual dining, corporate-driven (chain) restaurant industry segment, has moved all restaurant human resource practices up several notches.[2] Now significant time is spent training supervisors in techniques for interviewing. Competitive forces require restaurants to be guest-driven in design/decor, food product offering, and service delivery, which is directly related to human resources practices. Psychological tests may provide excellent background information, but the individual responsible for the staff member's performance or direct report should have final say as to the hiring of the individual after the interview, so long as illegal reasons for excluding an applicant for employment are not used.

Interview Techniques

Three widely accepted reasons for interviewing are: (1) to get information (attitudes, feelings, personality, general temperament, appearance, speech patterns, etc.); (2) to give information (i.e., to sell the job and the establishment and company); and (3) to make a friend (the applicant may become a staff member or a guest). The interview should be viewed as a two-way process, as both the interviewer and the interviewee have something to sell. Some interviewers use their roles to intimidate the applicant and to delve further than necessary into the applicant's life. This attitude on the part of the interviewer can ruin the reputation of the business and could be illegal. Employers should review the employee-screening inquiries forbidden in the state in which the interview is being conducted. Moreover, if the applicant is hired, there may be resentment towards the supervisor if he or she is the person who conducted the interview.

When interviewing prospective staff members, the environment should be as pleasant as possible; this may be the interviewee's first impression of the establishment. If possible, the room should not suggest intimacy although privacy is required. It should be well lighted, adequately furnished, and large enough for ease of movement. The interviewer should prepare for the interview by becoming familiar with the applicant's résumé or employment application, as well as with the specifications for the job or jobs for which the person may be interviewing. The interview should be held at a time convenient for both, and ample time should be allowed for each interview. A short interview made in haste in order to "fill the squares" may result in short-term employment, which wastes time and money.

Tips on Interviewing

Have a plan or pattern for the interview and be attentive to and interested in what the applicant has to say. Put the interviewee at ease, and allow ample opportunity for the interviewee to respond to your questions and to volunteer information; do not interrupt when the interviewee is talking or thinking (framing a response), as they may reveal something important that you may not be able to ask legally. According to the Civil Rights Act of 1964, you may not use discriminatory remarks (regarding race, color, religion, sex, age, marital or family status, disabilities or handicaps, criminal charges or arrest record, or national origin), and neither may you discriminate in hiring for any of the above reasons. You may ask the person, if hired, to prove that they were at least 18 years of age, or to prove eligibility to work in the United States. You may ask what languages the candidate speaks or writes fluently if job related, and you may ask, "Are you capable of performing the essential functions of a server with or without reasonable accommodation?" While you may ask specifically, "Are you available to work Saturdays or Sundays if needed, " you must ensure that you *ask no more than that*, lest you infringe on the person's freedom to practice a certain religion without being discriminated against for a job. You may ask if the candidate has been *convicted* of any crime.

Take notes if possible during the interview, but do not allow your active note taking to cause you not to listen or to give full attention to the job candidate. Ask open-ended questions as follow-ons to a candidate's response, and follow the open-ended response by the candidate with this type of question: "Give me an example of how you . . . handled this situation . . . or felt about . . . and so forth." Probe for the candidate's behavioral responses or actions in situations by posing such critical situations or following up with any of the candidate's responses. Make use of how, why, when, what, where, who; and for example, for instance, in what way. Do not be afraid to probe, but ensure that you do not cross the legal line. Acknowledge the applicant's ideas: "uh-huh," "yes," "and what else can you add to that?" Use summaries and do not be judgmental. Before exiting the interview, let the applicant ask you any questions he wishes. Immediately after the interview and after the prospective staff member has left the room, record your impressions on an interview response sheet.

After the interview and before hiring, there are several subtle things you can do to test the suitability of one applying for a service job in a restaurant. Before conducting the interview, invite the applicant to have a seat in the dining room and to order whatever he would like. Notice where she sits—does she pick a table and sit where she can see what's going on? Or, ask the interviewee a silly question, "Were you born happy?" If the applicant smiles, the person may be well-suited for a job as a server, may demonstrate a sense of humor, and may be pleasant with guests. One restaurant operator asks the applicant to follow him somewhere. He intentionally walks fast; if the applicant keeps up, she is more apt to be alert and fast on her feet. Another operator is especially aware of body odors. If applicants have an odor on the interview, he assumes they will have an odor on the job.[3]

Simplified Interview Response Form

Interviewed by   Date

Remarks:

Neatness:
Character:
Personality:
Ability:
Position:
Reporting Date:
Salary or Wage:

Use a series of questions relating to the factors listed below in selecting servers.

Conducting Reference Checks

The most convenient method of conducting a reference check is by the telephone. It is preferable to talk directly to three previous employers if possible or all supervisors during the last few years, as well as personal references. Telephone references are easier to record for the person collecting the information as well as for the person giving information. Additionally, those giving information by phone are apt to be more candid than if they were to write the same information. The cost of the phone call is small in comparison to the time invested in the hiring process or the costs incurred if the employee is not suitable.

Some questions that can be asked of previous employers include: name of employer, job title, tasks performed, pay, length and dates of employment, reasons for leaving, quality and quantity of work, absenteeism and punctuality, accidents, personal characteristics, strengths, weaknesses, overall effectiveness, would you rehire? if not, why not? Because of certain legal issues, many former employers now refuse to give any references— either good or bad—except for verifying dates of employment. Verifying dates may reveal any discrepancies on the job application.

The police can give a record of convictions, if any, in the cities where the applicant has lived. Credit reporting agencies may also be used, but one must be knowledgeable of the provisions of the Fair Conduct Reporting Act. A full listing of the provisions is available from a local credit reporting agency. You must notify the employee within three days after ordering the investigation that a report will be made that it will include information about her character as well as her mode of living. If the applicant is denied employment on the basis of the information supplied by the agency, the applicant must be notified, and the name and address of the agency making the report must be given.

Using the knowledge gleaned from the employment application, the personal interview, and the reference checks, the supervisor is now in a position to decide which applicant to choose, or whether to hire a particular applicant under consideration. It is a good idea to hire employees on probation whenever possible. The importance of the job or the level at which the person was hired will determine the length of the probationary period. For example, a dining room hostess may require a one-or two-month probationary period, while an upper-level management position may require a six-month probationary period. Dining room attendants would require three or four weeks. In this amount of time, the employee's supervisors should be able to determine whether the new employee, with required training, is capable of handling the job and displays other job behavior characteristics that are appropriate and suitable. If you decide to terminate during the probationary period, do so *without cause*. As soon as you attempt to show cause, you will have allowed the probationary employee to rebut your contention(s). The day after an employee's probationary period has ended, you should terminate only for specific cause as stated in your employee handbook and use progressive discipline procedures. Seek qualified legal advice in your state for your employee manual and employment procedures.

Wages and Salaries

Tip credit allowance for employers and tip reporting require the employer to pay social security taxes on the amount of tips reported. This tip credit provision has been most helpful to restaurant operators because it reduces the minimum wage the operator must pay the employee if the employee works in a job in which tips are received. Employees benefit because the employer calculates base pay plus tip income before she contributes to employee's Social Security. Guests benefit since the cost of the menu items are, in fact, understated by some 10 to 25 percent. If the employer were required to scale his wages from the minimum wage, his labor cost would be higher, and prices would need to reflect the increased cost of doing business. To Insure Promptness (or TIP) creates immediate incentive for the service employee. Additionally, the guest may feel that he has more control over the service encounter. At present, the tip credit allowance is 40 percent of the minimum hourly rate.

The hospitality industry has historically combined low wages and salaries with long hours. Traditionally, entry level positions have been filled by immigrants and minority groups who were happy to find work. Because of various restrictions on immigration, laws restricting young people from working, government compensations, and regional economic activity, the employment situation is dynamic and changing rapidly. Wages will have to move upward. Employees are usually satisfied with the absolute amount of pay they receive if the job provides a sense of achievement and satisfaction for the work performed. The worker's demands vary with the individual's expectation, lifestyle, social background, and financial obligations, and an employee may not be satisfied or motivated to do a good job unless he or she feels the wage or salary is equitable. The major source for discontent, however, is not absolute pay (how much they actually make) as it is comparative pay (how much is Pat making for equal work—in my restaurant, or how much does Shelly, who works across town also as a server, make?). Since the anticipation of getting paid has a greater motivating force than the pay itself, regular increases in pay are helpful, but should be related, whenever possible, to the staff member's performance. Ideally, an effective employee should see that effective performance is rewarded, while poor performance is not rewarded.

In the absence of minimum wages set by federal or state governments or labor unions, wages in the hospitality industry are low. The restaurant industry as a whole stands to gain as the standard of living and status for each employee, many of whom are disadvantaged, can be elevated. On the other side of the picture, as wages and salaries in general in the United States have risen, so has productivity (i.e., the contribution one employee makes toward sales). In the service industries in general and in the labor-intensive food service industry, productivity has not kept pace with the rise in wages. The food service operator must investigate new methods for decreasing payroll costs by increasing productivity. Layout and design, robotics or automation, labor-saving equipment, menu design, and staff scheduling will become critical factors for keeping costs in line.

Pooling Tips

Some operations pool tips, a practice that has both pros and cons. Each staff member is given points that are determined by the function of his job. For example, the maître d'hôtel and chef may receive four points, the first cook or sous chef and captains may receive three points, the servers and cooks two points, and the dining room attendants and cook's assistants one point. All tips are totaled for the shift, and this total is divided by the total number of points (a total of all those working the shift). The money is then awarded on the number of points each employee has. Although all operations do not include production employees, some restaurants do. In some restaurants one point on a good evening may be worth $35 or $50! This system has an advantage when employee turnover is very low, promotions come from within the organization, the management enjoys a good working relationship with the staff, and the staff works well together. The disadvantage to pooling tips is that it may reduce individual incentive, especially in an operation that experiences high to moderate employee turnover. The workhorse does not feel that she is being adequately compensated for her level of contribution, while the loafer is reaping benefits from the efforts of her co-workers.

Performance Appraisal (Rating Systems)

A discussion of performance appraisal should not be limited strictly to service employees, yet it is important to do so because service employees enjoy a unique and pivotal job. A service employee cannot be evaluated strictly on his relations with guests, or strictly on his relations with other employees, or strictly on his relations with his supervisors. He must be rated on all factors. As a result, standard rating forms are inadequate for rating servers, captains, or dining room attendants. Rating, in and of itself, is always biased or subjective, as it is the rater's perception of the ratee who is being recorded. Rating staff members should be accomplished with as much objectivity as possible. Rating employees, however, offers a tool by which management can communicate with employees about their performance in specific job functions. While some accuse rating systems of producing resentment on the part of the ratee, many employers would agree that communicating to the employee about poor or excellent performance is preferable to keeping things in the dark. The staff member is being rated anyway, whether in the supervisor's mind or on paper.

The job description (i.e., a complete job description listing all tasks, responsibilities, and job-specific behaviors) should be the basis for employee selection and training and for any rating system. The rating form or procedure should be simple enough so that the employee can understand the basis for the rating. The various factors may be weighted, since some factors may be more important than others. There are various types of rating systems against which an employee's performance may be measured. Critical incident research can be used in situation-specific settings (i.e., varied for geography, style of restaurant, price of menu items, design/decor, etc.) that can yield an objective employee rating system in contrast to an absolute rating system, in which arbitrary values are assigned to task accomplishment. The critical incident rating system describes specifically an employee's behavior in a specific incident in several categories and at different levels of effectiveness. The rater indicates an actual behavior or a judgment on how they think a staff member would respond in the incident/situation listed. This system is less subjective since the rater rates an actual behavior, not a numerical value of an action or job task indicating level of performance. Although the rater can subvert the objectivity of this system, there is an enhanced opportunity for her to objectively evaluate a staff member.

The following system is very susceptible to subjective ratings since a true definition of the individual factors is vague. A rating sheet is marked where the staff member has demonstrated a specific behavior. When taking an order this server:

1	2	3	4	5	6	7	8

Does not smile: stands in one place while taking the order for the entire table.

Smiles and stands in one place while taking the order for the entire table.

Smiles and walks around the table speaking individually to each guest.

Perhaps fifty of this type question in various categories would be asked for each employee.

Absolute Rating Scale—an arbitrary value assigned to a trait or behavior.

1	2	3	4	5	6	7	8

Dislikes Work

Shows Interest

Shows intense enthusiasm and interest in all work.

Ranking is another system used within the industry to evaluate employee performance. Individuals are ranked, from the best server to the worst server, and may be assigned points for their particular position in the ranking. It is most difficult to measure the real effects of this type of rating system, and it does not allow for effective employee counseling— the new paradigm approach to management and leadership. An additional disadvantage to the ranking system is that many good employees are unable to be rewarded sufficiently.

The person closest to the individual's job, the employee's direct report, should complete the rating form. It has been found that as a person rises within an organization, he loses touch with the specific aspects of a job. In a large dining room the captains may be called on to rate servers. A better system allows a second level supervisor to focus his evaluation on an employee for a given day, spreading his evaluations out over the course of a year. He needs to evaluate only one person per day. This accumulated rating system will provide a broader overview of an individual's performance evaluation as compared to a snapshot or point-in-time evaluation. The total can be transferred and recorded on the employee's permanent record, and the tally sheet (service manager's rating sheet—see Figure 3–4) can be destroyed. The following categories outline the areas for which service employees can be held accountable:

Appearance: neat and in good taste, tidy, clean.

Accuracy: correctness of service procedures whenever possible.

Quantity of work: amount of service given during meal as well as amount of guests the individual could efficiently serve.

Dependability: punctuality, attendance, ability to perform required tasks with a minimum of supervision.

Cooperation (employees): willingness to work with fellow employees; sociability and warmth to fellow employees and supervisors.

Courtesy (guests): sociability, warmth, and attention given to guests.

Initiative: demonstrates the ability to be a self-starter.

Judgment: ability to make proper decisions.

Stability: ability to withstand pressure and remain calm under crisis.

Housekeeping and sanitation: ability to keep his/her station and tray orderly and clean; removes dirty trays regularly; follows rules of sanitation.

Safety: ability to function in a safe manner; keeps service areas free from safety hazards; follows safety rules.

Rating Errors

The *halo effect* is the tendency of a rater to prejudge the ratee (e.g., on only a few factors) and mark the entire rating form indicating superior performance or poor performance. The halo effect results in the rater not differentiating between factors on the rating form. The *leniency error* is the tendency to be a "nice guy" and rate each employee higher than her actual performance in the job. This syndrome has forced some organizations to dispense with the absolute system and adopt the forced-choice ranking system as an attempt to reduce "grade inflation." The *error of central tendency* exists when the rater does not differentiate between effective or ineffective job performance and rates all employees as average or only shades of differences from the average score.

FIGURE 3–4
Service Manager's Rating Sheet

Service Manager's Rating Sheet

_____   Circle one: Luncheon / Dinner
            Employee's Name

                                   Host/Hostess _____
                                   (Rating Official)

                                   _____
                                   Reviewing Official

Rate the member of the service staff on his/her performance for the day's operation. Total the scores for each day. Fill in this form for each employee at least once per month. This form should be completed at the end of each year.

Use this scale for point values:

0–65 = unsatisfactory   84–94 = above average
66–73 = satisfactory   95–100 = absolutely superior
74–83 = average

Day/Date	Appearance	Accuracy	Quantity of Work	Attendence and Dependability	Cooperation with (Employees)	Courtesy toward (Guests)	Initiative	Judgment	Stability	Housekeeping & Sanitation	Total Points for Overall Evaluation
1.											
2.											
3.											
4.											
5.											
6.											
7.											
8.											
9.											
10.											
11.											
12.											
Totals											

Promotion

Whenever openings occur, it is wise to search for replacements within the organization whether single unit or within the chain. This effort utilizes the experience and proven abilities of present staff members, which are also the best predictor of future job success. Promotion from within reinforces loyalty and the concept of "the devil I know is better than the angel I don't know." Offering advancement opportunities within the firm increases employee incentive by demonstrating a career ladder. Yet before one from within the establishment is promoted, she must possess the same minimum qualifications as anyone applying for the job either from within or outside the establishment or chain. Promotion on seniority alone is perhaps one of the worst measures for predicting managerial success. Seniority should be considered, but as a factor only, not as the sole determinant for promotion.

It is important to establish job specifications and to adhere to these specifications even (and especially) when promoting from within the organization. The practice of adhering to specifications will decrease the amount of favoritism that may damage morale and incentive among the other staff members. Whenever possible, current staff should be given the opportunity to train and practice for promotion. Assigning the safety director's job to a current staff member gives upper management a good look at that individual's organizational and managerial skills. Similar assignments will make it easier to identify management potential of others from within the current workforce.

Discipline

Management establishes rules and regulations and expects employees to follow them. The rules should define not only restrictions placed on the staff, but staff rights as well. Rules and regulations should be posted, and each employee should be required to read them and review them at regular intervals. Staff should be asked to sign a document stating that they have read and understand the establishment's rules.

When disciplinary action is required, a memorandum should be sent to the staff member or read in his or her presence. The memorandum should exclude extraneous matter and should be short and to the point. One copy should be sent to the next level of supervision, one to central personnel, and one kept for the writer's record as well as one for the staff member. A disciplinary memorandum should indicate

1. Action taken for particular offense.
2. Time period given for improvement.
3. Further action if no noticeable improvement is noted.
4. Specific performance incidents for which the action was taken.
5. Provision for the employee to acknowledge receipt of the warning.

Mr. Alan Katz of Baltimore, Maryland, lists 23 rules and regulations in the staff manual. Corrective action (counsel, dismissal, warning, etc.) is listed alongside each regulation, and employees are required to read, sign, and date a form indicating that they have read and understand the rules. Employees are required to review the rules every six months. At each six-month interval, the staff member must initial and date the original document indicating that he has again reviewed the rules and regulations. It is necessary to document all disciplinary action. A general rule of thumb says, "if you didn't write it down, it didn't happen." Indeed, if management does not have proper documentation for discipline action, it is leaving itself vulnerable to legal action. In times of high unemployment, legal suits are more prevalent when employers take spurious or indiscriminate disciplinary action or if termination is deemed necessary.

Terminations

Terminating employees is rapidly becoming obsolete as a management alternative. Indeed the cost of terminating an employee and then recruiting and selecting for the vacated work position may exceed $1,500 for a lower-level staff member. A new employee is not as productive as an old employee, and he or she is prone to accidents. In a direct service position, a new employee may negatively affect guest service because of his or her lack of job knowledge or behavioral deficiencies. A number of states restrict the employer's rights to fire an employee under certain circumstances. If you do business in those states, you should check with your lawyer before terminating anyone. If a decision is made to fire an employee, the supervisor should ensure that the staff member has been given every opportunity to enable him to do his job correctly. All terminations should be preceded by progressive warnings or discipline. Firing is an unpleasant managerial task and should be used only when all efforts to improve performance have been exhausted. Should this task become too simple or too frequent, the individual manager should take a closer look at herself, the organization's policies and procedures, or the culture of the organization. The following procedures should be followed when a staff member must be terminated:

1. Terminate in private. Do not apologize, and do not embarrass the employee.
2. Give the person several reasons for termination, but also highlight his strong points and offer to help him find another job (if appropriate). The termination process should not be long (15 minutes maximum).
3. Make sure that the offense is serious, or that the person has been warned previously.

4. Ask if he has any questions. Offer any assistance, and tell him that you will give him the best reference possible under the circumstances.

5. Pay him for all work to this point and ask him to take all his personal belongings from the establishment.

6. If you feel that an employee may become uncontrollable or even violent, seek a private place that is otherwise appropriately secure.

7. If you feel that sabotage may ensue, have the employee escorted from the premises, and if further necessary, obtain a restraining order. But do not overreact!

Training

Every restaurant has a training program; however, many operations are not proactively involved in training. Employees learn the answers to the following questions in an organized training program.

How do we meet our standards?

How do you know what is expected of you?

How can you decrease accidents?

How do you learn the correct serving procedures?

How do you learn to up-sell in the dining room?

How do you learn to provide correct wine service?

What about safety and sanitation?

How do you satisfy the guest?

How can you adapt to today's rapid changes?

Many restaurants advertise an "on-the-job training program," which is often a farce. Perhaps many on-the-job training programs should be called "earn-as-you-learn . . .(the hard way)" or "on-the-job work."

"But training costs a lot of money and a lot of time!" "My people get enough in one week when they follow one of my regulars around. I give them a small station to see if they can hack it. If they can, they've got the job!"

This relaxed attitude toward training may cause an establishment to lose whatever competitive edge it may have had. Indeed, *operators cannot afford not to train*. This concept, not being able to afford *not* to train, is identical to the quality management (QM) process which states that "There is no such thing as the economics of quality; its always cheaper to do it right the first time" and "The only performance measurement is the cost of quality!" A concentrated training effort translates to a positive attitude and resulting behavior from the staff member. The necessary job skills are more easily learned. In a classic article, Dr. Michael Gallagher charts a trainability curve and a cost curve.[4] It can be seen from these charts (Figure 3–5) that an operator achieves maximum training at minimum cost when training new employees. The trainability curve shows that employees with more time in the job are more difficult to train, and the cost curve shows that it is more expensive to train employees who have more tenure on the job. In short, it is harder to teach an old dog new tricks. You should inoculate and imprint new employees with the operation's standards of quality as well as its policies, procedures, and techniques.

As will be discussed later in this text, accidents result from or are caused by new employees in a majority of occurrences. Training not only reduces accidents, it has been proven that good training programs also reduce absenteeism and short-term illnesses, employee turnover, spoilage and waste, damage to equipment, overhead, and labor cost. Indeed training increases employee morale, productivity, job knowledge, sales, and customer satisfaction. People are not perfect with respect to organizational goals, and training continues to develop both supervisory and technical skills in an ever-changing organization.[5]

Every person hired must go through an orientation program. Many new employees are very uncomfortable in a new job, and the orientation program should serve, among other things, as a gradual introduction to the organization as well as the job. During the orientation phase of training, the new staff member will be given such things as

1. Company history, the objectives of the organization, as well as how the organization works.
2. What her hours, wages or salary, and benefits are; when the regular pay periods occur, and when can she expect her first check.

FIGURE 3–5

The trainability curve (t) and the cost curve ($)

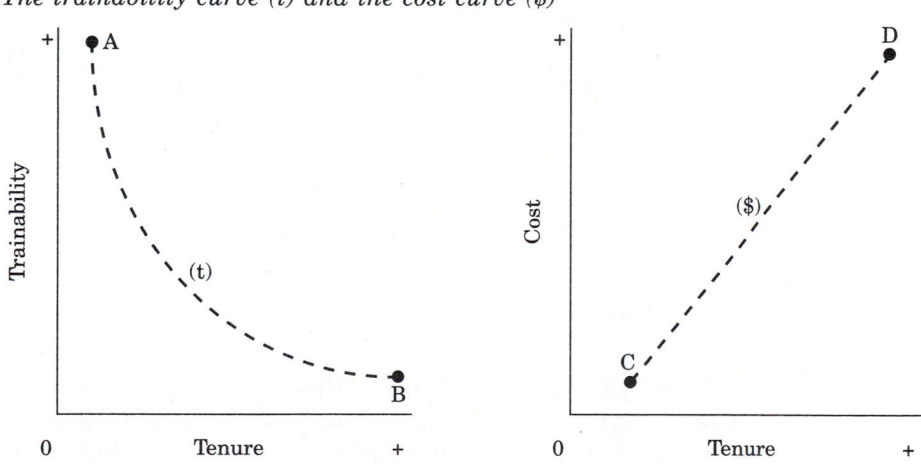

3. A brief description of her duties (including a basic direction in the job).
4. Policies and procedures forms (e. g., work permits W-4 withholding form, completed time card if applicable, rules and regulations).
5. Uniform and dress code.
6. Introduction to supervisor and co-workers.
7. Information about her work station, where the break area is, when she will be taking breaks, and where the restrooms are.
8. An overview of what (top) management thinks is important.
9. Ample time for any questions.

After orientation the employee must be trained to a minimum level of proficiency for her to be able to perform her job. For example, if trays are used, she must learn how to carry a tray, pour water, serve butter, serve cocktails, and so forth before being allowed in the dining room (see detailed service task procedures in Chapter 9). After this initial training, which is intended to bring the new staff member to a minimum level of proficiency, the new employee should be allowed to work for several shifts and then to ask questions of her supervisor on procedures she does not understand. After the initial training, which must be a well-planned and organized effort, the employee should attend refresher or continuation training with all other members of the service staff at regular intervals.

This whole process can be viewed as a wheel, with refresher training sessions offered on a biweekly or monthly basis. The frequency or repetition of the various programs should be determined by (1) the employee turnover rate, (2) the level of intelligence of trainees (i.e., the ability each has to retain knowledge, and (3) the complexity of the tasks. However, before entering this continuation training wheel, each staff member must attend an orientation training program as well as an introductory training program for minimum proficiency of required job tasks. Some employees may need not attend the required task sessions, but every new staff member *must* attend the orientation program. When a new staff member is bombarded with all of the things he is expected to know for his entire tenure in the particular job, he is overwhelmed, and sometimes very little information is actually retained by the new trainee.

A Systems Approach to Training

The development of a training program should follow the process outlined here. A whole book could be written to describe this topic, but such detailed treatment is beyond the scope of this text. The first step when developing a training program is to assess needs. Ask the questions: Do we have a training problem? Could he do it (the task) if his life depended on it? It must be remembered that training is not an end, but a means to an end. Yet training cannot be a one-shot approach; training must be continuous. One can see how the development of a training program is essential if the establishment intends to deliver a quality product and quality service. Indeed, the concepts on quality management are contained within the systems approach to training, and training is a subset of quality management (QM) (see Chapter 2).

Organization analysis is the first consideration within the assessment phase. Training must be started from the top down, as the major emphasis is to help the individual achieve the organization's goals (both long term and short term) and objectives. Many a trainee has come away from a training program saying, "I wish my boss would take this course." The organization's resources must also be analyzed as to finances, facilities, and human resources. Consider this example of an inadequate analysis from the organizational perspective. In two separate actions a manager mentions to his kitchen steward or training director that the dish machine operators need to speed up the number of pieces through the machine. He also talks to the purchasing agent about the same problem. The steward or training director perceives this as a training need, while the purchasing agent views this as a cue to begin looking for a new dish machine. Each expends considerable effort before secrets are revealed and the manager's desires are known.

In a well-designed assessment, the training director would quickly cease efforts or clarify organizational goals. The second investigation in the assessment phase is a complete task or operations analysis, and the third is the human performance analysis. The discussion of task analysis focuses on task-unit job descriptions, which is discussed in detail in the very next section. The human performance phase deals with comments such as

"I've got to teach her."
"He's got to change his attitude."
"We need a course to teach people . . ."
"Our waitresses can't sell wine."

Job Descriptions

A job description, complete with all tasks required in performing the job, must be written. The sources listed plus the job descriptions contained in this text as well as in *Tasks to Jobs* will serve as excellent guidelines. Additionally these descriptions must be tailored to the particular establishment by observing the staff members on the job in the establishment. The job description can be used not only as a guideline for the training program, but also for task-unit scheduling, performance appraisal, and wage and salary administration. From the job description, behavioral objectives should be determined. These objectives should indicate what the trainee will be able to do at the completion of the training. Behavioral objectives must be written for each desired task; for example, "The trainee will be able to demonstrate the correct procedure (as printed) for carrying, presenting, opening, and serving red wine."

An evaluation scheme must be developed directly from the objectives in order to measure instructional intent. Questions and other forms of examination are derived directly from the learning objectives, which are derived directly from the job, task, and human performance analyses. This reinforces the systems approach to training, since nothing is designed in a vacuum—each piece of the training program development is related to its predecessor phase. The reason that the evaluation scheme of the training program is developed *before* training begins is to ensure that the content of the evaluation plan is not polluted (contaminated) by anything during the actual training.

Standard criteria for measuring instruction in job-related training programs are inadequate (e.g., rank, standard scores, percentile scores, percentage, or "passing grades"). The best measure in a job training program is a criteria-based exam (i.e., derived from the objectives after a detailed analysis). The trainee must meet or exceed the level of performance described in the learning objectives or the job criteria established for effective performance. If the trainee cannot attain these benchmarks, either the training objectives are unrealistic or the trainee should not be placed in the work situation, especially where he might have to interact with guests.

Information gathered in the evaluation process must then be routed back to the development phase of the program where updates, changes, and modifications in the training program will be necessary. Information from the evaluation process should come from (1) trainees while in the training program, (2) graduates of the training programs at different phases or times after training (e.g., one year after completion, two years after completion, five years after completion, and so forth), (3) supervisors of the graduates of the training programs *as well as* from (4) guest surveys using the QM and the critical incident technique.

Before designing the training (lesson) plan, the trainer will select and sequence the training units. In selecting training units, trainers should remember that the content of the training program must be directly relevant to the job to facilitate the transfer of knowledge from the training setting to the job. Content must make a significant contribution to attaining the organization's objectives as well as the human performance objectives. (Use service procedures detailed in Chapter 8 to design a task-based training program for servers).

When sequencing instruction, consideration should be given to the arrangement of material based on (1) chronology (e.g., the order of service);

(2) general to specific (e.g., wine knowledge to wine service); (3) specific to general (e.g., basic wine service to knowledge of wines), and (4) simple to complex (e.g., taking a basic order to taking the order with embellishments of menu items and subtle up-selling techniques).

The training plan is the blueprint from which the training instructor works. It is the point at which the ideals of what the trainer would like to accomplish meet the realities of time, space, equipment, and money. A good training instructor will combine all the resources available to have the best training program for the least expense. The training plan describes how all factors will be combined so that the largest number of trainees will develop the highest degree of skill with respect to the facilities, time, instructor(s), and content. Planning the lesson is a time of reckoning—determining how to fit what needs to be done within time and money restrictions. The training plan calls for what the trainee will be doing during each phase of instruction, as well as the type of instruction (lecture, demonstration or four-step method, movies or video tape, interactive video, etc.) that will be used.

When selecting training instructors and when preparing the training environment, select the right person to do the training and make sure he knows how to train and has the ability to demonstrate, to impart knowledge, to inspire the trainees, and to appraise the trainee's performance. Have necessary training aids, audio-visual support, tools, and all required equipment at hand. Make sure the work place is in good order and that everything, including the trainee, is in the correct position. Ensure that the instructor has provided ample time for the instruction to take place and for the trainees to grasp the information being presented—he should display a friendly, helpful, interested, and unhurried attitude. For the instructional/training process itself, instructors should place the trainees at ease. A nervous, jumpy trainee is in no mental condition to receive or absorb new information or ideas. When conducting an individual human performance analysis, the training instructor should check what the learner already knows, and proceed to arouse the learner's interest while building up the learner's self-confidence.

Conducting Meetings with the Service Staff

Regular meetings with the service staff must be conducted in order that managers receive first-hand knowledge of guest reactions and guest desires. An agenda for each meeting must be compiled by the supervisor conducting the meeting. Otherwise, the meeting lacks direction and results in a boring affair for all employees. Groups should seldom exceed 30 or so members. If the group is too large, exchange among the members may be minimal.

The Four-Step Training Process

1. Prepare the worker for the job.
2. Explain the job.
    A. Give him any preliminary information that will be helpful.
    B. Show him how to do the job at full production speed.
    C. Then demonstrate how it is done, slowly if possible. Illustrate and question carefully and patiently.
    D. Stress and explain key points—give reasons.
    E. Point out safety precautions.
    F. Explain clearly and completely, taking one point at a time.
    G. Repeat operation full speed.
3. Get him started (tryout performance).
    A. Let him do the easy parts—you do the hard ones.
    B. Let him add the difficult parts—one by one.
    C. Have him tell and show you how the job is done; have him explain the key points.
    D. Point out where he may run into difficulties.
    E. Ask questions and correct errors.
    F. Continue until you know HE knows.
4. Put him on his own.
    A. Let him take over the entire job—but watch him. See that he is forming safe and correct habits.
    B. Leave him alone, but encourage him to come to you if anything bothers him.
    C. As he progresses, explain any additional fine points that may have been deferred at the start.
    D. Review his progress frequently.
    E. Check safety, quality, and quantity of production.

An effective method to begin a meeting is to introduce nonthreatening directives from management, as it has a settling effect on the group. Compliments and praise should be extended to those individuals who have performed well, especially when guests have recognized any server's performance. When necessary, negative comments should be covered next, but specific negative comments directed towards individuals should be avoided, and negative job performance evaluations should be conducted in private. From this point forward, a round-the-table discussion can be encouraged by the supervisor. Rather than saying, "Lani, anything to add?" the group leader may pick a specific thing that she knows Lani can talk about and say, "Lani, tell us about the guest who came in wearing a hat and refused to take it off." After the round table discussion, the supervisor may read or distribute a short incident or role-play. An effort must be made by the supervisor to withhold judgment of any individual staff member's handling of a situation. Invariably other staff members will offer suggestions that are acceptable, and the person who took an outlandish position will probably modify her thinking. Good ideas are usually embellished, while mistakes are pointed out. If the group is generally nonresponsive, this may indicate tension within the group. A cohesive team will tend to work together.

The following role-play exercises and incidents may be used to stimulate group discussion. These situations are easy to develop, and any supervisor should be able to generate one good incident per day.

Role-Play Exercises

Role-Play 1

Customer: You waited 10 minutes for your order to be taken; your coffee was not hot when served; your main course was undercooked; you did not get any butter for your rolls; and you were offered a refill on coffee only once. Your check is $4.59, and you do not feel that you got either the food or service promised in the advertising. The restaurant is near your work, and you would like to return again, but not if it is going to be like this time.

Cashier: You have had an extremely busy rush, the head server is home sick, and there are several new people on the schedule. This customer comes in to the restaurant often and usually finds something to complain about.

Role-Play 2

Manager: One of your best servers is coming in for work half hour early this evening so she can talk to you. She sounded upset on the phone. Mary does an excellent job. She is honest, reliable, and has helped you train other servers.

Server: The new server, Polly, is a thief. Ever since she started working, your tips and the tips of the other servers have been decreasing. Polly always seems to cash in large sums of change at the end of the night. You have not actually caught her in the act, but one of the other servers said she saw Polly take a tip off a table that was not hers. You think your manager should know.

Role-Play 3

You are an assistant restaurant manager. Your host is incapable of handling a large crowd, and there are convention delegates swarming into your restaurant. You were helping seat guests and answering the phone for reservations.

Mr. Alexander's secretary called for reservations, and you told her you were filled to capacity. She informed you that Mr. Alexander was already on his way over! He is a regular and important customer. When Mr. Alexander entered, you told him that you could not seat him or his five guests. He became quite indignant. To make matters worse, the host remarked to you in Mr. Alexander's presence, "You could have seated Mr. Alexander if you had just planned things a little better." The host has always been envious of you.

What do you do?

Role-Play 4

You are a shift supervisor in a coffee shop. A guest just got up from his table and grabbed a handful of paper napkins from the counter. Gladys (a middle-aged waitress with ten years longevity) proceeded to reprimand the guest and remove the napkins. The guest explained that his two children were messy eaters, and he needed the napkins. Gladys showed no sympathy to the guest. The guest registered a complaint to you personally.

How do you handle the guest? How do you handle Gladys?

Role-Play 5

You are a young assistant food and beverage manager at a 125-seat American service restaurant. In addition to your responsibility for supervising dinner (6:30 P.M.–10:30 P.M.), you volunteered to supervise the training program your corporate headquarters has designed for service personnel. You have great rapport with almost all of your service staff. However, Gertrude has refused to cooperate with the standardized system you are teaching. She informs you that she has been "quite successfully" waiting tables for 22 years. Her tips are better than your average server's tips. Your manager has told you, "Get Gerty up to standard or get rid of her!" Firing Gerty is not an alternative.

What would you do? What factors need to be taken into consideration?

Conclusion

The personnel function in service management is multifaceted. Consideration of the organizational structure, recruiting and selecting service employees, interviewing, and conducting reference checks weigh heavily on the manager. The techniques listed will assist the service manager in selecting and organizing her service staff. Rating systems for tipped employees seldom reflect wages paid as they do for supervisory personnel, but the ratings are important for evaluating the individual's worth to the organization. It is important for managers and all service staff members to know their individual strengths and weaknesses.

Promotion from within the organization provides career opportunities within the organization. This may decrease staff turnover, which will stabilize the work environment. While discipline and termination are difficult to deal with, it is important that management develop guidelines for treating each of these areas. Training is a necessary function. Many operators feel that they do not have enough time or money to train when they really cannot afford not to train. The guidelines for conducting employee meetings will assist supervisors in this effort, and conducting an effective meeting is an excellent training session.

Endnotes

1. D. E. Lundberg and J. P. Armatas, *The Management of People in Hotels, Restaurants, and Clubs* (Dubuque, IA: Wm. C. Brown Company Publishers, 1989), p. 115.

2. P. Dukas and D. E. Lundberg, *How to Operate a Restaurant* (New York: Ahrens Publishing Company, 1960), p. 162.

3. D. E. Lundberg and J. P. Armatas, *The Management of People in Hotels, Restaurants, and Clubs,* 3rd ed. (Dubuque, IA: Wm. C. Brown Company Publishers, 1974), p. 105.

4. M. C. Gallagher, "The Economics of Training Food Service Employees." *The CHRAQ,* May 1977, p. 56.

Additional Readings

Hinkin, T. R. *Cases in Hospitality Management: A Critical Incident Approach*. New York: John Wiley & Sons, Inc., 1995.

A Hospitality Industry Guide for Writing and Using Task Unit Job Descriptions. Tourism Education Corporation. Boston: Cahners Publishing Company, 1976.

Mager, R. F. *Analyzing Performance Problems*. Belmont, CA: Fearon Publishers, 1962.

Preparing Instructional Objectives. Belmont, CA: Fearon Publishers, 1962.

Mager, R. F. and P. Pipe. *Analyzing Performance Problems*. Belmont, CA: Fearon Publishers, 1964.

Marvin, B. *Restaurant Basics*. New York: John Wiley & Sons, Inc., 1992.

Tanke, M. L. *Human Resources Management for the Hospitality Industry*. Albany, NY: Delmar Publishers, Inc., 1990.

Tasks to Jobs. The International Labor Organization. Geneva. 1983.

Wilson, A. and R. J. Goodman, Jr., "Task-Unit Scheduling." *Cornell Hotel and Restaurant Administration Quarterly*, August 1984.

FIGURE 3–6

Dining Room Organization Chart for Formal Á La Carte Service

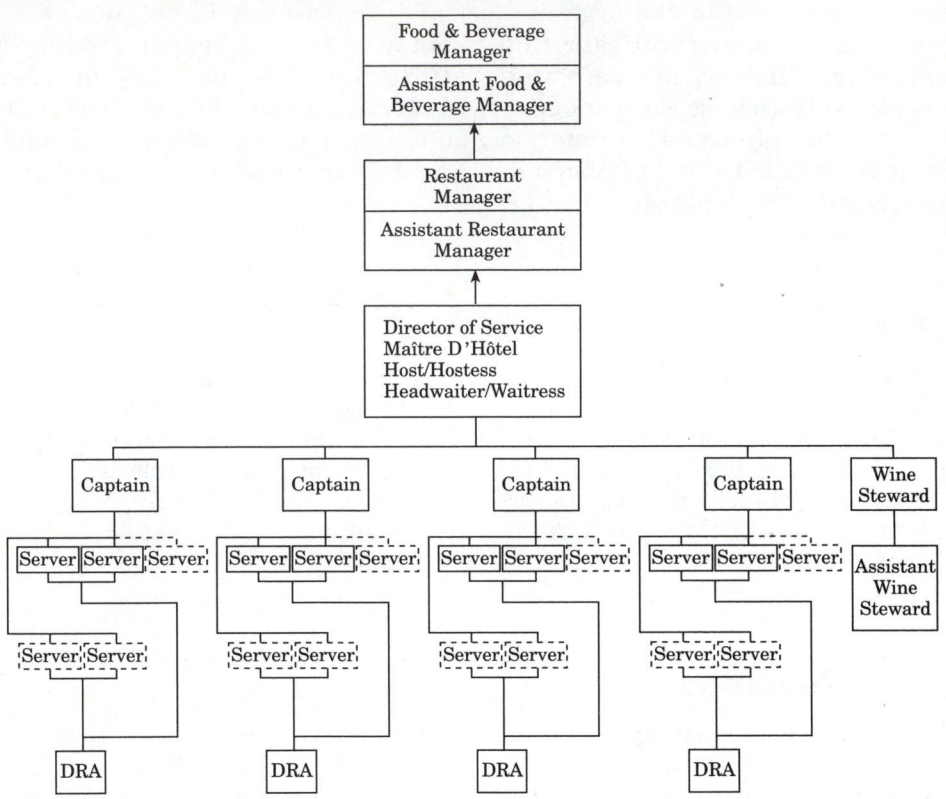

DRA = Dining Room Attendant

CHAPTER 4

Types of Service

Chapter Outline

The Types of Service
Cart Service (Gueridon/Trolley)
Platter Service
Plate Service
Family-Style Service
Buffet Service
Banquet Service
Conclusion

Learning Objectives

After studying this chapter, the student will be able to . . .

1. Define the following types of service (as named by function): Cart Service, Platter Service, Plate Service, Family Service, Buffet Service, and Banquet Service.

2. Outline the major characteristics of each type of service.
3. Compare the cost structure and market appeal of each type of service.
4. Evaluate the advantages and disadvantages of each type of service.

Key Words/Phrases

Platter service
Russian service
Plate service
American service
Cart service
French service
English service
Butler service
Tableside cookery

Banquet service

Chef de rang

Commis de rang

Captain

Busser

Classical restaurant

Wine steward (sommelier)

Expediter

Annunciator

Pantry

Gueridon

À la carte

Cost structure

Space per guest

Occupation cost

Increased residence time

Turnover

Rechaud

Poor quality control

Service cloth

Underliner

Cover

Banquette

Lower left, raise right

Planked platters

Shrinkage

Service à la Ritz

Market appeal

Rules of service (etiquette)

Plus sales

Food cost percentage

Rule of seven minutes

Through-put

Derivative product

The Types of Service

Restaurant table-service styles in the United States primarily use three types of service. Although **platter service** (sometimes referred to as **Russian service**) is used primarily as an upgraded style for banquets, **plate service** (or **American service**) and **cart service** (or **French service**) are used primarily for à la carte dining. Perhaps by tradition only, restaurateurs in the United States adopted European terminology for naming the types of service. The European terms refer to the various styles of service as French, Russian, American, and **English service** (or **butler service**). There seems to be some confusion when these service terms are used. In an informal survey of approximately 100 European students, the name used to describe the type of service depended on where the individuals naming them were trained. People have been known to argue vehemently as to what the correct name for a particular type of service is: French service and Russian service are the two types of service most in dispute. It seems that these arguments are futile.

To communicate with other professionals in the industry, it is easier to name the type of service by the function being performed. In this text and to ease the confusion, the major types of service will be referred to as: *cart service* (**tableside cookery** and service), *platter service*, *plate service*, and *family service*. Additionally, *buffet* and **banquet service** will also be discussed in this chapter. Yet even this discussion as to the types of service is academic. Rarely will one see a restaurant in the United

States, except in large cities or formal banquets, that strictly adheres to a particular type of service. In order to plan and to make decisions it is important to define the types of service, and a well-educated restaurateur should be aware of the managerial advantages and disadvantages of each, enumerating each type of service's cost structure and marketing appeal.

Cart Service (Gueridon/Trolley)

Cart service is called *French service* in the United States and in Germany; yet in France, Cart Service is referred to as *Russian service*. To highlight this confusion, a banquet server, when applying for a banquet job, is asked if he or she knows French service. What is really being asked is, "Do you know how to use a fork and spoon in order to transfer food from a platter to a guest's plate?" Yet some texts make it clear that Russian service is erroneously called French service. What distinguishes this type of service from the others is that the food is brought to the guests' table in either a raw state or a semiprepared state and finished (either warmed, sauced, flambéed, or carved) on a cart, in front of the guests in the dining room. This personal attention is elaborate and delivers individualized dining service to the guest.

The final food preparation is performed by the **chef de rang**, and she is assisted by a **commis de rang**. Although the chef de rang has been called a **captain** or a server (waiter/waitress), she performs some of the tasks performed by a traditional server and some of the tasks a captain usually performs. The commis de rang is referred to as a dining room attendant (busperson or **busser**), but he performs many more service-related functions than are usually given a traditional dining room attendant. A demichef de rang is a commis de rang who has recently been promoted and is given a small station and the assistance of a commis. The chef de rang and the commis work together as a team in a station of approximately 20 guests. The chef de rang prepares the food and places the food on the plates, while the commis actually serves the guest. Each of these two individuals must be highly skilled, since the chef de rang is performing many of the functions in the dining room that the cook performs in the kitchen.

Duties of the Staff

In a **classical restaurant** the headwaiter (chef de salle) or maître d'hôtel will greet the guests at the door and pass the party to a chef de rang, who will also greet the guests, lead them to a table in his station, and seat them. He will then take the order for cocktails or appetizer wines. He may pass the order to the commis, especially if cocktails will be served, or he may serve the cocktails or wine himself. In the absence of a **wine steward (sommelier)**, the chef de rang will serve the dinner wines. He must be able to cook menu items at the tableside and also needs to be able to flame these foods, carve meat, and bone fish and poultry. After he prepares the food, the chef de rang will plate and garnish the food while the commis actually serves the guests.

The commis de rang assists the chef de rang in seating the guests; and while the chef takes the order, she offers service to guests by serving relishes, butter (informal meal), and water (customary in the United States). After the chef de rang takes the order from the guests, the commis will place the order with the **expediter** or **annunciator** in the kitchen (**pantry** and range). When the food is ready for serving, the commis brings the food either to the guests (i.e., preplated appetizers) or to the chef de rang for preparation and plating. As mentioned previously, after the chef prepares the food, the commis actually serves the guests.

Characteristics of Cart Service

Cart service is characterized by a cart (trolley or **gueridon**) or light, movable table (some with wheels on only two of the four table legs) at tableside as well as quality personalized professional attention and service. Since there is very low guest turnover, menu items must be priced higher in order to cover the restaurant's fixed costs. Additionally, more service personnel are needed per guest. Food is served from the right side of the guest with the server's right hand. In cart service a minimum cover (silverware setting) usually consisting of a dinner knife and a dinner fork (see Chapter 9 for detail on place settings) is set, and additional silver is brought with the specific course being served.

Cost Structure and Market Appeal of Cart Service

If it were determined by survey or in a feasibility study that there is a market for elite clientele and the restaurant owners wanted to attract this type of guest willing to pay a relatively high menu price, then cart service would be the best type of service to employ. In fact, when main course menu prices exceed 30 to 40 dollars per cover **à la carte**, something more than plate service is usually expected by the guest. In Europe and parts of Asia as well as other parts of the world in a restaurant of any caliber, guests would not accept having a plated meal brought from the kitchen and simply placed in front of them. In many other countries, plate service is associated with a café. From the managerial point of view there is an additional advantage to cart service: It may be used only on slow nights, and therefore some of the kitchen staff may be released. This may be beneficial, because salaries paid to service personnel are generally lower than those paid production personnel since service personnel are compensated via gratuities. Of all the major types of service, cart service has a higher **cost structure** than the other major types of table service. Service delivery costs are higher to institute and maintain a cart service system.

In the classical approach to cart service, a highly skilled staff is required, and skilled servers may be either difficult to find or nonexistent in certain geographic markets. If the primary market segment to be served suggests that the use of cart service is warranted in the operation, an extensive service training program must be planned, developed, and maintained. Another disadvantage to cart service is that more **space per guest** is required. A general rule used in planning and designing restaurants is to allow 15 square feet per person in the dining area (i.e., if the restaurant seats 150 people, 2,250 square feet are required). In restaurants offering cart service, *18 square feet* per person is required as a minimum. More room is needed to roll carts around the dining room, and additional space is required to keep a safe distance between the cart and the table during food preparation, especially if food is to be flamed at tableside. Menu pricing must be adjusted upward since there is a higher **occupation cost** (rent or mortgage). As an example, a 150-seat restaurant offering cart service would require 2,700 square feet or 450 square feet more than if plate service were offered. Dining space rule-of-thumb marginal costs run approximately $100 per square foot. For the space only the cost is increased by $45,000.

Menu pricing must also be adjusted upward since cart service is slow, with leisurely service (**increased residence time**) resulting in fewer guest **turnovers**. A 150-seat restaurant with a busy plate service could expect three turns, while the same restaurant offering cart service may expect only two turns. If a certain sales figure is required to cover costs plus profit (and it usually is), the menu price must reflect the fewer number of turnovers. A 150-seat plate service restaurant with an $12 cover average and three turns would bring in $5,400 for an evening. The cart service restaurant with two turns would need to increase the cover average to $18 to bring in the same dollar volume. Besides these two factors there will be some additional costs required to purchase carts, flaming lamps (**rechauds**), pans, platters, and so on. These costs must be calculated into the menu price, even though they are not as substantial, as the occupation costs are higher, the sales volume is lower, and there are fewer guest turnovers. These equipment costs will be slightly less than the cost of additional service equipment for platter service. However, the production of food in the dining room may decrease, ever so slightly, the amount of kitchen equipment required.

Another slight disadvantage in performing tableside cookery in the dining area is that the dining room may smell of stale food unless it is aired out or vented. This is especially noticeable if the room has large draperies or tapestries that may absorb the odors. Since there are several individuals in a dimly lit dining room, as compared to only a few in a well-lit kitchen preparing food, the managerial control over product quality is reduced in cart service. In other words, a cart service restaurant has **poor quality control**. Poor quality control should not be confused with poor quality. Indeed, many restaurants offering cart service have the finest quality available. However, it is more difficult for management to observe (and control the quality of) the production of each item or the plating of each menu item. It is also more difficult for the chef de rang to determine degrees of doneness of the meat, adjust seasonings, or regulate the thickness of sauces as he is working in the dining room. In short, it is difficult to cover up any mistakes while in the presence of the guests. Each dish prepared in the kitchen may be inspected by an expediter before presentation to the guest. It would be ludicrous to have each dish prepared at tableside inspected by a quality control individual before presentation to the guest. Portion control can also be poorer in a cart service system than in a plate service system, although the high-cost items such as steak can be controlled with minimum effort.

Cart Service—A Modern Approach

A modern approach to tableside cookery and service follows with explanations of the staffing requirements and the equipment and utensils used in the preparation of food as well as service at tableside. Several tested, standardized recipes appear at the end of Chapter 8, but their inclusion is not intended to make this text either a professional's guide or a cookbook. Rather, the simplified method presented here is proof that tableside cookery need not always entail unnecessarily slow service complete with elaborate tableside presentations—the traditional, classical approach to cart service.

This modern, practical approach to tableside cookery and service is not a contradiction to the previous discussion, rather it is evidence that a facsimile of classical cuisine can be presented as a cost effective alternative to the customary plate service while maintaining flare and panache.

Classically, formal servers were expected to spend at least a year in the kitchen of a first-class hotel or restaurant, and even more time as an apprentice or commis de rang in the dining room. The singular feature that distinguishes cart service is some form of preparation in the presence of and before serving the guests. Historically, only restaurants with high-priced menus, working off higher profit margins, could absorb the costs involved with tableside cookery and cart service. These costs traditionally included low guest turnover, poor portion and quality control, more dining space per guest, and excessive training time for the service staff.

Sequential Service for Formal à la Carte Meal*

- Settings (minimum cover).
- Maître d'hôtel or chef de rang seats guests and presents menu.
- Water served (optional).
- Take food order.
- Offer wine list and/or suggestions.
- Serve appetizer (in center of cover) on cover (service) plate.
- Remove first-course dish (leave cover plate).
- Serve soup from cart in center of cover on cover plate; offer soup garnish.
- Remove soup dishes and cover plate.
- Food (fish course) served from platter or plates filled from gueridon and placed in center of cover.
- Clear fish course.
- Serve and clear Sorbet course.
- Main course served as fish course.
- Remove main course dishes, order as follows:
  1. Relish dish.
  2. Condiments.
  3. Dinner plates.
  4. Vegetables dishes.
  5. Empty wine glasses.
  6. Extra flatware.

- Serve salad (formal service) in center of cover with fork at right (refrigerated forks are impressive).
- Remove salad dish.
- Crumb table.
- Silver for dessert course placed right of cover.
- Serve dessert in center of cover.
- Remove dessert course.
- Serve coffee (may be served with dessert).
- Offer brandy or cordials.
- Present check at a reasonable time after cordials (or coffee), ensuring that guest does not feel hurried.
- Take guest's money or card to cashier and return change or card on dish (if card, offer pen for signature). Thank guest for tip.
- Server helps guests as they rise to leave and checks that nothing is left behind.
- Remove tip and tray.
- Clear table and relay.

---

*Steps may be deleted as level of formality is reduced. Casual theme restaurants would edit these steps to suit the specific service system and the clientele or specific target market.

The modern approach allows servers with very little knowledge of tableside cookery to prepare foods with complete confidence in the presence of guests. The method is simplified because the ingredients are preprepared and preportioned in the kitchen, recipes are standardized for the particular operation, and the method section in each standardized recipe describes procedures in simplified terminology.

There are several advantages to the modern approach when compared to the classical. Since menu items are prepared as much as possible in advance, the residence time per guest is decreased, which increases the guest turnover rate. Since all ingredients are preportioned, quality and portion control are enhanced. Recipes are not left to the individual whims of the captain preparing food at tableside. Most important, however, is that captains and servers need not spend excessive time in training. The checklists for dining room setup (mise en place), cart setup, and simplified procedure at the tableside make the service staff's job as easy as possible. (See tableside cookery recipes in Chapter 5.) The most difficult aspect of tableside service, especially with a combination of service styles, is the coordination required between the service staff and the kitchen staff, and among the service staff who must work together in teams.

If all tableside food preparation and service are from the cart, little coordination is required from service to production. With a combination of service styles, however, one server must bring vegetables or other items not prepared at tableside from the kitchen as the other service team member finishes the food preparation at tableside. The manager must be fully aware of the staffing considerations for this modern method of tableside cookery and service.

Staffing Requirements

In any staffing situation, each operator must determine his staffing requirements based on the individual need of the particular establishment. Yet the functions, tasks, or duties that need accomplishing are similar from one property to another. For example, it is necessary to prepare the dining area for service (mis en place) whether in an elegant restaurant, casual theme restaurant, or in a coffee shop—the functions are the same, the specific tasks will differ. In addition to setting up the dining room, the kitchen must also be prepared for service. Guests must be greeted and seated, and orders must be taken, placed at the range, picked-up, and served to guests or picked-up and prepared for the guest at the tableside. It is essential for management to detail and to define all the tasks that need to be accomplished from the time the first employee arrives for his shift until the last employee leaves.

The many tasks in the kitchen and dining room are divided among the various employees and supervisors. Almost all of these duties must be accomplished during the service period, yet the person who is designated by management to accomplish these tasks may vary from location to location. For example, the captains usually prepare foods at tableside and serve the wines (in the absence of a wine steward) in most restaurants. Serving wine, however, can be accomplished by any of the employees in the dining room. The manager should designate tasks to the various employees in the operation. A restaurant operator who decides to use tableside cookery in his property should look at several factors with reference to staffing and scheduling.

In a normal plate service style operation a server should be able to efficiently wait on 14 to 18 guests at one time. The 14 to 18 guests would be seated in rotation and not seated simultaneously. However, if tableside cookery and service is being used, the server cannot efficiently serve the same 14 to 18 guests. The recommended rule of thumb for tableside service is approximately 10 to 12 guests for one server working alone. The station division can be made several ways:

- Two stations of 15 or 17 with one person flaming for two stations.
- Three separate stations with each server serving and preparing food at the tableside.
- One server per station of 13 to 15 guests with one dining room attendant for each of two servers.

A staff member preparing food at tableside should be designated for each of two stations, as the second method listed above may tie up a server at one table and force her to neglect her other guests. Additionally, when tableside cookery menu items are served at the same table where items prepared in the kitchen will *also* be served, the team system allows one server to be working at the tableside while the other picks up food in kitchen. The guests in one party will then be served simultaneously as much as is possible. Managers must determine which pay scale is beneficial, as dining room attendants may receive more in hourly wages from the establishment than servers. It would behoove management, if this is the case, to dispense with the dining room attendant designation and call everyone a server with different tasks and different responsibilities.

The number of tableside items and the popularity of these items should also be taken into consideration when staffing or scheduling. If the restaurant offers Fresh Spinach Salad Helen and Steak Diane as the only two tableside preparations in the restaurant, the stations need only be decreased by two or three guests per station, and the server serving the station may also prepare foods at tableside. However, if only these two tableside items are offered and they prove to be very popular, the number of guests in each station should be decreased as necessary to provide efficient service. (See Chapter 5 for recipes on tableside cookery.)

The configuration of the dining room and of the stations will also be a factor in staffing and scheduling. For example, one restaurant with approximately 25 to 30 seats in a rather small room could not accommodate more than two service personnel serving in this room. If an additional service person were placed in this small room, the room would be too crowded, and servers would actually be bumping into each other while trying to serve. If this restaurant, however, offers many items that are prepared at tableside, the purpose of offering tableside service is to give personalized attention to the guest. Increasing the size of the stations significantly somewhat defeats the purpose of offering table-side service. Yet the restaurant would lose some valuable revenue-producing seats if they were to decrease the number of covers in this room. This decision can be made only by a manager who is fully aware of the guests' desires, the service they are receiving, and the operation's income statement.

Timing the Order

Recipes should have a time listed that measures the time from lighting the rechauds to serving the guest. Two and one-half minutes should be allowed on both ends of this calculated time to set up the cart and clean the used cart for a total time factor. It should take no more than five minutes total for setup and cleanup (i.e., two and one-half for setup and two and one-half for cleanup). However, it is difficult to determine when the tableside item will be ready in order that all guests at the table will be served simultaneously. The difficulty arises when there is a waiting line of servers at the range picking up their food, and the server needs the order because the food is ready at the tableside. The recommended procedure here is to allow the server to go to the head of the pickup line when tableside items are being served at a table in the server's station.

Another method for coordinating this effort includes the following: when the server picks up his semiprepared tableside cookery item, the range crew can plate the corresponding vegetables, cover, and hold (in a warmer) for the server's call. Food coming off the range and off the cart at tableside at the same time is difficult due mainly to mixing the styles of service. Exactly when does the server inform the range to "final prep" the menu items that will be served simultaneously with tableside items? When does the server preparing food at the tableside inform her partner to pick up the other food items or side dishes at the range to accompany the tableside items?

If everything were cooked at the tableside, the service procedures might be simpler. Difficulty arises when different styles of service are mixed. Yet an attempt should be made to speed the laborious process of classical tableside cookery without sacrificing flair and flamboyance. A description of the proper sequence follows in the boxed General Procedure for Flamed Items that follows, but each person should practice in order to master this sequence in the operational environment.

Platter Service

Platter service is generally referred to as Russian service in the United States and in Germany. In France it is referred to as French service or silver service. Platter service is universally accepted in fine restaurants

General Procedure for Flamed Items

Salads, Entrees, and Desserts

1. Server informs captain that he is picking up the required items for flaming. (Place a five-minute call for nonflamed items at this time, which indicates to range that they should perform final preparation and plating of nonflamed items and hold for service.)

2. Captain will prepare her cart and then wheel to guests' table.

3. Captain will wait for server to bring ingredients for preparation.

4. After server brings ingredients for flaming, he will return to kitchen to pick up nonflamed items.

5. Captain begins preparing flamed items at the tableside per recipe.

6. Server should return to dining room, serve guests eating nonflamed entree, and assist captain as necessary.

7. When captain has finished preparation, server will present food to guests.

Specific Procedure for Steak au Poivre Flambe

1. Server takes order from guests, including desired degree of cooking (well, medium, etc.).

2. Orders be turned in to the range, who will prepare all nonflamed items as normal. At the same time he will perform all kitchen preparation (e.g., portioning brown sauce into gravy boats, portioning clarified butter into pitcher, browning steaks, and so forth) on a tray with specific ingredients needed for server's tableside items. These will include the garnished steaks, butter, scallions, and brown sauce (from the steam table). Should the order require a well-done steak, preparation of cooking will be done in the kitchen so that steak only has to be finished on the cart.

3. Server informs captain he is picking up items needed for flaming. When he picks up these items, he will place a five-minute call for nonflamed items. Captain will prepare her cart with the other ingredients needed for tableside preparation (Worcestershire sauce, Madeira, brandy) and wheel to guests' table and wait for ingredients from server.

4. After giving the captain the ingredients, the server will return to the kitchen for nonflamed items along with plates for the steak au poivre, which will have vegetable and potato already on it. Captain will prepare flamed item.

5. Server will return to dining room, serve guests eating nonflamed entrees, and assist captain as necessary.

6. When captain has finished preparation, server will serve the steak au poivre, making sure "medium steak goes on plate with baked potato and zucchini," etc.

the world over. As mentioned earlier, many restaurant patrons would not accept plate service in standard service restaurants; and when cart service is not feasible, platter service is implemented.

Characteristics of Platter Service

In platter service the food is fully prepared in the kitchen by a cook or chef and placed on platters for service to the guest. The server brings the platter of food—entrees, vegetables, sauces, and so on from the kitchen into the dining room and may place the food at or on a secondary warming surface. He places hot empty plates in front of each guest and then serves the food by transferring the food from the platter to the guest's plate. The hot plates are usually kept hot in a warming stand in the dining room and placed from the guest's right side. While holding plates in his left hand protected with a **service cloth,** the server walks around the table clockwise as he places the plates. This movement around the table makes the flow more fluid as he need not stop and back up for each guest as he would if he were moving counterclockwise. The server serves the food from the left side of the guest while holding the platter in the left hand (close to the guest's plate) with the left foot advanced forward for balance and manipulating the fork and spoon with his right hand. The server moves around the table counterclockwise while serving the food for the same reasons stated above.

Soup is served in a silver soup cup, which is brought to the table in a soup bowl on an **underliner.** The soup bowl is on an underliner with soup cup in it; it is then placed on the service plate where the server inverts the silver cup pouring away from the guest and allowing the soup to fill the bowl. She then removes the emptied silver cup, and the guest may begin eating, usually after all guests at the table have been served. An alternate method for serving soup is similar to the cart service method, where a tureen is brought to the table and the server ladles soup into the hot, empty bowl that has previously been placed in the center of the **cover.** It is customary to set a complete place setting with all flatware required for that particular meal when platter service is the service system being used.

Cost Structure and Market Appeal of Platter Service

As a formal presentation and service of food, platter service has many advantages. Although slightly less personalized for the guest than cart service, platter service allows the guest to experience more personal attention than the same guest may experience when plate service system is used. This form of service may be quite elaborate if ornate silver platters are used. Less space per guest is required in the dining room than in cart service, as additional space is not required to roll carts through and around the room. The tables should be slightly larger than for plate service as 30 inches per cover is usually allowed as compared to 24 inches per cover for plate service. Service personnel must be able to move comfortably between guests when serving from a platter. If larger tables are required, special consideration must be given to the placement of these tables in the dining room. Adding an extra foot of dining room space along the length of a wall may make space for an additional row of tables, whereas removing a foot may not make the dining room any more crowded. This decision may be addressed during the value engineering phase of design. It is difficult to serve **banquette** or booth tables from a platter.

Although service personnel must be well trained, the level of proficiency needed for servers is not as extensive as that required for cart service. The difficulty arises not in the manipulative skills required with the fork and spoon, but the speed with which one must serve as a result of the numerous tasks required. One service person can handle more guests in an evening than if cart service were being used, since platter service allows for more guest turnovers. Platter service is more efficient since it is a faster form of service. Yet the station size for platter service need not be any larger than the stations required for cart service. If service is à la carte (as opposed to banquet service with a preset menu), one server should be able to serve 10 guests effectively. On the one hand, platter service is not particularly suitable for à la carte service, as it is time-consuming to take the orders, place orders at the range, pick up orders at the range, enter the dining room and place the platters on a secondary heating surface or cavity, pick up hot plates which are usually kept in the dining room, place hot plates in the center of the cover, return to secondary heating area and pick up platters, and finally serve the guests their food. On the other hand, it is an excellent type of service for banquets or for preset menus, and is, therefore, frequently used for formal banquets. The rules of thumb change for banquets or preset menus, and a server should be able to serve up to 20 guests efficiently for a preset or banquet menu. Management must assist the server in giving good service by using service teams when appropriate and by having all necessary equipment, utensils, and silverware available and handy.

Platter service offers excellent quality control, as each dish is prepared, placed on a platter, and garnished in the kitchen. The server must only transfer food from the platter to the plate since he does not have to prepare food at the tableside as is necessary in cart service. There can be good portion control; however, in practice, more food is usually placed on the platter than is required or sometimes even purchased by the guest, which ultimately results in waste and higher food costs.

There are some inherent disadvantages to any form of service, and platter service is no exception. A high initial investment in silver (platters) must be considered, although alternative metals/china (polished aluminum, polished pewter, stainless steel, and so forth), may also be used. These other metals or china are less expensive than silver or silver-plated equipment. It is also difficult to control the silver (platter) inventory, and replacement as well as repairs and maintenance (soldering, replating, and so forth) may be costly. Another notable disadvantage is the appearance of the platter after serving has begun. If each person in a party of four ordered Beef Wellington, the chef or line cook would plate the entree and vegetables, and garnish the platter for presentation in the dining room. By the time the fourth guest to be served saw the platter, he would be looking at a picked-over, unappetizing plate.

Plate Service

Although plate service can be referred to as German service, most agree that serving food that has been plated in the kitchen is called American service. In order to remain consistent, the term plate service will be used throughout this text, but the reader should be aware that *plate service* and American service are synonymous and are accepted as such universally. The distinguishing characteristic is that food placed on the plate in the kitchen will ultimately be placed in the center of the cover in front of the guest exactly as it was plated in the kitchen. The particular emphasis with this type service is speed. The service stations are usually arranged to give fast service. A characteristic of plate service is that food is served from the left and removed from the right (**Lower Left, Raise Right**). All beverages (coffee, tea, iced tea, milk, soft drinks, water, cocktails, and wine) are both served and removed from the right. Perhaps this rule (serve from the left) came about because Americans consume more of a wide variety of beverages than was the classical custom. Hence with the positioning of the cups, water glasses, and a variety of other drinking containers, it is easier to serve food from the left.

Restaurants offering plate service primarily may also borrow from the other types of service systems for certain items, such as (1) cart service—flaming entrees, desserts, and beverages and (2) platter service—**planked platters** (wooden boards usually decorated with potatoes and vegetables) and casseroles that are plated in front of the guests and served by the servers.

Cost Structure and Market Appeal of Plate Service

Plate service has only two disadvantages. First, it is not as elaborate or as personal as cart service or platter service, and hence may not be acceptable in certain types of restaurants or in certain parts of the world. Second, the service personnel may be bored with their tasks since a high degree of technical skill is not required. This may lead to a more difficult job on the part of management. The manager must continuously motivate his staff due to the monotony of the job from a technical or creative perspective when compared to cart or platter service. The operator may experience a higher employee turnover rate, a higher absenteeism rate, and a higher number of short-term illnesses. Plate service is technically more simple to perform as compared to cart or platter service since the service personnel need only to place a plate upon which food has been placed and garnished in front of the guest. As a result, a skilled staff, while desirable, is not essential, making hiring easier (larger pool of labor) and training for specific tasks less time consuming. Nonetheless, dining room servers and managers do appreciate the vast amount of people skills required to be truly effective servers. Managers may have an easier task motivating the service staff when there is a higher degree of technical skill required such as manipulating a fork and spoon correctly, opening a bottle of wine adeptly, or preparing foods at tableside with flare. Servers may experience the professionalism inherent in the job rather than seeng it as *just a job*.

In a remote area or developing area where there is an excess of unskilled labor, it might be foolish for managers to institute or require a formal service system. Some hotels in developing countries that cater to the European market have tried to use cart and platter service with difficulty, when plate service would ease the pressures on both the staff and management. Also if management desires elaborate service and there are too few servers on the floor able to serve the guests efficiently, the elaborate service turns into poor service. Using plate service would allow servers to quickly accomplish their tasks, place the food (on a pre-plated plate) in front of the guest, and have more time to address finer points of service.

Plate service is incredibly fast since many of the classical server's functions have been eliminated. The rule of thumb for staffing a plate service restaurant changes depending on the establishment's particular service system. One person can serve up to 18 guests effectively, and the range of 14 to 18 is a comfortable number of guests to serve for most service personnel. This rule of thumb applies to à la carte service, as a server should be able to serve 25 or more guests efficiently when a preset menu or banquet service is being used, especially when enhanced by a team service system.

Less dining room space is required for each guest when plate service is the service delivery system, and 15 square feet per person is the general rule of thumb used when laying out and designing dining room space. Yet in major metropolitan areas, less than 15 square feet may be designed, and in a rural or suburban area where cost per square foot is less, more than 15 square feet may be offered. The individual cover size, smaller than the size used for platter service, should be 24 inches across by 15 inches deep. The smaller covers allow for smaller tables, which translates into more seats within a given area. Since more people can be seated in a given area (lower rent or mortgage payments) and the service is considerably faster than cart or platter service, the menu prices for a given quality food product should be lower than the same quality product in a restaurant offering cart or platter service.

Sequential Plate Service

- Settings (standard American—two forks, two knives, two spoons).
- Host seats guests and presents menus.
- Pour water for each guest and place butter.
- Take cocktail order.
- Serve cocktail from right (beverage).
- Take food order.
- Bread is placed on table.
- Offer wine list and/or suggestions.
- Remove cocktail glasses if empty.
- Serve appetizer (center of cover).
- Remove first-course dish.
- Serve soup in center of cover.
- Remove soup dishes and show plates (if used).
- Serve salad, remove salad dishes.
- Serve main course, place in center of cover.
- Clear table, order as follows:
  Condiments.
  Dinner plates.
  Vegetable dishes.
  Empty wine glasses.
  Extra flatware.
- Crumb table.
- Present dessert and cordial menu.
- Serve dessert course (center of cover).
- Remove dessert course.
- Serve coffee (if not served with dessert).
- Serve cordials.
- Present check.
- Thank guest.
- Help guests as they rise to leave and check that no personal articles are left behind.
- Remove tip and plate or tip tray. Do not count tip.
- Clear table and relay if necessary.
- Refill water glasses when less than two-thirds full. Be sure to refill all water glasses to same level when refilling one.

Plate service offers excellent portion control. Since every food item the guest has ordered is plated in the kitchen and served to the guest in that form, he pays for what he gets and gets what he pays for. Whatever leaves the kitchen on a plate is precosted, priced, and controlled, so there is less chance for any **shrinkage** between the kitchen and the dining room. In this way it is easier to control items on a plate than items on a platter or cart. Quality control is excellent and the same for plate service and for platter service, since all food is prepared and plated in the kitchen.

Family-Style Service

Family-style service is more commonly called English service but has been referred to as French or Russian service in some areas. The particular characteristic of this type of service is that all food is brought to the table in dishes or on platters. The food is carved, dished, or plated and passed to each individual at the table, or the food is passed and each guest helps himself. In a home where domestic help is available, the maids or butlers may pass the dishes, approaching each guest from her left and allowing the guest to serve herself while the maid holds the platter. This form of family-style service may be used in commercial establishments, but it is not common.

Several restaurants use the form of family-style service where the plates and platters with food are placed on the table, and the guests help themselves. This type of service can be compared to an American Thanksgiving dinner where all the guests are seated at one time, the turkey is carved (before or after all have been seated), and the food is passed around the table. Asian restaurants typically use a modified form of family-style service, as the various entrees in an Asian restaurant are shared by the guests at the table. Yet in finer Asian restaurants, the guests do not plate their own food, rather deferring to a server who portions the various preparations at tableside, usually working from a tray on a traystand or from a cart.

Service à la Ritz is sometimes referred to as luxury English service and is very similar to family-style service. The host's or server's duties, however, are assumed by a highly skilled person who serves the food with flare and panache.

Cost Structure and Market Appeal of Family-Style Service

Hiring a technically qualified staff is not required when family-style service is being used. For example, a restaurant operator could hire high-school-age servers in the dining room, since service is informal and the staff needs only to place empty plates on the table and place large platters of food on the table. Even the skill required to serve a particular guest the meal she ordered is no longer necessary. Additionally, this type of service can be very fast. No time is required to mix and match entrees and vegetables either at the range or from a cart, and there is less talk time required when actually taking the order. As a result, menu prices can be lower, which, with all other things being equal, may increase the volume of business. Since all the food is prepared in the kitchen, family service offers excellent quality control; however, portion control is apt to be poor.

Tables should be as large as for platter service, since additional table space is required for the dishes that are placed on the table. As with platter service, family-style service can require dining room space of more than 15 square feet per person unless the larger tables are carefully arranged. Guest turnover is likely to be high since the service is fast, and this fast service decreases residence time for the guest. Depending on the length of the menu (i.e., appetizers, soups, fish, entrees, salads, desserts, etc.), one server could efficiently serve more than the standard 14 to 18 guests; however much more than 20 guests at one time (à la carte) might significantly decrease service effectiveness.

The most notable disadvantage for family service in a commercial establishment is that the guest may not get the feeling that he is being waited on, since food is placed on the table and the guests help themselves. Also, the dirty dishes at the table will make the table look messy, and again the guest may not experience a restaurant setting. These disadvantages are not as critical in an Asian restaurant, mainly because a precedent has been established in Asian restaurants and guests are accustomed to this form in order to taste the different dishes. Family-style service may not be a viable alternative as a type of service for a commercial establishment, save for Asian restaurants or large, informal, rural dining establishments where family service is customary. There are, however, successful restaurants offering this style of service where there is **market appeal** and an identifiable market segment demanding this style of service. In select markets, several Italian and Mediterranian restaurants have begun serving pasta and other selected menu items family style and with great financial success and market appeal.

Buffet Service

In buffet service the guest helps himself from the buffet table. The buffet itself and the display of food on the table can range from a very simple buffet, such as a soup and salad bar, to an elaborate buffet, such as those seen aboard luxury cruise liners. Many commercial restaurants build their reputations on the elaborate buffet table they offer. Buffets are effective sales tools and can be used to the operator's benefit, especially when offered during holidays or Sundays. Since fewer production and service staff are required to efficiently serve a given number of guests as compared to à la carte service, both production and service staffs may be given days off without damaging the reputation of the business. The food quality can be high, and each server can serve more guests efficiently for buffet service, since the guest is performing some of the server's functions. Food production workers can also be more productive, as food preparation can be spread over a longer period of time and produced in quantity versus made-to-order, individual portions.

Service personnel may enjoy working buffets since the service is easier to deliver and they can serve more people and earn more in gratuities. The guest seldom distinguishes between buffet and plate service and usually tips the customary 15 percent. Yet managers and servers should be aware of an additional responsibility when working buffets. Menu items can be changed or substitutions can occur during the course of the meal, sometimes very frequently, and it is each server's responsibility to check the buffet table for these changes in order to keep the guests informed. The service staff or a designated runner should watch the buffet table to be sure the food stays hot and appears appetizing.

Some Disadvantages of Buffet Service

Unless the service and production staffs are made aware of the appearance of the buffet table, the food can become unappetizing while sitting on the buffet line. One solution for this problem, however, is to produce food in smaller batches and regularly change the dishes on the buffet. Food cost can be high, as there is excessive waste when the food becomes unusable due to exposure. Sanitation laws regarding requirements for buffet lines may be stringent depending on the individual state. Food must be covered (sneeze guards), and top heat as well as bottom heat is essential to keep food hot and out of the danger zone (40° F to 140° F). Before installing a buffet or soup and salad bar, the restaurateur should investigate the state and local or county laws regarding the service of wholesome food to the consumer.

Banquet Service

No other type of service requires as much planning as banquet service. There are many advantages to this form of table service, which will be explored here along with its characteristics. Since banquet service is simultaneous service, that is, all guests being served at the same time, all arrangements, menus, beverages, wines, and timing must be carefully scheduled well in advance of the actual event. A staff briefing and sometimes even a "dress rehearsal" is essential to ensure that the timing of the event and all arrangements are communicated to each staff member to include setup, peripherals, miscellaneous equipment, supplies, audio-visuals, sound systems, additional services, entertainment, decorations, protocol if required, and so forth.

Banquet service usually involves a preset menu with place settings that reflect it. For example, if the menu calls for soup, salad, main course, dessert, two wines, and coffee, the place setting should have a soup spoon, a fork for the salad, a fork and knife for the main course plus steak knife if required, a butter knife, a utensil for dessert (spoon or fork as required), teaspoon for coffee, a water goblet (in the United States), and two wine glasses. In addition to having each place setting designed for the meal, the tables should also be preset for the menu including any accompaniments. Accompaniments to the meal, bread, butter, salad, salad dressings, and so forth *should not be preset on the table*, but should be ready for service before seating the guests begins. Adhering to this strict service etiquette of not presetting food or condiments may be *modified if time is critical* or if the banquet is particularly *informal*. If a server forgets to set butter for service during à la carte dining room operations, some delays will result; however this will not completely destroy the timing of the meal. If someone forgets to set the butter for service during a banquet for 400, the delay could ruin the banquet because all guests are served simultaneously.

The same **rules of service (etiquette)** apply during a banquet as during à la carte service, except that servers seldom engage in conversation with the guests. (See Chapter 9 for service procedures and techniques.) For à la carte service, the server must converse with the guest if only for just taking the order. Since service is simultaneous, the rule of thumb for simultaneous service is that from the time the first guest is served, any particular course until the last guest is served the same course, no more than seven minutes should elapse. If production cannot plate 400 meals in seven minutes, they should vary the plating process, such as create an automated or double production line or preplate some of the meals, keep the food warm, and serve these meals first while continuing to plate the balance.

When a head table at a banquet is designated, this table should be served first, and staffing for the head table should be somewhat better than just adequate. Speakers, guests of honor, and other dignitaries are usually seated at a head table. Those occupying the head table have duties to attend to, sometimes before and during but frequently immediately after the meal, and many speakers and introductions are conducted after those at the head table have finished eating (but before all others at the function have finished). If speeches, introductions, award presentations, and so forth are part of the banquet, the banquet manager should direct her service staff to move quickly *and* quietly during these periods. She should coordinate with the banquet host or meeting planner to ensure whether service should either continue or be suspended at particular times during the banquet.

Advantages and Disadvantages of Banquet Service

As an addition to à la carte service in an establishment, banquet service can be very profitable on many different dimensions. Banquet service is very fast—one server can serve almost twice as many guests efficiently as compared to à la carte plate service. Employee morale among the banquet service staff employees may increase as their efforts are usually well rewarded with gratuities. Since the number of people to be served (allowing for minor adjustments) is known, the staff wastes little time in setting up. A staff member may come on shift at 10:30 A.M., set up the tables and the accompaniments in one hour, take a 20-minute lunch break, finish setup, serve the meal, break down, and be out by 2:30 P.M.. Meanwhile, she could have served 28 guests an $22 meal and collected more than $100 in gratuities (or an average of $25 per hour). The fact that the number of covers is known in advance makes scheduling much easier than for à la carte service. And, the fact that additional part-time servers can be scheduled solely on the known volume rather than on a forecasted or estimated volume makes banquet service more efficient—more like a production manufacturing setting than a typical service organization.

Banquet sales can be considered **plus sales** and can be very profitable; **food cost percentage** is typically much lower in banquet service since it is easily precalculated, and waste, from overproduction is minimal. Operators can give better value to the consumer because of the above-mentioned factors, yet many operators take this profitable opportunity to cover inefficiencies in their à la carte operation.

Kitchen personnel usually have little to gain from additional banquet sales. When a commercial kitchen is improperly designed or there is no a banquet kitchen, equipment is sometimes overused to prepare for a banquet, especially when à la carte service is simultaneous with the banquet service. Managers are hesitant to add additional production personnel to cover the banquet preparation, and as a result production personnel morale declines. Additionally, many of the other types of equipment used by service personnel, such as water pitchers, silverware, and glassware, are in short supply during a large banquet, thus the ongoing à la carte operation may suffer if each à la carte guest receives poor service.

The following two areas, perhaps, present the largest challenges to banquet managers: banquet buffets and banquet beverage service. While banquet buffets optimize the staffing function in both the front and the back of the house, many operations do not provide adequate buffet offerings to service the number of guests efficiently. The **rule of thumb** to serve the same course within **seven minutes** to all banquet guests is often grossly violated during banquet buffets. Frustrated guests wait patiently *and not so patiently* while other banquet guests meander through the smaller-than-required buffet. While banquet buffets do optimize the operation's staffing requirements, the slow service the guest receives may prove counterproductive—guests may never return either for banquets or for à la carte dining. Banquet managers should determine the through-put (how fast all guests will take to traverse the buffet line) and then determine if the buffet line should be doubled or if the **through-put** is so long that plate or any other table service system would be more efficient. The simultaneous service conundrum is what presents this problem so vividly for banquet service. Indeed, for à la carte service, the periodic use of the buffet table allows for efficient and a less frustrating flow for the guests.

Banquet beverage operations suffer the same problem described for banquet buffets. Usually there is an insufficient number of bartenders or wine stewards to adequately service the guests in a timely manner. Again, guest frustration ensues. Banquet managers must design the service system to accommodate the simultaneity challenge for banquet buffets, banquet bar service, and banquet wine or beverage table service. The wine service issue and the beverage table service issue become even more acute when guests must also pay cash, individually, for wine and beverage service either at the bar or at table.

Conclusion

All too often service and the service-delivery system is given little attention during the planning phases of a food service establishment, and, as pointed out, there are some definite advantages and disadvantages to the various types of service. The personal types of service such as platter and cart service present more disadvantages on the surface, yet this added touch may be that single factor that distinguishes one restaurant's success from another's failure. Indeed, service is the **derivative product** that becomes the competitive advantage.[1] Before the decision is made to determine the service delivery system, surveys should be conducted as part of the feasibility study to determine the market for such a venture.

Questions

1. List the various types of service reviewed in the text and define each type relative to its use in different countries.

2. Discuss how you would prepare the mise en place for cart, gueridon, or trolley service in both the back of the house and front of the house. In what ways is the mise en place critical to the delivery of both quality food and service to the guest?

3. Through a chart or spreadsheet, compare the following characteristics for each type of service: dining room space (square footage) required, equipment cost, personnel skill level staff training requirements, restaurant style or environment, promptness of service/turnover rate, portion control, required space, menu price points, presentation of food, quality of food, and quality control.
(Service types are cart service, plate service, family service, buffet service, and banquet service.)

4. Describe and discuss some of the special challenges faced by banquet managers.

5. Develop a menu for an evening meal. Prepare tabletop setup schematics for serving the menu with each type of service defined in this chapter.

6. Collect the service equipment required for each type of service and demonstrate the techniques used in serving the guest.

Endnotes

1. The "derivative product" concept was introduced by Bruce Axler in *Foodservice: A Managerial Approach*. (Chicago: National Institute for the Foodservice Industry, 1979).

Additional Readings

Axler, B. and C. Litrides. *Food and Beverage Service*. New York: John Wiley & Sons. 1990.

Claiborne, C. *Dining Etiquette*. New York: Simon and Shuster, 1992.

Durocher, J. and R. J. Goodman, Jr. *The Essentials of Tableside Cookery*. Ithaca, NY: The Cornell Hotel and Restaurant Administration Quarterly.

Depew, V. ed. *The Social List of Washington, D.C.*, Kensington, MD: Jean Shaw Murray, 1980.

Meyer, S., E. Schmid, and C. Spuhler. *Professional Table Service*. Translated by Heinz Holtmann. New York: Van Nostrand Reinhold. 1991.

McCaffree, M. J. and P. Innis. *Protocol: The Complete Handbook of Diplomatic, Official and Social Usage*, Englewood Cliffs, NJ: Prentice Hall, 1977.

Post, E. *Emily Post's Etiquette*, New York: Funk and Wagnalls, 1969.

Tsuji, S. *Professional Restaurant Service, Ecole Technique Hoteliere Tsuji* (in English), New York: John Wiley & Sons. 1991.

CHAPTER 5

Equipment Used in Service

Chapter Outline

China
Glassware
Silverware or Flatware
Tablecloths and Napkins (Napery)
Accessories and Other Equipment
Tables
Chairs
Function Room and Banquet
 Furniture
Buffet, Serving Ware, and
 Gourmet Display Equipment
Tableside Service Equipment
Recipes

Learning Objectives

After studying this chapter, the
 student will be able to . . .
1. Explain how front-of-the house
 equipment supports the overall
 restaurant concept.
2. Outline the factors controlling
 the selection of any front-of-
 the house furnishings and
 tabletop architecture.
3. List the factors controlling
 required quantities for china,
 glassware, and flatware
 purchases.
4. Describe the criteria used
 for selecting table linens
 (tablecloths and napery).
5. Define the variety and
 characteristics of tabletop
 accessory items available in
 the marketplace.
6. Identify front-of-the-house
 production and service
 equipment used to support and
 augment the restaurant
 concept and service of food.
7. Give examples of the types and
 characteristics of furnishings
 used in function and banquet
 areas.
8. State the characteristics of
 equipment used for displaying
 and merchandising menu
 items.

Key Words/Phrases

Initial cost	18/8
Tabletop architecture	Natural fibers
China	Napery
Turnover rate	Wash-and-wear
Par-stock	Crocking
Replacement cost	Accessories and other equipment
Glassware/crystal	Holloware
Mass-produced glassware	Electronic cash registers
Silverware/flatware	Deuces
Hotel plate	Table configurations

Chapter 1 includes the paragraph, "When someone comes into your restaurant, she is looking for something more than satisfying the basic hunger or thirst need. Today's sophisticated restaurant guests are looking for far more than gustatory satisfaction when they choose a place to dine. 'They are seeking an experience—a sensory envelope of sight, sound, taste, smell, and touch that matches a mood or reinforces an image of self. As the mood and the image vary, so does the restaurant experience. . . .' (Colgan) After the professional restaurateur (who develops the concept) and the architect, interior designer, and contractor have created the intended experience . . ." STOP! This paragraph is repeated to underscore the importance of selecting front-of-the-house equipment that supports or renews the image of self and how the selection of the equipment used in service is an integral component of the design—indeed the entire feel of the restaurant.

Many owners/managers and their designers become totally involved in the selection and purchase of equipment since it supports the image of the restaurant so forcefully. Equipment is quite expensive, and many are appalled at the high cost, even though they may be purchasing in quantity and at wholesale prices. For example, one chair costs more than $100, with many models costing over $250. This means that the chairs alone in a small 60–75-seat dining room may have cost $15,000 or more. This should bring two considerations to the owner/manager and designer's attention: (1) What is my **initial cost**? (2) Can I replace the items I purchase, and how much will they cost in the future? In fact, an owner/manager and restaurant designer should always be aware not only of initial cost but replaceability as well. Some operations use customized china, silverware, and glassware, which may lend a touch of class to the operation. Yet customized equipment and utensils are (almost always) more expensive than open stock items, and customized amenities may be taken by guests and employees as souvenirs. The owner/manager and designer must decide if the initial additional cost and the concomitant inventory shrinkage is worth the increased investment.

The following discussion of restaurant equipment will be limited to the dining room or front of the house. Specifically, discussion focuses on china, glassware, silverware, flatware, holloware (pitchers, wine buckets, etc.), and accessories, such as linen, tables, chairs, and buffet or gourmet display equipment. Manufacturers and marketers of tabletop amenities have coined the term **tabletop architecture** to emphasize the design/decor/image concept.

China

As with other types of equipment, the initial purchase or replacement of **china** is most important. The managerial considerations in the initial purchase and replacement of china are more important than the purchase of other types of equipment. China may have a shorter life than silverware, but it usually has a longer life than glassware. China is quite expensive; for example, standard dinner plates cost from $45 to $150 per dozen, and a standard place setting (dinner plate, cup and saucer, butter plate, and two miscellaneous dishes) may cost more than $25. When you consider that for each seat in the restaurant you may have to purchase three place settings, the cost per seat for china alone approaches $75–100. In order to determine the proper quantity, however, several factors must be considered:

- **Turnover rate.**
- Type of dish machine (i.e., rate at which items can be washed).
- Number and type of menu items and frequency of service of particular items.
- Which dishes can be used for more than one purpose or more than one menu item.

When a manager of an existing operation decides to add more of the same pattern to his present stock, he must also consider several other factors. His restaurant may have been renovated, and the present pattern no longer fits the restaurant's mood or image. Since the particular pattern in use may be very costly, it might be wiser to retire the present stock, reserve it for special occasions or private parties, and purchase an entirely new pattern for daily use. A particularly well-known restaurant purchased gold-rimmed china years ago when the price of gold and the price of labor were lower. Before a decision was made to purchase more of the same pattern, an enterprising manager investigated the costs and found that it would be less expensive to purchase a new pattern than it would be to bring the old pattern up to **par-stock** levels. Another exclusive restaurant keeps the molds for their unique design under lock and key, and the **replacement costs** are quite high.

Selection of China

No one can dispute that restaurants are selling a product (food) to the guest, and the guest purchases this product in a package. Packaging, here, is considered in a marketing and global context. It is not a cardboard or plastic package; nonetheless, the presentation of the meal on a plate or the transfer from a platter to the plate is considered packaging. How the guest perceives this package preconditions his acceptance or rejection of that product. The restaurant caters to a specific type of customer, and the restaurateur should choose the tabletop product that appeals to the largest number of the type guests and specific market segments he expects to serve. Good restaurant china is very resistant to breakage, chipping, and scratching. It is usually broken by china hitting china. Seventy-five to 80 percent of all breakage occurs in the soiled dish area, and the manager should consider the durability of the china before purchasing a particular pattern or brand. Sales personnel can be excellent sources of information, but tend to overrate their line over a competitor's line. It is a good idea to use (on a trial basis) china in one's establishment before purchase, but this is not always possible. Another idea is to ask other restaurateurs about their experiences with either the pattern, the manufacturer, or both. Local or regional associations offer the opportunity to exchange ideas with other operators.

Heavy or thick plates are not necessarily more durable or more resistant to chipping or to breakage. However, heavy china does hold heat longer. The manager should consider the following items with regard to thickness and weight:

- The ease of handling for servers, dishwashers, and other kitchen staff.
- The extra storage space required for thicker china.
- Freight costs.
- The suitability of the china for the individual restaurant.[1]

A manager must look at many other factors in order to make wise decisions in the purchase of china. When replacement costs for china and glassware range on an annual basis range from .7 percent to .3 percent of sales, it behooves one to know as much as possible about the product being purchased. Factors for functional considerations of particular concern include durability; chemical composition; thickness and weight; engineering and construction; resiliency to shock; resistance to warping, scratching, and fading; porosity; cleanability; thermal characteristics; microwave and salamander/broiler usage; and breakage patterns. Design concerns include size, shape, thickness, and pattern and color.[2] Certainly one of the most important factors in the selection, purchase, and replacement of china is cost. Open stock items are less expensive, are held for immediate delivery by manufacturers, and can usually be replaced within a month. Undecorated china costs less than decorated china, and china with a sprayed-on design, printed design, decal design, or hand-decorated design follow in cost in that order. Machine prints are lower in cost, while anything requiring hand painting is more expensive. Since gold and silver designs are painted on after glazing, they do not wear as well as designs applied before glazing.

Item	*Amount (multiply number of seats by)*
Dinner plates	2.5–3
Salad plates	3–4
Bread and butter plates	3–4
Cups	3–4
Saucers	3–4

China breakage may run to 2 percent of gross sales per year, and this is a direct increase in expense and a loss in bottom-line profit. If breakage can be cut to even 1 percent, an operation with a million dollars in sales could realize $10,000 more in profit. Perhaps one-half of this $10,000 (or $5,000) can be passed on to the dish crew as an incentive. The restaurant still profits by $5,000 that would otherwise not be there. China can be cared-for and breakage can be reduced (1) by reducing handling as much as possible by having good storage facilities that avoid cross traffic, (2) having an adequate inventory in order to prevent rushing to get the china back in service, and (3) having a good kitchen design with proper equipment to unload, sort, and store the china as it is cleaned. A well-trained dish crew with proper guidelines for unloading, sorting, and stacking as well as incentives for reducing breakage is essential.

Glassware

The factors and considerations mentioned previously in the discussion of china also apply to the selection and purchase of **glassware**. Replaceability costs on the average for glassware are in the same range as those of china. However, the percentage for glassware could be considerably higher for an individual operation if expensive leaded **crystal** were being used for service. Although some leaded crystal goblets may cost $25 or more per stem, most restaurants do not use this type crystal in their dining rooms. As with china, but perhaps to even a greater extent, glassware is a package that the restaurant manager is using for her product. Appearance and durability play equally important roles in the selection of glassware. Yet in an effort to have individual glasses for every different wine or cocktail on the menu, the manager is forced to spend excessive time keeping inventory at par-stock levels for each different style, and she must spend additional time training the beverage and service staff as to which glass should be used for which drink, cocktail, or wine. The countervailing argument here is the visual appeal specialized glassware adds to the value of the beverage.

Some operations use only one type of glass for all cocktails, and this practice has both advantages and disadvantages. Because of the size of the chosen glass, certain cocktail recipes and total liquid amount may not appear to fill the glass. Moreover, a bartender may find it difficult to maintain strict portion control and may overpour liquor in an effort to make the glass look as though it has a sufficient amount of spirits. If glasses such as brandy snifters are used, it is difficult for guests or employees to take them off the premises—they do not travel well.

Selection of Glassware

Most restaurant operators purchase glassware that is **mass-produced** (or pressed) and consequently is lower priced than either hand- or machine-blown or custom-made crystal. Fine crystal glassware can range in cost from $4 to $120 per stem. Yet there is blown crystal on the market, which some consider to be a cut above the mass-produced variety. Costs for the mass-produced product run from $.50 to $3 for a particular piece, while the blown glass may run $3–5 for the same piece. The mass-produced glassware is usually thicker glass, which upon close inspection, will reveal some lines and bubbles in and around the glass, especially where it is fused (glued). An examination should be made to see if all parts are well fused. The edges and brims are usually rolled, and this makes the glass more resistant to chipping. The blown glass may also have either a bead-less, rolled, or straight brim (hand beveled or ground down). Although the beadless edge creates an upgraded beverage service package, the straight (sharp) brim is not recommended for commercial use as breakage due to chipping may be excessive. Some manufacturers, however, guarantee their tumblers and stemware against chipping on the glass's rim. Blown glass is usually thinner than the mass-produced variety, and imperfections can be seen in small air bubbles in the thicker sections of the glass and stem. Glasses are strengthened (to reduce breakage) by a rolled bead, a thicker glass, and a barrel or a bell shape where the brim curves back to center of the glass. The process of tempering or heat treating and rapidly cooling the glassware further strengthens the product against thermal or mechanical shock. Heat treating is usually performed after the glass is formed on its upper portion where most of the abuse occurs. Lead oxide may be added to the glass production process to give the glass added brilliance and clarity as well as the characteristic bell-note sound. Stemmed glassware is weaker than glassware without a stem, although the glass can be strengthened (thereby reducing breakage) if a thick, short stem instead of a long, thin stem is used. A weighted bottom increases stability so the glasses will not tip as easily, and during an earthquake, or aboard a ship, plane, or train, stability is important.

It is difficult to recommend one type of glass over the other as each has advantages and disadvantages. Some designers choose inexpensive glassware because they feel that guests do not appreciate fine crystal and it breaks more easily. Conducting a value-engineering or value-design analysis, designers sometimes choose to spend more money on items they feel are most visible to (and appreciated by) the guest, such as individual center settings and expensive linen. Such items have a longer life as well. Certainly other operators may feel that guests do appreciate fine crystal when dining out. The individual designer, owner, or manager must make the decision on the type of glassware based on the purpose for a particular glass, what she can afford, and which best complements the ambience in the dining room. In a rating of wine glasses by the *Wine Spectator*, the following quote illustrates the concern of aficionados regarding glassware.[3]

> Clear glass and a thin-rimmed bowl reduce the barriers between the wine lover and the wine. The better the clarity, the richer the colors appear. The thinner the rim, the less the glass distracts from the wine as it enters the mouth.
>
> The stem should be long enough so that the hand doesn't touch the bowl. That avoids obscuring the wine with fingerprints or warming it above the proper serving temperature. But if the stem is too long, the glass will be tipsy. We preferred glasses with stems about as long as the bowl was tall.
>
> Swirling the wine releases essential aromas . . . and a slightly in-turned rim keeps swirling wine safely in the glass. A large bowl and a narrow opening work together to magnify the wine's bouquet.

How Much to Purchase

It is most difficult to establish glassware requirements for purchase, however two of each type glass selected, per seat, for use should be more than adequate as an initial purchase. This can be reduced to one-half to one glass per seat for beer, cordials, brandy snifters, and some specialty wine glasses. Water goblets, iced tea, collins, highball, cocktail, and on-the-rocks glasses are used frequently and two glasses per seat are recommended.

Silverware or Flatware

The decision to select **silverware** over stainless steel **flatware** is usually much easier than selecting glassware. The cost of silverware is much more (perhaps 5 to 10 times the amount) than the price of stainless steel flatware. The choice of silverware or flatware supports the restaurant's concept and target market. Too frequently a restaurant selects a cheaper grade flatware pattern, which may deflate the image the restaurant is attempting to project and takes away the guests' enjoyment of the dining experience. The feel of the utensil in the hand and in the mouth sends a sensual message to the guest. A burr on a fork or spoon that nicks the lip or tongue undermines the sensual experience of eating delicately prepared and meticulously served food. Very elegant establishments and upscale hotel dining rooms may use sterling silverware. However, the number of establishments using sterling is quite limited. Most elegant operations or formal dining rooms use silver-plated flatware (**hotel plate**), which is considerably less expensive than sterling, but considerably more expensive than stainless. A dining room could not be considered an elegant dining room if stainless steel flatware were used. In any case, good quality stainless steel is preferred over poor quality silver plate flatware as the latter will chip and peel and interfere with the sensual dining experience. Stainless steel flatware is being used more and more, as the patterns are varied so as to match the restaurant theme and the metal is strong, durable, and difficult to dent, scratch, or stain.

> Lower quality stainless steel flatware contains roughly 13 percent chrome, while high quality . . . contains 18 percent. . . . The highest grade of stainless flatware combines 18 percent chrome with 8 percent nickel. The resulting **18/8** is highly resistant to corrosion, and it will maintain its luster over an extended period of time with proper care.[4]

A buyer may check strength by

- Placing a fork tine on a hard edge and putting pressure on it to bend it.
- Bending a spoon where the bowl joins the handle.
- Noting junctures of stainless steel blades into handles, noting whether the blade is cemented or soldered in or is solid with the handle (cemented blades loosen easily).
- Trying to dent a spoon bowl by striking it a hard blow with a hard, sharp object.
- Checking junctures to see if they are secure, well-plated, and well-burnished; tacking should not be permitted.[5]

Selecting a pattern that affirms the restaurant's concept is important, as is finding a pattern that the manufacturer will continue to produce. (See page 122 for the types of flatware pieces commonly available.) If a manufacturer discontinues a pattern, the operator will be forced either to have mismatched table settings or to incur considerable expense in completely restocking the flatware inventory. The following table is based on a general operation for normal service. Quantities and items will vary according to the individual operation. To work out a proper service, consideration should be given to number of uses of the seats and rate of washing and drying, as well as the quantity to be held in reserve. In most cases, reserve stock should be at least 25 percent of that in active service, and reorders should be placed as often as practical.

Item and description	Amount (multiply by number of seats)
Spoons	
Tea	5
Dessert/utility	2
Table or serving	¼
Iced tea	1½
Demitasse	2
Bouillon	2
Forks	
Dessert/utility	2
Dinner	4
Salad	2
Fish	½
Oyster	1½
Knives	
Dinner/utility	3
Dessert	2
Butter	2–3
Steak (individual)	½
Fish (individual)	½

Tablecloths and Napkins (Napery)

Historically, elegant restaurants and hotel dining rooms used only white linen tablecloths and napkins, and white is still the choice for formal service. Yet with the advent of colorfast dyes, restaurants began to use colored tablecloths and napkins. In fact, the reason white was used in the past was because the dyed fabrics could not withstand the excessive use and subsequent cleaning that restaurant linens underwent. When colored linens were used, they could not be cleaned adequately lest the color fade. The two primary **natural fibers** used for tablecloths and napkins are cotton and linen. Mercerized cotton is relatively inexpensive, has a good sheen, and has a long life since it holds up well in soaps, detergents, and bleaches. Yet 100 percent cotton fabrics wrinkle or crease easily unless the cotton fabric is treated to be wrinkle free. Linen is relatively expensive and does not have as long a life as cotton: it does not hold up as well in soaps, detergents, and bleaches. It has a moderate sheen and crisp texture (it wrinkles and creases even more easily than cotton), but linen absorbs moisture quite well, sheds dirt easily, and is lint free. These characteristics make linen very suitable for napkins and towels. "All **napery** should be non-chlorine-retentive (chlorine weakens the fabric) and be able to be washed at 160° F with bleach."[6] Most laws require that fabrics must be treated so as to be nonflammable. Polyester fibers (Dacron) are usually combined with cotton (50:50) for tablecloths and napkins. This product resists wrinkling, but may produce an excessive amount of lint. Because of its no-press, no-iron characteristics (i.e., **wash-and-wear** fabric), some restaurants have purchased wash-and-wear tablecloths and napkins and installed small commercial laundries in the restaurant for all their laundry needs.

A restaurant operator in New England installed a laundry for her inn (200 + seats and a 50-room motel) and estimated that the payback period (over laundry costs for the same time frame) will be less than two years. Initial investment for wash-and-wear linen and washing machines and dryers for a 200-seat restaurant may range from $40,000–$60,000, yet this investment can be recouped in less than two years.

Napkins made of a Dacron and cotton blend are not as absorbent as napkins made of 100 percent cotton or linen, and they tend to spread liquid around the guest's mouth instead of absorbing the moisture. Service cloths or side towels should be very absorbent, lint free (so as not to spread lint on the service person's clothes or on glassware or silverware), and capable of withstanding frequent bleaching. They are usually made from linen, cotton, rayon, or their combinations. Some of the fabrics mentioned above dye easily while others do not. To check for dye that rubs off (**crocking**), rub a piece of dyed fabric on your hand when it is slightly moist. If the dye comes off, do not purchase the fabric. Some dyes will bleed or leach during washing, which results in fading. Requirements for linen vary according to the individual requirements of the operation. Several factors to be considered when linen is being supplied by a linen supplier are

- How many covers (to determine number of napkins).
- How many tables (number of tablecloths).
- What type of tables.
- How long between deliveries.

In any case, it is wise to overestimate linen requirements, since there is no way to substitute another product as would be the case with food.

Accessories and Other Equipment

There are many pieces of equipment that are used in a food service operation. Time and space do not permit a detailed description of all equipment used; however, a brief description of some of the more common pieces follows.

Salt and Pepper Shakers, Pepper Mills.   Shakers should not have cut glass areas or excessive indentations as this makes them difficult to clean.

Pepper mills should be decorative but also as smooth as possible to facilitate cleaning. Holes in the top of the pepper shakers should be large enough to release the standard pepper grind, and purchasers should not buy the large grind pepper when the shakers will not easily dispense the pepper.

Ashtrays.   Ashtrays are relatively inexpensive. The safety ashtray is recommended over other models since it has two ridges and the cigarette rests on both. When the cigarette burns down to the first ridge, the cigarette falls into a trough rather than onto the table and snuffs itself out.

Holloware.   This includes pitchers, creamers, sugar bowls, ice buckets, and so forth. **Holloware** can be made of silverplate or stainless steel or any other composite material. "Edges should be turned in to give extra strength and reduce chances for denting. Seams should clean easily. Handles should be separated from the unit by insulation if the container is to hold hot items. . . . insulation should be guaranteed against loosening. Points of juncture should be well soldered with silver or hard solder . . . spouts on pitchers . . . should be of the nondrip type."[7].

Coffeemakers.   The automatic, 12-cup (glass bubble) pot coffeemakers are recommended for most standard à la carte restaurant use. This type of equipment will reduce waste, and the coffee is usually much fresher than the large one- or two-pound automatic coffeemakers that are necessary when large banquets are being served. Also, for à la carte or lower volume operations, waste can be excessive when using the one- or two-pound automatic brewers. Upgraded coffeemakers include single-head or dual-head versions with standard or special tall airpot brewing machines (called airpot brewers) or the pour-over model that automatically empties the brewed coffee into an insulated container with a pump, usually for guest self-service. This style is particularly popular when a restaurant offers hot and fresh specialty premium and flavored coffees. For establishments that serve a variety of flavors and styles of coffees, the airpot, pump-style servers provide more flexibility than the traditional 12-cup style. Additionally, the reduced oxygen environment keeps the coffee significantly fresher for much longer periods of time. The coffee does not evaporate, which concentrates the coffee, and, in the presence of oxygen, coffee becomes more bitter. Other machines brew larger quantities of coffee than the 12-cup type but less than the traditional 3-gallon banquet-style or diner-style coffeemakers. These coffee servers are the portable reservoir server with a pour spout identical to the traditional one- and two-pound coffeemakers. These can range from one gallon to two gallons and are designed to nest safely on top of a square warming plate. As with the airpot or air-void type, these coffeemakers have brewing mechanisms similar to the 12-cup type, but the brewing spout is higher than the 12-cup style that allows either the airpot, air-void, or portable reservoir to fit under it.

Espresso Machines.   Espresso is a favorite after-dinner coffee drink. Espresso-based products (cappucino, latte, cafe au lait, and so forth) are sweeping the country in popularity. Several espresso models are available; the automatic, by-the-cup, vending-machine-type coffeemaker is available for restaurant use when there is no one either specifically designated for or knowledgeable about making espresso, although the initial cost of these automatic machines is very high. The manual machine or espresso coffee machine may also be used for dining room operations, but caution to the operator who slows down his entire service system when servers (instead of a designated person) are required to make individual cups of espresso. The automatic vending machine is maintained quite easily and yields a consistent product. For coffee or espresso purists who drink coffee in a coffee shop, cafe, or coffee bar, only the large, hand-fashioned copper machines or sleek, modern, Italian design machines will create the desired image. Some restaurateurs have mounted small espresso machines on carts. They roll the carts to the tableside and make a pot or a cup of espresso in front of the guests. This merchandising technique increases after-dinner beverage sales significantly and reduces the dram-shop liability when compared to high-proof, spirited after-dinner drinks.

Generic Definitions

Espresso—a concentrated (very small—demi tasse) cup of coffee (1.5–2.5 ounces) brewed under steam pressure using an espresso roast (dark roasted bean).

Cappucino—brewed in a small cup (smaller than a regular cup of coffee, but larger than a demitasse) with 1/3 cup espresso and 2/3 cup of steamed milk with milk foam (made from steam) on top and can be sprinkled with powdered chocolate or cinnamon.

Cafe latte—brewed espresso in a regular-sized coffee cup with more steamed milk, proportionally, than cappucino.

Cafe au lait—sometimes espresso but usually regular coffee with milk, sometimes all whipped together.

Cafe mocha—cafe latte with chocolate flavoring added.

Toasters.   There are two types of toasters on the market with which service personnel should be familiar. Servers operate toasters as often as any other person in the kitchen, since it is one of their tasks especially when serving breakfast. One type of toaster is a conveyor belt or rotary rack and another type is the pop-up toaster. Multiple units of pop-up toasters can increase the capacity so that, with respect to volume, one type has no advantage over the other. However, rotary or belt toasters use more energy, as they remain on during the entire serving period, while the pop-up types use energy only when activated to make toast. The pop-up type of toaster is preferred by servers since there is no waiting to load the unit(s) to capacity.

Soft-Drink Dispensing Machines.   These machines are ideal to increase server productivity if they are self-service, and they can be more profitable than single-service (can or bottle) drinks, especially when premeasured (robotized—as used in quick service restaurants) dispensers are used in lieu of the manual type. Labor productivity is maximized using the robotized dispensers. Many employees, however, may take advantage of "free" drinks since it is difficult to restrict employee consumption in most restaurant operations. The cost, however, is minimal and may promote employee morale. Records of employee consumption and waste should be tabulated in order to control soft drinks.

Cash Registers, Electronic Cash Registers, Point-of-Sale Computers.   This vast subject area cannot be discussed here in detail—for as soon as this book is published, the information would be outdated. Certain key concepts will assist the food service manager in determining electronic equipment. This equipment is of particular concern to the restaurant manager because it is the system for gathering management information such as a daily sales analysis report and staff sales and productivity analysis. **Electronic cash registers** are designed to improve customer service (speed and accuracy), reduce costly errors (human error in tallying guest checks can sometimes run to 20 percent), expand the flexibility and controls available, and yield more usable management information. Machines can be programmed to the menu and reprogrammed whenever the menu changes. Programming allows for an accurate count of items sold (the menu mix), an accurate count of items depleted from inventory (as with a perpetual inventory system), as well as automatic pricing and tallying of the menu items. Machines may have memory keys that automatically pick up a previous balance for a particular table. Some machines offer dual-purpose keys (i.e., the same menu item can be programmed at two prices, one for luncheon and one for dinner, or one for happy hour and one for regular hours). In addition to yielding menu counts and the like, the guest check is printed in such a manner that guests can easily verify their guest checks. Some models also offer built-in digital clocks that print the time the order was placed on the requisitions (with remote printers to the kitchen, pantry, or service bar on a precheck machine) as well as the time payment was received. This assists management in determining turnover analysis and peak-period staff scheduling.

Tray Stands.   These should be portable but should remain stationary during the serving period if space permits. The practice of picking up folding tray stands and setting the tray down on the tray stand near the guest's table is less formal than having a tray stand in a relatively permanent position in the room. The chrome or metal tray stands that have a shelf below allow for extra storage space for such items as cups, saucers, underliners, monkey dishes, and water pitchers, but they do take up extra space in the dining room, which would reduce the number of available restaurant seats.

Side Stands.   Stands should be centrally located in the dining room and can range from complete (i.e., coffeemaker, icemaker/bins, roll warmers, water faucet, and storage space) or simple (i.e., slotted drawers for silverware and shelves for underliners, etc.). When possible, side stands should be secluded from guests' view; however, doors (hinged or sliding) on side stands decrease server productivity by tying up one hand just to open and close the door. Doors also present a safety hazard, as sliding doors can catch fingers and hinged doors may be left open or may swing open causing one to trip over or otherwise hit the door.

Ice Machines.   These can be purchased in various shapes and sizes and in several models that produce ice cubes of different sizes and shapes. Machines that produce the small ice cubes (half-inch cubes) are preferred for cocktails, since they expose maximum surface area. They are also solid and fit well into any type of glass. Because of the fit, spirits poured into the glass fill the glass more completely than with other types of cubes. Chipped or shaved ice is not recommended except for frappes or as a base for caviar, oysters, clams, and so forth, since too much surface area is exposed causing the ice to melt rapidly. When used for cocktails, chipped or shaved ice waters down the drink too quickly, and this may be perceived by the guest as an inferior or weak drink. Tube ice does not fit well into glassware or goblets and is not recommended for dining room service. Half- or quarter-moon shaped ice cubes are satisfactory for ice water and wine buckets, but are not as suitable for cocktails for the aforementioned reasons.

Many other accessories must be purchased and each operator must select, based on her individual needs, the equipment and accessories required.

Tables

Whether to purchase **deuces**, fours, or sixes, and rounds, squares, or rectangular tables is the decision of the individual operator in concert with his architect, designer, and food facilities designer/equipment specialist. The mix of deuces to fours and other **table configurations** and the like should be determined in part by the feasibility study, in part by the menu, and by the meal to be served. Luncheon business usually requires more deuces than four tops, whereas dinner may need the reverse. When the restaurant is adjacent to areas where business entertaining prevails, larger tables may be required. Square tables that can be converted to rounds with drop-leaves offer flexibility to the operator. A 36-inch square table can be configured by opening the leaves to a 53-inch diameter to seat up to seven guests (perhaps slightly crowded), six guests, or two guests comfortably by folding down the leaves to the 36-inch square to make the table smaller and more intimate. Recently a franchise restaurant chain discovered that many of the seats at their four tops were unsold as a result of the customer mix during luncheon. Since they could expect only two turns (i.e., two separate groups at a table at different times) during the short luncheon service period, a considerable amount of revenue was being lost. Surprisingly, many luncheon guests were being turned away; yet, they could not increase the number of covers in this short period because of the table configurations.

Deuces are ideally $30'' \times 36''$ (minimum of $24'' \times 30''$). Round deuces should ideally be $36''$ in diameter (minimum of $30''$). Fours or threes are ideally $42'' \times 42''$ (minimum of $36'' \times 36''$) or $36'' \times 48''$ (minimum of $30'' \times 42''$). It is not advisable to purchase round tables for only four, as they should be large enough for six ($54''$ diameter), and preferably they should have drop leaves to be convertible as mentioned previously. Sixes are best seated at round tables ($54''$ in diameter desirable, $48''$ in diameter as a minimum, and $60''$ in diameter as a maximum); however rectangular tables for six are satisfactory ($42'' \times 72''$ preferred, $42'' \times 60''$ minimum, and $84''$ in length absolute maximum). Eight people should be seated at round tables ($66''$ in diameter very comfortably, $60''$ comfortably), and not at rectangular tables if at all possible.

When larger parties (i.e., 12, 15, or 20 guests) frequent one's restaurant, plywood tops can be cut, curved, hinged, and otherwise fitted to rest on the operation's existing tables to accommodate any number of guests. In all cases, a minimum of 18" should be allowed for the chair (measured from the edge of the table) and a $24''$ minimum aisle space between the backs of two adjacent chairs. Total distance, therefore, from the edge of one table to the edge of another table should be $60''$ at the minimum ($18'' + 18'' + 24''$). Tables may be covered with or made of wood, acrylic, vinyl, glass, plexiglas, or leatherette. Depending on the formality or elegance of the restaurant, the operator should select tables that fit the decor if tablecloths will not be used.

Chairs

Restaurant chairs are very expensive; a single chair may cost more than \$125–\$150. It is important, therefore, to select chairs that are suitable for the operation from the decor perspective as well as for utility and durability.

Depending on individual needs, the operator may choose high backs, armrests, or upholstered chairs. Chairs with armrests are particularly helpful to older adults and should be used when the primary market segment includes older adults. Upholstered chairs add elegance to a dining room, but they may require more upkeep or maintenance, not to mention initial cost, than plain wood or metal chairs. Upholstered chairs also may be more comfortable than wood or metal chairs. This raises an important point: the comfortability of the chair may help determine the rate of guest turnover. If chairs are very comfortable, guests may linger a while, and this may tie up a table. Coffee shop operators, especially for their counters, may sometimes design chairs so that they are slightly uncomfortable—guests will spend less time at the table or counter. One quick-service chain is known for designing seats that slope forward so one has to keep moving back in the seat to avoid falling on the floor. These design factors tend to increase the guest turnover rate. This concept is euphemistically termed "the fanny factor."

Function Room and Banquet Furniture

Rectangle

Round

Oblong or Oval

Serpentine

Quarter-round

Half-round

Trapezoid

Folding tables can be purchased with various-shaped tops, but can also be purchased quite narrow (15″ or 18″ wide) for seminars and meetings (classroom-style). Wishbone-style folding legs allow for maximum seating with more comfortable knee and foot room in contrast to the straight or pedestal leg. Knock-down cabaret tables with pedestal tops (center column) and bases offer considerable flexibility. Different sizes and shapes of tops may be interchanged with the same column or base, and because of styling, many of these types of tables do not require tablecloths.

Chairs that stack have almost entirely replaced folding chairs, as they are much safer, easier to handle, look neater, and last longer since they have no moving parts. Some general guidelines:

- Strength and durability. Be aware of the weakest link (mechanical or folding devices), safety for guests and employees (sharp edges), and ease of cleaning.
- Ease of handling. Lightweight, but durable. Use of dollies for transporting furniture.
- Ease of storage. Ensure against non-mar stacking. Storage space is a critical concern, since it reduces the amount of space that may be used for generating revenue. Storage space can limit function room the amount and type of furniture one could purchase. However, too little storage space may also require improper stacking and storing, which may result in damaged furniture or decreased life of the function-room furniture.

- Flexibility (e.g., knockdown tables with different tops). There is much additional equipment that can be and must be used in setting up function rooms and banquets; however, an extensive discussion or a listing of advantages and disadvantages would go beyond the scope of this text.

The following list of the equipment may prove useful:

- Folding platforms.
- Portable dance floors.
- Portable bars (discussion in Chapter 11).
- Folding and portable lecterns.
- Trucks and dollies.

Buffet, Serving Ware, and Gourmet Display Equipment

The previous discussion of china, silverware, glassware, and furniture applies directly to a discussion of buffet and gourmet display equipment. In particular, the choice of this type of equipment can enhance the visual and tactile appeal in the same way that china, silverware, and glassware do. Buffet and display ware must also be highly functional to maintain proper serving temperature during the meal period (when appropriate). These products are manufactured in varying sizes and shapes (rectangular, oval, circular, and so forth), metals or other raw or composite materials (stainless steel, copper, silverplate, plastic or acrylic, glass, crockery, and so forth), and filigree. Chafing dishes and soup tureens may be purchased in silverplate, chrome, stainless steel, or crockery, and are priced according to the design and the material used to fabricate the particular dish. A large silver chafing dish with stand, insert, and lid may cost more than $1,000.

There are many styles on the market from which an individual operator may choose. They may be heated by one of several sources: canned gels, liquid fuel, denatured alcohol, bottled gas, or electricity. Most chafing dishes use canned gels or denatured alcohol. As this secondary heat source is needed only to *maintain the heat*, the heat source need not be as hot as that required for primary heating such as tableside cookery. In order to keep food hot for any length of time (that is, buffet for a dining room, as compared to a banquet), top heat supplied by a heat lamp is necessary lest the food get cold. Portable buffet tables come with electrically heated units and canned-gel heated units. Some are designed to fit on top of a table, while others are on wheels and can be rolled and placed into a desirable location.

Recent models have wood-grain finishes and can be designed to accommodate different pan-size combinations. Sneeze guards are highly recommended if not mandatory, and purchase of any of these units should include sneeze guards as part of the unit or above the food display. As with chafing dishes, it is necessary to have top heat (infrared lamp with reflectors) over each well. Cake tiers, large shell bowls, serving stones, mirrored or glass gourmet display trays, beverage housings and ice pans, ice carving pedestals, drip collectors, cubes and columns, and rainbow glows offer the *pièce de résistance* to any buffet and are quite useful for displaying all types of food on ice, salad, molded gelatins or ices, hors d'oeuvres, dips, wine or beer on ice, and fresh fruits. Some are made of a molded sturdy high heat plastic, some of which resembles crystal, while others are opaque white. The fabrication material must be very durable and easily washable, and if possible, washable in the dish machine.

Tableside Service Equipment

There are distinct advantages and disadvantages for each of the pieces of equipment used in the dining room for preparing food at tableside. The total investment for the equipment necessary for tableside cookery and service is less than might be anticipated. For example, a 100-seat restaurant could invest $4,000 to $6,000 in equipment, offer two items to be prepared before the guest, and provide tableside exposure to more than 60 patrons over a two-hour meal period. Enumerated below are the pieces of equipment required for tableside cookery.

Carts

While functional considerations are the most important when choosing a serving cart, the basic features of the cart must complement the decor of the dining room. Having selected a cart that blends with the ambience of the dining room, the restaurateur should verify the equipment's practicality in light of several factors. Carts should be structured for versatility, permitting the use of a single cart for the service of appetizers, entrees, salads, desserts, and cordials. Hinged side leaves or drop leaves provide maximum work surface when required but allow the cart to be folded into a more compact unit for storage. A low ridge around the perimeter of the cart's work surface prevents items from falling off easily, but requires special attention when cleaning. Carts should be easily maneuverable through the aisles and must fit through doors in the dining area and kitchen. If there is tiering in the dining room, it is advisable to provide carts for each level. Large diameter caster wheels, each swiveling independently, should be made of rubber to reduce noise, especially if portions of the dining room are not carpeted.

All parts of the cart should be tight-fitting, both to facilitate the preparation of food at tableside and to reduce noise. Carts must be well-balanced with the center of gravity not too high on the cart, which may cause the cart to tip over easily. A simple test will determine whether the cart is well-balanced and has proper casters. Roll the cart around a room that has no carpets and a few cracks in the floor. If the cart chatters, the casters are poor. Similarly if fixtures on the cart are loose-fitting, the cart will rattle and be quite noisy. Second, clear the cart of all equipment, provide ample space in the room, and spin the cart around. If it tips over, the cart is not balanced and could cause problems in the dining room, especially when loaded with flaming lamps, food, and bottles of spirits. The weakest link in most carts is the brace(s) that suspends the drop leaves. Is this equipment sturdy? Is it easy to operate? Is it sharp? Can someone pinch his hand on it? Does it fasten the leaf firmly to the main part of the cart when extended? If the answer to any of these questions is yes, the purchaser is compromising something, and therefore the purchase price should also be compromised.

It is strongly recommended to purchase carts with hinged or drop leaves, since the cart will be easier to store as well as providing more work space while in the dining room. Another weak link in the cart is how the tiers or shelves and the top fasten to the supporting posts. If glue is the only thing holding the posts to the horizontal shelves, do not purchase the cart. They should be fastened with screws that *pass through* the shelves.

One safety factor that should be considered is the type corners used on the cart. If they are at 90 degrees, someone may catch a corner in a thigh. It is recommended that the corners be rounded at approximately three-quarters to one inch, which will also give the cart a nice appearance with smooth lines rather than sharp points. Sharp corners are more easily damaged, as well as causing damage to walls and other furniture because they impact directly as opposed to glancing blows. The plastic coverings on some sharp cornered carts have been known to chip because they are formica-covered and butted rather than molded. All-purpose, plain carts range anywhere from $500 to $1,500. If the cart costs too much, ensure that you are not paying for things you do not need. Carts with built in rechauds are considerably more expensive and offer less flexibility. A simple hole can be cut in the top of an all-purpose cart and a rechaud may be dropped in. The hole can otherwise be covered for dessert or cordial display.

The restaurant designer must be aware of storage space for the carts. It looks awkward to have rolling stock strewn all over the dining room, and the equipment can be damaged if not stored properly. Poorly stored carts present a safety hazard since they may block aisles. Purchase only the number of carts needed.

Carts can sometimes be small tables approximately 24″ × 36″ with wheels on either one set of legs or on all four legs. These small tables are always covered with a tablecloth and placed close to the guests' table for tableside preparation and plating.

Special Carts, Trolley, or Wagons

Special carts include a wide variety of equipment used to display food in the dining room or rolled to the guests' table to serve from the cart. These special carts are effective for merchandising food and beverages with the opportunity to increase per-person check average and ultimately the restaurant's gross revenue. Special carts include dessert and pastry carts, cheese and fruit carts, liqueur and cordial carts, special after-dinner coffee and beverages carts, roast beef-carving carts, wine and decanting carts, soup or tureen carts, breakfast or omelette carts, salad, appetizer, and hors d'oeuvre carts, and any other item a creative restaurateur feels could benefit by its visual impact. Often, these special carts are not rolled around the dining room. Although mobile, they remain essentially stationary, and they are strategically located in the dining room.

Flaming lamps, or rechauds, should fit the style of tableside service, complementing the carts selected for the operation. For example, a tall flaming lamp placed atop one of the higher carts available would bring the cooking vessel to a level that would make the server's work difficult. Further, it would defeat the purpose of tableside cookery, making it difficult for the guest to see the food being prepared. Of the numerous models available from different companies, each rechaud has its own advantages and disadvantages.

Some flaming units use clean-burning fuel (canned gels), while others utilize denatured alcohol. The clean burning fuels leave no carbon deposits on cooking utensils and are especially desirable when producing flaming coffees. Butane or propane burners (either in cans or refillable tanks) are becoming more popular and have their distinct advantages and disadvantages.

Alcohol Burners.   The small double-burner, denatured-alcohol rechaud with one-inch diameter, with holes one-half inch away from center circling the center opening has a distinct advantage: it produces a very large flame after the unit heats up, but does not produce an excessive amount of heat. Recharging the unit is very efficient, quick, and simple. It takes almost no time to recharge, and refueling can be accomplished after one or two tableside preparations. The amount of fuel that each heating unit takes is minimal and therefore there is little wasted fuel. The large flame is quiet, erratic, wispy, and romantic as the flame curls around the pan. It seldom overcooks the product. Incidentally, the large flame makes it easier to ignite the spirit: when the flame curls around the edge of the pan, it will ignite the spirit when the spirit is at the proper temperature. By not having to shake or move the sauté pan, the spirit is kept apart from and not diluted in the sauce, which makes the spirit easier to ignite.

If volume cookery is required, this unit requires more time at the tableside. It is recommended to use a preheated pan for all tableside cookery for all rechauds, but most of all for alcohol burners as this shortens the time at tableside but does not decrease the presentation at tableside for the guest. The alcohol burners produce large deposits of carbon, which typically collect on the bottom surface of the pan. This carbon is difficult to clean and makes an unsightly pan.

Another disadvantage to the alcohol-burner rechauds is that the flame is difficult to control or adjust since it is controlled only by airflow. The only adjustment is the opening or closing of the smaller holes that encircle the larger opening. While this is not a major disadvantage, the heat produced by the flame is minimal in relation to the flame size. However, unless the following procedure is adhered to when the unit is hot, *the flame is very difficult to extinguish*. After the major cooking (flaming) has been accomplished, the flame should be lowered immediately. Although it does not respond immediately when the air supply is reduced, the flame will eventually subside, and only after it subsides can the flame be extinguished. Several unsuccessful attempts to extinguish a billowing flame will appear unprofessional if not dangerous.

Another type of alcohol burner that offers more heat and a greater ability to adjust the flame has a major opening of slightly greater than two inches with holes around the edge. The flame control adjustment on other similar models not only has rotary control (i.e., opening or closing the small holes around the major opening), but it has a push-pull mechanism, which opens or closes the opening of the center hole. Yet an extreme disadvantage here is that the unit sometimes *cannot* be extinguished. As the flame heats up the unit, it becomes increasingly difficult to extinguish the flame; however, the size of the flame can be reduced significantly. Loose-fitting parts allow the alcohol to vaporize, where well-constructed units will not leak and can be extinguished more easily. Another disadvantage is that the unit requires at least one pint of fuel (denatured alcohol) before it will work satisfactorily. Evaporation in this type of rechaud will waste expensive fuel for an establishment with a limited tableside menu.

Denatured alcohol solvent has a very distinctive, strong odor that can be objectionable. The person preparing foods at the tableside may frequently experience tearing (like tear gas) since the eyes are particularly sensitive to fumes of the burning alcohol. Yet, experimentation with several fuel sources revealed that, although considerably more expensive, the burning of Sterno liquid fuel diminished the odor significantly. Isopropyl alcohol is absolutely pungent and should not be used in the dining room. Neutral spirits (ethyl alcohol from petroleum or grain source) also produced a putrid odor, but not as overpowering as isopropyl alcohol.

Solid Fuel (Gel) Burners. The solid fuel burners have two distinct advantages. There is no odor while the fuel burns, and only a very small amount of carbon residue is deposited on the cooking vessels. Yet the heat source is insufficient unless the fuel is spread over a wide area. Simply opening cans of gel (normally used for buffet chafing pans) and burning from the can (with the small opening) does not produce adequate heat, and the time spent in preparation is excessive. Additionally, the quality of the food products may be less desirable because sauté items may not brown—food tastes warmed-over rather than sauteed. However, heat intensifiers (available from suppliers) and purchasing the gel in bulk and using larger quantities of gel than is available in cans helps eliminate the low-heat problem. Flaming beverages in glasses is the best use for the canned fuels (gel). The can of fuel can be shrouded in a silver bowl or supreme dish and placed on a cart *as is*. The heat is quite adequate since undiluted spirits are being ignited, and it is a clean burning fuel. Another use for the canned fuels is for chafing dishes on buffet lines or for hot plate warmers, which can be used in tableside cookery and service.

Bottled Gas Fuels (Propane/Butane). Rechauds using canned gas or refillable bottled gas have several distinct advantages. The fuel burns cleaner than denatured alcohol, but not quite as clean as the gel. The size of the flame can be low or high (depends on the element), but the amount of heat in each case is relatively high as compared to the gel or the alcohol. This may present a minor problem, as the food may cook quite rapidly while not allowing the normal time sequence for the service team member to pick up items in the kitchen not prepared at tableside. This high-heat type unit is useful for blinis, crepes (the pancake itself), or omelettes that are to be prepared at tableside.

The small-flame, bottled-gas rechauds are not recommended for two reasons. First, they hiss rather loudly, which can be disturbing in a quiet room. Second, although the heat (BTU output) is high when the flame is small, it is more difficult to get the spirit that is in the pan to ignite. Usually the pan must be tilted to the flame, which results in inevitable spills; or if the spirit mixes with any sauce in the pan as a result of tipping the pan, the now diluted spirit may not ignite. Additionally, the flame is not as theatrical or romantic as the large, erratic, billowing flame produced by the alcohol. If a decision is made, however, to purchase propane or butane rechauds, the unit must have a spreader mechanism at the flame source to more evenly distribute the heat. If a spreader is unavailable, do not purchase the unit, as the heat will concentrate on one section of the pan, scorch the pan, and cook the food unevenly.

An electric rechaud is a common piece of equipment used in Switzerland and other western European countries to facilitate tableside service. Dense, rectangularly shaped metal plates with insulated handles are kept hot at a sideboard using electricity. Just prior to service, they are placed on the cart or service table resting on the insulated handles. They are used to warm plates, platters, and tureens or other serving vessels while carving or portioning food onto plates at tableside, or to keep plates or side dishes warm while the main course is being prepared or finished at tableside. The heat is usually insufficient to cook or flambé products at tableside, but it is most adequate for any other form of tableside service.

Sauté Pans, Crepe Pans, and Sauce Pans. The selection and purchase of the pans to be used for preparing the various menu items at tableside deserves careful consideration. Of utmost importance is that the pan be copper, heavy gauge aluminum, or stainless steel, never a thin aluminum or thin stainless steel. The heat sources are quite variable and tend to concentrate in sections of the pans. A light, flimsy, thin-bottomed pan will not distribute the heat adequately, and the food products will be inferior. Similarly, the pan will not sustain the rough treatment usually found in commercial operations, and the pans' appearance is important because the pan is being used in the dining room in front of guests. Copper is preferable to stainless, as it makes a good presentation and distributes the heat more evenly. Yet copper is difficult to clean, since it must be washed, scoured, and polished. The lining of copper pans should be stainless steel. The steel wears considerably better than tin or any other inert metal and most likely will last for the life of the pan. Stainless steel is also easier to clean.

Copper pans with tin linings produce a superior food product because tin does not react with food products as does aluminum, which may cause discoloration or off flavors. Yet the tin wears off very rapidly and needs to be resurfaced (retinned) frequently. High-acid (low pH) food products such as a tomato sauce react with copper, which then produces toxic food. If there is a person in the local area who can retin the pan, then purchase of these pans may be advisable. However, this added task for a busy operator is uncalled for, and stainless steel pans are recommended.

Several shapes and sizes of sauté pans are available, and the size and shape should be compatible with the rechauds. It is an acceptable practice to use a rectangularly shaped pan on a round rechaud, but it is preferable to use the rectangular or oval shaped pan on a rectangular rechaud. The heat is utilized more efficiently, diffusing rather than concentrating on specific areas of the pan. For most entree-type foods, the rectangular or oval pans are preferable. There is more usable space in the pan, and this area can be used to separate items (meat and vegetables or sauce and spirit) in the pan while cooking. The size pan should be determined by the operator based on the menu items and the size of the portions offered. Standard sizes can be obtained from the various companies. The recommended size for all-purpose use is the 8″ × 13″ size. Do not purchase oval or rectangular pans without long handles, and *never attempt tableside cookery from a pan without a long handle*. It is foolish and dangerous to grasp the sides of the pan with a side towel lest the towel catch fire.

The round, open skillets come in diameters ranging from 6 to 12 inches. The 8- and 10-inch pans are recommended over either the smaller or the larger pans. The large pans (larger than 10 inches or 11 inches) are too cumbersome to use at the tableside, while small skillets are not practical for preparing entrees at tableside. The small skillets may be used to ignite undiluted spirits for pouring over cherries jubilee. Small sauce pans (one quart) may also be used for igniting undiluted spirits, while larger, deeper sauce pans should be used for flaming beverages such as cafe diable.

Crepe pans should be used primarily for crepes suzette; however, they are useful for cooking other desserts at the tableside such as bananas flambé, peaches flambé, or cherries jubilee. Crepe pans should be rather large (11 inches to 12 inches in diameter) compared to skillets, and the ridge should be near vertical or perpendicular, short (3/4 inch or less), and the pans should be made of heavy-gauge metal. The large surface area is used to thinly distribute the sauce around the pan or to separate the sauce from the spirit so the spirit will ignite. It is difficult to flame crepes suzette when the spirit has been mixed with the butter, sugar, and citrus juices. There are several models of all stainless steel crepe pans, which are as eye-appealing as the copper-coated models. From the aesthetic viewpoint, the copper on the crepe pans is not as essential as on the sauce pans, since the small ridge is hardly visible on sauté pans or skillets.

Carving Tools and Equipment.   The basic tools required for carving at tableside are knives, forks, and a steel. There are several different types of knives available, as well as different types of forks and steels. Although a chef's knife is used in the kitchen for cutting vegetables, not meat, it becomes a useful tool for cutting some meats at tableside. The wide blade is most effective when removing the breast from the bone of a capon or roasted chicken because it keeps the meat in large pieces. A boning knife, although most desirable for boning raw chicken, is not as useful as the chef's knife for carving cooked product, and may be clumsy at tableside. A smaller, 8-inch chef's knife is recommended for boning chicken at tableside; large knives with blades greater than 8-inch are unnecessary and obtrusive when used at tableside.

The blade should be stainless steel or nonstain, high-polished carbon, since carbon tool steel blades stain and may look dirty or unsanitary. Stainless blades do not hold edges as well as carbon blades, and the nonstain, high-polished carbon is preferred. Plastic, single-mold handles are recommended for several reasons: sanitation, ease of washing (they can be washed in a dish machine), and safety (the rough surface and contoured shape of the handle provide minimum slipping). Their appearance, however, is not as aesthetic and bone-handled carving knives should be considered for front-of-the-house use.

Several models of forks are available for tableside use. The small cook's fork, with a short handle is acceptable for carving roasts, rack of lamb, and chateaubriand, and recommended for carving whole roasted chicken or capon. The distance between the tines of a two-pronged fork is of some concern to the person carving at the tableside. If the tines are separated by an inch or more, the fork is of little use in attempting to carve a whole baked chicken. The bones of the chicken are so small that the tines straddle the food rather than hold it steady, and large forks are cumbersome and gaudy for tableside use. An oversized or a standard dinner fork is a suitable tool for carving at tableside, especially for baked chicken. The metal of a carving fork should be compatible with the metal selected for the knife unless the decision is made to use the standard dinner fork.

The steel is a useful and necessary piece of equipment which is *used for finishing the edges of a sharp knife* as well as removing tiny, microscopic metal burrs that result from sharpening the knife on a diamond sharpener or whetstone. Many people use the steel in lieu of a whetstone for sharpening the knife, but this practice is not recommended. Several steels on the market are poorly designed: those with a flat (top view) or oblong (cut-away view), with the guards (around the handle) protects the user only if he or she is using the narrow edge to hone the knife. Many users would choose the flat or larger surface, and hands would not be protected from the blade if the knife were taken beyond the handle/steel juncture. Additionally, if used correctly, the steel would wear very quickly, as the narrow edge exposes little surface. This model is not recommended. Another model has only two guards extending from the handle/steel juncture. The steel itself, however, is round. This limits the safe use of the tool as only two areas may be used.

The best steel has three guards extending from the handle, and this provides maximum protection from injury on all of the round steel surface that can be used safely for honing the edge. The size steel used should complement the knife, especially for use at tableside. Using a 14-inch steel for a small knife looks foolish at tableside, while using a small steel 8 to 10 inches with a roast-beef slicer with a 14-inch blade is dangerous. The composition of the blade may be either ceramic, stainless steel, or nonstain, high carbon. Carbon tool steel is not recommended since it will tarnish and look unsanitary. If absolutely necessary, knives may be honed in the presence of guests, but it is preferable to have the knives sharpened, honed, and ready for use before serving the guests. Obviously the steel is necessary on buffet lines when carving roast beef, ham, turkey, and the like.

Proper use of the steel requires the heel of the knife blade and the tip of the steel to meet with an angle of the blade on the steel of about 25 degrees. The knife is moved toward the heel of the steel, with the tip of the knife ultimately reaching the heel of the steel simultaneously. The knife should be removed from the steel and the process repeated on the opposite side of the knife. The steel should be held rigid. Many run the knife blade back and forth on the steel, but this method is improper. The minute particles that make up the blade edge of the knife should all be aligned the same way, and this can only be accomplished by using the above-mentioned procedure. After the knife has been honed, the blade should be wiped clean with a cloth with the sharp edge facing away from the individual's hands or fingers.

Spoons used in tableside service should be the same design as well as complement the dinner forks in size. A standard serving spoon should be used, as soup spoons are too small and do not fit properly with the dinner fork. Ladles may be used for spirits or gravies and sauces, but should not be used in lieu of using a fork and spoon properly.

Boards and Platters.   When selecting boards for carving at tableside, consideration must be given to the platter that must be used under the board. Liquid invariably runs from the product and must be trapped so that it not spill on the cart or on the floor. Composition cutting boards are recommended over wooden boards, and the operator should investigate the state laws before purchasing any natural wood product. Well and tree designs with carved-out portions for collecting the juices are not recommended for commercial use because they are difficult to clean. Additionally, the carved-out portions create a void when one attempts to cut through a product leaving gaps, tearing the carved item and slowing service. The board size should complement the product being carved. It would be foolish to place a small trout on a board designed for a steamship round. Any product brought on a board for presentation to the guest should be garnished. Even a large product on a small board needs garniture. Garnitures such as suet or a butter carving may be reused since they are never served and should not come in direct contact with the food.

Several platters are available for presenting raw or partially prepared product to the guest. Oval platters, rectangular platters, round platters, and special-design platters are available from several suppliers. Perhaps the most important consideration in platter selection is the size relative to the product(s) being prepared. Shrimp scampi would look foolish on a 10- or 11-inch platter unless there is an appropriate garniture. This decision should be made by the designer or the operator after selecting the menu items featured for tableside preparation and after a standardized presentation platter has been designed for the operation. The composition of the platters, whether silver, china, stainless steel, or polished pewter, should complement the decor of the dining room. In an elegant room a stainless steel platter might be out of character, as would a silver platter in a restaurant with English Pub decor. The final decision as to shape, size, and composition must be made by the designer or restaurateur.

Vegetable platters may be presented separately from the entree or may be displayed on the same platter. With a small cart, however, it is difficult to heat the entree and the vegetables in the same pan or even on the same rechaud. It is perhaps preferable to present the entree on one platter and prepare the entree at tableside. While a server is finishing the food preparation, the other service team member may fetch the hot vegetables from the kitchen or the pre-cooked vegetables may be kept warm using an electric hot plate on a sideboard or the hot metal warmer discussed above in the section on rechauds. Vegetables may be transferred to the guest's plate while the plate is on the cart; or, by using a combination of types of service, the server may serve the entree to the guest on a properly garnished plate and then transfer the vegetables from the platter while the plate is in front of the guest. Vegetables may also be served properly in separate dishes simultaneously with the entree.

Condiment holders, such as the small dishes referred to in the recipes, may either be made of china, stainless steel, pewter, or silver. These dishes should complement the platters used for presentation of the entree. If china dishes (monkey dishes) are used, it is essential that they have under-liners (saucers). Metal is preferred to the china for appearance and for breakage. It is not necessary, however, to have underliners for such items as Worcestershire sauce, pepper mills, and so forth, as this would unnecessarily clutter the cart.

The equipment and utensils used for preparing salads at the tableside is the same equipment used in preparing other tableside items, with the exception of the salad bowls. The fork and spoon should be the same utensils used for preparation of other entrees, and the condiment holders should also conform to the aforementioned criteria. Salad may be served appropriately on 8- or 9-inch plates—avoid using smaller plates. If salad bowls are used, they should conform to the sanitary standards established by the state in which the restaurateur is in business. Wooden salad bowls may have more eye-appeal than other models; however, clear glass, china, ceramic, or simulated wood may serve as suitable substitutes. The important aspect for managerial consideration is cleaning and sanitizing the soiled salad bowl. Salad bowls should be able to stand dish machine temperatures. To maintain a professional environment in an upscale dining environment, salad should not be served in salad bowls or with the large wooden fork and spoon commonly used in the home. However, in a casual theme environment, this style of service is particularly appropriate.

Recipes

Fresh Spinach Salad Helen

Yield: 2 Portion: Fills a 9″ plate			Temp: Time:
Ingredients	*Weights*	*Measures*	*Method*
Spinach	5 oz. A.P.		Wash spinach well. Remove large stems and dry well.
Mushrooms, fresh medallions		6 medium	Tear into bite-size pieces.
Bacon, thin slices chopped	2 oz.		Partially pan-fry bacon, reserving the fat.
Onion, 1/4 diced		1/4 c.	Add onions to bacon when bacon is clear and sauté until onions are transluscent and bacon is crisp.
Vinegar, wine, or cider		1 tsp.	Reserve bacon, onions, and fat. Do not poor off fat. Keep bacon and onions warm. Bacon fat must remain liquid.
Pepper, freshly ground		TT	Place spinach leaves in salad bowl. Add mushrooms to spinach and toss. Add bacon and onion mixture to spinach and toss. If required, add salad oil as needed and toss. Add vinegar and toss. Plate, sprinkle with fresh pepper, and serve.

Steak Diane

| Yield: 2 | | | Temp: |
Portion: 3.2 oz. filet			Time:
Ingredients	*Weights*	*Measures*	*Method*
Beef, tenderloin			Ignite burners of rechaud at tableside.
steaks, 2 oz.	12 oz.		Place clarified butter in heated pan.
Shallots, minced		2 tbsp.	Add Worcestershire sauce to butter.
Mushrooms, medallions	1 oz.		Place filets, shallots, and mushrooms in pan, keeping filets separate from shallots and mushrooms.
Lemon		1/4	Place lemon in cheesecloth and sprinkle steaks with juice. Season steaks with salt and pepper.
Butter, clarified	1 1/2 oz.		
Garlic, powdered		1/4 tsp.	
Mustard, dry		1 tsp.	Season "vegetables" with mustard and thyme. Turn steaks when browned on bottom. Continue to cook to desired degree of doneness.
Thyme		1 tsp.	
Cream, heavy		2 oz.	
Parsley, chopped		1 tbsp.	Add cream to vegetables, stirring until hot and thick.
Parsley, sprig		2 sprigs	Pour brandy in pan and flame.
Brandy		1 oz.	Lower flame.
			Serve.
			Extinguish flame.

Dessert Crêpe Batter

Yield: serves 8 **Portion:**			**Temp:** **Time:**
Ingredients	*Weights*	*Measures*	*Method*
Flour		1 1/4 c.	Stir in flour, sugar, and eggs into mixing bowl.
Sugar		3 tbsp.	Gradually stir in milk and liqueur.
Eggs		4	Beat with wire whisk until flour lumps disappear.
Milk		1 3/4 c.	Rub through a fine sieve in another bowl and stir in oil.
Grand Marnier or Cointreau		1/4 c.	Cover and refrigerate batter for at least two hours before using.
Oil (Wesson or other)		2/3 c.	To fry crêpes:
Butter (clarified)		as needed for pan	Warm 4–5″ crêpe pan or skillet over high heat until drop of water evaporates instantly.
			Lightly grease bottom and sides of pan with oil.
			Stir batter lightly and pour about 2 tbsp. of batter into pan.
			Roll batter around pan so it quickly covers bottom.
			When batter firms up, pour off excess by tilting pan.
			Cook crêpe until light brown rim shows on edge. Turn over and cook for one minute on that side and then slide crêpe onto a plate.

Crêpes Suzette Flambé

Yield: One serving for 2 Portion: 3 crêpes per person			Temp: Time: 6 min.
Ingredients	*Weights*	*Measures*	*Method*
Sugar, granulated		1/2 c.	Light burners of rèchaud at tableside.
Butter		12 pats	Put butter into pan and allow to melt.
Orange, fresh		1/2	Add the sugar to the melted butter, stir
Lemon, fresh		1/2	and allow to dissolve.
Orange, grated peels		1 tsp. (optional)	Add the rind of the orange and the lemon.
Lemon, grated peels		1 tsp. (optional)	Wrap the orange in the celery cloth, hold above the pan and squeeze juice into the pan. Repeat the procedure with the lemon.
Grand Marnier		1 oz.	
Brandy		1 oz.	Stir mixture until it begins to bubble (avoid carmelization) and add crêpes,
Crêpes		6	one at a time. Turn crêpe in sauce using fork and spoon, being very careful not to tear or rip crêpe. Then fold it into quarters and place to one side in the pan. Repeat the above procedure with the rest of the crêpes. When all are folded in the sauce, move them toward the center of the pan, add the Grand Marnier, and stir gently. Then add the brandy to flame.
			Spoon sauce over the crêpes. Use fork and spoon to dish crêpes onto 9″ plate (3 per plate) and spoon the sauce over them. Serve.
			Extinguish flame.

The Flaming Isle of Skye

| Yield: 2 | | | Temp: |
Portion: 6 oz. coffee and cream			Time:
Ingredients	*Weights*	*Measures*	*Method*
Lemon, wedge		1/4	Rim the brims of each 8-oz. wine glass with lemon juice from the wedge; dip the brims into the sugar to coat.
Whipped cream		6 tbsp.	
Sugar, granulated		1/4 c.	Light flame.
Drambuie		1 1/2 oz.	Warm glasses over flame by rotating glasses.
Scotch		1 1/2 oz.	
Coffee		9 oz.	Pour 3/4 oz. Drambuie into each glass. Ignite spirit in glasses and continue rotating.
			Add Scotch (3/4 oz. each) to glasses, ignite and rotate.
			Pour in hot coffee and top with whipped cream.

Notes
Igniting an undiluted spirit produces a large flame. Insure that it is not too hot or you will get an explosion, not a flame.
Tea may be substituted for an unusual flaming beverage.

Cafe Diable

Yield: 4 cups (demitasse) Portion: 2 cups (demitasse)			Temp: Time: 6 min.
Ingredients	*Weights*	*Measures*	*Method*
Lemon peel		1 whole	Cut the peel from the meat of the orange and the lemon so the whole peel is intact and resembling a corkscrew worm.
Orange peel		1 whole	
Coffee, strong		10 oz.	
Cloves, whole		as required	Insert whole cloves into the peels on the outside surface. Attach both peels to the fork.
Brandy		1 oz.	
Triple sec		1 oz.	Portion coffee into coffee pot.
Brown sugar		1 tbsp., 1 tsp.	Light rèchaud.
			Place brandy and triple sec into small sauce pan over flame.
Cinnamon, stick (broken lengthwise)		1/2 stick	Add cinnamon stick to spirits.
Lemon zests		2	Add peel to spirits, but keep attached to fork.
			When spirits are warm (not hot), remove spirits with ladle to flame and ignite.
			Take flame to spirits in saucepan and ignite.
			Stir with peels and ladle flaming spirits over peels while holding peels over and above saucepan.
			Add coffee into saucepan, add brown sugar, and stir.
			When sugar is diluted, fill cups and garnish with zest of lemon.

Caution! Igniting an undiluted spirit produces a large flame. Insure that it is not too hot or you will get an explosion, not a flame.

Questions

1. Choose a restaurant with which you are familiar and determine the quality and amount of *all equipment and supplies* for that particular operation. After you have made your choices, defend your selections on ambience/decor, quality, and quantity.

2. Would you rent linen or have your own laundry? Why?

3. Establish criteria and specifications for tableware in a casual dining theme restaurant. Select three china companies and evaluate how their product line(s) do or do not meet your needs.

4. Discuss the glassware characteristics that affect a purchasing decision for an up-scale restaurant operation.

5. Compare and contrast the flatware characteristics that would be selected for an up-scale gourmet dinner house and for a casual dining chain operation.

6. Discuss the types of equipment, other than tabletop, needed for an operation functioning primarily as a caterer for large groups (weddings, banquets, cocktail parties).

7. What characteristics of the restaurant operation influence purchase decisions for tables and chairs?

8. Review spec sheets for several types of gourmet display equipment. Discuss how and why you might decide to use and purchase each of these equipment pieces.

9. Collect information and prices for several espresso machine models. Develop a spreadsheet showing beverage types, costs, sales forecast for each beverage type per day, margin between cost and sales, and total sales forecast and margin per week. Select one of the espresso models and calculate how long will it take to pay back the cost of the equipment from the margin between cost and sale of the beverage.

Endnotes

1. E. M. Bowden. "Managerial Considerations in the Selection of Restaurant China." *The Cornell Hotel and Restaurant Administration Quarterly,* May 1977, p. 43.

2. Ibid.

3. "Glassware," *Wine Spectator*, November 22, 1992, pp. 35–36.

4. J. Durocher. "Flatware." *Restaurant Business Magazine*, May 1, 1991, p. 200.

5. J. M. Stefanelli. *Purchasing: Selection and Procurement for the Hospitality Industry*, 3rd ed. (New York: John Wiley and Sons, Inc., 1992), pp. 181–83.

6. L. H. Kotschevar. *Quantity Food Purchasing* (New York: John Wiley & Sons, Inc., 1975), p. 166.

7. L. H. Kotschevar. "Non-Food Supplies," *Quantity Food Purchasing* (New York: John Wiley & Sons, Inc., 1975), p. 653.

Additional Readings

American Restaurant China Council. *Questions and Answers—Purchasing Tableware.* Alexandria, VA: The American Restaurant China Council

Colgan, S. "Restaurant Design," *Restaurant and Hotel Design International Magazine*, 1987.

Guide to Function-room Furniture. Philadelphia, PA: Institutional Products, Inc., 1995.

Kotschevar, L. H. "Non-food Supplies." *Quantity Food Purchasing.* New York: John Wiley & Sons, Inc., 1975.

Peddersen, R. B. *Food Service and Hotel Purchasing.* Boston: CBI Publishing Co., Inc., 1981.

Stefanelli, J. M. *Purchasing: Selection and Procurement for the Hospitality Industry.* New York: John Wiley & Sons, Inc., 1992.

Warfel, M. C. and M. L. Cremer. *Purchasing for Food Service Managers.* Berkely, CA: McCutchan Publishing Corporation. 1985.

Numerous catalogues and promotional material are available from manufacturers and dealers of restaurant equipment and supplies.

FIGURE 5–1

Flatware piece identification

 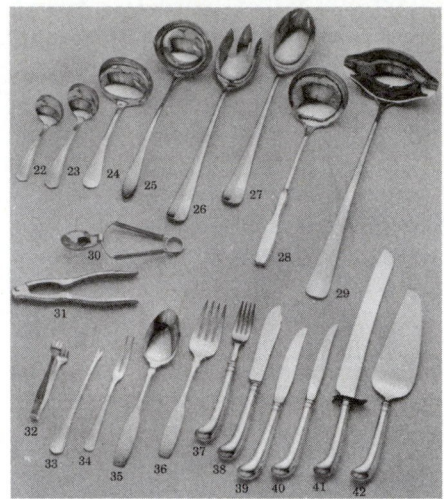

Spoons	Forks	Knives
1. Coffee or Demitasse	8. Seafood/Oyster	14. Butter Spreader†
2. Teaspoon	9. Fish*	15. Dessert‡
3. Bouillon	10. Dinner	16. Dinner‡
4. Round Bowl Spoon	11. Dessert	17. Steak*
5. Dessert/Soup Oval Bowl	12. Serving/Cold Meat/Buffet	18. Dinner*
6. Tall Drink/Parfait	13. Salad	19. Fish*
7. Table/Serving		20. Dessert*
		21. Butter Spreader*

22. Sauce Ladle, 4 1/2″, 1/4 oz.
23. Sauce Ladle, 6 1/2″, 1/2 oz.
24. Soup Ladle, 7 1/2″, 2 oz.
25. Punch or Soup Ladle, 11″, 4 1/2 oz.
26. Buffet ServingFork, 13″
27. Buffet Serving Spoon, 13″
28. Soup Ladle, 11 1/2″, 2 oz.*
29. Punch Ladle, 15″, 4 oz.
30. Escargot Tongs, 6″
31. Lobster Cracker, Chromeplated only
32. Sugar Tongs, 4″
33. Lobster Pick, 6″

34. Escargot Fork, 6 1/4″
35. French Service Spoon, 8 1/2″ (Tablespoon)
36. French Service Fork, 8 1/2″ (Cold Meat Fork)
37. Fish Fork, 7 7/8″
38. Fish Knife, 9″
39. Dinner Knife, 8 7/8″
40. Steak Knife, 8 7/8″
41. Ceremonial/Wedding Knife, 13 1/2″
42. Pie Server, Offset Handle, 10 5/8″

*   **Hollow Handle** – The handle of a flatware piece, usually a knife, is made from two identical halves permanently bonded together and carefully polished to give a smooth, seamless appearance. The blade is inserted between the halves and also permanently bonded for the life of the piece. Grace, balance, and ease of handling are characteristic of the Hollow Handle knife.

†   **Solid Handle** – The knife (blade and handle) are made from one piece of metal stock with the handle being somewhat thicker than the blade.

‡   **Flat Handle** – The knife is made from the same piece of metal stock like the solid handle but there is negligible difference in thickness between the blade and handle.

CHAPTER 6

Sanitation and Safety in Service

Chapter Outline

Sanitation in Service
What can Management Do?
What Can Management Look For?
Safety in Service
Ultrahazardous Activity
What Is an Accident?
General Safety Advice

Learning Objectives

After studying this chapter, the student will be able to . . .
1. Demonstrate how service personnel are responsible for the prevention of food-borne illness.
2. Describe examples of restaurant areas that suggest a high level of sanitation practices to the guest.
3. Define how temperature control affects the healthful quality of the food served.
4. Identify the characteristics of a safe food handler.
5. Evaluate the characteristics of a safe work environment.
6. Formulate a plan of safety practices for service personnel.
7. Set up emergency medical services for both employees and guests.

Key Words/Phrases

E. coli
Food poisoning
Food-borne illness
Salmonellosis
Sanitation inspectors
Litigation
Botulism
Trichinosis
Hepatitis
Toxins
Staphylococcus
Streptococcus
Dangerous temperature zone
Centers for Disease Control (CDC)
AIDS (Acquired Immunodeficiency Syndrome)
Americans with Disabilities Act (ADA)
HIV positive
Outbreak

Occupational Safety and Health Act
  (OSHA)
Worker's compensation
Ultrahazadous activity

Fire Inspection Checklist
Emergency procedures
Cyanosis
Cardiopulmonary resuscitation (CPR)

Sanitation In Service

In early 1993, Jack-in-the-Box Restaurants served rare hamburgers throughout the northwest United States and infected numerous customers with a virulent strain of **E. coli**. Several individuals died and many others were hospitalized as a result of eating the infected meat which was traced to a meat processing plant. Jack-in-the-Box was not responsible for the infected meat, but they failed to heed the warning issued by the government to fully cook ground meat to kill any pathogens. Two weeks after the incidents occurred, the *Wall Street Journal* reported that expansion plans for Jack-in-the-Box restaurants were placed on hold in order for the company and its parent, Foodmaker, to fully assess the damaged reputation and its effect on the firm's profitability. In the spring of 1995, Foodmaker settled out of court for a large but undisclosed amount with the victims.

In April 1995, 50 tourism professionals attending a three-day meeting in Massachusetts fell ill with most signs pointing to **food poisoning** resulting from a dinner served during their second evening by an outside caterer. Apart from the obvious irony—one local paper described it "a public relations disaster"—the incident underscores the heavy responsibility of meeting planners who must safeguard the well-being of their attendees.

In May 1995, over 100 passengers on a Princess Cruise Liner were hospitalized for **food-borne illness** that the line claims was contracted during meals taken off ship at one of their ports of call.

These sad, but true, vignettes underscore the risks all food-service operators experience and the importance of ensuring safe food handling practices. A recent segment titled "Salad Bar Sickness" aired on *Dateline NBC* on May 3, 1995, and the following day in *USA Today* an article was featured regarding sanitary tests conducted on communion wine and hosts (wafers). This publicity further heightens the general public's awareness about communicable diseases, especially through food-borne transmission. The dining public is ever more aware of food sanitation practices and will no longer tolerate gross operator error.

Every person has been stricken with food-borne illness (disease carried or transmitted to human beings by food). Food poisoning is, perhaps, as common as the common cold, and several million cases of food-borne illness occur each year in the United States. In spite of the effort by operators, processors, and government agencies, food poisoning continues at an alarming rate, and a majority of the incidents are a result of poor food handling. The entry-level characteristic of many food-service employees places the onus of training the staff on the management of the food-service operation. Food poisoning often goes undetected; for instance, people will remark, "I think I've got a little bug. I don't feel too well." They probably have food poisoning. You can be particularly suspicious if several or many people "get the stomach flu" simultaneously and for a short period of time—one day—and then recover quickly (after the toxins were expelled from the body). We see clear evidence of this in the sports news when an athletic team, all of sudden, is stricken with "a little flu" all at the same time!

Many types of bacteria cause food-borne illness. Some bacteria produce illnesses with only mild effects, while others produce more severe effects. Some are of a short duration—the illness may last for only a few hours, and sometimes the illness may be very prolonged (e.g., **salmonellosis**) and severe; people may become seriously ill and even die. If the person who has become ill is otherwise healthy, perhaps the effects of the illness will disappear rapidly.

Who is responsible for the prevention of food-borne illness? The manager of an individual food service establishment is directly responsible for the prevention of food-borne illness because (1) it is the law and (2) the stakes for noncompliance are high. Local governments are usually responsible for inspecting food service establishments for sanitary conditions and safe food handling practices. If the establishment is involved in interstate commerce through its purchasing or other activities, however, the federal government may have jurisdiction.

The United States has proposed that specific guidelines and uniform standards for sanitation be established for the food-service industry. This information is available from the the U.S. Government Printing Office and should prove useful, if not required, reading for any food-service operator. For example, one of the new provisions of this document says, "tableware should be set prior to serving a meal only if glasses and cups are inverted, and knives, forks, and spoons are wrapped and otherwise covered." If strictly enforced by **sanitation inspectors** at the local level, this provision will create havoc with food service operators, especially in fine dining and other table service environments.

Food sanitation is a very important issue with government and the consumer, and it behooves each operator to become a professional in his industry. Minor violations are seldom brought before the public, and operators are usually given ample opportunity to improve unsanitary conditions. (See *Food Service Establishment Inspection Report*.) In New York City, however, the local news media have begun publishing in newspapers and announcing over television and radio the particular food service establishments that have violated codes for food-service sanitation. Food-service operators and their employees are responsible for the health and well-being of the public and must ensure that they are serving wholesome food. The most important factor is the risk an operator takes by running an unsanitary operation. If a person becomes ill after eating in your establishment and brings suit, it may cost the restaurant millions in **litigation** expense, and the bad publicity may be sufficient to eventually close the operation. Unfortunately, good sanitation and employee hygiene are not a competitive advantage—every guest demands wholesome food. Cleanliness, however, can be marketed effectively, and many quick-service as well as causal dining chains actively market cleanliness, and they subtly market sanitation.

Several years ago an incident occurred concerning a soup cannery in whose product **botulism** was found. One person died from eating the soup, and the particular food-processing company is no longer in business. A famous movie actor brought suit against a restaurant for supplying undercooked pork from which he claims he contracted **trichinosis**. The director of in-flight services (food) for an international airline took his own life after an outbreak of food-borne illness on a flight for which his in-flight kitchen provided food. Winning or losing the case in litigation was not material at that point. The damage had already been done.

Guests are particularly aware of the clean appearance of a food-service establishment and have rated cleanliness very high as a concern for selecting a restaurant. Eighty-nine percent of those responding to a NPD/CREST survey (for COEX '90), specified that proper food handling is important to them, and 27 percent said that cleanliness and food safety are determining factors in restaurant selection.[2]

Some particular areas that management should concentrate efforts on are the sections in the restaurant most visible to the guest. These include:

- Clean menus.
- Clean, unstained, and pressed linen with no holes.
- Clean salt, pepper, ketchup, mustard, and other condiment holders.
- Clean floor with carpet vacuumed or swept frequently.
- Chairs, table legs, and so on, clean and dusted.
- Spotless silverware and glassware.
- Entry, waiting area, and restrooms picked up and clean.
- Ample trash cans and ventilation in the restrooms—an absence of odor is preferable to that of intensely perfumed chemicals.

- Display shelves, hanging fixtures, pictures, etc., clean and dust-free.
- Server uniforms clean and pressed.
- No smoking by any employee in guest's view.

But clean is not necessarily sanitary, which is hygienic and free from food-borne pathogens or any other toxicant.

What Can Management Do?

All food must be kept free of contaminants which means that the true food infectors, such as salmonella or **hepatitis**, must be held in check. Bacteria capable of producing **toxins** that result in food poisoning are everywhere. All food, unless sterile, has **staphylococcus** and may have **streptococcus** germs, and the task for food-service managers and their employees regarding these and other food infectors is to prevent or retard bacterial growth. This can be accomplished by reducing assembly or preparation time in the **dangerous temperature zone**. Food should be kept below 40° F (7° C) or above 140° F (60° C). Although bacteria may grow at a temperature below 40° F, the rate is slow enough that the danger of producing enough toxins to cause disease is minimal. In every case, bacterial food poisoning is the result of mishandling food (i.e., leaving food in the dangerous temperature zone for too long or by allowing one who is ill to work with food). Service managers in particular should be aware of these facts because the front-of-the-house person is usually responsible for keeping watch on a buffet table.

Maintaining proper temperatures on buffets is not an easy task if heating equipment is inadequate. The physical equipment aspects are important, but so are the people aspects. A manager should be on the lookout for poor personal hygiene among the service staff and the production staff. A clean person sheds approximately two hundred bacteria per minute by just breathing, and a dirty person sheds considerably more. The manager should also be cognizant of infected food handlers. Infected food handlers transmit diseases of the respiratory tract via the nose or mouth (coughing, sneezing) and via the hands. Respiratory-tract diseases can also be spread when smokers touch their lips and then handle food or food contact surfaces such as silverware, glassware, or china. Diseases of the intestinal tract and infectious hepatitis are transmitted when the infected person does not thoroughly wash his or her hands after using the toilet.

The safe food handler must:

- Be in good health (people who are sick or infected must not handle food—better safe than sorry).

- Handle food safely.
- Practice sanitary personal habits.
- Wash hands (and fingernails) effectively after using the restroom, touching any part of the body, smoking, eating, or touching unsanitary equipment or utensils.
- Wash hair and body frequently.
- Cover all cuts or open wounds with an antiseptic, waterproof bandage.
- Wear clean work uniforms at the workplace. Avoid wearing uncovered street clothes when working with or serving food to guests.
- Never work with or serve food when ill.

Dining room service personnel do not pose as serious a problem with respect to transmitting food-borne illness as do food-production personnel. The reason for this is that by the time the server handles food, the bacteria will not have had time to grow. However, servers infected with salmonella or hepatitis can transmit their disease. Yet a recent case at Johnson and Wales University, an internationally recognized culinary school, underscores the responsiblities now being placed on service personnel. A sizeable sum was awarded to the family of a student who died after eating a shrimp egg roll at a school cafeteria. The student asked for a *vegetarian* egg roll when he ordered his meal. He inadvertently was served a shrimp roll, and he suffered an acute allergic reaction and died en route to the hospital. While in this case the server was a cafeteria worker, dining room service personnel will be held responsible for placing a correct order with food production and serving the correctly ordered food item(s) to the appropriate guest. Indeed, the food-production personnel must also follow the order given them by the service staff because they, too, bear responsibility for injuring a guest if they do not prepare the item as advertised or printed as such in the menu.

Practices in service are necessary for sanitation and safe food-handling practices and also for aesthetic reasons; the guest would hardly like to see the server's thumb in his soup. Yet the cook's thumb in the soup can do far more damage—especially if his thumb is in the soup during the earlier stages of food production. Service personnel can pose a problem, however, when their duties take them into the kitchen and when they assist in food preparation or otherwise handle food. The food-service manager and the service manager in particular may observe much when conducting a preemployment interview with respect to sanitary habits.

- Does the prospective employee look dirty?
- Does he have skin infections or lesions?

- Does she display nervous habits by picking at her face or other body surfaces?
- Does she bite or show evidence of biting her fingernails?
- Does he cough, sneeze, wheeze, or appear to have a runny nose?

This list should not imply that the person seeking employment should not undergo a physical exam; quite the contrary. Yet a physical by a physician may mention nothing about biting fingernails or picking at one's face or stroking one's hair. A preemployment physical examination is desirable to screen out possible disease carriers, but this is no guarantee of the permanent health of the employee. Physical examinations are not required by most states in the United States, yet other countries may require physical examinations.

The **Centers for Disease Control (CDC)** in Atlanta has not categorized **AIDS (Acquired Immundeficiency Syndrome)** as a food-borne illness since, as yet, there has been no documented case of AIDS being transmitted through casual contact. At present several U.S. government regulatory bodies, whose regulations are in conflict, require resolution. On the one hand, the Civil Rights Act of 1964 and the **Americans with Disabilities Act (ADA)** protect the rights of individuals with AIDS or who are **HIV positive**. On the other hand, the Food and Drug Administration (FDA) prohibits food-service operators from employing workers, in any capacity, with communicable diseases that can be transmitted by foods or who carry an organism that could contaminate food or a food-contact surface. Nonetheless, employing an HIV positive or AIDS-infected person in a food-service establishment could create a marketing nightmare for the business. This situation presents a serious dilemma for the restaurant manager.

What Can the Manager Look For?

Managers must assume that the customer is a dirty, disease-infected person since many customers may be diseased. The manager must protect all other guests from those that may be infected. Although employees are examined by competent medical authorities for illness, the customer cannot be so examined. When a guest enters your establishment, he may not have washed his hands after using a toilet. He may have infections that can transmit germs, and each guest must be protected from other guests with respect to contaminating food. It is up to the individual manager to protect one guest from the other by covering displayed food, as much as possible, from sneezes, coughs, and hands. Never serve food (butter, rolls, bread, etc.) to anyone after the food has been served to another table. Food displayed on a buffet table must be displayed so that one guest cannot contaminate food that is subsequently eaten by another guest.

How can a manager tell if her operation is consistently performing in an effective manner in sanitation? Truthfully, she cannot. Yet there are indicators. Are there frequent complaints that the food served has foreign objects in it? Are guests leaving food on plates? This may indicate that portions are too large or that food is aesthetically unpleasing (e.g., off taste). Is the air-conditioning system working properly? Dirty filters will not remove stale odors from the dining room, and this is irritating to the guest and provides food for breeding vermin. Are there frequent complaints that the food is cold? Does the service staff spend an inordinate amount of time polishing spots that have collected on glassware and silverware? Do the water goblets have a a cloudy appearance or a fishy odor? This indicates a faulty dish machine. Do the guests ask for replacements for dirty, cracked, or chipped china or glassware—good breeding grounds for food-borne illness bacteria? Are the drapes or window sills dirty or dusty (with *old dirt*)? Are windows streaked, grimy, or greasy? Are the walls clean and uncracked? Are there cobwebs? Are floor tiles loose? Is the carpet stained or soiled?

What can the dining room manager do to reduce the risk of a food-borne illness **outbreak** in his establishment? Provide adequate hand-washing facilities that are well supplied with a disinfectant soap in all areas where hands are likely to become contaminated, and provide clean and sanitary locker rooms. Provide for sanitary garbage disposal and an adequate number of durable trash cans with lids, and schedule frequent garbage and trash collection. Keep rodents and insects out and under control. Spraying with pesticides may be necessary, but this must be supplemented with the best prevention, which is a clean establishment. Provide adequate supplies and ample separate storage for toxic cleaning materials. Ensure that there is adequate labor for proper and correct cleaning of the dining room and the kitchen. Check for dark, damp areas and areas where food spills are cleaned frequently (e.g., service stations, side stands, or tray stands). Provide adequate checklists and cleaning instructions for all equipment. Excellent cleaning procedures are listed in the classic text by Longree and Blaker, *Sanitary Techniques in Food Service*, and can be supplemented for newer equipment with the manufacturer's manual. Provide hot and cold holding equipment that will keep food out of the danger zone of 40° F–140° F (7° C–60° C). Food should be heated to 165° F (74° C) before being placed in a steam table or chafing dish for buffet service. Are salad dressings, cream, or other condiments left on the service stands, the guest's table, or the buffet table without refrigeration?

Provide for adequate training of all employees preparing and handling food; suggest training films or filmstrips. Impress upon each employee the importance of good sanitation habits and practices, and as a supervisor, show that you appreciate and reward the efforts of your staff to maintain a clean and sanitary restaurant.

A Checklist for Sanitary Practices for the Service Staff

- Keep yourself in good health; report illnesses to your supervisor.
- Bathe daily, use deodorant, wash hair at least twice a week, and wear clean clothes; change undergarments daily.
- Practice frequent, thorough, and correct hand washing (30 seconds rubbing with soap).
- Cover open cuts or abrasions with antiseptic bandages and waterproof protectors.
- No smoking (contamination from hand to mouth to hand).
- Don clean uniforms at establishment.
- Wear no decorative jewelry.
- Avoid using a handkerchief or tissues in dining room; use only if involuntary sneezing or coughing occurs. Wash hands immediately.
- Do not touch food-contact surfaces such as fork tines, spoons, knives, and so on.
- Never touch food; butter, bread, ice, and so on. Use plastic or latex gloves if touching food is unavoidable.
- Handle glassware by the base or stem.
- Handle cups by the handle.
- Handle plates with the fat part of the thumb; do not place thumb on the plate.
- Do not serve on soiled, chipped, or cracked china or glassware.
- Never reuse any silverware or china placed on a table at which guests have been seated.
- Do not use anything that has dropped to the floor.
- Do not touch head or hair or other parts of the body; wash hands if you accidentally touch your face or body.
- Keep fingernails short and clean.
- Never spit in the kitchen or dining room.
- Change tablecloths when soiled, preferably after each guest turnover.
- Do not use service cloth to wipe perspiration from body or face.
- Do not wipe hands on apron or clothes.
- Use clean menus, not soiled ones. Requisition pads and guest check books should be clean.
- Clean and wash chairs frequently; wash tables with warm, soapy water (with sanitizing agent) after each guest turnover, and wipe dry with a clean cloth or paper towel.
- Condiment containers should be wiped and clean for each service period.
- Remove gum from under tables and counters (before and after service).
- Do not invert glasses over bottles or stack cups or glasses so that the bottom of one touches where the guest's mouth would touch.
- Use a hairnet to maintain hair above the collar.

Safety in Service

Restaurants have the special honor of recording the most injuries on a dollar cost basis of any industry—in part because of the large labor force.[3] The **Occupational Safety and Health Act (OSHA)** passed in 1970 specifies in detail many rules with which a food service operator must comply. Some conditions are not specifically covered, and in this case a general duty clause states: "Each employer shall furnish to each of his employees employment and a place of employment which are free from recognized hazards that are causing or are likely to cause death or serious physical harm to his employees; and shall comply with occupational safety and health standards issued under the Act." The Department of Labor requires that employers of 10 or more employees must submit a "written employer safety and health program" (RSA 281-A:64 *Safety Provisions*). Guests and employees are continuously exposed to safety hazards in our hospitality environments. Hazards such as sharp objects, extremely hot surfaces, heavy lifting, and slippery surfaces are all potentially dangerous. Guests are more than likely to be involved in slips and falls according to the National Safety Council, which reports that one-third of guest accidents are from slips and falls.[4]

While the basic management functions of planning, organizing, staffing, directing, and controlling describe the basic tasks of management, areas of safety and accident prevention do not really fit into any one of these areas. This subject and an awareness of safety are most important to management and to all employees. Accidents not only decrease productivity, they lead to higher workman's compensation/insurance premiums (ranging from 3.5 percent to 8 percent or even 16 percent of payroll in some areas) and expensive litigation. Experts feel that restaurateurs must take safety seriously as the insurance premiums and litigation equal only 14 percent to 25 percent of the direct costs. Indirect costs of 75 percent to 85 percent include money spent for (1) lost time, (2) worker's compensation, (3) increase in insurance premiums, (4) the cost of retraining or replacing an employee, (5) time spent by other employees to aid the victim, to observe what happened, and to discuss the incident, and (6) damage to equipment or facilities is quite high.

Many restaurant operators blame insurance companies, the government, lawyers, and doctors (and the continuing rise in costs of medical care), but a self-assessment is clearly warranted. Indeed, many insurance companies are rejecting the **_worker's compensation_** business as it loses money for the insurance carrier. Accidents cost untold dollars, and an OSHA violation could cost the business $10,000 in fines if the violation is considered serious or willful. Criminal penalties are also provided for in the Act, which may be punishable by a fine ($10,000), imprisonment for not more than six months, or both. While the U.S. government mandates must be complied with, the operator will also experience significant increases in her worker's compensation rate as discussed above. This premium is also factored by the individual property's "loss experience." The experience rating is derived from two factors: frequency of accidents and severity of accidents. Indeed, it is crucial that food-service operators take a proactive stance with regard to safety both for their guests and their staff.

The October 10, 1991, issue of *Restaurant Business Magazine* reported that Burger King Corporation initiated a safety training program to eliminate or, at least reduce, accidents and offered incentives to unit managers. It discovered that 4 percent of the chain's restaurants were the cause of 60 percent of the losses due to injuries. After installing the program, Burger King significantly cut its losses due to accidents by both employees and guests. Claims dropped from 7 per unit in 1985 to 3.2 in 1990. Savings flowed directly to the bottom line with an estimated savings of $11 million over the five-year period; the safety program costs approximately $1 million per year. With slips and falls leading the injury list, Burger King isolated hazardous areas and continued to follow up to ensure safety program intensity. Employee accidents also revealed many cuts to the skin surface; Burger King provides special gloves to reduce cuts and also established a centralized purchasing department for all safety-related equipment items.

FIGURE 6–1

Cost of workplace injuries

Condition	Percent of Claims	Average cost per claim
Back strain	31%	$23,916
Other sprains/strains	19	13,611
Fracture	11	23,138
Concussion/bruises	11	12,055
Laceration/puncture	10	9,722
Dislocation/crushing	3	47,249
Hernia	3	24,499
Burn	3	12,833
Infection/inflammation	2	13,805
Amputation	1	40,249
Occupational disease	1	31,305
Cumulative injury	1	29,166

Source: National Council on Compensation Insurance (NCCI).

Ultrahazardous Activity

Any restaurant engaging in **ultrahazardous activity** as defined by the law is liable for the manager's behavior and the behavior of its employees. If flaming foods are on a restaurant's menu, the operator should be sure that he is adequately and appropriately covered with liability insurance. Additionally, the operator should train and make a record of training sessions in order to prove in a court of law that he has exercised reasonable care in offering tableside foods. Proof of, and adherence to, the procedures listed in Chapter 10 of this text may help an operator prove that she has exercised reasonable care in flaming foods at the tableside.

What Is an Accident?

An accident is a suddenly occurring, unintentional event that causes injury or property damage. An accident may be the result of an unsafe act or an unsafe condition. An unsafe condition may result from either poor housekeeping or poor maintenance, and the majority of accidents are the result of unsafe acts. To begin an accident prevention training program to help prevent unsafe acts, the manager should approach accident prevention from two lines of thought—the psychological and the physical. Low morale and a poorly trained person are ripe conditions for accidents. Over half the accidents in the food-service industry involve new employees who have been on the job for less than two years. The emotional condition of a person under stress could present a dangerous situation, and stress conditions are very real possibilities in service industries; the work is a high-tension, rush-and-slack-period type job. Physical fatigue also creates a potentially hazardous situation, and the service person who must work a double shift falls into this category.

Unsafe Acts include

- Poor housekeeping, failure to remedy unsafe conditions.
- Overloading, overcrowding, bad storage or handling.
- Repairing or adjusting equipment, and using dangerous material under pressure.
- Failing to use personal protective clothing or safety devices.
- Operating machinery at unsafe speeds.
- Not using machine guards.
- Using defective equipment.

As an industry serving the public, the hospitality industry has an additional burden of protecting the guest. Correcting sloppy housekeeping or shoddy maintenance will do much to correct hazardous situations and to protect guests and employees. Rarely are safety efforts and accident prevention supported by a desire to anticipate, prevent, and avoid accidents. Carelessness is usually blamed first and punishment is usually the remedy. The way to protect against accidents is proper training. Although the responsibility for safety and safety awareness is everyone's, management and ownership have the ultimate responsibility. Lip service is inadequate; the manager must make a concerted, planned effort for instituting safe practices.

A standard checklist should be available to each employee, and each should be able to follow instructions. Procedures and information in case of emergency include the following items:

- Personnel to notify in case of an emergency.
- Civil disturbance instructions.
- Fire evacuation procedures.
- Release of kitchen CO_2 system procedures.
- Death (do not remove the remains; cover with blanket; call local authorities; call management or persons on emergency list; discourage assembly of crowd).
- Disorders (do not get involved; call management; call local authorities if situation is out of hand).
- Elevator malfunctions (find location of car; if passengers are in car, ask them to remain calm; assure them that help is on the way; call maintenance personnel; call management).
- Post a list of first-aid instructions; make the *Red Cross Standard First-Aid Guide* accessible.
- Gas, steam, or water-leak procedures.
- Power failure or electrical arcing procedures.
- Policies in case of sickness or injuries in addition to first aid.

Management should encourage local fire-inspection officials to visit the property regularly to advise of any unsafe or illegal practices. There is a substantial history of restaurants, lounges, nightclubs, and other hospitality organizations that have violated laws by locking fire escape doors or blocking exits with equipment and other violations that have caused multiple deaths and injury. A **fire-inspection checklist** may resemble the following, while the individual establishment should customize an inspection checklist and **emergency procedures** for its own occupation.

Departmental Fire Inspection Checklist

Corridors

1. Are there obstructions to free passage in the corridors?
2. Is the wall finish in good repair so as to prevent fire extending into any concealed space?

Stairways
1. Are stairs in good repair?
2. Is there storage of any type on or under the stairs?

Exits
1. Is each exit indicated by EXIT signs?
2. Are the EXIT signs continuously illuminated day and night?
3. Are exits free from all obstructions?

Fire Extinguishers
1. Is the proper type of extinguisher provided for the area?
2. Is each extinguisher in its proper place?
3. Is each extinguisher charged?
4. Are the seals intact on each extinguisher?

Stand Pipe System
1. Is each hose station well marked?
2. Does the hose appear to be in good condition?
3. Is the nozzle attached?

Electrical
1. Are electrical wires, conduits, panels, or junction boxes warmer than surroundings?
2. Are extension cords used where permanent wiring should be installed?
3. Are the power cords to all electrical appliances free of breaks and obvious defects?
4. Does the electrical system appear to be in otherwise good condition?

Special Areas and Hazards:
1. Is there evidence of careless smoking?
2. Are all first-aid kits properly stocked?

Some Guidelines on Safety Training

Identify significant safety hazards (the problem or problem areas in your operation) and determine why they exist. Then choose a solution to the problem or problems, apply the solution(s), and communicate the solution to others. The most important of these guidelines is finding or identifying the problem.

An anecdote highlights the need to identify the problem correctly before applying any solutions. In a high-rise condominium, there were frequent complaints that the elevators were too slow. A team of engineers was called in to analyze and solve the problem. Everything seemed to be normal and in accordance with design specifications, but the engineers decided to speed up the opening and closing of the doors; they also installed electric eyes in the elevator door crevices to reduce the time that the elevator doors would remain open. A few weeks passed, but complaints kept coming in. The engineers were called back again to solve the problem. As much as possible, they sped the elevators up so that they would move more rapidly between floors. Complaints still came in. Management was truly frustrated; short of buying new elevators, which would be a major expense, they did not know what to do. They called a psychologist to analyze the problem. After considerable study and consternation, the psychologist analyzed the problem: How do we stop the flow of complaint letters? To heck with the speed of the elevators. She began studying this problem and decided to install mirrors in the elevator lobbies or vestibules on each floor. The complaints stopped altogether!

Designing a safety training program is a major task. It is helpful to know that there are many people who can design programs or assist managers in designing specific safety training programs. These include

- Trade associations (national and local or regional restaurant associations).
- State agencies.
- U.S. government agencies (e.g., the Department of Health, Education, and Welfare).
- Insurance companies (use caution as they could be looking for insurability).
- Consultants (within any particular area, there are many people who could participate in or direct a safety program).

A safety director or officer could be appointed to set up and administer a program, and a safety committee could be established; there could be cross-department inspections. An emphasis on safety will be felt by all, and this, in itself, will encourage everyone to be conscious of safety and safe practices. Additionally, a safety training program will give employees an opportunity to have some additional responsibility. An employee designated as safety director may be observed by management and used as a testing or proving ground for a possible promotion. When an OSHA inspector arrives, the food-service manager or authorized representative of the employer and a representative authorized by the employees should accompany the inspector.

Be sure to check the inspector's identification. Respect her authority since she assesses fines and you pay. Cooperate with her by showing her whatever she wants to see, and learn from her by asking questions.

A Checklist for Safety Practices in Service

Safety in the kitchen and in the dining room is of great importance. Safety consciousness is part of the job. With training, with the right attitude and with alertness to hazardous situations and conditions, accidents can be reduced to a minimum and, in many cases, eliminated. Accidents cause much lost time, and lost time costs you and your employer money. Advise your employer and other employees of any safety practices you have learned. Report any accident, however slight, to your supervisor.

Dining Room

- Stack dishes properly in bus boxes or on trays. Be sure that dishes will not slide off. Do not overload.
- Keep swinging doors and drawers to side stands shut.
- Inspect food for foreign objects before serving. Do not put hands in food; get another plate.
- Be sure you use the correct door entering or exiting the kitchen or dining room; do not stop or backtrack.
- Never hurry. Walk briskly, but never run. Keep to the right when rounding corners. Notify and warn guests when serving hot plates and hot beverages.
- Remove and report any broken furnishings that may injure you or your guests (torn or loose carpets or rugs; curled carpet edges; defective or splintering chairs).
- Remove and destroy broken or chipped glassware or china.
- Remove knives and forks from a child's reach.
- Keep your station clean. Clean up spills immediately and pick up everything you drop.
- Throw nothing. Always make a positive exchange.
- Use a dry service towel when handling hot dishes.
- Know the location of and how to use fire extinguishers.
- Know where the first-aid equipment is and how to use it.
- Unplug electrical equipment before cleaning.
- Wear proper footwear—sturdy toes and nonslip soles.
- Never scoop ice with glass.
- Never clean up broken glass with your hands—use a broom or a service towel and place in garbage or special broken glass receptacle, not in bus box!
- Be aware of traffic flows—warn others when passing behind, and announce that you are passing through when approaching a large crowd.

Accident Report   Check [✔]
Please Fill Out Completely [ ] Employee or Customer [   ]
Check [✔]

A.M.[   ]

Store-Name & Number   Accident Date   Time   P.M.[   ]

Name   Occupation   Age

Address   Zip Code   Phone #

Social Security #   Employment Date

What Happened?

Was First Aid Treatment Given Yes/No What?

Date Injured Returned to Work   Time   Date   How Long Off?

Nature of Injury

Name and Address of Doctor

And/or Hospital

Names and Addresses of Witnesses

Employees or Customers

Check [✔]

	Permit	Full Time or Part Time	Married	Single
Yes [ ] No [ ]	[ ]	[ ]	[ ]	[ ]

Please Give Us Your Suggestions on How This Accident Could Have
Been Prevented:

Restaurant

Manager Signature
Sign

Injured Employee or Customer

Report Date

(Use Other Side for Additional Information)

HOW TO LIFT SAFELY

The factors that contribute to safe lifting are...

1. Approach the load and size it up (weight, size and shape). Consider your physcial ability to handle the load.

2. Place the feet close to the object to be lifted 8 to 12 inches apart for good balance.

3. Bend the knees to the degree that is comfortable and get a good handhold. Then using both leg and back muscles. . .

DETERMINE IF OBJECTS CAN BE LIFTED AND CARRIED SAFELY.

Stack material in such a manner as to permit full view while carrying.

When lifting and carrying with another person—teamwork is important.

The load should be equally distributed. Movements must be coordinated so you both start and finish the lift action at the same time and perform turning movements together.

When two persons carry a long object, it should be held at the same level by both and on the same side of the body.

The following safe practices should be observed in order to avoid injury.

4. Lift the load straight up—smoothly and evenly. Pushing with your legs, keep load close to your body.

5. Lift the object into carrying position, making no turning or twisting movements until the lift is completed.

6. Turn your body with changes of foot position after looking over your path of travel making sure it is clear.

7. Setting the load down is just as important as picking it up. Using leg and back muscles, comfortably lower load by bending your knees. When load is securely positioned, release your grip.

Avoid strain by storing heavy objects at least 12 inches above the floor.

Avoid awkward positions or twisting movements while lifting.

Overreaching and stretching to reach overhead objects may result in strains or falls.

Use a ladder instead of chairs, boxes, etc.

Source: National Institute for Occupational Safety and Health

- When flaming food, keep the flame as small as possible (ensure that pan is not too hot), pour from a wide-mouthed container, warn the guest when prepared to ignite, and be sure you are a safe distance from all guests and other employees.
- Remove obstructions (handbags and briefcases) from aisles.

Kitchen

- Use caution when opening or closing plate warmers or steam tables.
- Remove lids from pots so the steam will exit away from your face or hands.
- Do not use any piece of equipment you do not know how to operate.
- Grasp knives by the handle. If a knife is falling, do not grab for it—jump away.
- Clean up all spills (food, drinks, and broken dishes) immediately. Use caution in wet or greasy areas (near dishwashers, stoves, ice machines).
- Walk in the kitchen—DO NOT RUN.
- Horseplay is dangerous—don't.
- Do not touch electrical appliances or equipment if standing in water.
- Make sure all traffic areas are cleared of rolling stock or other equipment. Do not block exits.

General Safety Advice

Each restaurant operator should have available the standard first aid and personal safety book published by the American Red Cross. Someone on each shift must be trained in first aid in order to handle any emergencies. (This is required by law if hospital or clinic is more than 10 minutes away even in heavy traffic conditions.) Burned out lightbulbs should always be replaced, and those that cannot be reached safely should be reported. Frayed electric cords should not be used and should be replaced immediately upon discovery.

Heart Attack

A person having a heart attack may exhibit the same behavior as a guest who is choking on food. However, a heart attack victim will usually be able to speak, and a choking victim will not be able to speak. Figure 6–4 indicates the early warnings of a heart attack and how to help a heart attack victim.

How You Can Save the Life of Someone Choking on Food

The following maneuver is the effective way to dislodge food caught in one's throat and has been used successfully since its introduction.

Symptoms

- Violent choking—victim cannot answer if spoken to
- Unsuccessful attempts to inhale (victim cannot breathe)
- **Cyanosis** (i.e., blue lips, face, and neck)
- Collapse
- Unconsciousness
- Death—imminent if not corrected

Persons Most Susceptible

- Children
- Denture wearers—chewing sensation is diminished
- Inebriated persons—chewing and swallowing sensation diminished
- Older adults—difficulty in chewing

Procedures (per Figure 6–3)

1. Sitting or standing

   a. Stand behind victim with arms around his waist.

   b. Grab fist with other hand and place fist in victim's abdomen above navel and below rib cage.

   c. Move fist quickly into abdomen with an upward direction.

   d. Procedure may be self-administered and repeated as many times as necessary.

   e. Consult physician as lung infections may result.

2. Lying down

   a. Kneel over victim straddling his hips.

   b. Place one hand atop the other with heel of hand on victim's abdomen above navel and below rib cage.

   c. Move fist quickly into abdomen towards victim's rib cage.

   d. Consult physician as lung infections may result.

Early Warnings of a Heart Attack

Pain, in one form or another, almost always accompanies a heart attack. Pain ranges from a mild ache to unbearable severity. When severe, pain is often felt as constricting, like a vise on the chest. Pain also often includes the burning and bloated sensations that usually accompany indigestion. Pain may be continuous or it might subside, but don't ignore these indications even if the pain does subside.

FIGURE 6–3

FIRST AID FOR CHOKING

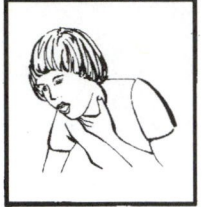

UNIVERSAL CHOKING SIGN

If victim can cough, speak, breathe ➡ *Do not interfere*

If victim cannot
COUGH
SPEAK
BREATHE
IS BLUISH

HAVE SOMEONE CALL FOR HELP

PHONE:_____

TAKE ACTION: FOR CONSCIOUS VICTIM•SITTING OR STANDING

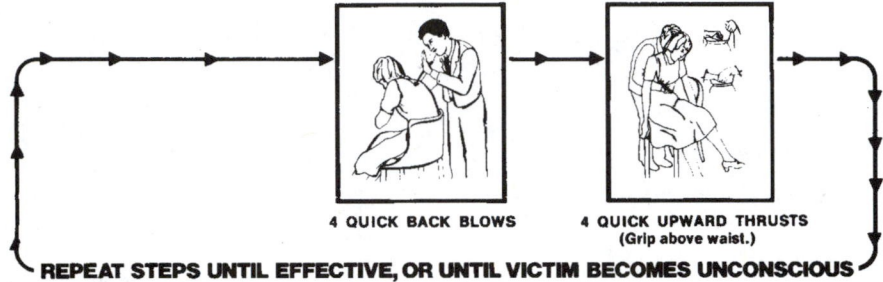

4 QUICK BACK BLOWS

4 QUICK UPWARD THRUSTS
(Grip above waist.)

REPEAT STEPS UNTIL EFFECTIVE, OR UNTIL VICTIM BECOMES UNCONSCIOUS

TAKE ACTION: FOR UNCONSCIOUS VICTIM

REPEAT STEPS UNTIL EFFECTIVE

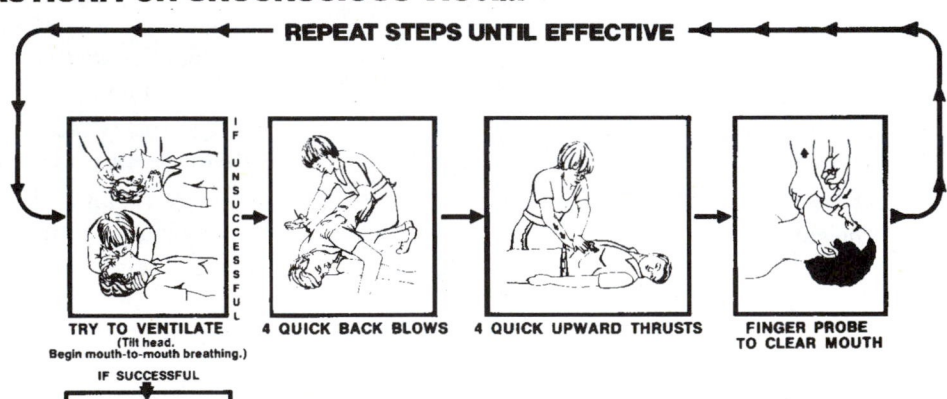

TRY TO VENTILATE
(Tilt head.
Begin mouth-to-mouth breathing.)

4 QUICK BACK BLOWS

4 QUICK UPWARD THRUSTS

FINGER PROBE
TO CLEAR MOUTH

IF
UNSUCCESSFUL

IF SUCCESSFUL

CONTINUE
VENTILATION
IF PULSELESS
PERFORM C P R

The National Research Council/National Academy of Sciences publication—*Emergency Airway Management 1976* is the reference for the procedures described on this poster.

Everyone should learn how to perform the first aid steps for choking and how to give mouth-to-mouth and cardiopulmonary resuscitation. Call your local Red Cross chapter for information on these and other first aid techniques.

CAUTION: Abdominal thrusts may cause injury.
Do not practice on people.

NATIONAL RESTAURANT ASSOCIATION

FIGURE 6–4

Symptoms of heart attack

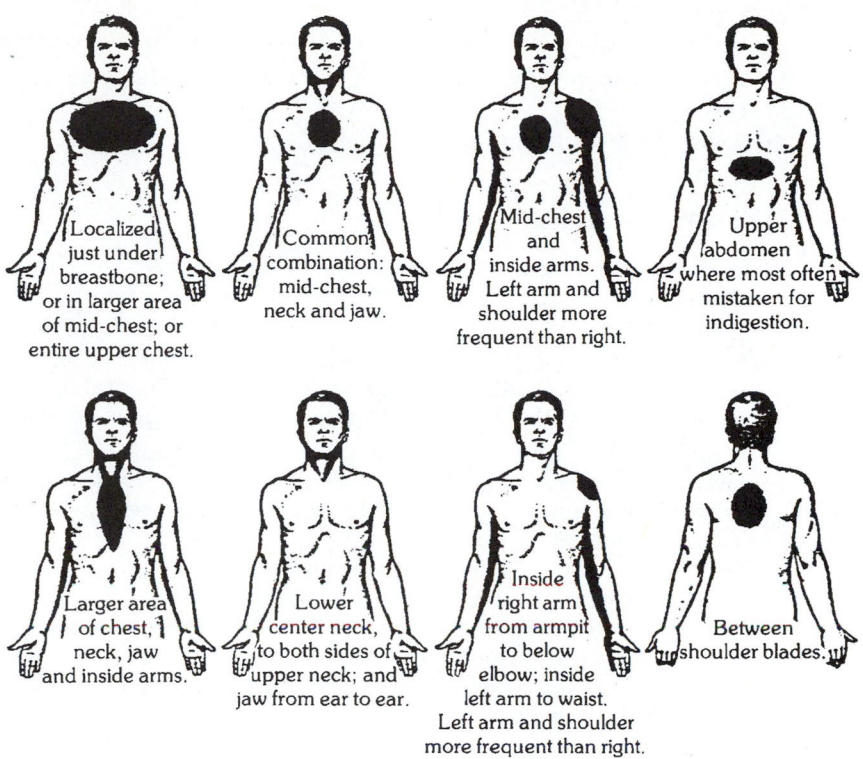

Checklist of Other Heart Attack Early Warnings

None of the following symptoms is conclusive proof of a heart attack. But the more of them present, the more likely it is that the patient is undergoing a heart attack.

- Difficulty breathing
- Palpitations
- Nausea
- Vomiting
- Cold sweat
- Paleness, weakness, or anxiety

How to Help a Possible Heart Attack Victim

You can best help (and possibly save a life) if you know in advance what to do. The following procedures were developed to be taught by local chapters of the American Heart Association and the American Red Cross:

Prior to a Heart Attack

- Know where the nearest hospital equipped to handle heart attack emergencies is.
- Learn and know how to do **cardiopulmonary resuscitation (CPR)**.
- Know how to quickly call a doctor, the hospital, and/or an ambulance.
- Know the fastest route to the hospital.

During a Heart Attack

- Help victim to least painful position—usually sitting, with legs up and bent at knees. Loosen clothing around neck and midriff. Be calm, reassuring.
- Call ambulance to get victim to hospital via your local rescue squad, police, or whatever other method available. Speed is vital. Once the ambulance is on the way, notify the family physician, if known.
- If ambulance will arrive in a few minutes, wait, comforting the victim. Otherwise, carry victim to car trying to keep victim's exertion to minimum. If possible, take another CPR-trained person with you. Victim should sit up—not lie down.
- Drive cautiously to hospital. Keep close watch on victim (or have passenger do so). If victim loses consciousness, stop car, pull victim to hard surface outside, perform CPR. Call for help. Keep up CPR until resuscitator or ambulance arrives.
- If patient retains consciousness to hospital, make sure he is carried, not walked, to emergency room.

Questions

1. "Very few people actually become ill from food poisoning." Discuss.
2. Who is responsible for food-borne illness in a restaurant?
3. Why so much concern for sanitation?
4. Why is the customer a dirty person?
5. What should the manager be on the watch for (*a*). with respect to his employees (*b*). with respect to the physical facilities?
6. "Pre-employment interviews have become a formality as very little is actually revealed." Discuss this statement as related to sanitation in service.
7. Where does money go when accidents occur?
8. What two things may cause an accident?
9. What is usually the first (but erroneous) response to an accident?
10. Who should be called on to assist in designing a safety training program?
11. How can employees be involved in an accident-prevention program?
12. What should you do if you are the manager and an OSHA inspector arrives?

Endnotes

1. *Applied Foodservice Sanitation,* 4th ed. (Chicago: The Educational Foundation of the National Restaurant Association, 1992), p. 4.
2. Marc Gordon, *Restaurant Business Magazine,* December 10, 1990, p. 72.
3. Stan Luxenberg. "An Ounce of Prevention," *Restaurant Business Magazine,* October 10, 1991, p. 98.
4. National Safety Council, *Accident Prevention Manual,* 5th ed., chapter 3.

Additional Readings

American National Red Cross. *Standard First Aid and Personal Safety.* New York: Doubleday, 1975.

Health and Safety for the Hospitality Industry. The Educational Institute of the American Hotel and Motel Association, 1991.

Health and Safety Guide for Hotels and Motels. U.S. Department of Health, Education and Welfare, National Institute for Occupational Safety and Health, Division of Technical Services, 1975.

Longree, Karla, and Gertrude G. Baker. *Sanitary Techniques in Food Service.* 2nd ed. New York: Macmillan, 1982.

Marriott, Norman G. *Principles of Food Sanitation.* 2nd ed. New York: AVI, 1989.

Perkins, Charles E. "What Every Supervisor Should Know about Hotel/Motel Safety."

Safety Operations Manual. National Restaurant Association, Technical Services Department, 1988.

Scarpa, James. "Oops! Is Your Restaurant an Accident Waiting to Happen? *Restaurant Business Magazine,* February 10, 1992, pp. 66–76.

Serving Safe Food: A Guide for Foodservice Employees. Chicago: The Educational Foundation of the National Restaurant Association, 1990.

Safety Training and Education Organizations and Agencies

U.S. Department of Labor
Occupational Safety and Health Administration (OSHA)
Region 1
133 Portland Street
Boston, MA 02114
617–565–1161

The National Institute for Occupational Safety and Health (NIOSH)
Technical Information Branch
4676 Columbia Parkway
Cincinnati, Ohio 45226
513–533–8382

National Restaurant Association
(NRA)
Public Health and Safety
Department
1200 17th Street, N.W.
Washington, D.C. 20036
202–331–5900

American Hotel and Motel Association (AHMA)
1201 New York Avenue, N.W.,
Suite 600
Washington, D.C. 20005-3931
202–289–3100

National Fire Protection Association (NFPA)
Batterymarch Park
Quincy, MA 02269
617–770–3000

National Safety Council (NSC)
444 North Michigan Avenue
Chicago, IL 60611
708–285–1121

Sales Is a Service Function

Chapter Outline

Definition
What Does the Service Staff Need
   to Know to Sell
Conclusion
A Quick-Reference Checklist for
   Increasing Sales in the
   Dining Room

Learning Objectives

After Studying this chapter, the
student will be able to . . .
1. Describe personal selling.
2. List the characteristics of a
   "neat, clean personal
   appearance."
3. Demonstrate the difference
   between pressure selling and
   suggestive selling.
4. Calculate financial benefit to
   both server and management,
   the difference between a
   nonselling check and a positive
   sales check.
5. List the areas of knowledge
   that service staff must have for
   competent selling.
6. Demonstrate both positive and
   negative sales techniques.

Key Words/Phrases

Sales personnel
High-pressure sales approach
Check average
Tips
Profitability
Reward structure
Nonaggressive selling
Residence time
Guest turnover
Convenience food products
Made-to-order menu items
À la carte (menu items)
Preprepared (menu items)
Production time
Accompaniments
Sullivan nod
Visual picture
Menu terminology
Plate presentation
Plus sale
Wine steward
Carafe service
Choice of yesses
Menu briefing
Special of the day
Team contests

Definition

Selling is the personal or impersonal process of assisting and persuading a prospective customer to purchase a commodity or service, or to act favorably upon an idea that has commercial significance to the seller. The first thing that a salesperson in any industry must do is sell himself or herself. There are certain things a person can do to accomplish this.

One must be interested in one's job and in people and must have a neat, clean appearance.

- Shoes: clean, shined.
- Hair: neat, clean, restrained.
- Body: clean, if fragrance is used, only use a small amount.
- Fingernails: clean, short, neutral or very light colored polish.
- Makeup: light lipstick, no heavy eye makeup.
- Teeth: clean and polished, unstained, and straight with none missing.
- Jewelry: none is best, but wedding ring and simple watch are maximum acceptable.
- Uniform: clean, unstained.
- And a smile!

Army officers at West Point rated the appearance of entering cadets solely on the basis of each cadet's statement of his name and home address, taking 5 to 10 seconds per cadet. The combined ratings correlated positively with the aptitude for service ratings made by peers and superiors after 14 weeks at the Academy. People's opinions based on momentary first impressions are positively related to overall service success. Appearance and manner can and do affect ratings of job performance.

It is important, therefore, that each individual working in the front of the house have a neat, clean appearance and a pleasant manner. The guest's impression of the establishment and of his service person is determined, in part, by his first impression of the server.

Service personnel in some restaurants are called **sales personnel**. This has both pros and cons, as it will remind servers that their job can be improved upon if they are good at selling in the dining room. On the other side, this terminology may remind the service person to be overly aware that he is a salesperson and not involved with giving service. But good service sells, and excellent selling is felt as good service.

When discussing sales with your service staff, it is important to tell them that sales in the dining room are not high-pressure sales (i.e., using a **high-pressure sales approach**), but personal, suggestive selling. The guests have already made the decision to come into the particular establishment to eat. Therefore, the job of selling is that of making suggestions to assist the person in ordering and to increase the check average.

In a study of server behavior, sociologists Suellen R. Butler and William E. Snizek found that pressure selling increases the **check average** and hence **tips**. On different occasions they subjected some diners to high-pressure sales and others to no sales, and found that selling does increase the tip, which gives the server a measure of control over the guest-server relationship.[1] However, caution should be exercised. High-pressure sales may increase the check average for the moment, but will the guests return? In other words, this may be a short-term effort and damage the long-term effectiveness and **profitability** of the operation. Managers should also be aware that servers operate in an independent environment, since they obtain more of their **reward structure** (financial and psychological) from the guest than from management. It is easy to convince service personnel that higher sales actually put money in their pockets *as well as* benefiting management. In fact, the server gets much more of the sales dollar than does ownership.

This example shows each server where the restaurant's total sales dollars are going. Additionally, the increase in sales should be computed on a weekly and monthly basis to make a larger impression on the server.

Nonselling Check	**Check with Positive Sales Effort**
$10 Entree	$3 Cocktail
	$3 Appetizer
	$10 Entree
	$4 Wine/person
	$2 Dessert/person
	$3 After-dinner beverage
$10	$25
4.7% x $6 = .28	15% x $10 ~ $1.50
4.7% x $25 = 1.18	15% x $25 = $3.75
Difference that goes to management	Additional gratuity that goes to service

In the example above, even if you only increased your sales by 2 dollars per person, you serve 20 people in an evening. This figures out to 30 dollars extra per week, or 120 more dollars per month. In addition to making the service person happier by increasing sales, the guest will enjoy her dinner more. Wine complements the food—it makes the food taste better. An after-dinner espresso or capuccino, brandy, or dessert wine can be that final touch that distinguishes a very good meal from an absolutely superb meal—one that the guest considers incomparable to anything she has had in the past. Additionally, the guest perceives quiet, **nonagressive selling** as attentive service. Servers should not try to sell too much. If a particular establishment enjoys a very rapid and high **guest turnover**, increasing the residence time (or delaying the guest) by offering dessert, cordials, coffees, and so forth, may prevent the establishment from maximizing revenue. Also, it will increase the time that other guests must wait for a seat and can certainly cause guest frustration. High-volume, casual-theme restaurants, such as Pizzeria Uno, Applebee's, TGI Friday's, Bennigan's, Olive Garden, and Red Lobster do not take reservations and may have one table (or more) of guests waiting in the bar for seating in the dining room (several no-reservation restaurants now allow a phone call so that the guest's name can be placed on the waiting list). A similar situation exists in a diner or coffee shop operation that depends on rapid guest turnover; extending the **residence time** may decrease profitability. Plus sales or add-on sales may not necessarily increase the guests' residence time.

What Does the Service Staff Need to Know to Sell

Proper training of the service staff translates into dollars for management and staff. The service staff must be competent at selling the restaurant and its menu. Frequently managers are overheard in attempts to spur their service personnel to sell, "You are in partnership with management, if you do well we do well." Many, however, fail to communicate to their service staff what they need to know to be good at selling.

The staff must know the basic ingredients and preparation of the menu items. They must know the quality of the raw products used. Is the fruit fresh? Is the soup homemade? What grade of beef is used (prime, choice, etc.)? Is the seafood fresh, fresh frozen, or **convenience**? The service staff must know when to play up particular items on the menu. Many low-cost steak houses would not do well in advertising the source or quality of the beef they use. The term *fresh frozen* may be used to describe certain items such as brook trout.

Today's consumer is very aware of quality and value. It would not only be illegal but also foolish for either the manager or the server to misrepresent the food products actually being served. Most restaurant patrons do not object to convenience foods (processed) if priced accordingly. Many are upset, however, when convenience foods are passed off as being "made in our kitchen by Alfredo, our award-winning chef."

The staff must know the time required to prepare the various menu items, especially made-to-order items. **Made-to-order items** are just that: they are made when the guest places the order (classically speaking, this is termed **à la carte**—priced separately). This is not to say that menu items cannot be **preprepared**, but they are not cooked or finally prepared until the waiter places the specific order at the range. Such items as chicken or veal cordon bleu may be stuffed and breaded; but they are not fried/baked until the order is placed. Roasts, stews, and certain items en casserole are prepared in advance, kept warm, and only need to be placed on the plate or platter for service. Other items must have all preparation done when the order is placed. For example, the **production time** for broiled chicken takes 25 to 30 minutes, whole boiled or steamed lobster is done in 20 minutes, and broiled steaks require 10 minutes preparation time.

The staff must know that ready-to-serve items are prepared in advance and what the ready-to-serve menu items are, so that if a guest is in a hurry, they may suggest these items. The chef should inform the host and he or she in turn should inform each service staff member of the menu items that are ready-to-serve, and how long each of the made-to-order menu items will take.

The staff should know when to offer another cocktail. The time to offer the second drink is when the first drink is three-quarters finished. The guest will then feel that he has the time to drink another before he is served his entree. Regular drinkers usually do not need coaxing, but the casual or social drinker can be offered and sold this second cocktail at the right time with a fair amount of success. If servers present menus, they could bring the menus when asking for the next drink order. If servers do not present the menus, some other task can be accomplished (filling water, serving butter or relishes, etc.) as an unobtrusive excuse to approach the table. The time to suggest another bottle of wine is when the first bottle has just been emptied and the main course has either not yet been served or is just being served.

The staff must know the various accompaniments to the various menu items. At this time, high profit à la carte items can be suggested. "Sir, our sautéed mushrooms are fresh and would really taste good with your steak." The staff must be instructed and made aware of all the various à la carte **accompaniments** to menu items to increase sales and profitability. Managers must inform all service staff personnel what the accompaniments would be for each menu item during the menu briefing. Jim Sullivan, a well-known restaurant sales speaker, recommends a three-minute session with the service staff to increase add-on, complementary menu items or desserts sometimes highlighting the daily sales specials. Using the **Sullivan nod**, it goes like this:

Guest: . . . and a Pepsi, please.
Server: Large? (slowly nodding the head up and down)
Guest: Yeh, large.
Guest: And I'll have the New York Strip—medium rare.
Server: Good choice. Can I bring you a bowl of our French onion soup (slow head nod) or homemade vegetable soup to start?
Guest: Yeh, French onion soup sounds good.[1]

The staff must carry through with order taking. Carrying through with order taking means that the service person must back up to the beginning of the menu, taking control of the guests' ordering in a quiet way, and suggest appetizers and hors d'oeuvres as in the preceding example. When the server approaches the guest for an order, the guest will probably say, "I'll have the strip steak medium." It is up to the service person to say, "Would you care for a shrimp cocktail?" The service person should make specific suggestions. "Would you like an appetizer?" does less for the guest than suggesting any specific food item. The idea here is to give the guest a **visual picture** of the food. "Appetizer" means little; "shrimp cocktail" means something specific.

Timing is also very important when suggesting appetizers. If the guest appears to be in a rush, he would be less likely to order an appetizer. If, on the other hand, the entree selected by the guest will take some time to prepare (i.e., a made-to-order item) the server should indicate this and offer an appetizer. "Madam, the veal cordon bleu will take about 20 minutes to prepare; may I suggest a small dish of our sauteéd chicken livers, which I'll bring to you quickly?" The guest will perceive the server's behavior as good, attentive service. If a server forgets to offer an appetizer, he could return to the table saying that he had placed the guest's order in the kitchen and that it should be ready in number of minutes. "Would you care for a cup of our French onion soup now?" he might ask.

The staff should know menu terminology and descriptive words for the menu items. A poorly managed restaurant was noted as having a most unappetizing term, "disjointed chicken," as a description on their menu. The service person should be aware of the **terminology** he or she is using to describe certain dishes. Managers will be well advised to furnish several descriptions for the various menu items so that a server will have this terminology available. Although the menu could have descriptions, servers should not just restate what is already printed on the menu.

Guest: Well, what does the scrod taste like?
Wrong: It's bland.
Right: It is a very delicately flavored fish served under an
excellent sauce.

The staff must know the correct and proper service for all menu items. This practice may also improve relations between service and production. The chef is very concerned and proud of the appearance of the food she prepares, and the server can destroy her work. If the server presents a delicately decorated sauced menu item to a guest and carelessly slants the plate when setting it down, covering the plate with the sauce or destroying the design, the result is a poor **plate presentation**; for example, the stew should cover only a portion of the rice (i.e., slightly overlapping). This brings the contrasting colors out, which makes the food more appetizing to the guest, and this is a much preferred presentation.

The staff should be able to anticipate the guest's likes and dislikes. This is a difficult thing to do, but no harm is done if the server misreads the guest. If a guest is overweight, the waiter *may* suggest a low-fat or low-calorie menu item but should simultaneously offer a high-fat or high-calorie dish so as not to offend the guest. If the restaurant caters to the general public, a stew or meat and potatoes may be suggested to a construction worker. Each item of the menu may not appeal to a particular server, but *the server should never show distaste for a guest's selection.* Liver and onions may disgust the particular service person, but he should not react negatively to a guest's choice.

The staff must know the proper service technique for wine. If the service person does not feel comfortable opening a bottle of wine in front of the guest, he will hesitate selling a bottle of wine for fear that he will be embarrassed. Management's responsibility is to teach the proper service procedures, as this will instill confidence in the server. Servers who are adept at opening wine will want to sell more. Servers enjoy showing their better side. If a server can put on a little show by properly and professionally handling and opening a wine bottle, this increases his tip for two reasons. First, the check is increased, and second, the guest perceives this as professional, attentive service (see Chapter 10 on wine service). If wine is served promptly, the guests may drink more, and this increases sales and gives the guests more enjoyment of the meal.

Wine is a **plus sale** (add-on sale) when nothing else can be sold. The guest has already ordered her meal and all its food accompaniments. Unlike appetizers, dessert, and beverages that are served before or after the meal, the wine is served with the meal and greatly increases profit. The sale of wine usually does not increase residence time (the average amount of time a guest sits in a chair). When a guest orders wine, the service person should bring a full bottle unless the guest specifically requests a half bottle. In other words, the server should assume that the guest wants a full bottle. Management should stock only a limited variety of wine in half bottles. This reduces costly inventory and makes the task of taking inventory considerably easier.

When the wine bottle is empty and the guests are still eating, the server or **wine steward** should not whisk away the wine bottle or wine bucket, but should bring another bottle, without having to be asked by the guest, and offer it to the host at the table. If the guest rejects the bottle, the server should withdraw quickly and should certainly not offend the guest. Champagne or sparkling wine (especially a semisweet sparkling wine such as Asti Spumonte) is a delightful accompaniment to dessert. Server should be shown this pairing of dry sparkling wine (brut or natural) and semisweet (extra dry/brut, semiseco, or deux) in tasting sessions. The server may suggest a glass of dry sherry, vermouth, or wine spritzer as an aperitif in lieu of a cocktail (i.e., martini, manhattan, highball, etc.). This is especially successful for luncheon, as sherry and other appetizer wines are not considered a "hard drink" and may have more acceptability during luncheon. Correspondingly, the server should offer espresso or cappucino, a sweet sherry, or other dessert wine (port, Tokay, etc.) if any or all of the guests in the party have refused a brandy or cordial.

Many operators who have found it difficult to train their service personnel in proper wine service have found that **carafe service** significantly increases their wine sales. It is quite easy for a server to suggest "red, white, or rose" and serve by the carafe as compared to wrestling with the terminology and the service of wine by the bottle. This suggestion does not apply to all operations; however, if wine sales are floundering, carafe service may bring the sale of wine out of the doldrums.

The server should give the guests a **choice of yesses**. If the guest is able to say no, it is easier for him to say no than if he is not asked a yes/no question.

> *Wrong:* Would you like an appetizer?
> *Right:* Would you care for shrimp cocktail?" (no, but specific request)
> *Best:* Would you care to start with a shrimp cocktail or a fruit compote?" (a choice of yesses.)
> *Wrong:* Would you like wine with dinner?
> *Right:* Would you prefer our house wine or a bottle of pinot chardonnay with your chicken?
> *Best:* I would suggest the mountain Burgundy or the Valpolicella with your steak.
> *Wrong:* Coffee?
> *Right:* Would you like ice cream or our fresh baked apple pie with your coffee?

Conclusion

Managers cannot expect their service personnel to know all of this information. It is the responsibility of management to train and instruct servers, and the manager must insist on several important steps. There should be a **menu briefing** with the service personnel and the chef or his representative *before each service period;* service personnel must be at work in time to receive this briefing before service. The menu briefing should include all of the items mentioned in this chapter and especially a **special of the day** for which service staff receive a team bonus. Change the sales special daily: Sautéed mushrooms one day, any soup the next day, a special salad complement the day after that and so forth. Keep it fun and interesting! Managers can help servers sell by having display racks for wine, dessert carts, and cordial carts as well as point of sale information on the tables, in the menu or in other places where appropriate.

Selling in a restaurant is not pressure sales. It is soft, suggestive selling, and a sale should never be forced. Managers should also ensure that their servers do not get discouraged if they do not sell well; the law of averages will take care of the "yesses" and the "noes." It is important for each server to keep trying to increase the check average even when it may seem that he is not getting sufficient response to his suggestions. A contest may be used to promote sales, but care must be taken so that the competition is healthy and not cutthroat. **Team contests** seem to work better. When individual sales contests are held, invariably, the same person repeatedly wins the sales contest. Counting the number of people served in a given period or on a given day seems to excite restaurant operators and employees. In the classroom situation each class wants to outdo another class; while in operations the goal is to "outdo what we did

on Mother's Day last year compared to this year." This can result in some difficulty, since a good restaurant develops return business on quality (value), not just quantity. The same holds true for each service person. "Well, we have this great server; she can handle 50 people at once!" The question that should follow is "how well can she handle them?"

Whenever a particular restaurant is having a promotion, management should first communicate this to the staff. The staff must be aware of the promotion, but additionally the personnel are consumers and can offer many useful suggestions. Good sales techniques begin with the individual selling himself. If an individual looks good and is proud of himself, he has more confidence and his attitude and manner will sell the restaurant.

A Quick Reference Checklist for Increasing Sales in the Dining Room

- A nice phone voice.
- Know menu terminology and descriptive words.
- Serve wine promptly.
- Don't let staff get discouraged; the "noes" will average out.
- Know how to sell wine.
- Smile.
- Know the correct and proper service for all items.
- Have a good appearance.
- Never show distaste for a guest's choice.
- Be accurate with the guest's orders.

- Leave a copy of the menu on the table.
- Anticipate the guest's needs.
- Anticipate the guest's likes and dislikes.
- Know the major ingredients, quality, and preparation.
- Don't force a sale.
- Know time required to prepare made-to-order items.
- Suggest cocktails or appetizers, sherry, or other aperitifs.
- Know ready-to-serve items.
- Carry through with order taking.
- Know accompaniments to the various items.

Questions

1. Explain what selling oneself is.
2. How could a manager prove that good sales techniques can help the service person's salary?
3. Is it true that a higher check average can increase guest enjoyment of the dining experience? Explain.
4. What should service personnel know to be better sales persons? Embellish three of the ideas presented in the chapter.

Endnote

J. Sullivan, P. Roberts. *Service that Sells*. (Denver, Colorado: Pencom Press, 1991), p. 86.

Additional Readings

Carlson, K. "Reciprocity in the Marketplace: Tipping in an Urban Nightclub" in J. P. Sprodley and D. W. McCurdy. *Conformity and Conflict: Readings in Cultural Anthropology*, 3rd ed. Boston: Little, Brown and Company, 1977, pp. 337–47.

Department of Health, Education, and Welfare. *Training Food Service Personnel for the Hospitality Industry*. OE-82018. Washington: U.S. Government Printing Office, 1969.

Marvin, B. *Restaurant Basics*. New York: John Wiley & Sons, 1992.

Sullivan, J. and P. Roberts. *Service that Sells*. Denver, Colorado: Pencom Press, 1991.

CHAPTER 8

The Director of Service

Chapter Outline

Learning Objectives

After studying this chapter the
student will be able to . . .
1. Describe the desirable
   characteristics for a director
   of service.
2. Explain how a checklist
   approach is useful in
   performing a job function.
3. Demonstrate the use of a
   reservation system.
4. State the guidelines for
   greeting and seating guests.
5. Outline the basic principles for
   scheduling employees.
6. Identify the factors controlling
   the dining room division into
   stations.
7. Discuss the methods for
   financial control within the
   dining room environment.

Key Words/Phrases

Upper management
Maître d'hôtel
Host
Headwaiter
Service director
Opening checklist
Menu briefing
Point-of-sale (POS) system
Reservations
Reservation record
Average residence time
Turnover
Countdown method
Walk-in guests
Scheduling software
Scheduling slots
Split shift

Skeleton crew
Fixed labor component
Variable labor component
Gantt chart
Run chart
Histogram

Service stations
Side stand
Tray stand
Private stock check
Split ring technique
Buddy discount

The approach of this text so far has been directed at the **upper management** of a particular food-service establishment. For service to function smoothly, the individual directly responsible for the service staff and its tasks must possess a considerable amount of knowledge. In smaller restaurants, the manager may be the person directly responsible, and the manager/owner's personality pervades the establishment, giving the particular establishment its personality. If the host greeting guests is stuffy, the other service personnel are apt to follow her style.

Correspondingly, if the host is a cordial, warm person, other service staff will tend to emulate her. The larger the business becomes, the more dependent owners/managers become on the staff. Each food service establishment has a standard of service quality and certain tasks that must be accomplished to support the service quality standards. For example, if it is determined that the guest will be escorted to his table, someone must perform this function. In a formal atmosphere, this task may be accomplished by a captain after receiving the guest from the **host**, **headwaiter**, or **maitre d'hotel**. In a less formal dining room, the host might escort the guest to the table, seat the guest, pass menus, and make some appropriate comment, such as, "I hope you enjoy your meal." He would leave the table while the server or dining room attendant would take over by greeting the guests, pouring water (United States), serving butter, and perhaps serving rolls or bread.

The **service director** must determine which tasks are appropriate for the particular establishment and the level of service quality desired and assign duties accordingly. The job descriptions presented below include many of the tasks that should be performed, and he assigns them to particular individuals within the service staff. Yet, a service director may delete tasks as required for the particular operation (perhaps a less formal service environment) or assign them to another person within the organization. The task of presenting guests with a copy of the menu may be performed by the host, the captain, or the server. The descriptions presented in this chapter are organized so that they may be put into operation with only minor adjustments for any particular food service establishment.

Note: Many of these functions may be assigned to the assistant manager or the manager, and this description implies that the director of service is additionally acting as host. Although the most competent director should

Job Description

Director of Service (Dining Room)
(Maître d'hôtel, Host,
Headwaiter)

Job summary: Greets guests, supervises and directs the efforts of captains, servers, and bus personnel. The host must ensure that gracious service is given to all guests.

Work responsibility: The director is responsible for service in the dining room, coordinating the kitchen and dining room staffs, and ensuring that proper service techniques are being followed.

Specific tasks:

- Supervises captains, servers, and bus personnel.
- Assigns pre-opening side duties to service staff.
- Takes guest reservations; handles details for private functions.
- Schedules service staff for duty.
- Assigns service stations to service staff.
- If point-of-sale (POS) or electronic cash register or computer terminal is used, pre- or reprogram with daily specials or revised prices.
- Ensures that par stock items are at proper level. Requisitions or secures linen; condiments; various supplies

such as sugar, salt, pepper, etc.; and requisitions additional china, silver, or glassware if required.

- Informs management, maintenance, or housekeeping personnel of required actions: paint touch-ups, carpet cleaning, faulty electrical systems, broken furnishings, etc.
- Supervises the setup of buffet table.
- Greets guests and escorts them to appropriate tables (balances stations).
- Handles guest complaints and has total responsibility to make suggestions to guests for food or beverage.
- Ensures that all closing duties are completed and that all tables are reset.
- Dismisses individual service personnel at appropriate time.

Reports to: Restaurant manager or her assistant.

Special considerations: The director must remain cheerful and professional under the most adverse conditions or any difficult situations that occur in the dining room. The personality of the establishment rests with the director.

know every aspect of his job as well as the job of each person that works for her, an **opening checklist** should be constructed for the individual establishment as this gives the director and the service staff a guide from which to work.

Proper use of the checklist does not require the host to read the checklist and then perform the particular instruction. The director should perform his functions in the usual manner, but then refer to the checklist to ensure all critical tasks prior to or during the serving period have been performed. The list should be revised or updated frequently and adjusted to fulfill the restaurant's mission statement and desired level of service quality.

Opening Checklist for the Director of Service

- Record names and assign stations on dining room station assignments and duties sheet.
- Check total reservations and tables that must be set or reset. Memorize names and number in each party.
- Check function sheets for private party settings and details.
- Assign side duties on station assignment sheet to service personnel and check that each is properly attired and in full uniform.
- Requisition all par-stock supplies required (i.e., linen and condiments).
- Supervise table setting check and opening side duties.
- Check buffet table and salad bar setup progress (if applicable).
- Specify time for menu briefing.
- Assign reservations to tables.
- Get **menu briefing** and specials pricing from chef or his representative. All service staff should be present. Check menu items for shortages or excesses.
- Pre- or reprogram **point-of-sale (POS)** system
- Check windows (blinds, drapes), lights, and air conditioning.
- Check for proper number of clean linens and condition of menus.
- When ready for service: open doors (assuming set service periods) and begin seating guests.
- During service circulate dining room and function rooms. Check for courteous, prompt, and correct service: water filled; butter/bread supplied; condiments available; proper service of all items; table cleared of unused and unnecessary silverware, china, or glassware; table crumbed; coffee hot; buffet checked for quantity of food, appearance, and heat.
- Checks are paid as guests leave.
- Bid guests farewell. Check with server or captain to ensure guests have not left belongings. Assist guests with coats or jackets.
- Supervise closing duties and release staff as required (ensure tables and function rooms are reset if required) .
- Add list of closing duties per particular establishment.

Kitchen
- Ice refilled/water pitchers filled.
- Coffee urns filled (decaffeinated if required), cream filled, coffee and tea bag supply adequate, cups and saucers available, tea pots available.
- Iced tea (made) filled, fresh lemon wedges available, underliners supplied.

- Roll area prepared: baskets, napkins or cloths, fresh rolls, warmer on.
- Soup/salad area: cups, bowls, utensils, underliners, garnish/crackers.
- Pantry and range pick-up areas clean.
- Trays clean, in proper place.
- Supply of side towels available.
- Service bar or beverage pickup area clean: cocktail napkins, stirrers, garnishes handy, trays wiped.
- Butter preset: individual portions, chips or pats broken out, iced.
- Sour cream, ketchup, mustard, mayonnaise, and other condiments available.
- Plates, underliners, glassware, silverware restocked.

Dining Room
- Plates, underliners, glassware, silverware, ashtrays, matches, napkins all restocked in side stands.
- Linen stocked for resetting.
- Candles, mints, condiments, doilies, sugar, salt, pepper supplied and restocked.
- Table check: aligned, balanced (see Laying the Tables); proper cloth size and proper side up, spotless, pressed, lines even; proper number of settings, evenly spaced on tables; silverware/glassware spotless; settings neat and correct; center settings proper, complete, and balanced.

The checklist serves an additional function. If the director cannot be present for a particular service period, his substitute will have an excellent guide to follow. The checklist may also serve as a guide for other management personnel to evaluate the director.

Reservations

The location of a particular property will determine whether **reservations** should be honored at all, honored on time or not. If the property is located in a resort area, more leeway may be allowed on honoring reservations. Conversely, if the property is catering to business people on a luncheon hour or catering to theatergoers, reservation times must be honored exactly on time. Many restaurants realize the expense of operating a reservation system and have discontinued taking reservations while seating guests on a first-come, first-serve basis or in order of arrival. Many casual-theme restaurants take names at the door and ask guests to wait in a waiting area or at the lounge. As a competitive advantage, several chain restaurants have begun taking names over the phone and adding the names to a wait list. In other words, they are taking reservations, but they are not guaranteeing seating times.

Yet, reservations have a function, and only the individual manager of an establishment can make the decision of whether a reservation system is desirable or undesirable and whether it is cost effective or not. If management decides to use a reservation system, several methods to **record reservations** should be investigated. If a manual system is used, a bound book is preferred, especially for a small property or a property where the person taking advance reservations is also on duty in the dining room. An automated or computer database system or single, preprinted sheets for individual meals may be used for multiunit operations employing a full-time, central reservations person to take reservations such as in a large hotel or resort. Whether a database system, bound book, or single sheet system is used, the method for recording reservations should be standardized, providing for required information (name, time, number in party, telephone or room number, method of payment, etc.). If reservation times are to be honored, the reservation form should have times preprinted. Seating control may be established if times are limited (i.e., three slots at 6:00 PM, three at 6:15 PM, and three at 6:30 PM) to determine whether the property will have a table to seat the guest(s).

Video display seating charts are now available that duplicate the manual systems of the past. These can be most effective in restaurants with large or multiple dining areas where communicating an available, reset table to the host's stand requires excessive travel time by a service staff member. Significant savings can be enjoyed by increasing the throughput of guests and dining room productivity facilitated by this technology.

An **average residence time** (how long guests stay at a table) should be calculated for each restaurant. Smaller tables generally **turnover** more quickly than do larger tables. If guest turnover is expected, then the preprinted times may be repeated after the average residence time has elapsed. A **countdown method** may also be used for properties with single seatings (i.e., dinner theater or nightclub operations). A set of numbers with each number representing a table configuration or number of seats at each table in the dining room may be stamped or written on the reservation form. Each number is marked-off or slashed when a reservation is confirmed.

~~222~~   As tables of the various configurations are

222

~~444~~   confirmed, these numbers would be crossed off.

444

~~669~~

If reservations are taken, tables may be assigned one of several ways. If the operation does not take **walk-in guests** at all, tables may be assigned by name with assurance. There could be a potential problem with six stations in the dining room, six sets of reservations for 8:00 PM, and six sets of reservations for 8:30 PM. If each table is blocked or assigned by name, the following could result.

Mr. Kowalski with reservations at 8:00 PM arrives 15 minutes late while Mr. Barasch with reservations at 8:30 PM arrives 15 minutes early. Both have been assigned to the same station. Assuming an otherwise normal evening with other reservations and other tables occupied, this method will have caused one server to be unnecessarily busy. The guests may not get efficient service as a result of this reservation method if no other adjustments are made when the guests enter. As an alternative, tables may be blocked-off (marked), but not specifically designated by the name of the guest (unless a special guest requests a specific table). The host will always have a table that will accommodate a particular party with a set number of guests with reservations as he makes specific table assignments the moment the guests arrive; he is better able to balance the stations among the service staff using this method.

An improved variation on the blocking system, however, does exist. The reservations may be assigned by *marking reservation times*, not the specific guests' name, on the appropriately configured tables. As a guest enters with a reservation, the host notes the proposed time listed for the reservation, locates a table with a time and configuration identical to the guest's requests, and seats them at that table. This will allow for more flexibility in seating guests and allows for a better service station balance thereby distributing a more equal number of guests per service person in a specific time period. These systems work best with a seating chart or computerized display of the tables in the dining room.

Greeting and Seating Guests

Greeting and seating the guests requires a particular flair on the part of the host. The host's behavior is critical to establishing the environment the restaurant intends to project. Some guests feel uncomfortable when they first enter a restaurant. It is up to the host to greet them with a smile and in a cordial manner. He should look directly at the host of the party, making positive eye contact. This is necessary to let the guest know that you are talking to him. Since many hosts must eventually check the reservation sheet or begin finding a table at which to seat the guests, they forget to establish eye contact with the guest. An appropriate greeting should follow or be coincident with eye contact, "Good evening (afternoon), sir (madam)." At this point the host should pause allowing the guest(s) to speak. The host should not assume a table for one, two, or ask for whether the guest had reservations at this initial greeting time. After the guest responds, "Table for two," or "Reservations for Lee Jones," then the host should answer, "How many in your party," or "Yes, sir/madam," or "Yes, Ms. Jones."

During this brief greeting the host should be unencumbered. He should have nothing in his hand—no menus, pen, or pencil. He should be standing upright, not using the host's stand as a crutch. If necessary the host should assist in removing coats that have not been checked. After assisting with coats, the host should glance at the reservation sheet (if necessary), check off on the reservation sheet that the Jones party is in the house, locate a suitable table, and escort the guests to the table. Immediately after the initial greeting, the host should inquire if there have been any changes in the number in the party for whom reservations were made, if indeed reservations were made. Another table may be more suitable if the group has changed in size. It is very important at this point for the host to know if he does have a suitable table. If for any reason, however, the host assumes a table vacant and then finds it occupied after checking the chart, video display, or on reaching the table, he should *immediately* and quickly locate a table in the dining room and seat the guests. A mistake has already been made, and any adjustments must be made after seating the party. Do not leave guests standing in the dining room or escort them back to the host's stand to find a table.

At no time should the guest(s) be left standing in the dining room without escort. If there is any doubt in the host's mind, he should excuse himself *before* inviting the guests to follow, locate a suitable table visually, and then invite the guest(s) to be seated. When escorting guests to a table, the restaurant's host should accomplish all administrative tasks (gathering menus, locating a suitable table, etc.) before inviting the guest to follow. When he has finished doing this, he should look the host of the party directly in the eye again, offer an inviting gesture with his hand (not his finger) and make a suitable comment, "Would you follow me please, sir." As the restaurant's host ventures into the dining room, he should walk slowly and after a few steps should turn to see if the guest(s) are in fact following. It is very embarrassing for the host to have walked the length of the dining room alone while the guests are still standing at the entrance.

After seating all guests (see the following Host's Greeting and Seating Guidelines), the host should pass the menus, attempt to establish eye contact and excuse himself by voicing some suitable comment—in most European dining rooms, the maître d' usually says "bon appetit." He should check back at the table within five minutes (absolute maximum) to ensure that a server has approached the table to begin service.

The host should be available throughout the duration of the meal. He should not spend time in the kitchen unless absolutely necessary. After guests have been served the main course, the host should check the table. He should not inquire about the meal unless spoken to by one of the guests, but he should make it obvious that he is available for comment. It is trite for the host to say, "How was your meal?"

Host's Greeting and Seating Guidelines

The time spent before guests are seated is not as critical an interval as the time spent waiting for service and for food after being seated. The capacity of the dining room at a given time is determined by the number of and the capabilities of the service staff. The capacity of the dining room is not determined by the number of seats in the restaurant. Giving guests attentive and timely service is significantly important from the customer service perspective and for optimal/productivity.

In an elegant establishment the maître d'hôtel should have memorized names and know how many guests are in the party (reservations) and at what table(s) he is going to seat them. In a casual-theme restaurant, an attempt should be made to associate the name with the party when the guests arrive at the door to place their names on a reservation or waiting sheet. The host should inquire if a guest(s) has reservations. Seat well-dressed people in conspicuous places whenever possible and balance the dining room so as not to overburden one station. This offers better service to the guest and an even distribution of gratuities to the staff.

Seat parties of more than two at larger tables; it is easier to pick up settings than to lay them. Always pick up additional place settings if no additional guests are expected. In addition to following appropriate rules of etiquette, this is a nonverbal cue that alerts other servers as to the specific table configuration. Research indicates that the restaurant will achieve a better seating utilization over time if tables are occupied when available—even if the party being seated has fewer guests than a table is configured for. Holding a four-top and causing a couple to wait for a vacant deuce annoys the guests and, in the long term, decreases the total number of guests served and the restaurant's productivity.

Offer the best seat (facing the dining or best view) to the woman in a party of two (this is a traditional custom), or the eldest woman in a larger party, assuming normal etiquette prevails. As modern etiquette and full equality in the treatment of gender becomes the norm, guests may be offended by the preference given to women. Use judgment when seating older adults. Many times older adults prefer to conform the traditional treatment of gender—deferring to the women.

At wall or booth tables of four, seat the women on the sofa seats facing the dining room. Pull the table out (rotate if on pedestal) so they can slide in easily. Although the restaurant's host may offer a seat to her female guests in particular or males as required, the host should remain at the table until all guests present are seated, assisting guest(s) with their coats, briefcases, umbrellas, or purses. Present the menus closed from the left and assist the guest with the napkin if necessary. Some guests may sense a violation of their personal space if a server attempts to place a napkin in a guest's lap. While some texts suggest presenting the menu open, the menu may be difficult to manipulate if it is large, and the design of the menu front piece is negated if the menu is not presented closed.

The server should be assisting the host in seating the guest or standing by after the host leaves the table. The server or a dining room attendant should fill water glasses, take cocktail orders, serve cocktails, and place bread and butter on the table. While guests are reading the menu, whenever possible the server should attend to them, announcing the specials, offering suggestions, upselling when appropriate (see Chapter 7), and so forth. He should not serve another table if at all feasible; however, this practice is most difficult to accomplish in many busy restaurants.

Scheduling the Service Staff

Scheduling service employees is a difficult job for many directors, while some may not have problems scheduling the service staff. Scheduling can be eased by using a **scheduling software** program such as *Time-boss 3*, which is also designed to control labor costs. There is much variability of business in certain types of restaurants, making it very difficult to forecast covers. A manager must determine his overall staffing needs by following the rules of thumb listed below, and by following these basic scheduling principles:

- Know the standard of service quality desired and the qualities and abilities of the service personnel.
- Know the reliability of your personnel.
- Make good forecasts. Forecasts should be made by taking the following factors into consideration:
- Number of people served on the same day last year.
- Number served on same day last month.
- Number served on same day last week.
- If in a hotel or proximate to a lodging facility, what is the occupancy and what effect does that occupancy have on the dining room forecast.
- Goings on about town.
- The weather.

The purpose of scheduling is to optimize labor availability to ensure that the guests receive the standard of service quality established for the restaurant's dining room and to simultaneously optimize the service staff labor cost. Scheduling is working backward. The staffing guide reflects the number of **scheduling slots** determined by the type of service, the menu, and by good forecasts. After the staffing guide (number of service slots) has been determined, the service staff is fitted to the time slots. **Split shifts** allow for some flexibility, but they are not always possible either because of personnel practices or because of union contract stipulations. An example of a split shift is when a server works from 10:00 AM until 3:00 PM and again the same day from 6:00 PM until 9:00 PM for an eight-hour shift; allow some flexibility, but labor laws as well as labor unions may place restrictions on split-shift scheduling.

FIGURE 8–1
Staffing Chart for a 144–Seat Dining Room

Forecasted Hourly Volume in Dollars*	Number of Guests per Hour*	Number of Servers	Number of Bussers	Number of Hosts
Up to $270	13–18	1	0	1
$270–540	18–36	2	0	1
540–810	36–54	3	1	1
780–1080	52–72	4	1	1
975–1350	65–90	5	1	1
1170–1620	78–108	6	2	1
1365–1890	91–126	7	2	1
1560–2160	104–144	8	2	1

*Where forecasted amounts overlap, manager should interpolate either conservatively or aggressively, depending on service level desired.

Assumptions:

Minimum of 13 Guests per server	Average of 3–4 Servers per Busser
Maximum of 18 Guests per Server	$15 Check Average per Guest

Operators should schedule a **skeleton crew** (theoretically, the skeleton crew is the **fixed labor component** needed to operate the restaurant if only one guest came into the restaurant). In addition to the skeleton crew, the director should schedule additional staff to service the customer demand (**variable labor component**) and have the opportunity to call in part-time employees as needed with little or no advance notice (standby crew). Many of the factors discussed for dividing the dining room into stations are extremely useful for scheduling purposes as well.

In addition to the standard scheduling formats such as times against names of service personnel or names against times, a modified **Gantt chart** may by used, which displays the person or persons being scheduled against a start and an end time. Schedules can also be overlaid on a **run chart** or **histogram** to match staffing needs against customer demand. The schedule and staffing guide should reflect the number of service staff required to meet the establishment's standard of service assessing customer demand on an hour-by-hour basis.

Figure 8–2

Histogram* of number of servers required for hourly volume in $

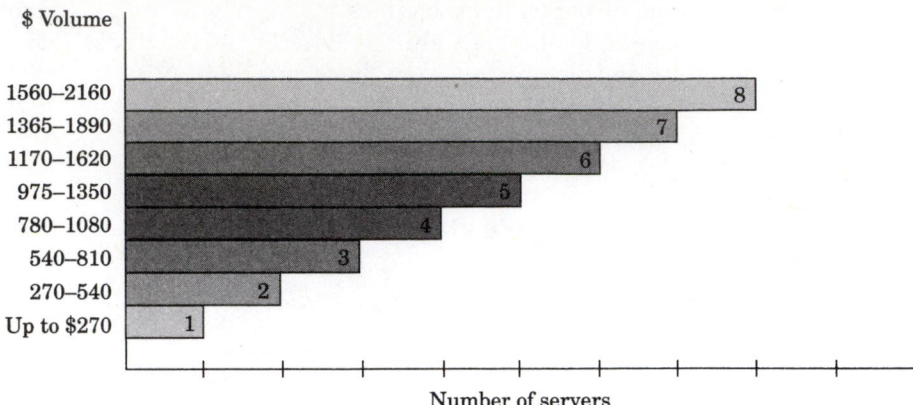

*Histogram—a basic bar chart with each bar (square or rectangle) representing a number or frequency in proportion to the other bars on the chart.

Figure 8–3

Run chart* of forecasted number of guests per hour

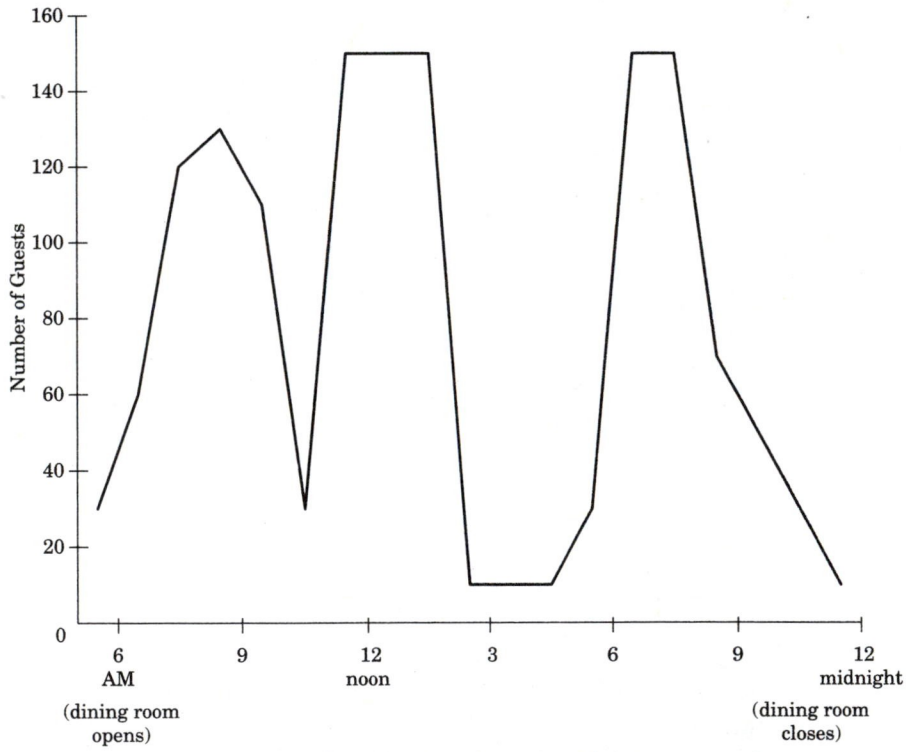

*Run chart—a simple plot of some item (number of guests, sales volume, days absent, etc.) over time.

These rules of thumb may be used as a guide for scheduling and dividing the restaurant dining room into stations:

Strictly plate service—A server should be able to efficiently serve 14 to 18 guests à la carte at one time. A dining room attendant for typical plate service should be able to service four servers efficiently.

TABLE 8–1

Activities Required

Activity	Description of Activity	Immediate Predecessor
A	Bring tables and chairs up from basement and arrange in hall	–
B	Pick up tablecloths from laundry and place on tables	A
C	Arrange place setting and decorations	B
D	Fill water glasses	C
E	Turn ovens on and perform equipment check	–
F	Prepare and cook main course	E
G	Prep salad and store	–
H	Seat guests	D
I	Plate salad and serve	G, H
J	Plate dinner and serve	F, I

TABLE 8–2

Activity Time Estimates in Hours for Gantt chart

Activity	Most Optimistic Time	Most Likely Time	Most Pessimistic Time
A	2.30	3.00	3.50
B	0.40	0.50	0.75
C	0.75	1.00	1.25
D	0.30	0.50	0.75
E	0.28	0.30	0.35
F	3.00	3.25	3.50
G	1.00	1.25	1.50
H	0.50	0.75	1.00
I	1.00	1.25	1.30
J	1.25	1.50	1.75

FIGURE 8–4

Gantt chart for special functions (simplified analysis)*

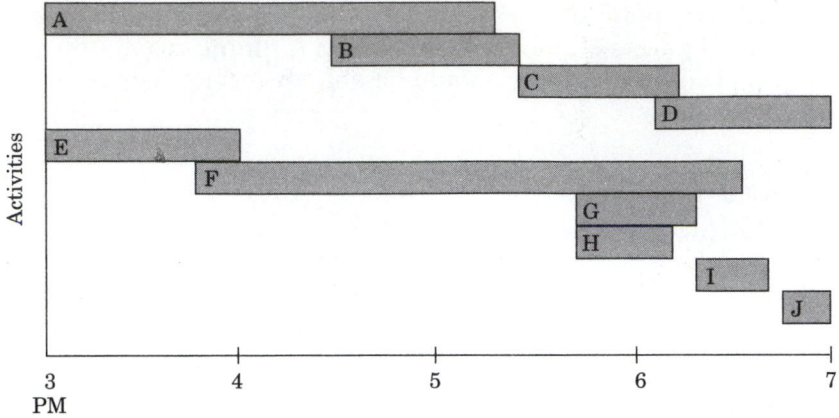

*Gantt chart—sequencing device for tasks, jobs, or activities relative to due date (or time) and scheduled completion date (or time).

Plate service with some flamed items or tableside service—This should be scaled downward accordingly. If the server is to perform normal service and also flame items (not a recommended practice), the stations should have fewer guests. The actual number will depend on the frequency of tableside preparation. Generally in a cart or tableside service restaurant, 10 guests *per service staff* member is recommended.

Strictly platter service—A server should be able to service 8 to 12 guests efficiently for à la carte service.

Strictly cart service—A server should be able to serve 10 guests efficiently. Many establishments require their staff to serve more than 10 guests per person, but this defeats the purpose of cart service, which is to provide personal, attentive service. Stations for this type of service should contain approximately 20 guests, as the servers work in pairs with a chef de rang and a commis de rang.

In a cart service dining room, a station of 30 guests may be designated with a captain and two servers or a captain, a server, and a dining room attendant. If the physical facilities allow, this distribution may be most efficient.

If a dining room manager desires, she may establish scheduling guidelines based on her dollar volume of business, which is only a variation in scheduling the forecasted number of covers (working backward from the average per person guest check) and the total dollar volume of business forecasted. (See Figures 8–1 and 8–2.) In a plate service dining room for example, if she estimates $5,500 gross revenue on Thursday night and her check average is $23 dollars per person, she expects to serve approximately 239 covers. If her establishment seats 100 people, she expects 2⅓ turns that night, and using the rules of thumb, she should have approximately five or six servers on the floor assisted by two dining room attendants and a host for the dinner shift beginning at 6 P.M. and ending at 11 P.M. A scheduling chart may be created to determine the number of service staff required for either a certain forecasted dollar volume or total covers forecasted for the evening, and exact staffing needs should conform to the guest demand on an hourly basis. Using peak demand scheduling allows for staggering the shifts with fewer staff during opening and closing with maximum staff during peak hours. Indeed, staggered shifts optimize the dining room's total labor cost. Preopening and closing duties, or service preparation duties for the following shifts, as well as certain food preparation duties, may be combined with service responsibilities to maximize labor productivity and minimize labor cost. During low-volume periods, combining jobs and job functions can be of critical importance.

Dividing the Dining Room into Stations

Several factors must be taken into consideration when dividing the dining room into stations. Some establishments have physical divisions such as walls or different rooms or sections of the restaurant. Some properties have one large room that must be sectioned for the most efficient service.

The following factors will assist the director for any type of food service establishment. The particular design of a restaurant may dictate the size of the **service stations**, and this is an important factor that may be overlooked during the initial planning and design phases of an operation. The director should use the rules of thumb for the number of seats in a particular station as a guideline for dividing the dining room into stations.

Distance of Stations from Kitchen. If a station requires that a server walk a long distance, this station should be smaller than one that is closer to the kitchen. The size tray, the type of tables, or number of seats in the station also determine the optimum size. If the trays will accommodate six covers comfortably with all accessories, it would be best to have tables as multiples of six: a deuce and a four, a six, or two three-tops. A table of eight would be difficult to service if the table were far from the kitchen or pick-up area and the trays were small. On the other hand, if a table of eight were close to the pick-up area, the service person could make two quick trips without greatly affecting the flow of service.

Location of Station. If station 1 were close to the kitchen or door (i.e., a relatively unpopular station), and if station 4 were by the window (i.e., a popular station), station 4 should be slightly smaller than station 1. Station 4 will probably turn over several tables more than station 1 and each server should wait on as close to the same number of guests as possible over the entire shift.

Type of Tables. Seven deuces at one time (à la carte) might overburden a server, but serving one six-top and two four-tops would be within the acceptable range. Therefore, the mix of table configurations is very important, and the number of seats and the type of tables must both be considered.

Number and Distance of Side Stands/Tray Stands to the Stations. Since some **side stands** and **tray stands** are portable, this factor may not be of importance, yet the specific configuration of a dining room may limit the portability of either a tray stand or a side stand. If a side stand is some distance from a station, this does limit slightly the number of people a server can serve efficiently. The rules of thumb must be adjusted upward with more guests per server if there is a preset menu. It takes a considerable amount of time to take orders, record the choices, and have such plated properly and distributed correctly. A server should be able to serve 20 or more guests in a plate service banquet with preset appetizers, soup, and main course with vegetables, dessert, and coffee.

Type of Service. The number of seats is an important factor when dividing the restaurant into stations. Along with the restaurant layout and design, the type of service should be considered as a major factor in dividing the dining room. (See Chapter 4.)

Quality of Staff. Another major factor in dividing the dining room into service stations is the quality of the service staff. If one's property is located in a metropolitan area with a relatively high check average and a low employee turnover rate among the service staff, the stations can be larger because the servers may be more efficient and better trained. If one's property is located in a rural area and only open seasonally with a very high employee turnover rate from season to season, these stations might need to be smaller.

Internal Control in the Dining Room

One of the functions of management is to control the operation. Although the control function in management includes the control of people (scheduling, discipline and so forth), internal control refers to financial control. The discussion of financial control here is only a primer. A complete discussion can be found in *Internal Control* by Neal Geller. Detailing a food and beverage control system here is well beyond the scope of this text, yet internal control as it relates to service is included. Indeed, many establishments assign the job of cashier to the host who then has a dual function.

The purpose of sales control is to ensure that all food prepared in the kitchen and served in the dining room generates revenue for the operation, and that revenue must be recorded correctly by servers and cashiers. The operator can lose money in several areas. The customer can walk out without paying; he can sneak out undetected; he can complain that the food is unsatisfactory due to taste or claiming foreign objects are in the food; or he can claim that he did not consume four cocktails, but only three. The operator can lose when the server makes errors either intentionally or unintentionally.

There are several ways a server may take money from the restaurant, the guest, or a credit card company. If the server returns change to the guest on a tip plate, he may pocket some of the change (usually in round amounts of one, two, or five dollars) before returning it to the guest. If no receipt is given, the guest may not remember the exact amount of either the check or the amount he gave for payment. The server may also simply present the wrong (and higher) check, overcharge for certain items, pocket the overcharge, and then correct the restaurant's copy of the guest check. A crafty waiter was known to have guest checks printed on his own that were identical to the establishment's checks. He would slip one of his preprinted checks to the guest for payment, discard his **private stock check**, and pocket the full amount.

A similar situation may arise when a server has two identical orders (such as a buffet) and presents the same check to two separate parties. He pockets payment from one party and deposits the other payment with the proper guest check to the cashier. If a cashier is not used and when the servers collect money and deposit the money into one central cash drawer, the operator is leaving himself open to theft because she may not be able to assign responsibility to any person.

A cashier could also use the **split ring technique** in which a guest presents $2.79 payment for items that are not accompanied with a guest check (i.e., coffee shop type operation); he rings "no sale" and then quickly rings $.79. He takes a $5 bill, deposits $.79 in the cash drawer, gives $2.21 change to the guest, deposits the five in the cash drawer, and secretly records the amount he will eventually pocket. He later pockets his overages.

Perhaps one of the slickest tricks yet involves credit card theft and/or misuse. The server watches for guests who appear to be in a hurry (i.e., checking the time frequently, tapping hands nervously on the table, or a mention about an engagement such as the theater, a movie, or a concert) and who pays by credit card. She returns the card, but slips it under a soiled napkin or dirty plate. If the guest leaves his card, she pockets the card and does one of two things. She (1) holds the card for several days and returns the card, reporting the lost card as found, and collects her reward. She (2) trades cards with her buddy across town (this makes tracking the theft of the card more difficult) and imprints several record of charges (ROCs) from the restaurant she works at with her buddy's card from across town or keeps the card to run in through the magnetic reader. When a guest pays for a check with cash, she pockets the cash, writes in the amount and forges the signature on the ROC or does the same with the computer-generated slip. The restaurant is none the wiser until and unless the credit card company issues a charge-back. And, the charge-back occurs only if the card is reported missing or if, some months later, the guest refuses to pay for an unauthorized charge.

A more common theft technique is for the server to intentionally (or unintentionally) forget to write certain items (extra cocktail, appetizer, dessert, etc.) on the check for payment. This can be a **buddy discount** or he may expect the guest to notice the omission and compensate him accordingly in the form of a larger gratuity. Sometimes the server may even alert the guest that he is not charging for something for any number of reasons or to gain favor with the guest. If not stated, guests seldom are aware of the omission and usually tip 15 percent of the total guest check anyway. In this scenario, the server actually cuts himself out of a gratuity. Another deceitful practice is for the server to pad (i.e., adding more items on the guest check or guest receipt) the guest's receipt and split the difference with a patron who is on an expense account.

The following styles can be taken to ensure proper revenue control:

- Preferably all checks should be totaled on a cash register, electronic cash register, or computer (point of sale or POS system), or (less preferably) on an adding machine or calculator. Some have estimated human error in simple arithmetic at 15 percent.
- A dual system (i.e., precheck rung by server) on a POS system or a duplicate check or food requisition system is essential.
- Cash received should equal the amount totaled on the guest checks (less any adjustments). The amount requisitioned on the guest checks should equal the number of portions sold. Also, the host's total cover count (number of guests served) should equal the cashier's and the kitchen's.
- If a manual system is used, prenumbered guest checks are a must, and if a separate means is used to requisition food from the kitchen (i.e., a requisition "req" or "dupe"), these should also be prenumbered. Each guest check or requisition must be accounted for at the end of the shift. It is also suggested that the checks (if not computer generated) be printed by a reputable firm

not located in the immediate area. If guest checks are computer generated or generated by an electronic cash register system, the computer automatically assigns a guest check number, which is used to track items ordered by a party of guests.

- Service personnel must be required to sign for requisitions or guest checks (if checks are used as requisitions). The requisitions must be controlled by the host and/or the cashier. Many establishments assess a heavy fine (illegal in some states) to the service person if a guest check is lost. This has an additional advantage because the server is also responsible for skippers or walkouts.

- No erasures should be allowed on either guest checks or requisitions. Mistakes will be made, but lining through errors will suffice. It would be preferable to void the requisition or guest check and complete a new one. Additionally, each check should be rung up separately.

- The person requisitioning for and filling out guest checks should not be allowed in the cash box unless each server maintains his/her own bank (see detail listed below).

- Excessive "no sale" rings should be investigated.

- The cashier should not have a key or card enabling her to total the cash register, and only one person per cash drawer should be allowed.

- Exceptions to procedures must be OKed by an authorized person such as a manager.

- All customers must be given receipts with the correct total.

- Hire a spotter to test your system and your staff.

- Review your system frequently.

Although some quick fixes to guest and employee theft can be offered, the design of an internal control system must be done by a professional. A professional can design a control system for food cost control, purchasing, and the like as well as cash receipts control. Anyone who wants to steal probably will find a way. However, a professionally and properly designed control system makes theft difficult to accomplish.

There are several advantages to electronic cash control systems, which are essential in any operation with moderate volume. Several of these advantages are as follows:

1. Speeds service—can automatically dial for credit card authorization.
2. Preset keys (or PLUs [price look-ups]) help:
   a. Reduce costly errors.
   b. Expand flexibility and control.

   c. Customer service as guest gets printout of his meal and, because of wide use, most guests know how to read machine abbreviations of menu items.

3. Can be used for requisitioning as a perpetual inventory system—bringing inventory to par-stock levels.

4. Yields significantly more management information:

   a. Employee/drawer accountability and productivity.

   b. Menu item analysis.

   c. Volume reports for totals as well as during peak demand periods on an hour-by-hour basis.

   d. Tax and tip summaries (sales, food, excises, etc.)

   e. Easier to isolate food and beverage items, which assists in inventory control.

Controls are essential, yet no control system should cost more than the items being controlled. Each strip steak should be accounted for; each pea should not. Additionally, controls should not be so designed that they inconvenience the guest by slowing service. Many establishments control wine excessively, with the result being slow wine service and a decrease in total wine sales. Other operations use POS systems intended to speed service, but they do not have an adequate number of terminals, creating bottlenecks at the terminals. This simultaneously reduces guest contact and the time and opportunity to up-sell the menus thereby increasing the check average.

Conclusion

The job of service director is all-encompassing, as he or she must be able to manage people and be well mannered in order to greet guests. Since the job has so many facets to it, the person designated as service director should use a checklist as a reminder. The particular style and flair that the host must exhibit in front of the guest can be learned and must be consistent with the formality of the restaurant. The host must have confidence in himself, and he must like people. Accepting and assigning reservations, whether in advance and/or over the phone or in person as a guest enters the restaurant, can be accomplished haphazardly, or reservations may be standardized. Handlng reservations may be customized to fit to any establishment, or reservations may not fit the market at all.

Scheduling service personnel is a difficult task. With a knowledge of the menu, the type of service, and the staff's capabilities, and the rules of thumb, and by maintaining good forecasts, the director of service should find it easier to schedule her service staff. Dividing the dining room into stations is a very important function. This may determine whether the guest gets good or poor service. It can also have a direct effect on the morale of the service personnel. Service personnel must feel they are being treated equally. If one server always gets the good station, the other staff members may feel discriminated against.

Although controlling the financial operations is the duty of the cashier, the host in many establishments does in fact perform this function.

Questions

1. Who decides what tasks should be performed and who should perform them? Why?
2. What are the basic tasks of the service director as outlined in the chapter?
3. Why is a checklist helpful? List some things that the service director on the floor should do.
4. What is perhaps the most important thing a host should do when the guest walks in?
5. What should the host do if the table he had chosen for a particular party is occupied when he approaches?
6. List five guidelines the host should follow when seating guests.
7. What are the three systems mentioned in the chapter on assigning reservations? Describe each.
8. Simulate assigning reservations at a restaurant of your choice and defend your ideas.
9. What makes scheduling the service staff such a difficult job?
10. What are the major factors that must be taken into consideration when dividing the dining room into stations?
11. What design factors determine the size of the service stations?
12. List the rules of thumb for scheduling for plate service, platter service, cart service.
13. List the major factors a dining room manager should be concerned with as related to service.

CHAPTER 9

The Service Staff: Responsibilities, Procedures, and Techniques

Chapter Outline

Job Descriptions
Checklist for Setting a Table
The Order of Service (A Checklist for Plate Service)
Operational Procedures
Tips for Good Service

Learning Objectives

After studying this chapter, the student will be able to . . .

- Outline position summaries for dining room personnel.
- Set the standards or specs (specifications) for the tabletop for formal, casual, and buffet dining.
- Outline the order of service for a Plate Service operation.
- Demonstrate the following service activities:
  —Carrying a large tray.
  —Carrying a cocktail tray.
  —Lifting heavy trays.
  —Changing table linens.
  —Using a service cloth.
  —Preparing a standard place setting.
  —Greeting and seating the guest.
  —Presenting the menu.
  —Taking the guest's order(s).
  —Serving the table—beverage and food.
- Demonstrate the following clearing and reset activities.
  —Clearing and reset with guest present.
  —Stacking plates on tray.
  —Unloading a tray.
  —Crumbing the table.
- Describe the recommended procedure for serving special menu items, i.e., steak tartare, raw oysters, caviar, escargot.
- List 10 tips or procedures for providing good service to the guest.
- Explain the importance of a written servers's checklist.

Key Words/Phrases

Etiquette	Place setting
Dictionary of Occupational Titles (*DOT*)	Center setting
	Banquette
Captain	Service plate/show plate/base plate
Service station	Entremet setting
Sommelier	Cocktail order
Server	Service cloth
Runner	Standard place setting
Back server	Requisition forms
Server bank	POS system
Dining room attendant	Expediter
Busperson	Bus tub
Dumbserver operator	Crumber
Table balance	Underliner
Silencer/undercloth	Monkey dish
Cover	Gooseneck

The delivery of dining room service is filled with detail, and there are countless duties that must be performed. It is necessary for a manager to know the specific duties within the jobs she is supervising. Historically, a manager was expected to be able to demonstrate the highest degree of skill in the jobs she was supervising before being promoted to supervisor. Today's manager recognizes that a good or excellent server does not necessarily make a good dining room supervisor. And an excellent supervisor may be a lousy server. While the supervisor cannot be ignorant of the skills required for effective job accomplishment, the manager is responsible for training and maintaining standards and for formulating policy and originating standards, not necessarily *doing* the tasks.[1]

Gracious behavior, correct etiquette, and proper service are of utmost importance. Careless, rude, or improper service can ruin good food and the chef's art, and even mediocre food can be enhanced with superb, caring service. The emphasis in this chapter is not intended to train people to become proficient service staff members, but rather to become effective managers by being keenly aware of service **etiquette**, service standards, the proper method of setting tables, and serving various menu items used in first-class dining rooms, and to be aware of standards and procedures that can be modified for the casual dining environment. Lest she

---

Supplemental service procedures and techniques for informal, casual restaurants were adapted from service training manuals generously offered by Applebee's International, Inc., and Uno Restaurant Corporation. The author expresses his thanks.

be at the whims of a classically trained maître d', it is essential for a manager to know the proper methods in order to supervise effectively. The many tasks required of the service staff, captains, servers, dining room attendants, and banquet servers may be allocated for maximum productivity and efficiency from the service staff both singly and collectively. Although the job descriptions that follow are complete and workable, individual job descriptions must be designed specifically for a particular operation. As with standardized recipes that must be customized for a particular kitchen, service staff job descriptions must be tailored to and standardized for a specific dining room operation.

Job Descriptions

The following job descriptions are distributed among the job titles and expanded from the ***Dictionary of Occupational Titles*** (***DOT***), published by the U.S. government, and task descriptions listed in *Tasks to Jobs,* published by the International Labor Organization. Both of these publications can be either purchased or found in most major public or university libraries.[2]

Dining Room Captain

Job Summary.   Provides proper greeting and service, coordinates the tasks of two or more service staff members, including servers and dining room attendants (bussers) in the dining room. The captain is the leader of the service team.

Work Responsibility.   The **captain** is responsible for gracious and proper service usually at two or more **service stations**. At capacity, the captain may be responsible for 35 to 50 guests. He or she is primarily responsible for taking the order and, therefore, selling the menu, and will offer and serve wine in the absence of a wine steward or **sommelier**.

Specific Tasks
1. Greets guests.
2. Ensures that server or dining room attendant pours water and serves butter.
3. Takes guests' order.
4. When serving alcoholic beverages, ensures responsible practice.
5. Serves guest all courses in proper sequence.

6. Ensures that service personnel clear soiled dishes and silverware properly and in a timely way, as well as performing all of their duties properly.
7. Presents check.
8. Bids guest farewell.
9. Ensures that table is clean, sanitized, and reset.
10. Ensures that station breakdown is complete at end of shift.

Reports to: Host or Dining Room Manager

Special Considerations.   The captain must be capable of performing all tasks required of a **server**, teaching these tasks, and directing the efforts of servers.

Server (Waiter/Waitress)

Job Summary.   Sets tables, prepares dining room, counters, coffee shop, or lunch room for service, and serves meals to guests. She or he must know proper rules of etiquette in order to furnish gracious service, working in both formal and informal settings.

Work Responsibilities.   The server is responsible for gracious and proper service at the assigned station. Each station may seat more than 20 guests (depending on type of service).

Specific Tasks.
1. Reports to captain or host to receive necessary instructions for the shift and for any menu changes.
2. Sets assigned tables and ensures that service area is stocked (linen, silver, glassware, and china, etc.). Sets up any special displays that may be used for that meal period.
3. Greets guests and may assist captain or host in seating guests. Serves butter, fills water glasses, serves cocktails utilizing responsible beverage service practices, answers questions about menu items, and (in the absence of a captain) makes suggestions about dishes and wines if customers so request or desire.
4. Writes orders on check, inputs into POS or computer, or memorizes order, and turns in order to cooks with consideration to timing of preceding courses. Picks up all food and all other needed items from various stations in the absence of a **runner** or **back server**.

5. May garnish and decorate dishes prior to serving.

6. May carve meats, bone fish or fowl, and prepare flaming dishes or desserts at guest's table in absence of a captain.

7. May serve guests from a platter at guest's table.

8. May ladle soup, toss salads, portion pies and other desserts, brew coffee, and perform other services as determined by establishment's size and practices.

9. Replenishes wine, water, and butter and bread supply, or has dining room attendant do it.

10. Observes guests to fulfill any additional requests such as extra napkins and wet-naps if finger foods and to perceive when meal has been completed.

11. After all the guests have finished each course and before the next one is served, server should remove all soiled dishes or ensure that dining room attendant does.

12. When guests have finished meal, table should be cleared. Guests may be asked if he wants to have leftover food wrapped for takeaway.

13. Server may now present check and again inquire to see if the guest is satisfied. Server may receive immediate payment and may take check to cashier, or makes correct change from own **server bank** *not in presence of the guest*.

14. May reset table or counter at the conclusion of the meal and ensures that table or counter is clean and sanitized before resetting.

15. Server checks out cash or charge receipts, coupons, house charges, or gift certificates to balance server bank.

16. Server will perform other tasks as directed by the supervisor. May be asked to perform as a captain, dining room attendant, host, or banquet server.

This is a composite description, and tasks or functions may be deleted or placed under other jobs should the manager so choose.

Reports to: Captain, Host, or Dining Room Manager.

Special Considerations.   Server must be thoroughly familiar with the establishment's menu (American, some foreign dishes) and all types of alcoholic beverages. Must know how to pronounce names of foreign preparations on the menu and what beverages best complement them. Must know proper methods of serving meals of all kinds. In a meal consisting of several courses (and especially when accompanied by wines), the server needs to learn how to achieve proper timing between courses and must know which wine goes with what course. To prevent the guest from feeling neglected, the server needs to know how long it takes to complete each course so as to be able to regulate the service of several different tables at the same time.

Server's Personal Equipment.   Bottle opener/corkscrew; ballpoint pen or two pencils (five-inch length minimum); matches or a lighter; service cloth (optional in some establishments).

Dining Room Attendant (Busperson)

Job Summary.   Assists servers, maintains cleanliness, and keeps dining room supplied with clean utensils, china, glassware, condiments, and ice. Clears soiled dishes, removes them to kitchen, and resets tables.

Work Responsibility.   The **dining room attendant**, or **busperson**, will be responsible for proper service, assisting from one to four servers.

Specific Tasks.
1. Assists servers in their tasks.
2. Removes dishes from dining room to dishwasher in kitchen.
3. Replenishes supply of clean linens, silverware, glassware, and dishes in the dining room.
4. Replenishes butter supply for guests.
5. Fills and refills water glasses for guests.
6. Resets tables. Replaces soiled table linen and sets table with silverware, china, and glassware.
7. Assists in carrying food trays to the table.
8. Makes coffee and tea and fills ice bins and fruit juice dispensers.
9. Supplies service bar with food, such as soups, salads, and desserts.
10. Dusts furniture and cleans and polishes glass shelves and doors of service bar and such equipment items as coffee urns and cream and milk dispensers.
11. May wait on and bring items to guests.
12. May transfer food and dishes between floors of establishment using dumbservers and may be designated **dumbserver operator** (gender-neutral terminology for dumbwaiter).
13. May run errands and deliver food orders to offices and be designated a **runner**.
14. Assists in breaking down service stations.

Reports to: Server, captain, and host.

Special Considerations.   The dining room attendant must know the prescribed methods for clearing dishes, setting tables, and cleaning the dining area.

If the preceding descriptions are insufficient or if a specific breakdown is required for union or wage administration or for the operation's needs, please refer to the appropriate documents.

The following checklist for setting tables may be used as a guideline for banquet and a la carte operations. Realize that each individual establishment may have particular methods that do not conform to the standards listed below. This does not decrease the importance of the standard; however, the new or young manager should not try to impose the standard on an existing and prosperous operation. Change may best be effected gradually.

Checklist for Setting a Table

Tables

1. Check table for proper position in the room; check alignment and spacing.
2. Check **table balance** (use cork if table is uneven, not matchbooks).
3. Use drop leaves or table extensions as required to adjust size of table and configuration.
4. *If tablecloths are not used,* ensure that the table grain or decor (e.g., airbrush-designed, acrylic-topped tables) is facing in the proper direction.

Tablecloth

1. Center **silencer** or **undercloth** on table; make sure it is clean.
2. Center tablecloth on table; make sure the fold lines are straight and that proper size is being used. The cloth should extend a minimum of 10 inches beyond the edge of the table, but should not touch the floor. Be sure the tablecloth is "face up," that is, shiny or crest side up and that hems on the edge are always away from the face (hems down).
3. Some operations set two cloths, one of which will remain on the table throughout the service period.

China, Glassware, and Silverware

A **cover** describes an individual place setting (24 inches × 15 inches minimum).

1. Tables should be set by balancing the individual **place settings** and the center settings (sugar, salt/pepper, ashtray/matches, relishes, crackers, or flowers). Each **center setting** should match, throughout the dining room, the placement and organization of the center settings of like tables.

2. Do not handle silver by food contact surface; carry on a plate covered with a napkin or in a clean service cloth.

3. Handle glassware by the base or stem; never grasp by the brim.

4. Covers should face each other for an even number of settings. Odd numbers face an open space.

   a. If two places are set at a **banquette**, they should face the dining room.

   b. Covers are set between table legs whenever possible.

   c. Chairs should just touch the tablecloth when placed at the table.

5. Balance additional condiments if preset (i.e., butter, sour cream, salsa, dressings).

6. If a **service plate**, **show plate**, or **base plate** is used, ensure that the crest faces the guest.

7. Place forks on left, tines up (except for informal luncheon settings when forks and spoons may be set on the right). *(Note: In Europe the spoons may be placed face down and the fork tines down, especially when using oversized silverware—silversmiths mark is usually on the concave portion of the utensil.)*

8. Place knives and spoons to right with knife edges facing the plate, and spoons up and to the right of (outside) the knives.

9. Lay silver at right angles to the cover. Although silver may be placed following the contour of a round table, this destroys the appearance at the top of the cover.

10. Place silverware evenly one-half inch from edge.

11. Dinner knife and fork are placed next to plate.

12. Place individual butter plates above dinner forks, centered on and one inch above the forks. An acceptable alternate method is to place butter plate to side of forks.

13. Place butter knife on right side of plate or on top edge (see Figure 9–1).

14. Generally, butter and/or bread plates are not used for formal service during the meal.

15. Carry stemmed glassware inverted in the hands with stems between fingers, and carry regular glassware only by the base.

16. Place water glass centered on and one inch above the knife closest to the dinner plate.

17. Place other glassware as specified (see Figure 9–2) .

18. Glassware should be right side up before guests are seated (standard etiquette). Sanitation requirements may require that glassware be placed down until after guests have been seated.

19. Place settings should not have too many pieces. As a rule of thumb, three forks, two knives, three spoons, and four glasses plus the dessert (**entremet**) **setting** should be maximum. If more glassware or silverware pieces are necessary, they should be presented just before the course being served.

20. If dessert silver (entremet setting) is laid, place parallel to cover with handle of fork left and handle of spoon right. Spoon is placed above fork.

21. Parfait or iced tea spoons and dessert knives should not be preset.

22. Crackers, melba toast, relishes, butter, and water should never be placed on the table before the guest(s) is seated if following formal etiquette. To speed service in casual dining, some food items may be preset on the table before guests are seated.

23. Place napkin in middle of cover on top of showplate (hors d'oeuvres plate) in formal service. If preset menu item (i.e., for banquets), napkin should be folded on butter plate, in one of the glasses, or placed behind the preset food.

24. Never place bread on a napkin.

For informal or plate, platter, buffet, and banquet service, silverware is usually preset. For cart service, silverware is usually brought with each course.

Correct Method for Placing Wine Glasses

The following diagrams (Figure 9–2) depict the correct placement of wine glasses and the place settings for the courses or foods to be served (Figure 9–3 to 9–23). One should not spend time memorizing the place

FIGURE 9–1

Three acceptable methods of placing butter knives on bread and butter plates: (1) most preferred (2) acceptable (3) acceptable (not recommended)

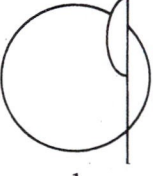 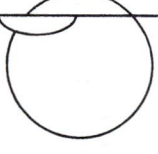 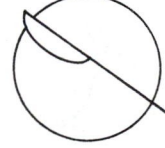

1   2   3

FIGURE 9–2

Correct method for placing wine glasses on the table. The guide runs up and down the dinner knife (knife closest to dinner plate). The guide glass should be placed so that the edge of the base is centered on, and one inch above the dinner knife. Glasses must be removed (cleared) before the next wine is served.

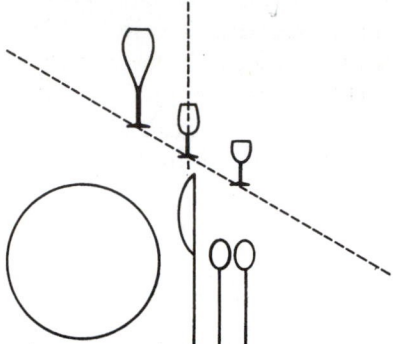

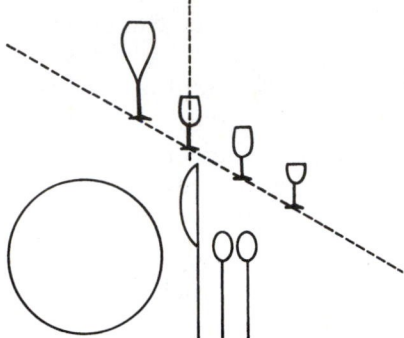

3 Wines: (From right to left in order of consumption) white wine (rhine wine glass) red wine (All-purpose wine glass) sparkling wine (tulip champagne glass)

4 Wines: (From right to left in order of consumption) white wine (rhine wine glass) light red wine (all-purpose wine glass) heavy red wine (all-purpose glass) sparkling wine (tulip champagne glass)

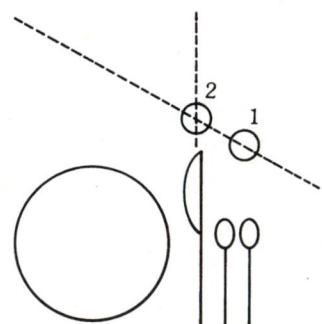

2 Wines

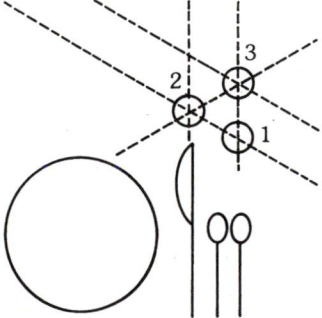

3 Wines

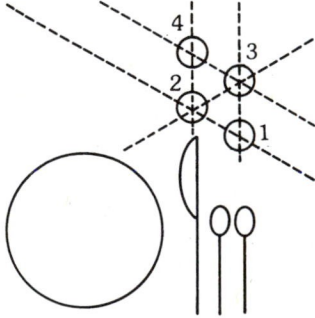

4 Wines

FIGURE 9–3

Complete breakfast

FIGURE 9–4

Hot Cereal

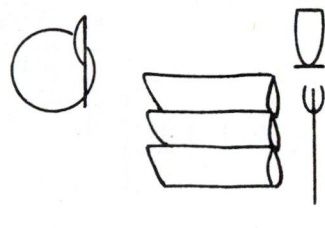

FIGURE 9–5

Standard plate service

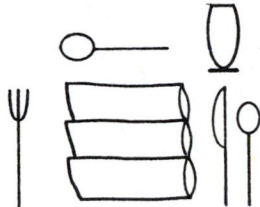

FIGURE 9–6

Variation of standard plate service with added bouillon spoon

FIGURE 9–7

Informal luncheon. Note: No knives, forks on right

FIGURE 9–8

Standard plate with cocktail fork resting in bouillon spoon

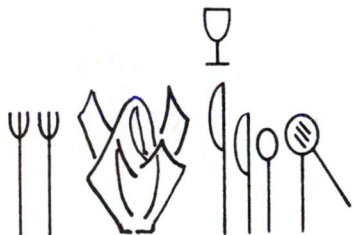

FIGURE 9–9

Minimum cover, also called simple or French cover

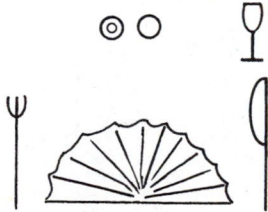

FIGURE 9–10

Standard plate service with entremet (dessert)

FIGURE 9–11

Basic à la carte (French)

FIGURE 9–12

Soup, fish, meat, and dessert

FIGURE 9–13

Hors d'oeuvres

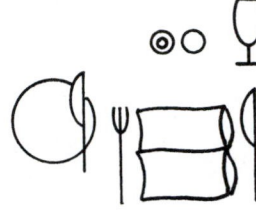

FIGURE 9–14

Smoked salmon

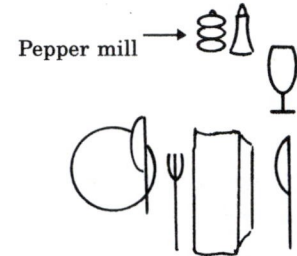

Pepper mill →

FIGURE 9–15

Smoked fish in general

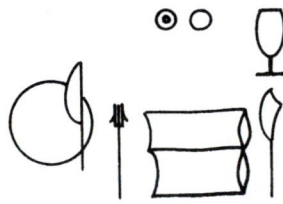

FIGURE 9–16

Oysters

FIGURE 9–17

Cold lobster

FIGURE 9–18

Bouillabaisse

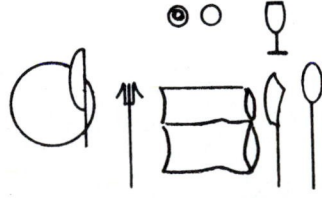

* ⏐ denotes fish fork;   ⏐ denotes fish knife;   ⏐ denotes oyster/seafood fork

FIGURE 9–19
Stew

FIGURE 9–20
Cheese

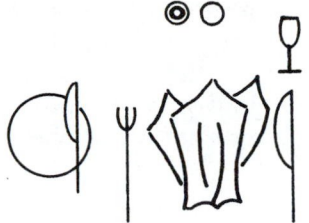

FIGURE 9–21
Melon half

FIGURE 9–22
Melon slice

FIGURE 9–23
Grapefruit half

setting for lobster, the place setting for escargot, etc., but should have ready access to a reference in order to set the table properly for each course. On the other hand, each server should know the standard setting for each course on the menu of the establishment. Correspondingly, a server should be able to design a place setting using the standard rules of etiquette (Checklist for Setting the Table) when given a menu. The service person must, therefore, know which utensil(s) is used for a particular food. These diagrams are sketched so that any manager could duplicate these line drawings in order to communicate to her service staff. For example, a banquet manager (or headserver) may sketch the desired place setting on the function sheet, and the server could set the table correctly from this simple line drawing.

The following task procedures can be used to train servers in the proper methods for serving a specific menu in a formal dining room and can be modified for casual dining. The manager should be able to either duplicate or modify these standard tasks for the operation as well as tailor the tasks to the menu in the dining room. Many of the tasks listed can be transferred to other operations, but the specific cocktails and menu presentations should reflect, more specifically, the operation in question.

The Order of Service (A Checklist for Plate Service)

1. Tables set ready for service.
2. Host seats guests and presents menus.
3. Greet guests with a genuine smile.
4. Pour water for each guest. Refill water glasses when less than 2/3 full. Refill all glasses to same level around the table.
5. Serve butter (if anticipate several rounds of cocktails, serve butter after taking the food order).
6. Take **cocktail order**.
7. Serve cocktail from right on cocktail napkin in center of cover.
8. Serve bread now or wait until salad is being served.
9. Take food order from host or from the left side of each guest.
10. Offer wine list and/or suggestions. Take wine order.
11. Remove cocktail glasses when empty. If wine is not ordered, offer more cocktails.
12. Serve appetizer (center of cover).
13. Serve wine if matched with appetizer or soup.
14. Remove appetizer dish.
15. Serve soup in center of cover.
16. Remove soup dishes and show plates (if used).
17. Serve salad; offer rolls or bread; remove salad dishes.
18. Serve entrée; place in center of cover. If side dishes are used, place on left of the cover. Offer rolls or bread again.
19. Remove main course dishes using the following order.
    a. Condiments.
    b. Dinner plates.
    c. Vegetable dishes.
    d. Empty wine glasses.
    e. Extra silver.

20. Crumb table.
21. Present dessert (on cart or tray, by menu, or verbally).
22. Serve dessert course (center of cover).
23. Remove dessert course.
24. Serve coffee (if not yet served).
25. Serve brandy or cordials.
26. Present check.
27. Thank guest.
28. Help guests as they rise to leave and check that no personal articles are left behind, and bid guests farewell.
29. Do not count tip.
30. Clear table and reset if necessary.

Operational Procedures

The following are step-by-step procedures for performing various tasks.

Carrying a Large Tray

1. Carry above shoulders.
2. Use left hand (preferable since most doors open to the right).
3. Lift with palm; can use fingertips if desirable. Fingers should be at a 45-degree angle to front of body.
4. Use right hand to balance until proficient.
5. Tray should be clean.
6. Place clean cloth on tray to prevent slippage.
7. Balance items on tray, heaviest toward center or in center where hand is (glassware, etc., to edges away from the body).

Carrying a Small Tray

1. Carried waist high with left upper arm close to body. Forearm outstretched (90 degrees) with hand under the tray.
2. Remove and serve with tray held in left hand.
3. All items removed or served with right hand.
4. Bend with knees; do not lean over from the waist.
5. Small trays must always remain on the left hand. They should never be set down in the dining room.

Lifting Heavy Trays

1. Bend with knees.
2. Place tray in approximate position for carrying on shoulder.

3. Lift by straightening your knees and move tray into place with shoulder and hand.
4. Lift with legs, not your back.

Lifting Heavy Objects (Boxes, etc.)

1. Bend down with knees.
2. Grasp with one hand close to body, other hand on opposite side of object.
3. Keep back straight.
4. Lift object with legs, not arms or back. (See Chapter 6.)

Changing Linen

1. Move center setting close to edge of table nearest you.
2. Take clean cloth with double fold between thumb and index finger and single folds (2) between index and middle and middle and ring fingers.
3. Spread arms as wide as the table, if possible.
4. Drop hemmed edge (bottom of your cloth) over the back edge of table.
5. Grasp soiled cloth with butt of your palm and little finger.
6. Gradually release the double fold (between thumb and index finger) and pull to center of table while continuing to hold the soiled cloth.
7. **Stop!** Move center settings to opposite side of table (i.e., on clean cloth side).
8. Grasp clean cloth between thumb and index finger and soiled cloth with butt of hand and little finger.
9. Pull remaining hemmed edge toward you; grasp soiled cloth again at edge nearest you. Center the clean cloth. Remove soiled cloth by continuing to grasp at both ends to keep crumbs and paper litter from falling. Check that all folds are even on top of the table.

Table Setting and Preparation (Informal)

1. Many operations no longer use tablecloths, but use cloth place mats or glass tops that cover a decorative tablecloth or undercloth. Natural wood grain, composite, Formica, and acrylic tops are also being used with the place setting simply on the table.
2. Before setting the table, these surfaces must be cleaned and sanitized to maximize infection control. A proper, nontoxic sanitizing agent must be provided for use by dining room personnel.

3. If spray bottles are used, they should be used carefully so that spray does not reach any guests dining in the restaurant. Spraying into a clean cloth or paper towel will minimize guests getting a whiff of sanitizing agent or cleanser.

4. Both paper and cloth place mats must be single-use items. *Do not reuse a soiled place mat.*

Preparing the Bread Tray or Bread Basket

1. Place properly folded napkin in bottom of tray or basket.
2. Place rolls or assorted breads as required.

Filling Salt and Pepper Shakers

1. Remove shakers from tables.
2. Wipe all shakers clean.
3. Remove tops.
4. Use specially designed refill jugs or small funnel (or make funnel out of paper).
5. Place several pieces of rice in salt shakers to absorb moisture (in geographical areas where there is very high humidity).

Filling Water Pitchers

1. Determine the number of water pitchers required for the service.
2. Place on rolling table (with soiled table cloth on table). Place sheet pans on top of cart, and place service cloth in side sheet pan.
3. Place pitchers inside sheet pans (on towels).
4. Fill with ice.
5. Pour water into pitchers (have installed and use flexible hose to speed the process).

Carrying the Service Cloth

1. Select a **service cloth** that is clean and unstained.
2. Be sure that the cloth has no holes in it or that the edges are not frayed.
3. Fold so that edges are not visible—fold edges under.
4. Place cloth on left forearm, draped with edge on fat part of thumb.
5. Never place service cloth under arm, in pocket, in belt, or on the shoulder.

Carrying Hot Plates with Service Cloth

1. Place folded cloth over edge of plates and ensure that edges fall down the sides and would fit under the number of plates to be carried.

2. Lift plates close to body, but do not touch your body.
3. Do not attempt to carry too many plates.
4. Wiggle tails of cloths from underneath the plates when setting down so as to not make noise when removing cloth.

Using the Service Cloth to Handle a Hot Plate

1. After folding and holding cloth as specified in Carrying the Service Cloth, slide cloth over hand and fingers near one end of the cloth.
2. Grasp hot plate with cloth.
3. Hold other end of cloth with right hand so as not to drag it over guest's lap.

Serving the Guest

1. Ensure that you *know what each guest ordered*, and serve each guest what he or she ordered. *Never* approach a table and ask who gets what—always know!
2. Serve each guest from the left (plate service standard etiquette) using your left hand and *do not touch the top of the plate* with any part of your hand or body.
3. Do not stack plates on top of plates, and ensure that food (especially sauces) does not slide all over the plate.
4. If plate is hot, *inform the guest*.

Polishing Silverware (Clean Water Spots)

1. Never grasp silver by any part of utensil other than the side of the handle. Touching the food contact surface is unsanitary, and touching the handle itself leaves fingerprints.
2. Be sure that the cloth is clean and sanitary.
3. Moisten cloth slightly with clean water (a dilution of water and white vinegar is sometimes helpful) or pass utensils over steaming water to moisten.
4. Wipe until polished.
5. If silver has stains or food on it, get another silver piece.

Cleaning or Changing Ashtrays

1. When an ashtray has more than one or two crushed cigarettes in it (per operating standard), place a clean ashtray on top of the soiled ashtray on the table.
2. Remove the two ashtrays *together* using the clean ashtray to cover the soiled ashtray so ashes will not wisp onto the table.
3. Replace clean ashtray on table.

Note: Never empty onto a plate, paper place mat, cloth place mat, or tray, or clean out or wipe an ashtray in presence of guests. Always bring a clean ashtray from the back to replace a dirty one.

Polishing Glassware

1. Grasp glass by stem or lower to midsection of straight glass, never by the brim.
2. Polish as with silverware—slightly moisten cloth. Insert in glass.
3. Wipe clear. Be sure no lint remains on glass. *Note:* Best to use a lint-free cloth or lint-free paper towel.

Setting the Table (Standard Place Setting)

1. Place napkin in center of cover.
2. Place silverware (dinner knife and dinner fork) approximately five inches apart and one-half inch from the table edge to establish the center of the cover.
3. Knife blade is toward the plate, facing the inside of the cover.
4. Place second fork parallel to and just touching the first fork.
5. Place butter knife and spoons parallel to dinner knife.
6. Place water goblet centered on the dinner knife (unless water is to be served on request only, in which case the water goblet is not preset).
7. If wine glasses are preset, center on the dinner knife or water goblet.

Host Greeting (at the Door)

1. Use "Sir" for men and "Madam/Ma'am" for women.
2. Address yourself to the group as opposed to one person and say "Good evening," "Good afternoon," or some appropriate salutation.
3. If you do not recognize the party (host), ask the person in whose name the reservations were made.
4. If no reservations, inquire as to how many are in the party and find an appropriate table or include name on waiting list; state a realistic wait time—it is better to err on the long-wait side (underpromise and overdeliver).

Captain's, Server's, or Attendant's Greeting

1. Give some proper salutation to the group: "Good evening," "Good afternoon," etc.
2. Introduce yourself as being their server for the meal—if standard operating procedure, use your name in the salutation; otherwise, be natural: "Good afternoon (evening), I will be serving you this afternoon (evening)."
3. Address the host (on the left), and take order for cocktails or wine for her guests. "Would you care for a cocktail, a beer, or a glass of sherry/wine?"

Seating Your Guests

1. Pull out a chair as a gesture for the guests to be seated (in general) or for the women (traditional service) or the eldest, as the case may be, in the group.
2. Push chair in by lifting rear of chair slightly and pushing forward with your foot on the leg and your hands on the top of the chair.
3. Face women toward the dining room (traditional etiquette)
4. If seating guests in a booth, offer buffet seat to the women (traditional etiquette).
5. Pull table away from the seats to facilitate access by the individual being seated; replace table to original position. *Note:* See Greeting and Seating Guests in Chapter 8.

Presentation of the Menu

1. Present each guest (at least those old enough to read) a menu.
2. Present the menu (closed) from the guests' left beginning with the person on the right of the host and moving counterclockwise around the table.
3. Be sure that the menus are clean and not soiled, tattered, or torn.
4. Present the menu with left hand—if guest does not grasp menu, gently place in the center of the cover.
5. Do not carry menus under your arm or tucked in your belt or waistband (especially in the back belt or waistband).

Pouring Water (Formal Dining)

1. If necessary (i.e., you cannot easily reach the glass with the pitcher) move the glass closer to you by grasping the base or stem.
2. Do not lift the glass from the table (formal etiquette).
3. Pour water in glass (about three-fourths to seven-eighths full).
4. Do not normally cross in front of guest, but excuse yourself when necessary (i.e., when you must cross in front of guest).

Pouring Water (Informal, Casual Dining)

1. Bring water goblets with ice and water already in the glass to the table and serve as with any beverage. Glasses may have been prepared, in advance, for the service period.
2. Use a cocktail tray for service, and *do not* grasp glasses by or around the brim.
3. When refilling, picking the glass from the table is acceptable—this procedure departs from classical etiquette.

Taking Cocktail Orders

1. As with all orders, ask host if she will order.
2. If not, ask each guest (standing on guest's left) what he would care to drink.
3. Order drinks from bar or service bar by filling out beverage requisition/check or entering such on POS machine.
4. Use the small tray for cocktails.

Serving Cocktails, Mocktails, or Beverages (General)

1. Cover cocktail tray with cloth or napkin.
2. Place beverages on tray and distribute weight evenly and toward your body.
3. Obtain one cocktail napkin for each person.
4. From the right, place napkin in center of cover with crest/logo facing guest.
5. Place beverage glass on napkin and back away.
6. Do not grasp glass by rim.

Taking the Food Order

1. Address yourself to the host on his left if a host is apparent.
2. If no host is apparent:
   a. Address yourself to the man when a man and a woman are eating together (traditional etiquette).
   b. Address yourself to the elder if your guests are of the same gender.
   c. In large groups a host should be apparent who decides whether he or his guests individually will give their orders.
3. In large groups begin with the person on the host's right, and on that person's left.
4. Keep sequence so as to serve guests in correct order without having to ask guests who gets what. (See Picking Up a Food Order [Specific] on page 205.)

Filling Out Food Requisitions (Manual Forms in Triplicate with Separate Cashier)

1. All food orders must be on **requisition forms**. Prenumbered pads are available from cashier.
2. Take orders per above—write clearly (press hard for carbon).
3. Note table number.
4. Original copy goes to cashier.
5. Second copy goes to range.
6. Third copy is for server.

7. Take dessert orders on server copy and give to cashier immediately after dessert and beverages are served.

   Note: Cashier will not prepare final check until server's dessert copy is received.

8. Cashier will prepare final check and hold for server's call.

Taking the Order Using POS Systems

1. All food and beverage orders must be entered into the **POS system**.
2. Follow POS procedures established by the operation in conjunction with the operator's manual of the electronic system being used. Take orders per Taking the Food Order on page 201.
3. Enter all guest requests in the POS system.
4. After taking dessert order and serving dessert/coffee or after dinner drinks, ask guest if he or she would like the check.
5. Total check and present in appropriate folder or on tip tray/small plate.

Filling Out Beverage and Wine Requisitions

1. Write all beverage (cocktails) orders and wine orders on beverage requisition.
2. Follow same distribution procedure as for food requisitions.
3. Fill out requisition completely, with table numbers and server's initials/number.

Passing Requisitions to Main Range

1. Fill out requisition completely except for dessert.
2. Present pickup slip to **expediter** at main range.
3. See procedure handout for placing and picking up orders.

Order of Service for Buffet

1. Greet the guests.
2. Pour water.
3. Serve butter.
4. Take cocktail/wine/beverage order.
5. Place bread.
6. Take food order.
7. Remove cocktail glasses when empty—ask for another round.
8. Serve appetizers.

9. Invite guests to buffet.
10. Serve à la carte items to guests who do not choose the buffet when buffet guests return to table.
11. Serve wine.
12. Pour coffee if desired by guest.
13. Remove dishes only when all have finished.
14. Crumb table.
15. Offer dessert .
16. Serve dessert—pour coffee.
17. Remove dessert if luncheon meeting ensues.
18. Present check promptly—do not wait for guest's call for check unless luncheon meeting ensues.

Note: Guests eating luncheon are usually in a hurry as compared to dinner service. Do not wait until they have finished cocktails before proceeding with their food order.

Clearing the Table with Guests Seated

1. Clear all dishes with the right hand and from the right side. Leave the water goblet and the silver required for dessert and coffee (leave coffee cup and saucer if already served) on the table.
2. Clear dishes completely from one person before proceeding to the next. Do not inconvenience the guest by reaching across or in front of the guest, and keep the plates lower than guest's eyes while in the vicinity of the table before raising for removal.
3. Ensure that all table trash, empty portion-pack containers, and other items are cleared frequently.

Resetting the Table with Guests Seated

1. Carry clean silverware from the kitchen to the dining room on a cocktail tray or dinner plate covered with a napkin or service cloth. If resetting from a side stand, also use a plate or cocktail tray.
2. Lay the silver per standard etiquette—forks on the left and knives and spoons on the right side of the cover. Grasp the edges of the utensil, *never* touch the food contact surface, and avoid fingerprinting the handle.
3. Approach guest from side on which you are laying the silver on the table. Do not reach across or otherwise inconvenience the guest.

Note: Do not use any silverware that has dropped on the floor.

Stacking Plates on a Tray

FIGURE 9–24

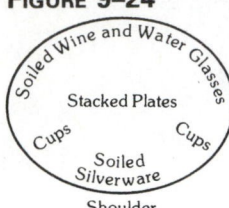

1. Heaviest dishes are laid in the center of the tray or where weight would be on your shoulder.
2. Glasses and light articles to the outside.
3. Dishes with food on them should *not* be piled up unless covers are used.
4. Stack according to sizes of plates—larger plates on bottom.
5. Cups are not placed on saucers (takes up too much room).
6. Tray should be covered with a clean napkin.

Unloading a Tray (Soiled Dishes)

1. Place tray down on unloading rack at dishwasher's station.
2. Save all unopened portion-pack condiments, crackers, and so forth.
3. Place silverware in presoak tub.
4. Place glassware in proper racks.
5. Place cups on cup rack.
6. If racks are full, inform dish machine operator (DMO) and then place an empty rack in its place.
7. Spray (if available) and wipe tray clean (top **and bottom**).

Loading a Bus Tub

1. Place **bus tub** on tray stand. It is improper to place a bus tub on a chair and a *serious breach of dining etiquette* is to place a bus tub on a table.
2. Separate items as much as possible in the bus tub.
3. Use caution with glassware to prevent breakage.

Note: Bus tubs are not usually used in front-of-the-house operations in finer dining environments, although they can be used in informal or casual dining following appropriate procedures.

Crumbing a Table

1. Clear all dishes except water glasses. Leave sufficient silver (if clean) for dessert course.
2. Use appropriate **crumber** or. . .
3. Fold dinner napkin small enough to fit comfortably in palm of hand.
4. Use folded side of napkin to sweep crumbs, table litter, or debris into small dish covered with another a folded napkin.
5. Perform this function from either side and do not inconvenience the guest.

Picking Up a Food Order (General)

1. First organize all serving equipment for food and accompaniments: lemon wedges, tartar sauce, mayonnaise, horseradish, etc.
2. Cold foods are picked up and placed on tray away from where hot foods go.
3. Hot foods should be picked up last and covered.

Picking Up a Food Order (Specific)

1. Diagram of placing plates on tray.
2. Stack plates per diagram placing the order of the last person served on the bottom of the tray.
3. If arm service, arrange plates on the arm so that the first person served can be served with the left hand from the left side.

Carrying Plates (First Method)

1. Place thumb over edge and hold plate between thumb, index finger, and middle finger—do not allow thumb to touch the top or eating surface of the plate.
2. Place ring finger and little finger up above rim of first plate.
3. Balance second plate on thick part of thumb, and ring and middle finger, not on wrist.

Carrying Plates (Second Method)

1. Place plate over the middle and ring fingers and under the index and little fingers.
2. Balance second plate on the tripod created by the thumb and the tips of the index and little fingers.

Removing Soiled Plates

1. When all guests have finished eating, begin removing soiled dishes from right of the person you served first (the person on the host's right) and transferring plates to your left hand.
2. Remove serving dishes first if on the guest's table and then the largest plates first following with smaller plates which can be balanced on top the larger plates. Use the following procedures for carrying plates and scraping food.
3. Clear all dishes except for the water goblet and the silver required for dessert and coffee (leave coffee cup and saucer if already served).
4. Clear dishes completely from one person before proceeding to the next person.

5. It is unnecessary to remove center setting items (e.g. salt and pepper, sugar/sweetener carrier, etc.) from the table and may be construed by the guest as encouraging the guests to leave.

Note: **Never** place anything on a guest's plate while the plate is on the guest's table. All soiled and loose silverware, china, or glassware must be lifted from the table and then stacked out of the direct sight of the guests. Do not lift silverware *off* the guest's plate—pick up the entire plate.

Scraping Food

1. Place plates, as in Carrying Plates.
2. Scrape food gently from second plate onto first plate (out of sight of guest), and place knife and fork on plate.
3. Place fork prongs up and at 11 o'clock position.
4. Place knife under prongs of fork with the handle pointed at 2 o'clock position with sharp edge toward you.
5. Remove third plate and place on top of second plate. Repeat procedure.
6. Using four plates as a maximum, place first plate on top of stack.

Serving Beverages

Coffee

1. Pick up empty coffee cups and saucers from storage area or sidestands and place on right side of guest with handle at 45-degree angle to guest's right.
2. Place all cups and saucers on table before pouring coffee.
3. Obtain coffee pot from sidestands or kitchen.
4. Pour coffee gently so as not to spill.
5. Never remove cup and saucer from table to pour. If necessary, slide cup and saucer closer to you for easy reach. Always carry cup and saucer as a unit—never separately .

Note: Coffee is a very hot beverage. Handle with extreme care so as not to burn anyone—guests or yourself. Carry hot coffee pots in your hands—not on a hand-held tray. It is more dangerous to remove a cup and saucer from the table to fill/refill with hot coffee than it is to move the cup and saucer closer to you while leaving it on the table to fill or refill the cup.

Tea (Pot Service)

1. Brew tea per operation's standard in pot. *Only use a pot designated for tea,* as pots that have been previously used for coffee impart an awful flavor to the tea. Infuse tea for specified

time—do not infuse for too long as bitter (high tannin content) tea will result.

2. Discard tea that has been exposed to air every 10 minutes.

3. Using a thermal carafe and minimizing exposure to oxygen will keep tea from tasting bitter and will last 30 minutes or more.

4. If thermal carafe is used, heat glass lining with hot water considerably before infusing the tea, and close lid tightly.

5. The above technique is far superior to filling the thermal carafe with hot water and then allowing a server or the guest to brew her own tea.

Note: Tea brewed with lukewarm water is not worthy of being served to anyone!

Tea (Hot—Individual Service)

1. Pick up empty cups and saucers from side stands and place on right side of guest with handle at 45-degree angle to guest's right.

2. Pick up silver or stainless teapot (short covered pot as compared to thin pot used for individual coffee service).

3. Rinse with hot water to warm up the pot. Pour out water.

4. Refill with hot water and place on tray with tea bag or loose tea infuser (either filled with loose tea or empty—depending upon the operation's standard).

5. Carry into dining room and place on appropriate underliner with doily.

6. Before serving guest, float infuser or tea bag in hot water with string or infuser handle/chain visible to the guest.

7. Serve guest from right and place pot to the right of the cup.

Note: Cup and saucer should already be in place on the table. Do not brew tea with lukewarm water.

Powdered Hot Beverages (Instant Coffee, Cereal Beverages, and Portion-Pack Service)

1. Pick up empty cups and saucers from side stands and place on right side of guest with handle at 45-degree angle to guest's right.

2. Pick up individual service pot.

3. Rinse pot as with tea.

4. Pour contents of package into pot and refill with hot water.

5. Carry into dining room and place on appropriate underliner with doily
6. Serve on guest's right, to right of the cup and saucer.

Note: Cup and saucer should already be in place on the table.

Presenting the Check

1. At a reasonable time after cordials or coffee, tally guest check and ensure it's correct—circle or rewrite the total. Then place guest check in guest check folder, on tip tray or plate face down—top with mints, chocolate, and/or guest comment card (per operating standard).
2. Present check to host by placing on table on host's left side.
3. Take guest's money or credit card to cashier or process payment *away from the guests' table* (cash, personal checks, gift certificates, coupons, and so forth) per operating standard.
4. Return change, card, and Record of Charge (ROC) on tip tray or plate with pen for signature (if card or card receipt).
5. If credit card is used, write type of card on check and ask guest to *sign guest check* as well as ROC.

Serving the Menu

Cocktails (See bar garnishes as server will garnish cocktails.)

Decanter Service (Note: Cocktails served in decanters will be specifically designated.)

1. Obtain wine or spirit from bartender in decanter.
2. Place filled decanter on tray or on ice in supreme dish.
3. Bring empty wine, sherry, or cocktail glass and cocktail napkin. From the right side of the guest, place napkin with logo facing the guest.
4. Place cocktail glass on napkin centered in the cover.
5. Place supreme dish down on table (just outside knife on right).
6. Remove water from bottom of decanter by circling the rim of the supreme dish with the bottom of decanter.
7. Pour spirit into glass and replace decanter in supreme dish or on the table.

All Other Cocktails, Mocktails, or Beverages

1. From the right side, place napkin in center of the cover with crest/logo facing the guest.
2. Grasping the glass by the base or stem, place full glass on cocktail napkin in the center of the cover. Use a clean napkin for each service of a beverage—use a fresh napkin for each round.

Note: Empty glasses should be removed from the right. A glass should never be reused unless the glass never leaves the table and is refilled at the guest's table as with coffee or iced tea.

Appetizers and Soups:

Fruit Juices/Fruit Cups

1. Place order on tray with cloth on tray.
2. Do not place on **underliner** until ready to place in front of guest.
3. Get underliner from kitchen, side, or tray stand.
4. Place juice or fruit cup on underliner with doily and place in center of cover.
5. If garnish is required (i.e., lemon or lime wedge for tomato juice), spear wedge with cocktail fork and place on right side of underliner with handle of fork at 45-degree angle.

Fresh Melon (honeydew, cantaloupe, papaya, casaba, etc.)

FIGURE 9–25

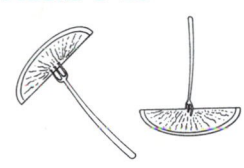

1. Place melon in a **monkey dish**.
2. Bring underliner for each melon. Do not place on underliner until *ready to serve*, but serve on underliner.
3. Spear lemon or lime wedge with cocktail fork and place on right side of underliner with handle of fork at 45-degree angle.
4. Cantaloupe does not usually require a lemon wedge.

Soup, Plate and Informal Service

1. Ladle soup into heated bowl or cup in kitchen. (A pitcher may be used for larger parties.)
2. Bring sufficient amount of soup crackers for each order.
3. Cover cup with saucer and bowl with underliner (heat retention, spillage). Bring additional underliners for guest service.
4. Remove underliner covers in dining room and replace with clean saucers or underliners and serve in center of cover.
5. Organize your tray with all required items before pouring soup.

Soup, Formal Service

1. Ladle soup into heated silver soup cup.
2. Cover with fitted silver lid.
3. Before service, place silver soup cup in heated soup bowl on an underliner with doily.
4. Set the three items in center of cover, remove lid, and pour soup into bowl by tilting cup away from the guest.

Note: Organize your tray with all required items before ladling soup for service.

Consommé

1. Ladle soup into double-handled cup (silver) cover with lid.
2. Place on underliner with doily.
3. Serve in center of cover. Remove lid.

Note: If soup is served in cups with handles, the handles should be on the guest's left and right not front and back. If one handle only, handle should be on guest's left side.

Shrimp Cocktail

1. Pick up order of shrimp cocktail from pantry or kitchen.
2. Place on tray.
3. Spear lemon wedge with cocktail fork and place on right side of underliner (see Figure 9–25 for accepted method of spearing lemon wedge on p. 209).
4. Place on underliner and serve in center of cover.

Other Menu Items, Plate Service Using Large Trays

1. Pick up plated entrée with vegetables (on plate) from main range (grill). Pick up steak knives for each person eating steak or chop.
2. Cover plates with heated metal cover. Stack if required.
3. Place on large tray and carry tray into dining room.
4. Place on tray stand, uncover, and serve from left.
5. Place plate in center of cover with main item on right side.
6. Whenever possible, all guests at a table should be served simultaneously. Minimize serving two separate tables simultaneously in formal dining environments.
7. Serving multiple tables all together in an informal, casual dining environment is acceptable.

Sauces

1. Place **gooseneck** or sauceboat on an underliner.
2. From the **left side** of the guest, spoon or ladle sauce overlapping item (i.e., seafood) and carrier (i.e., rice).
3. **Do not pour from a gooseneck**.

Perhaps the most critical phase in any à la carte food service establishment is the point where the server places the order with the expediter, annunciator, or cook at the range. The server is the best person to time the guest and the pace with which the guest wants to eat the meal or to be served. Server call systems somewhat defeat this idea unless the server knows exactly how long the most time-consuming item (of one table's order) takes to prepare. The server should then place the order when he knows when it should be served to the guest in proper time sequence. Using this method, the kitchen can begin preparation of the items for a table's order at its best pace knowing that the server has timed the placement of the hot food order. If a menu item takes a particularly long time to prepare (e.g. duck from a raw state, boiled or steamed lobster, and so forth), the server can place the order immediately after taking it, knowing that the guest will be ready to eat before it can be prepared in the kitchen or grill.

Each restaurant, especially casual-theme restaurants where speed of service is essential, should design a quality speed standard for the greeting and the service of the menu. For example, several casual-theme restaurants use two minutes as a maximum time from seating until server greeting. Using a modified Gantt chart (Figure 8–3) by plotting a service activity or task against a time line, the operator can specify a standard for service. How long before first round of beverages is served? How long before appetizers are served? Main course? Dessert? Table reset for guest turnover?

Proper server and production staff behavior in the kitchen is essential to a smooth-running operation. A server who argues in the kitchen makes everyone's job more difficult. Any server who botches the order, writes illegibly, picks up another's order, or otherwise confuses the system increases conflict and thereby decreases everyone's productivity. Servers should be empowered to ask the kitchen for items exactly as the guests ordered. If a mistake is made, the kitchen staff should correct the mistake without argument. If discrepancies arise, the arbitration should be resolved quickly, perhaps between the dining room and kitchen managers because the guest is waiting. Guest service extends to the production staff since **production is serving the server who is serving the guest**.

The *five-minute procedure* may allow the range more time to sequence orders and preparation while ensuring an ample supply of the menu items available for service. The server places all food orders immediately after taking the order from the guest, but the range does not begin final preparation until the server gives the five-minute warning. At that time, the range personnel will begin final preparation for the food or menu items to be served at a particular table. This system allows the range more time to sequence the orders and the preparation, and also ensures that there is an ample supply of the particular menu item before the server may return to the dining room. Additionally, there is more lead time to inform other service personnel of outages before the range is, in fact, out!

Another similar system for à la carte restaurants does away with the five-minute warning, and presenting the check or requisition at the range is synonymous with the five-minute warning. The above system requires that the server be more aware of the time it takes to prepare certain items.

If boiled lobster is to be served at the same table where a fillet of sole will be served, timing must reflect the span required to boil the lobster. In any case, the length of preparation time for each menu item must be communicated by the chef to all service personnel. This system also places more hardship on the range personnel, as they may have no idea about how many of any menu item is going to be needed until it is ordered.

If many of the menu items are prepared in advance (i.e., stew, roasts, lasagne, etc.), the five-minute warning system is unnecessary. Whatever system is adopted, it must be followed by all personnel. In large establishments with extensive menus, menu items may need to be picked-up at various stations in the kitchen. Expediters are essential to direct the flow, and they serve as a go-between between service and production.

Serving Various Menu Items

Mixed Hors d'Oeuvres (Antipasto), Cocktail Party, Cart or Platter Service

- Roll cart to guest's table. Get hors d'oeuvres plate from supply, side stand, or from the cart. Fill plate according to guest's instructions while holding it on the cart and serve plate from the left in the center of the cover.
- If serving guest from platter, hold platter in left hand and fill guest's plate directly in front of the guest.
- If serving guests at a cocktail party (i.e., standing), simply offer individual hors d'oeuvres to the guests. Servers must know what it is they are serving and a general idea of how the hors d'oeuvres are prepared. Have a supply of cocktail napkins handy.

Steak Tartare.   Served with Worcestershire sauce, Tabasco, salt, pepper, party rye, cooked, sieved egg yolk, minced onion, and capers.

- Roll cart to guest's table and present ingredients (not mixed) to guest. Combine ground meat with Worcestershire sauce, Tabasco, salt, and pepper in a mixing bowl. Then portion steak tartare mixture onto plates and garnish plate with party rye slices (or other crackers); cooked, sieved egg yolks; fresh, minced onions; capers; and fresh, minced parsley. Serve with an extra knife (butter) when serving steak tartare. *Note:* because of recent incidents with foodborne illness, particularly E. coli, steak tartare is a dangerous item to serve in a restaurant.

Caviar.   Serve in original tin buried in crushed ice in a silver glass or bowl. Serve with tongue depressor (preferable) or dessert spoon on the hors d'oeuvres plate or fish plate. Accompaniments to caviar include:

- Thin pancakes (blintzes) or hot toasts and thin slices of crustless brown bread, lemon, and chopped egg.
- Fresh pepper from a mill. Place a small butter knife to the right of the plate and finger bowl to left and above the cover.

Raw Oysters or Clams.   Serve in individual dishes (6 or 12 per order usually), which are placed in or atop crushed ice or sea salt. Place oyster fork on the extreme right of the silverware on the right, or if served as an à la carte order, place oyster fork to the right of silverware or on the plate per the operation's standard. Accompaniments to oyster service include (a) Crackers, vinegars, cocktail sauce, Tabasco, and horseradish; (b) Pepper mill; (c) Vodka.

Smoked Salmon or Lox.   Thin slices of salmon are served on bread (usually dark or rye). Usually served with fresh onion either sliced in rings or diced. Sometimes (for breakfast) served with cream cheese. Fresh pepper in a mill is essential to offer with smoked salmon or lox.

Snails (Escargot).   Often served in fitted dishes with snail clamps on the left of the cover and a cream soup spoon and an escargot fork on the underliner 45 degrees to guest's right or preset at right of spoon.
Note: Sanitation laws may prohibit the use of the actual snail shell. Alternatives are to place snail meat only in the fitted dish or use ceramic (china) cups that are made to look like shells or a china crock with indentations for the snail meat.

Melon.   Preset silverware for melon on table after taking the order. Serve melon on plate on top of service of show plate or on table per the operation's standard. The bottom of melon should be sliced so that melon does not rock on the plate (1). For formal service, the server or pantry worker should cut the melon at the rind from tip to tip (2), slicing the meat away from the rind. Then cut from tip to tip (3) with the knife perpendicular to the first cut. Then cut across the second cut (4) to resemble a checkerboard and alternate cubes of melon (see Figure 9–26). Offer pour-type salt shaker.

Grapefruit.   Serve in monkey dish on underliner with grapefruit teaspoon along right side. Individual grapefruit sections should be cut. Do not cut around the grapefruit, as this severs the section membrane from the rind and makes it most difficult to take the meat out. Pour-type salt shaker recommended.

Salads.   For formal service, salad should be served on china or glass plates. In an informal or casual environment they may be served in

FIGURE 9–26

How to cut a melon slice. Cut along dotted lines in order listed.

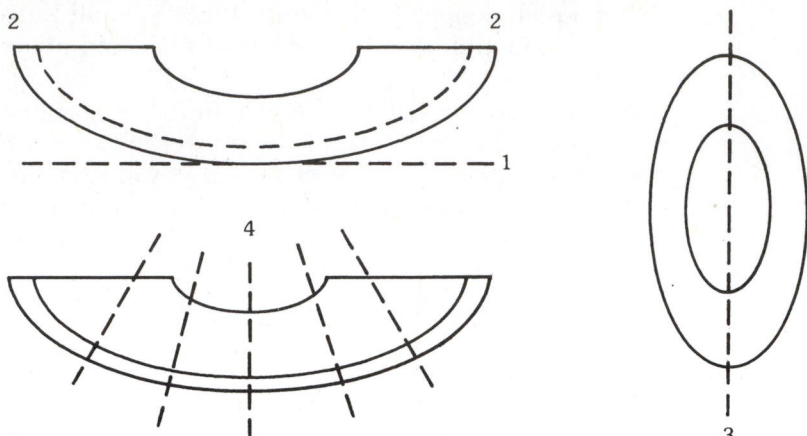

salad bowls. In a classical setting, salad is served in the center of the cover after the main course. Chilled salad forks may be offered with the salad course—a nice touch for formal service.

Desserts.   The dessert (entremet setting) spoon and fork should be moved from the horizontal setting to the vertical if they have been placed above the cover (entremet setting). Roll dessert cart to guest's table, or present dessert on (silver) tray. Plate the dessert in front of the guest per guest's instructions. Dessert knives should not be preset, but should be placed when serving dessert. Pies or cakes that will stand upright on their own should be served with the point facing the guest, and torts or cakes that will not stand on their own should be presented with the slope facing the guest.

Cheese.   Clear the table except for wine and wine glasses (red wine). Place a small clean plate and a small clean knife and fork at the guest's cover and bring fresh bread if required. Present the cheese on a platter, cheeseboard, or cart to each guest. Cut the pieces the guest desires using a cheese knife (tipped with two prongs) for cutting and placing the cheese on the plate. A flat cheese slicer may be used if guests are serving themselves.

Fresh Fruit.   Place a plate in front of the guest in the center of the cover, and place a fruit knife (steak knife) and fruit fork (dinner fork) crossed at the top of the plate with the tip of the knife in the prongs of the fork, both handles 45 degrees to the guest's right. Working from the left side of the guest, present the fruit (in a basket or silver platter) from the left, and allow the guest to serve himself or serve per the guest's desires. Grapes may be cut with scissors and then placed on the guest's plate by regripping small bunches with scissor blades. A finger bowl (with warm water and a lemon slice) should be placed to the left, slightly above the cover as this is a necessary accompaniment when fruit is served since it is eaten with the fingers.

Coffee (Formal Service). Clear and crumb before serving coffee, especially when serving coffee as a course after dessert. Place a coffee cup with saucer on a larger plate directly in front of the guest in the center of the cover. Angle the cup handle 45 degrees to the guest's right. Place a spoon on the underliner (not the saucer). Offer each guest coffee inquiring how he or she would like it. On a tray have sufficient coffee, cream, sugar cubes, and sugar tongs. To fill the coffee cup serving from right with service on left arm, (a) lower the whole service to the level of the table; (b) lower the coffee pot above the cup; (c) tilt the coffee pot without lifting it off the silver tray; (d) do likewise with the cream pitcher; and (e) serve sugar per guest's request.

Tips for Good Service

In addition to knowing the proper service for specific foods, the manager must know what constitutes proper behavior for the dining room staff. The recommendations listed are for an elegant dining room, and the individual manager should delete some of the rules if her establishment is less formal. Yet certain practices should be followed, as they relate to sanitation, safety, and etiquette, rather than formal, casual, or informal service.

- Never stand around in groups—stay at your station.
- Always greet your guests with a smile!
- Avoid conversations with other staff.
- Do not give loud orders.
- Never argue with anyone, especially a guest.
- Service cloth rules:
    - *a.* Don't mop your face.
    - *b.* Never carry under your arm.
    - *c.* Take a clean one once in a while.

    d. Never wipe silverware or glassware with a service towel in front of a guest.

    e. Use a clean, sanitary towel to polish silver or glassware before opening.

- Never put towel in your pocket, on your shoulder, or in your belt or waistband.

- Don't lean on chairs; don't put your foot on a chair rung or bend your knees to hear a guest. Stand erect or bend from the waist to hear.

- If you spill something on a guest, apologize, clean up the spill, and advise your supervisor.

- Talk only as necessary for politeness. In casual-theme restaurants, the server's personality may be encouraged to shine through.

- Don't smoke in areas where not allowed and never during the serving period or in any guest's view.

- Don't holler in the kitchen.

- Never use bad language.

- Take guest complaints to your supervisor if you feel uncomfortable and disempowered to handle the complaint.

- Say "thank you" when tipped, regardless of the amount tendered.

- Don't count money or jingle coins in pockets.

- *Never* hurry your guests

- Never eat during service.

- Don't carry pencils, books, etc., where visible, i.e., in pocket, behind ears, etc.

- Carry menus in your hands, not under arms or in pants, shirt, or jacket.

- Don't lean on walls or side stands.

- Don't put hands in pockets or on hips.

- Don't cross arms in front of chest.

- Don't add or write out checks or count out change in view of any guests.

- Don't complain about food to kitchen in general. Tell your supervisor unless a menu item needs to be corrected for a guest waiting to be served, and you are empowered to do so.

- Don't point in the dining room or gesture at a table. When necessary and required, use open palm and arm to point/direct.

- Always be courteous.

- Walk briskly, but never run.
- Don't walk briskly when leading groups to their seats.

Conclusion

A good server, and in turn a good manager, should be constantly on watch, looking for certain things in order to give good service. The following checklist can serve as a recapitulation of this chapter and includes portions of other important chapters related to serving the guest.

A Server's Checklist

In order to give good service, follow side duty assignments (opening and closing duties as assigned by host).

- Follow the order of service.
- Follow operational procedures.
- Condiments to accompany items before guest needs to ask.
- Water glasses full.
- Bread and butter supply adequate.

- Trays with soiled dishes cleared frequently.
- Serve food the way *each guest* ordered it (i.e., get the order right).
- Help the guest(s) order if he/she needs assistance with menu selection.
- All unnecessary silverware, glassware, dishes removed.
- Refill wine glasses frequently (half full for white and quarter full for red).
- Order more cocktails or wine if guest desires (i.e., ask if guest needs a refill).
- Check buffet table for food, appearance, and heat.
- Continue to follow up with service, but do not "bug" the guest.
- **Smile**.

Questions

1. List several important functions of the server, the dining room attendant, and the captain.

2. Where might one find a standardized listing of service tasks not covered in this text?

3. What is the preferred method of setting the butter knife on the butter plate?

4. Draw two ways to preset three wine glasses, and two ways to preset four wine glasses at a table.

5. List 10 (only) entries in the order of service in proper sequence.

6. Explain how to
   a. Carry hot plates with a service cloth.
   b. Change a table linen properly.
   c. Stack six plates (with covers) on a large tray for serving in the dining room.
   d. Load a tray with soiled china, glassware, and silverware.

7. What is the advantage(s) of a five-minute warning system for an à la carte restaurant? What is the disadvantage of a server call system?

8. How should the following menu items be served?

   a. Hors d'oeuvres.

   b. Melon (include method for cutting a slice of melon).

   c. Snails (escargot).

9. List 10 Tips for Good Service.

10. The local chapter of the *Chaine de Rotisseur* (an international gourmet group) is having their annual Christmas dinner in your hotel. Since you have been trained in service, the general manager has asked you to be the service coordinator/director for this very special event. The function sheet has called for a head table to seat 14 honor guests and 10 rounds with 10 covers each. The menu is as follows:

Lillet

Poached Eggs in Wine-Aspic, Mayonnaise Sauce

Beef Consommé "Carmen"

Chardonnay

Small Rock Lobster Tails, Lemon Butter

Champagne Sherbet

Santenay 1961

Medallions of Veal with Madeira Burgundy Sauce

Braised Leeks-Tangerine Rice   Artichoke Hearts Vinaigrette

Brie and Fruit

Moet et Chandon

Patisserie

Café

Napoleon V.S.O.P.

A. Per place setting, how many of the following silverware utensils would you requisition from the steward? Use zeros if you do not need an item. Blanks will not be considered correct.

dinner knife	cocktail or seafood forks	
dinner forks	dessert forks	
salad forks	lobster pliers	teaspoons

escargot pliers   steak knives   soup spoons

butter knives   lobster pick

B. Using the bottom line as the table's edge, draw (silverware only) one place setting according to the standards of etiquette for the *Chaine de Rotisseur* Dinner.

C. Should you bring refrigerated forks for the artichoke hearts?

  1. Yes   2. No

D. Which soup spoon should you set?

  1.   A round spoon?

  2.   An oblong spoon?

A. ○   B. ○

FIGURE 9–27

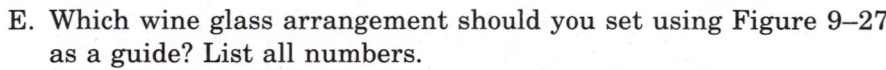

E. Which wine glass arrangement should you set using Figure 9–27 as a guide? List all numbers.

Endnotes

1. *The Waldorf-Astoria Manuals,* 111. (Stamford, CN.: Dahl Publishing Company, 1949), pp. 10–11.

2. *Tasks to Jobs* (Geneva, Switzerland: The International Labor Organization, 1979).

Additional Readings and References

Axler, B., and C. Litrides, *Food and Beverage Service*. New York: John Wiley & Sons. 1990.

Bickel, W. trans. *Hering's Dictionary of Classical and Modern Cookery*. Giessen, Germany: Fachbuchverlag Dr. Pfanneberg & Co, 1974.

Durocher, J., and R. J. Goodman, Jr. *The Essentials of Tableside Cookery*. Ithaca, NY: The Cornell Hotel and Restaurant Administration Quarterly.

The Essentials of Good Table Service. Ithaca, NY: The Cornell Hotel and Restaurant Administration Quarterly, 1975.

Meyer, S., E. Schmid, and C. Spuhler. *Professional Table Service*. Translated by Heinz Holtmann. New York: Van Nostrand Reinhold. 1991.

Tsuji, S. *Professional Restaurant Service, Ecole Technique Hoteliere Tsuji*. (in English) New York: John Wiley & Sons. 1991.

The Waldorf-Astoria Manuals, vol. 111. Stamford, Conn.: Dahl Publishing Company, 1949.

Wine and Beverage Service

Chapter Outline

Learning Objectives

After studying this chapter, the student will be able to . . .

1. List the major wine-producing countries of the world.
2. Classify wines according to origin, use, and general category.
3. Outline the order of wine presentation with typical meal service.
4. Recommend the basic equipment required for the service of wine.
5. Describe the procedure for decanting wine.
6. Describe procedure and demonstrate the service of red wine, white wine, and sparkling wine.
7. Outline the method for pricing wines.
8. List the types of distilled spirits available in a bar operation.

9. Describe the ways in which distilled spirits may be served with popular drink ingredients and garnishes.

10. Define liqueurs and cordials.

11. Differentiate between beer and ale.

12. Discuss the critical factors in determining the quality of beer.

Key Words/Phrases

Distilled beverage spirits
"White goods"
Vitis Vinifera
Vitis Labrusca
Appellation Controlee
Denominazione Di Origin Controllata
  (DOC)
Chaptalization
Residual sugar
Qualitatswein mit Pradikat
Aperitif
Aromatized or fortified wines
White table wine
Red table wine
Rose or blush wine
Serving temperature
Sparkling wine
Champagne method
Charmat method
Disgorge
Dosage
Vintage
Dessert wine
Wine steward
Tasting cup

Corkscrew
Serving basket
Decanter
Wine bucket
Champagne tulip glass
Cordial or pony glass
Brandy snifter or inhaler
All-purpose glass
Re-corker
Mark-up
Split
Mixed drinks
Highballs
On-the-rocks
Bar garnishes
Call liquor
Jigger
Shaker
Shot
Swizzle stick
Strainer
House well
Liqueur or cordial
Draught beer
Microbrewery

The study of wines continues to fascinate interest many people, and the consumption of wine has remained consistent during the last decade. This trend is especially delightful for the restaurateur or hotelier since **distilled**

beverage spirits have experienced some decline, and wine sales can add immensely to an operation's profit picture. As discussed in Chapter 7, wine is a plus sale when nothing else can be sold at that particular time. It is no wonder that a food service operator enjoys the trend of increased wine consumption. Larger market segments have moved away from the traditional pattern of hard drinking to more moderate and more varied. More people are drinking, and they are drinking a greater variety of alcoholic beverages, particularly wines and **white goods** (i.e., vodkas, rums, gins, and tequilas). The sale of hard spirits is more profitable for the restaurant operator. Beverage pouring (hard liquor) costs run between 15 and 25 percent, whereas wine may run in the 50 percent cost range. Since wine is much easier to handle and to dispense, an operator should look at his dollar profit rather than simply percentages in order to determine profit and give consideration for the plus-sale phenomenon.

Wine and Wine Service

The study of wines is complex with many texts, reference books, periodicals, and computer software covering the vast subject of the study of wines. The restaurant operator should know something about wines in general and should know about wines from many of the countries that are producing more and more wine, such as countries from the former Soviet Union (the country of Georgia in particular), South America, and Australia. Restaurateurs should expand their knowledge of wines not from one country alone, but from many of the countries that produce wines for export. It is beyond the scope of this text to present a course in the study of wines, but some mention of the product is interesting, useful, and essential for profitability and for service training.

The Classification of Wines

What is wine? Classically speaking, wine is fermented grape juice. Wine is classified by (1) the country in which the wine was produced, (2) its intended use, and (3) general category. There are several major wine-producing countries, and many other countries that produce wines that perhaps are not known as wine producers in the United States.

① country
② intended use
③ general category

By Country

The United States is a major wine-producing country, and the states in the United States that produce wines for national (and some international) distribution are California and New York, Washington state, and Oregon. Ohio, Maryland, and many other states also produce wines that are distributed nationally, but these wines are not as well known as the wines from California, Washington state, or New York. Several other states (more than forty) have vineyards and wineries, but the production from those wineries is usually distributed locally through retail sales at the winery store. The United States produces more varieties of wine than any other country in the world.[1]

California has several wine-producing regions with most California wines considered as premium wines. Although there are several large, commercial wineries in California, many of these wineries have begun to produce higher quality varietal wines, which are now being considered by some as premium wines. California has numerous wineries ranging from the large, commercial types to the small, boutique wineries that may produce only a few varieties. Many times these small wineries produce wines from vineyards from separate growers and limit the distribution of their products only to local markets.

New York state has also begun producing several premium wines, but these wines are not readily available nationwide and are generally reserved for local and regional consumption. New York produces several commercial wines that are available nationally, and New York sparkling wines enjoy a very good reputation. New York boasts among the oldest regions in the United States for producing wine commercially. Grapes grown in California are of the same type as the grapes grown in Europe—**_Vitis Vinifera_**—and hence are considered premium wines. Native New York grapes are of the **_Vitis Labrusca_** variety and have a very definite grapy or fruity flavor—much like Welch's Grape Juice. Nonetheless, New York wineries have introduced more *Vinifera* varieties within the last several years.

Washington state now has over 10,000 acres under cultivation for wine grapes, making it the second largest wine-producing region in the United States. Washington produces premium wines from the *Vitis Vinifera* variety, and most of these wines are produced in the Colombia Valley, which shares the same latitude as the most notable regions in France. Chateau Ste. Michelle wines dominate the offerings in restaurants for Washington state wines.

France, generally regarded as the leading wine-producing country in the world, produces an enormous variety of wine. French wine is controlled by a government agency, **_Appellation Controlee_,** which guarantees its authenticity if not its quality. Most of the French wine sold in the United States is appellation controlee wine, and most restaurants offer only French

Figure 10–1

Standard shapes of bottles used in bottling wines.

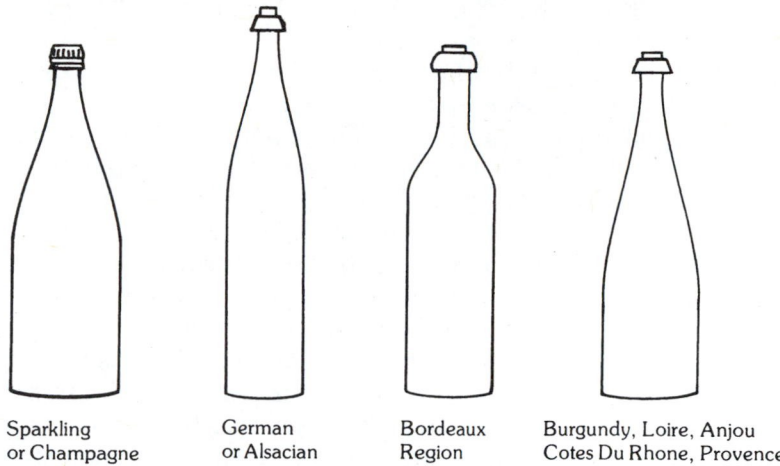

| Sparkling or Champagne | German or Alsacian | Bordeaux Region | Burgundy, Loire, Anjou Cotes Du Rhone, Provence |

appellation controlee wine, which dominates the market. French wine is *[region]* usually named for the producing region (e.g., Burgundy, Loire, Bordeaux, Champagne, etc.), which is the generic name. The French have also *[variety]* named their wines from the grape variety (Chardonnay, Pinot Noir, Cabernet Savignon, etc.), which is the varietal name. The wines from France are produced in the regions of Bordeaux, Burgundy, Champagne, Cognac, Alsace, Loire Valley, Rhone Valley, Armagnac, and Provence. Each of these regions is further broken down into the various districts (e.g., Graves, Beaujolais, etc.) and even further into communes, villages (e.g., Chablis, etc.), and then the vineyard proper. Generally the more specific the naming (i. e., "Les Saint-Georges, from Nuit Saint Georges in Burgundy" as compared to just "Burgundy") the better the wine. When the region appears between the words appellation and controlee, the production of the wine has been controlled more closely, and therefore the wine is apt to be of a higher quality. Usually the more specific the area designated between the two words (i.e., a village versus a district such as Medoc versus Bordeaux), the better the wine.

Italy produces the largest quantity of wine (in gallons) than any other country in the world, and Italians consume more wine per capita than in any other country. The United States imports more wine from Italy than from any other single country, yet the typical American knows little about Italian wines. The Italian government's controlling agency, ***Denominazione Di Origin Controllata* (DOC),** has helped increase the popularity of Italian wine in the United States, since quality is more consistent with price. Italian importers market Italian wines vigorously, and

[handwritten margin notes: "more specific / more better", "Italy highest producing / highest consumption", "DOC –"]

excellent values of quality wines are available from Italy. Chianti is among the most popular Italian wines for restaurant consumption in the United States. The Italian wines are divided into 22 wine-producing regions, which are not well known in the United States. Italian wine is more easily recognized by the name of the wine than by the regions. Popular Italian white wines include Pinot Grigio, Soave, Est Est Est, and Verdicchio. Popular Italian red wines include Chianti, Barolo, Gattinara, Bardolino, Barbera, and Valpolicella. Italy produces two wines worthy of note—Marsala, which is a fortified (greater than 14 percent alcohol by volume) wine similar in taste to a sherry, and Asti Spumante, a sparkling wine that is similar to champagne, produced in the Asti region. It is slightly more bittersweet than champagne and makes a delightful accompaniment to dessert.

The wines of Germany are delightful for sipping, and since they are generally mild and some very slightly sweet, they appeal to the American palate. German wines can be sold easily in many food-service establishments. Since they are moderately priced, as compared to the French, they therefore may find great popularity in commercial and family-type restaurants. German wines are divided into two major areas: the Rhine and the Mosel. Rhine wines are bottled in brown or dark amber bottles, which are taller and thinner than the standard French wines, but identical in *shape* to those from the Alsace region in France (see Figure 10–1). Some wine experts feel that the wines from the Rhine (e.g., Liebfraumilch) are good wines to complement food, but they do not feel that Rhine wine has the charm that is found in the Mosel wines from Germany or the white wines from France. Mosel wines are slightly fruity, very light, and are superb either with or without food. Mosel wines come in green bottles and the bottles are identical in *shape* and *color* to those from Alsace. German wines are very closely regulated. Due to poor sugar production in the grape as a result of diminished sun, sugar is added to aid the fermentation process (termed **chaptalization**). Chaptalization must be closely controlled so that producers may not illegally alter the wine—sugar can be added only *prior to fermentation* and must be completely converted to alcohol during fermentation. **Residual sugar** (after fermentation) is forbidden for chaptalized wines.

While French wines are graded on location (i.e., what vineyard produced the grapes), German (**Qualitatswein mit Pradikat** or quality wine with predicate) wines are graded on when the grapes were picked:

Kabinett—is the driest of the Qualitatswein.

Auslese—select picking (picking the best grapes).

Spatlese—late picking (the longer the grower waits to pick the grape, the more desirable the wine is considered).

Beerenauslese—grape that has been attacked by the "noble rot" or *Pourriture Noble* (a fungus) that makes the wine sweet.

Trochenbeerenauslese—a select picking of grapes that have been attacked by the noble rot.

— Eiswein (ice wine)—from grapes picked on the day of the first frost. This yields a very concentrated grape juice.

Each Qualitatswein has a coded control number on the label that tells the area the wine came from (first digit), the shipper or grower (next three digits), the cask number submitted for sample (digits five, six, and seven), and the date the particular wine was submitted for sample. Tafelwein is ordinary table wine and is usually not exported.

Tafel wein
Table wine

Other countries produce some very fine wines; however, the general use of these wines, with the exception of Spanish and Portuguese wines and, more recently, South American (Chile and Argentina) and Australian wines, is limited. South Africa, Austria, and Switzerland produce wines, but these wines are not widely distributed outside the growing region since they are consumed by locals.

By Use

Although most wine is used for drinking (i.e., table wine), wine can also be used for cooking and as a marinade; for celebrating various occasions such as weddings, toasts, christening ships, communion in church; for medicinal purposes; for flavoring; as a beauty aid; and for flavoring tobacco.

By General Category

Wine is categorized by general category or what the wine is. Wine complements certain foods, and food complements certain wines. A simple table pairs wine and food. The guest's preference, whatever he chooses to drink, is the correct wine to serve:

Food and Wine.   The following are in order of presentation in the meal.

Food	Wine
Canapes, hors d'oeuvres, cheese, crackers, relishes	Sherry (dry or cocktail), Champagne, Madeira
Soup	Sherry (dry or cocktail)
Fish	Dry white wine
Dark or fatty fish	Rose or light red
Fowl	Dry white, rose, or light red
Meat	Red or rose
Nuts, desserts, fruit, cakes	Tokay, Port, sweet or cream sherry, or Muscatel, Champagne
Cheese	Rich red wine

Appetizer (or **aperitif**) wines are sometimes called **aromatized or fortified wines** because of the additional ingredients added for flavoring and the additional alcohol (18 percent to 22 percent alcohol by volume), which is added to stabilize the wine. Drinking an aperitif is, classically speaking, the proper way to begin a meal, since the product is intended to sharpen the appetite. Since there is a higher profit margin in selling cocktails, restaurateurs do not aggressively promote the sale of appetizer wines. Since aperitifs are less expensive, they could be used to sell a banquet where the guest(s) might reject an open bar with beer or distilled spirits. Vermouth is a generic name, and it is the most common aperitif. The product ranges from the dry whites to the bittersweet reds. Dry or cocktail sherries are excellent appetizers, and the sweet or cream sherries *should not be served as appetizers* unless specifically requested by the guest. As with dessert wines and cordials, aperitif sales may be increased by merchandising the product by rolling a cart to the tableside with the wines displayed and offered to the guests.

Many other aperitifs are quite popular, and each has a common ingredient and characteristic—they taste bitter because of the added botanicals and quinine. Some of these are Dubonnet (red or blonde), which is produced in California from the original recipe; Lillet, St. Raphael, and Byrrh, which are imported French products; and Cynar and Campari imported from Italy. Cynar (pronounced che nar) is made from an artichoke base.

White table wines are usually served as accompaniments to fish and other seafood; light-meated fowl such as chicken, capon, or breast of turkey; or light meat such as veal or pork cutlets. White wines should be served chilled or approximately 50 degrees Fahrenheit (50° F) or 10 degrees centigrade (10° C). Some examples of white wines include generic, varietal, and proprietary names (named by the producer such as Blue Nun). Popular white wines include Chenin Blanc, Niersteiner Oldberg, Pinot Grigio, Bernkastel, Chablis, Sauternes, Chardonnay, Pouilly Fuisse, Pinot Blanc, Zeller Schwarze Katz, Rhine, Grey and Johannisberg Reisling, Liebfraumilch, Moselblumchen, Semillon, Montrachet, Soave, Verdicchio, White Chianti, Sauvignon Blanc, Sylvaner, Aurora, and Delaware.

Red table wines also include rose or blush wines. Very light red wines, such as the roses, blushes, Beaujolais, and Zinfandel may be served chilled, but most red wines are served cool or at cellar temperature—about 65 degrees (65° F) Fahrenheit or 18 degrees Celsius (18° C). While white wines outsell red wines generally, red wine consumption is gradually increasing its market share or percentage of the total from all wine consumed. This may result from its reputation as holding medicinal properties, not least of which is the reduction of cholesterol when red wine is consumed with high fat or red meat food products. Indeed, red wines are generally served to accompany red meats, dark-meated fowl, Italian or tomato dishes, or cheese or nuts. Some examples of red wine are Burgundy,

Bordeaux, Barbera, Bardolino, Barolo, Gattinara, Grignolino, Gamay, Beaujolais, Pinot Noir, Claret, Cabernet Sauvignon, Zinfandel, Chianti, Concord, Vino Rosso, Lambrusco, Brunello, Chateauneuf du Pape, Nemes Kadar, Petite Sirah, and Brouilly. Some **rose or blush wines** include white Zinfandel, Lancer's, Mateus, Tavel, Chateau St. Roseline, and Grenache Rose.

Sparkling wines can be served either as an appetizer wine, during the meal, or for dessert and should be served cold. As **serving temperature** is increased the solubility of a gas in a liquid decreases, which, if the wine is too warm, will produce an explosion and subsequent gushing upon opening the bottle of a **sparkling wine**.

Sparkling wines may go through a complicated production procedure (methode champenoise or **champagne method**), which, when combined with a higher tax than that of still wine, makes their total cost high. There are other processes to reduce the production costs considerably, namely the **Charmat** or bulk process method where the natural carbon dioxide (CO_2) is produced during the fermentation process in large vats instead of in the bottle. The sparkling wine is then bottled under pressure retaining the carbonation. Another carbonation process injects a still wine with carbon dioxide (CO_2) to make the still wine a sparkling wine.

The method champenoise or champagne method of producing sparkling wines is a long, slow process; however, the secret of champagne is the blending, not the method. Champagne grapes are pressed separately and blended later. Four pressings are standard: (1) vin de cuvee—finest of champagnes; (2) first tailles; (3) second taille; and (4) rebeche—used only for nonalcoholic beverages. The juice must be quickly separated from the skins, as the inside of the skin gives color to the wine. After the juice is placed in casks and then blended, a sugar/yeast mixture (cuvee) is added for the second fermentation where the (CO_2) gas (carbonation) is produced and the alcoholic content is increased. Capped bottles are placed in A-frame boards with the necks turned down. Each day the bottles are turned a quarter turn and tilted more neck down to loosen the sediment. All sediment will eventually collect at the cork, when the bottle is upside down vertically. The necks are then dipped in a cold brine solution, which freezes the sediment; the cork and with it the sediment is **disgorged**, and a **dosage** (another sugar/wine mixture) is added, which then determines the relative dryness of the champagne.

Type of Champagne	Percent of Sugar	Characteristic/Taste
Brut	.5–1.5 %	Very, very dry
Extra dry or extra sec	1.5–3.0	Fairly dry
Dry or sec	3.0–5.0	Sweet
Demi-sec	5.0–7.0	Quite sweet
Doux	7 or More	Very sweet

Sweet Champagnes are usually of lesser quality (sugar hides the imperfection) and are not found very often in the United States. **Vintage** champagne (85 percent of the grapes from the same year) is not necessarily of better quality, although vintages are declared only for exceptionally good years. **Vintage** champagne does have a distinctive character because it is not a blend.

[handwritten margin note: Vintage not a blend]

Sizes of Still Wine and Sparkling Wine Bottles

Miniature or Miniature (3.4 oz or 100 ml)

Split or small (6.3 oz. or 187 ml)

Tenth or medium (12.7 oz. or 375 m1)

Fifth or regular (25.4 oz or 750 ml)

Quart or large (33.8 oz. or 1. O liters [1,000 ml])

Magnum or magnum (50.7 oz or 1.5 liters)

Jeroboam or extra large (101.4 oz. or 3.0 liters)

Rehoboam (4.5 liters)

Methuselah (6. 0 liters)

Some examples of sparkling wines are Champagne (France), Pink Champagne, Cold Duck, Sparkling Burgundy, Sparkling Muscat, Asti Spumonte (Italy) or Spumonte, Sekt (Germany), and Mousseaux (France, from other than the Champagne region).

Dessert wines are served for or after dessert, and the distinguishing characteristic is that they are sweet. With the exception of Sauternes and late-harvest wines, most dessert wines are fortified. Dessert wines are not popular among restaurateurs; as with appetizer wines, they yield less profit than after-dinner cocktails, cordials, or brandies. With a deemphasis on alcohol consumption, the lower alcohol content (as compared to distilled spirits) of dessert wines may present an opportunity for restaurateurs to increase a check average while minimizing the risk of overserving alcohol. Dessert wines are usually served by the glass and chilled; and an excellent method of increasing dessert wine or cordial sales is to have a cart displaying the spirits rolled to the guests' table. Some examples include Port—red, tawny, or ruby; Muscatel—gold, red, and black; Black Muscat; Sherry—sweet or cream only; Angelica; Madeira; and Marsala.

Abbreviated Checklist for Service Personnel (Wines)

Wine complements certain foods and food complements certain wines. Yet the guest's preference, whatever he chooses to drink, is the correct wine to serve. Wine can also add to your tip.

Appetizer Wines.   Sometimes called aromatized or fortified wines. Vermouth (red or white), Sherry (dry only), Cynar, Lillet, Dubonnet (red or blonde), Campari, St. Raphael, Byrrh.

White Table Wines.   Usually served with seafood, light-meated fowl, chicken, etc. Serve at approximately 50 ° F. Chablis (dry), Chardonnay, Pinot Blanc, Rhine, Liebfraumilch, Semillon, Sauvignon Blanc, White Chianti, Light Muscat, Delaware, Niersteiner Oldberg, Pinot Grigio, Bernkastel, Sauternes, Pouilly Fuisse, Zeller Schwarze Katz, Grey and Johannisberg Reisling, Moselblumchen, Montrachet, Soave, Verdicchio, Sylvaner, Aurora.

Sparkling Wines.   Champagne can be served as an appetizer, during the meal, and with dessert. Serve cold. Champagne, Cold Duck, Sparkling Burgundy, Sparkling Muscat, Spumante, Asti Spumonte, Sekt, Mousseaux.

Red Table Wines.   Usually served for dark-meated fowl, red meats, Italian dishes, cheese, and nuts. Serve at approximately 65° F. Burgundy (dry), Barbera, Charbone, Gamay, Beaujolais, Bardolino, Barolo, Bordeaux, Brunello, Pinot Noir, Red Pinot, Claret (dry), Cabernet Sauvignon, Gattinara, Grignolino, Lambrusco, Zinfandel, Red Chianti (dry), Concord (sweet), Rose (dry to sweet), Vino Rosso (semisweet), Chateauneuf du Pape, Nemes Kadar, Petite Sirah, Brouilly.

Dessert Wines.   Generally served for dessert. Port (red, tawny, ruby), Muscatel (gold, red, black), Sherry (sweet or cream only), Black Muscat, Tokay, Angelica, Madeira, Marsala, Sauternes, or late harvest varietals.

Equipment and Glassware Used in Wine Service

In an elegant restaurant a **wine steward** (sommelier) and his or her assistants are responsible for the restaurant's wine cellar; this may include ordering wines, maintaining inventories, tasting new wines to accompany menu items, and ensuring that the wine is being handled and stored correctly. Additionally, the wine steward is fully aware of the wines in stock and should be most capable in discussing wines with restaurant guests. Wine in an elegant restaurant is a natural accompaniment to the meal; whereas in a medium-priced, theme restaurant, the wine list may not be extensive and those selling wines—captains and servers—need not be so aware of wines in general or of fine vintage wines. Indeed, even the opening of bottled wines is delegated to the bartender, and the ritual of

(i) host sip

having the host taste a small amount of wine before pouring for the entire table is ignored.

The wine steward may wear a chain around his neck with a **tasting cup** and key attached (actual key or symbolic key to the cellar). Most tasting cups are made of silver, aluminum, or other metal. This makes it difficult to see the clarity of the wine, and some cups have an arrangement of indentations (both convex and concave) in order to reflect light through the wine. The wine steward, upon opening the wine, sniffing and squeezing the cork, will pour a small amount for himself, swirl the wine, nose (smell) the wine, and taste it. He should then pour a small amount for the host who may do the same. Upon the host's approval, he should then pour for all guests at the table. (See wine service procedures.) As people drink more wine and become more knowledgeable about wine, they find wine that is more complex, more interesting, and more enjoyable. A wine just uncorked is more complex than a wine that has been allowed to breathe. Some guests may ask that a red wine be opened an hour or so before the wine is to be consumed. *New York* magazine conducted a blind test with several wine experts as the wine tasters with the following results. Wine that was opened and poured immediately was considered superior to wine that had been allowed to "breathe." The writers felt that the presumed improvement in the wine had little to do with the flavor of the wine and more to do with the fact that, by the time the wine had had an opportunity to breathe, the drinker's taste was impaired by the amount of alcohol consumed.

Corkscrews

Careful consideration must be given to selecting a **corkscrew** for opening wine with corks. If a corkscrew is not designed properly, the server, captain, or wine steward will have difficulty and will look clumsy in front of the guest. A "professional corkscrew" (see Figure 10–2) is the acceptable tool to use in the dining room, and it is the easiest to use with a little practice. The corkscrew must have a knife, and the knife blade should be *straight, not hooked*, to cut foil neatly below the bulge. The most recent addition to the professional corkscrew family substitutes two round metal pins with heads that resemble the head of a ¼-inch (0.7 mm) wide nail, but with sharp, filed edges (which substitute for the knife) that protrudes from the plastic frame/handle by a scant 0.2 mm—just enough to cut the foil. The lever should also be designed to remove bottle caps. More important, the lever must be relatively rigid. It must stay at any angle at which it is placed. A loose lever will flap on to the bottle's brim when the wine steward is trying to screw the worm into the cork, and this looks unprofessional or incompetent. The worm (borer or screw) should not have sharp edges, as this may cut the cork and thus prevent a smooth cork withdrawal. The point of the worm should follow the contour

FIGURE 10–2

Professional corkscrews

of the worm as with a helix. If it is a straight point, the corkscrew may pull through the cork and leave the cork in the bottle. Some screws have a small, smooth indentation on the outside of the screw, and this eases the task of drilling the screw into the cork. Indeed, some corkscrews are coated with Teflon, which also reduces friction easing the insertion of the worm into the cork. The portion of the lever that rests on the lip of the bottle should not have sharp edges. If the cork is stubborn, the glass may chip or crack before the cork can be removed. To minimize chipping the rim of the bottle, the wine server may depress the cork into the bottle just slightly (to break the seal) before inserting the corkscrew.

Corkscrews with wings (used to apply pressure on the lip in order to remove the cork) are absolutely not recommended for professional use. Corkscrews that look like the professional type, but with a bottle opener on the knife end, are not recommended either, since there is no knife to cut the foil, and there is already a bottle cap remover on the lever. The double-screw (double helix) corkscrew is minimally acceptable, but not recommended for restaurant use. The wooden-handle corkscrew, with an attachment that rests on the lip, is also minimally acceptable but not recommended for restaurant use. The two-pronged cork puller, which one wiggles down the side of the cork and then twists to pull the cork, is ideal for home use. The same tool can be used to reinsert the cork, and it does not damage the cork as the worm does. (This cork puller has been known as the dishonest butler). **One caution:** The prongs exert an outward force on the bottle and have been known to shatter the glass. To avoid this problem, wrap the top of the bottle with a napkin or service cloth before inserting the prongs into the bottle. The two-pronged cork pullers are not recommended for professional use at the table. It is a good idea to keep a two-pronged cork puller available for stubborn corks or those that may crumble with the insertion of the standard corkscrew. Cork removers that use air pressure or carbon dioxide (CO_2) are extremely dangerous. Still wine bottles are not stressed for pressure, and the bottle could explode if the cork is tight fitting and the bottle lacks integrity.

The Screwpull is a unique corkscrew with the helix coated with Teflon. It is inserted smoothly into the cork, and the plastic mechanism rests on the brim of the bottle. The worm is continuously twisted until the cork pulls itself out of the neck of the bottle. Screwpull has a pocket model as well as a sophisticated, one-step model that is excellent for banquet or preset functions.

Baskets

Although **serving baskets** are used for serving wine, this practice is not necessary or recommended. The basket serves two specific functions: (1) it is used to transport the wine (at approximately a 30-degree angle) from the cellar or wine storage area to the dining room, so as not to dislodge the sediment, and (2) it is used to hold the wine bottle for decanting. After decanting, the wine basket and empty bottle may be displayed on the guests' table. Baskets are made of wicker, silver/chrome covered wicker, or a decorative wrought-iron or silver/silverplated device that holds the wine bottle in a resting position with the neck slightly up.

Decanters

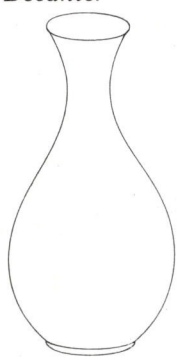

FIGURE 10–3
Decanter

The standard wide-mouthed (litre or half litre) carafe is ideal for serving wines by carafe, but should not be used for decanting fine wines. Fine wines should be decanted into plain (noncolored) **decanters** (Figure 10–3) and the decanters should not be cut glass, as this destroys the appearance of a clear wine.

Wine Buckets and Wine Stands

There are several different **wine buckets** on the market that are made of plastic, aluminum, stainless steel, and silver plate. Plastic (Lucite) or aluminum buckets are less expensive. Some silver wine buckets are quite heavy, especially when used with weighted silver stands and when filled with ice and water. They are difficult even for a strong person to carry. Stainless steel buckets and stands are compatible with the decor in most restaurants; perhaps only the elite, elegant restaurants should not use the stainless models. Whichever bucket is selected, the stand must be compatible with the bucket (i.e., it must fit). Smaller wine totes (made of ceramic, crockery or clay, marble, stainless steel, or aluminum) have become popular since they take up very little space and are less hazardous—they are not left in an aisle to trip on. Many restaurants no longer continue to chill white wine *after* it is opened—the bottle is left on the table. Many restaurant guests have begun to choose drinking white wine that is not so cold, and floating a bottle in a wine bucket with ice is both messy and dangerous and may sometimes render the wine too cold for proper enjoyment. This is *not true* for sparkling wine and Champagne, which *should* be served very cold.

Glassware

The companies that sell glassware produce countless varieties of glasses for many different purposes. Unusually shaped glassware is effective for marketing special beverages. Yet many operations need only stock a standard, eight-ounce wine glass that will be satisfactory for all the wines served. There are special glasses for the wines of Bordeaux, for the wines of Burgundy, and so forth, but this specialization is not required for many modern restaurant operations in the United States. The champagne saucer, which has been used traditionally to serve sparkling wines, is ill-suited for consuming sparkling wine. As the surface area is increased in the champagne saucer glass, there is an increase in the amount of effervescence lost. The **champagne tulip** or flute are much superior for serving sparkling wines, as the shape tends to retain the CO_2 gas. Additionally, the tulip or the flute is a more attractive glass, which will sell more product (because of appearance and size) than the saucer (see Figure 10–4).

The operator should also realize that large bowl glassware, while beautiful, elegant, and effective in marketing wines, may not be compatible with the dish machine or dish machine racks, and this may cause excessive breakage. If a restaurateur is anxious to stock several different kinds of wine glasses, the following are recommended:

Minimum stock should include (1) one of the all-purpose wine glasses (8-ounce size); (2) a dessert wine glass (3- or 4-ounce size); (3) a champagne tulip glass (6- or 8- ounce); (4) a **cordial or pony glass** (1-, 1½-, or 2-ounce); (5) a **brandy snifter or inhaler** (12- to 15-ounce).

Several factors should be considered when purchasing glassware:

1. Durability and compatibility—do the glasses have flimsy brims, stems, or feet? Will they fit into the dish machine easily?
2. Are they easily replaceable—will you end up with three different types or sizes of all-purpose wine glasses?
3. Are the glasses compatible with the decor and overall ambiance of the dining room—lead crystal would be out of character for the casual-theme restaurants and franchise steak houses.

Formal Wine and Champagne Service

Red Wine Service

Red wines should be served at cellar temperature (65° F; 18° C). Use extreme caution when handling vintage wines, as most vintage red wines throw a sediment. Decanting may be required (see separate procedure). Be sure that you use the proper glass for the type wine being served, that is, red wine or all-purpose glass. After wine has been ordered

FIGURE 10–4

All Purpose.
Use for reds or whites.

Brandy Snifter or Inhaler.
Use for brandy and some cordials.

All-Purpose Wine Glass.
Good for reds, roses,
and hearty whites.

Dessert Wine Glass.
Use for Ports, Tokay
other dessert wines,
sweet sherries.

Sherry Glass.
Use for dry or
cocktail sherries

Rhine Wine Glass.
Use for light whites.

Champagne Saucer.
Not recommended
for any beverages.

Champagne Tulip.
Recommended for
all sparkling wines.

Cordial or Pony.
Use for cordials
or liqueurs.

**Brandy Up
Glass.**
Use for cordials
or brandy.

left presentation

1. Present the wine to the host from the left side of the guest.
   Cradle the bottle in a towel and show the bottle with the label
   toward the host. The bottle must be unopened.

2. Open the wine after the host has nodded approval. Cut the foil
   or plastic wrap well below the lip and just below the bulge—this
   minimizes the addition of lead (for foil wraps) into the wine. Peel
   off the wrap. Wipe the cork and the exposed glass. Draw out the

cork with one motion and wiggle out for last half inch. Do not allow the cork to "pop" out. Place cork to the right of the host on a small dish with the wine producer's logo or label on the cork facing the guest. (After the foil is removed and the cork wiped, pressure may be applied to the top of the cork to break the seal of the cork and the bottle.) Wipe the mouth of the bottle again. (The guest's table may be used to rest the bottle when opening, or the bottle may be held in one's hands. Removing one's finger rings will reduce the clicking noise created when rings hit the wine bottle.)

3. Serve the wine by allowing the host to sample a small amount. After the host has approved, serve the person to the host's right and move counterclockwise around the table until all guests are served. The host should be served last—*but remember **to do** so!*. Fill red wine to no more than one-half full—less to ensure the wine makes it around the table (always underpour—never run out of wine before having an adequate amount for the host). Place the bottle on the table to the right of the host's wine glass.

White or Rose Wine Service

White wines should be served chilled (50° F; 10° C). After the host has ordered the wine, the server, captain, or wine steward may place the unopened bottle in a wine bucket with ice (and a wine stand) or with a smaller wine tote that is placed on the guest's table; the service cloth should be draped over the bucket or tote.

1. Present the wine after removing the bottle from the bucket or tote and wipe the water or moisture from the bottle. Show the bottle as with red wine.

2. Open the wine as with red wine.
   Note: The bottle may be replaced in the wine bucket *before* opening, and this is as acceptable as holding the bottle in one's hands, or resting the bottle on the table.

3. Serve the wine as with red wine. Be sure you are using the proper glass (i.e., Rhine wine glass, **all-purpose glass**, etc.).
   a. Fill to no more than three-fourths full—but it is preferable to fill only one-half full (always underpour—never run out of wine before having an adequate amount for the host).
   b. Replace the bottle in the wine bucket or tote, draped with a *clean* service cloth.
   c. Place bucket and stand to the right of the host (if possible) and ensure that the bucket is not in an aisle.

Champagne or Sparkling Wine Service

Champagne may be served during any portion of the meal and is a delightful accompaniment to any food. Handle gently so as not to increase the internal pressure. It should be served well-chilled (no more than 50° F). Bring an ice bucket with ice and water. A champagne tulip or flute glass is recommended for champagne service.

1. Present the champagne (unopened) as with white wine (see Figures 10–5 through 10–10B).
2. Open the champagne with caution, as the pressure can send the cork flying. Wrap the bottle in a service towel and tilt the bottle at a 45-degree angle.
   a. Locate the wire twist and place your thumb on the cork.
   b. Remove the wire (break or untwist) and foil in one action while still firmly holding the cork.
   c. Grip the cork firmly and *twist the bottle, not the cork itself,* to loosen. Continue to hold at a 45-degree angle—this reduces the force with which the cork comes out of the bottle.
   d. Allow pressure to push cork out, and place the cork to the right of the host.
3. Serve the champagne as with wine by allowing the host to sample a small portion.
   a. Begin with person on host's right and continue as with wine service.
   b. Pour in two motions by allowing foam to subside and refilling the glass to three-quarters full. (Always underpour—never run out of champagne before having an adequate amount for the host.)
   c. Replace bottle in wine bucket.

Decanting

Decanting should be performed on red wines that have 'thrown' a sediment. Decanting means to pour wine from its bottle to another container from which it will be served. Sediment is a deposit of dead yeast cells (harmless) and precipitated solids in the wine, which may impart a bitter taste and makes the wine appear dull or cloudy. Decanting also gives any wine a chance to breathe or oxidate. This rids the wine of the sulphur taste (called "bottle stink") that it may have. After the wine has been ordered

1. Select the proper bottle from storage using caution not to shake the bottle, and place the bottle in a wine basket or carry upright very carefully.

FIGURE 10–5

Presenting the bottle of wine to the guest. Cradle the bottle by holding the bottom of the bottle with the service cloth and the neck as shown.

FIGURE 10–6

Cutting the foil. Foil should be cut below the bulge. This prevents the wine from touching the foil as this may impart off flavors.

FIGURE 10–7

Inserting the corkscrew. The forefinger and the middle finger should be used to steady the screw. This also gives the server more strength where needed. The screw should be started into the cork at an angle (as shown in this figure) and after piercing, the screw should be moved vertically so that the corkscrew can be driven down the center of the cork.

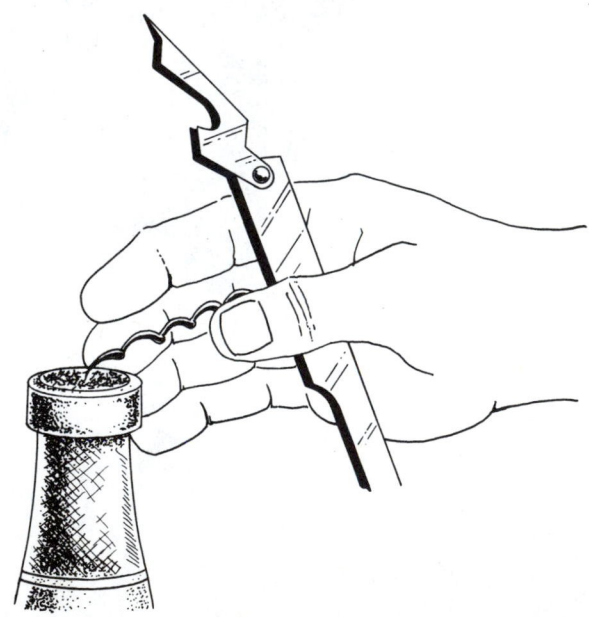

FIGURE 10–8A

Drawing the cork. One hand or finger should be used to steady the lever on the brim of the bottle while the other hand is used to draw the cork out of the bottle. Do not remove cork totally at this motion.

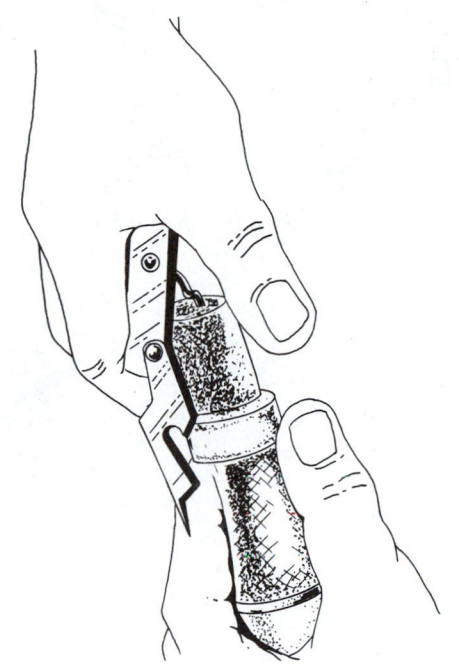

FIGURE 10–8B

Drawing the cork. With the fingers and the thumb, wiggle the cork out for the last one-quarter to one-half inch. Do not let it pop.

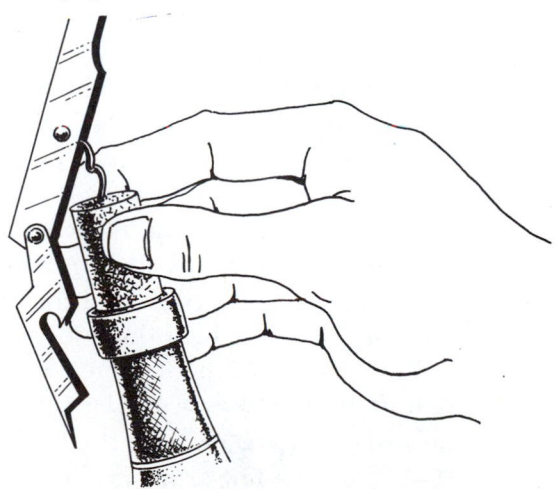

FIGURE 10–9

Serving the wine. Cradle the bottle in one hand and expose the label to the guest being served. Pour red wine with the neck of the bottle as close to the brim of the glass as possible, but without touching. Pour white wine from two inches above the brim of the glass. Simultaneously twist the bottle (counter-clockwise for right-hand pouring) when you stop pouring.

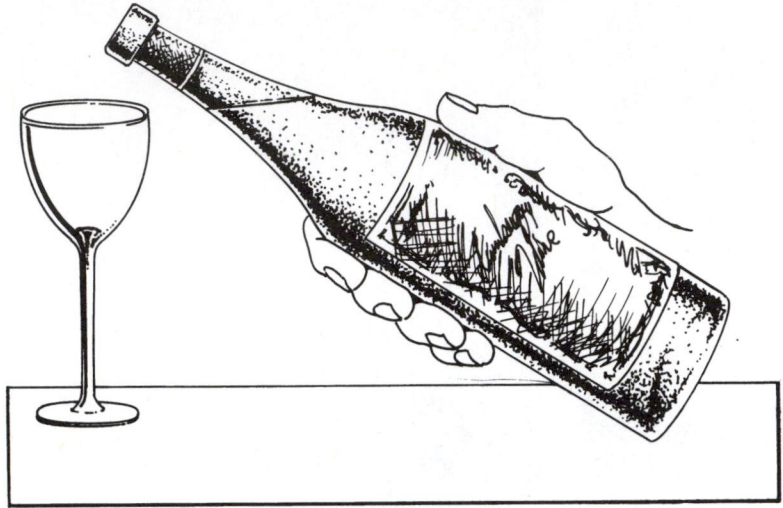

2. Present the wine in the basket or otherwise. After the host has approved, set wine on a service table or cart to the left of the host.

3. Open the bottle while it is still in the basket. The basket is generally not used for service.

   a. Cut and *remove **all** of the foil* using care to not move or shake the bottle, dislodging the sediment.

   b. Wipe the cork and the exposed glass.

   c. Draw out the cork and wipe as with red wine. Use caution not to rotate the bottle while inserting the corkscrew as the sediment may be disturbed. When the corkscrew is inserted through the cork, it may not be in the most convenient location, but do not move the bottle.

   d. Light the candle (or turn on a flashlight), but ensure that the flame does not heat the wine, but that the light is visible through the neck. (The candle should be offset from under the neck of the bottle.)

4. Decant by pouring the wine from the bottle to the decanter (see Figure 10–11). Pour a few drops into the decanter; stop pouring

FIGURE 10–10A

Champagne service. The foil need not be completely removed as shown here. However, as soon as the wire is moved (either by untwisting or breaking) the top of the cork must be controlled by the other hand and never released until the cork has been removed.

FIGURE 10–10B

Removing the champagne cork. The cork should be held firmly with one hand and the bottle should be twisted (by holding the bottom) with the other hand. The bottle should be at a 45-degree angle.

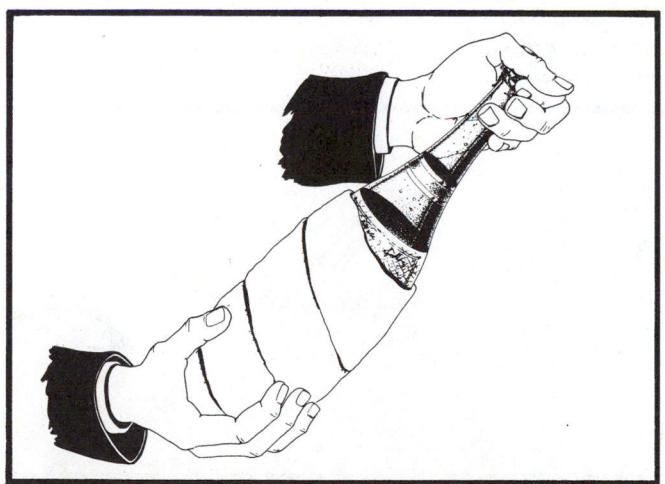

and swirl the wine in the decanter. Pour this wine into an extra glass. Then:

    a. Pour wine into the decanter in a steady, slow stream.

    b. Use a continuous motion or the wine will wash back into the bottle and mix with the sediment.

    c. Stop pouring when the sediment just begins to pass through the neck of the bottle.

5. Allow the wine to rest for a short time if possible before serving; old (madeirized) wines can go bad, turning to vinegar very quickly. Continue service from the decanter as listed in serving the wine in Red Wine Service on pages 235–237.

Note: The basket and bottle should be placed on the table to the host's right.

Equipment Required for Wine and Champagne Service

Needed are the wine, wine glasses (proper type, extra as required), corkscrew (professional lever-type preferred), service cloth, wine bucket or wine tote and stand (ice), decanter (clear glass preferred), wine basket (wicker or silver), candle and holder, matches, underliner for decanter (silver for fine service).

Wine glasses may be carried properly by inverting the glass and by inserting the stem of the glass between the server's fingers, holding the base of the glass. Single wine bottles should be cradled or carried with two hands. Holding and carrying the neck of a wine bottle with one hand

FIGURE 10–11

Decanting. The bottle and the basket should be held in one hand, and the decanter should be held in the other hand. Use caution with the candle as it should not be directly under the neck of the bottle lest it heats the wine.

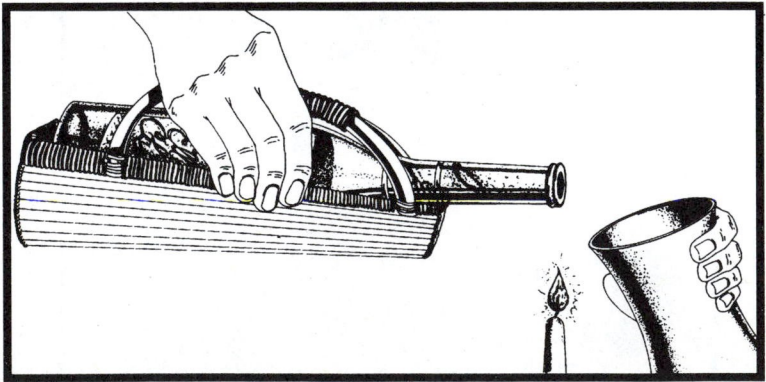

is improper. A cocktail tray may also be used to carry both bottles of wine and wine glasses simultaneously. When carrying a rose (blush), white wine, or sparkling wine to the table, the bottle may be placed in the wine bucket with ice, water, and a service cloth or a wine tote, and this entire setup may be brought to the table in this form. The ice bucket should be three-fourths filled with ice and half filled again with water. Water will increase the contact of the cold medium on the wine, and it will also allow the bottle to be submerged easily in the bucket. This is especially important if the white wine was not properly chilled or if a sparkling wine is being served (see Figure 10–12). Many wine totes are designed to either retain cold (when stored in a refrigerator) or cool the wine via evaporation when a crock or clay tote is used.

FIGURE 10–12

Temperature chart for wine service (Adapted from Hugh Johnson's POCKET WINE BOOK. Mitchell Beazley Publishers Limited: London, 1977. p. 17).

	° C ° F	
	21–69	
	20–68	
	19–66	
	18–64	Full-bodied, Mature Red Wine
	17–63	e.g., Bordeaux
Red Burgundy Wine	16–61	
	15–59	
Full-bodied White Wine, Port,	14–57	
Madeira	13–55	
	12–54	
Sherry	11–52	Light Red Wine
	10–50	
Dry White Wine	9–48	Rose Wine
Champagne	8–46	
	7–45	
Sweet Sparkling Wine	6–43	Sweet Sparkling Wine
	5–41	
	4–39	
	3–37	
	2–35	
	1–33	
	0–32	

To convert ° F to ° C:
Subtract 32 from ° F and Multiply by 5/9:

$$° F - 32 \times 5/9 =$$
$$° C$$

To convert ° C to ° F:
Multiply ° C by 9/5 and add 32:

$$° C \times 9/5 + 32 =$$
$$° F$$

Banquet wine service differs from à la carte wine service since the wines have been chosen in advance of the function. The wines are not opened in the presence of the guests, but are simply poured for the guests. It is helpful if one person is designated to serve only wines. The number of people one person can serve efficiently will vary, but an efficient wine steward should be able to pour wine efficiently for 40 or more guests.

The wine to be used for a large banquet should be checked well ahead of the function. If the wine is bad or has turned to vinegar, the beverage manager, or someone acting in her stead, will be able to purchase an additional supply. The operator may find it difficult to locate three cases of a particular wine on a moment's notice. Since the wines for banquets are opened in the back of the house and there are usually many bottles, an automatic corkscrew is recommended. With two swift motions the cork can be removed from the bottle *and* the cork removed from the corkscrew.

Sales Tips

Without repeating the factors discussed in Chapter 7, it is essential that the service staff know something about wines to be effective in selling wines. In reality, it is only necessary for the service staff to know the wines on the establishment's wine list, what those wines taste like (so that the server may describe them to the guest), how the names are pronounced, and which wines accompany or complement the foods on the menu. The best way to teach the service staff about the wines is to have regular and frequent tasting (not drinking) sessions. Entrée items should also be served, and the wines should be tasted with the food. Some operators serve a few wines to close their regular meetings with the service staff. The service staff must know how to open wines.

A successful method for teaching servers how to open wines is to purchase a **re-corker**, save empty wine bottles and corks, cork empty bottles (or bottles filled with water), and have each person practice, practice, and practice until fully competent. In a standard commercial restaurant, in contrast to an elite, elegant restaurant, only a few wines should be featured; each wine listed should have a brief description of the wine and the type foods the wine best complements. All wines, except for rare or vintage wines, should be kept readily available. Controls are essential, but the guest or the server should not be inconvenienced. Additionally, prompt wine service may mean selling another bottle. Bin numbers are very helpful for storing wines and are also useful on the wine list. The guest does not have to wrestle with clumsy pronunciation (Pouilly Fuisse), and communication between the guest and the server, and in turn the bartender, is facilitated. Wines should be priced realistically.

Wine is a plus sale when nothing else can be sold! No one has ever made a cent from tap water, but the fashionable alternative to alcohol is bottled water. Several rules of thumb have been suggested by some reputable wine experts:

Double the price for wines costing less than $5 and add one dollar to that figure for the selling price. For wines costing between $5 and $7, the **mark-up** should be 75 percent of cost plus $1 (i.e., a $6 wine should sell for $11.50). For wines costing more than $7, the mark-up percentage should be decreased as the dollar profit is more meaningful than percentage profit (i.e., a $10 wine can be sold for $15, and the operator will still make a comfortable profit). Find out what local package stores sell the wine you have on your list for. Add a few dollars (four to five only) for your selling price. Remember that your guests have a good idea of what the wine sells for in the package store (especially in controlled states), and they may feel "ripped off" if you try to make too much profit. In controlled states, certain wines may be available to restaurateurs but not generally available to the public in the state liquor stores. These should be used in finer restaurants, and a higher profit margin can be attained. There should be an inexpensive wine on the wine list that is no more expensive than the least expensive main course menu item. Carafe wines may accomplish this goal.

Know and have the service staff know the proper size bottle to recommend, although the server should never suggest a small bottle. At approximately three ounces per glass:

Split or small (6.3 ounces or 187 ml)—2 glasses (one or two guests).

Half bottle, tenth, or medium (12.7 oz. or 375 ml)—4 glasses (one or two guests).

Bottle or regular (24.5 oz. or 750 ml)—8 glasses (up to four or five guests).

Some Helpful Hints when a Guest Rejects a Wine

If a guest rejects a wine (costing less than $10) that the server, manager, or hostess feels is still a good wine, the wine should be exchanged without comment. This wine can be used for cooking or for the staff to build morale. Another bottle of the same wine should not be brought to the guest. A different wine should be offered with a comment such as "we probably have a bad shipment of Dogbreath wine, why don't you try the Floral Essence wine instead?" When a very expensive wine is ordered by a stranger (nonregular guest) who appears to be boasting, the server should take note. The manager or host may intercede and explain what a fine wine he has ordered. Perhaps she could strike up a conversation with the guest and ask politely if he has ever had a "Chateau Mouton" before. While explaining that the taste may be quite different than what the guest is used to, the manager should explain that if she determines that the wine is not sour, the guest is obligated to pay (this may also be stated as restaurant policy on the wine list or menu). For medium-priced wines, the operator must make her own determination as to how to handle the situation. In other words, how much loss can the operation absorb for expensive, rejected wines? Some restaurant operators assume all the risks of a bad bottle of wine younger than 25 or 30 years old. Moreover, most reputable distributors will give credit to the restaurant for a truly bad bottle of wine.

Spirits and Beverage Service

As with wines, a good manager must know his product before he can recommend any sales techniques to the service staff. The intent of this section is to increase the reader's knowledge about distilled spirits, and the service of these spirits. It is beyond the scope of this text to discuss beverage management planning, bar design, beverage cost control, beverage promotion, or a complete history of distilled spirits or to prepare one as a bartender. The reader should be aware of the books on beverage and bar management listed at the end of this chapter.

Whiskey

Whiskey is basically a spirit or potable beverage obtained from the distillation of a fermented mash of grain and aged in wood. The production of whiskey is a natural process and the skilled distiller guides the spirit through the four natural processes for the finished beverage. Mashing is the first process, which prepares the grain for fermentation. The grain is allowed to sprout and this is combined with a cooked mash, which is converted to fermentable sugars. Fermentation is the second process where yeast (a living organism) consumes the sugar, and the by-product of the yeast feeding on the sugar produces alcohol (and carbon dioxide $[CO_2]$). The product is then distilled, which is simply heating the product in a pot still or continuous still until the alcohol vaporizes. The alcohol vapors are cooled and condensed as whiskey. This whiskey is colorless and harsh and needs to be aged. When placed in charred oak barrels, the whiskey takes on an amber color, it loses some of its impurities, and the flavoring agents (congeners) mellow during the aging process.

Bourbon is a "distinctive product of the United States" by congressional resolution and must be distilled from a fermented mash containing no less than 51 percent corn, not to exceed 160 proof (160°). It must then be aged in new, charred-oak barrels for a minimum of 24 months; and before bottling, not reduced to below 80 proof. *Sour mash whiskey* is a bourbon, but producers of this product feel that it is superior to bourbon. Sour mash uses the residue of a previous fermentation recovered from the spent mash of a previous distillation. Sour mash is a full-bodied whiskey that is sweet, not sour. The process used to make it is akin to the back-yeasting process of making sour dough bread. Most bourbons are made using the sour mash yeasting method.[2] Some major commercial brands of bourbon are Wild Turkey, Bourbon Supreme, Ten High, Jim Beam, Old Grand Dad, I.W. Harper, Old Crow, Dant & Dant, Waterfill & Frazier, and Old Taylor. Rye is basically the same product as bourbon; however, rye, the grain, is used in lieu of corn.

Spirit Container-Sizes

Miniature or miniature (1.7 fluid ounces or 50 ml).

Half pint or small (6.8 fluid ounces or 200 ml).

Pint or medium (16.9 fluid ounces or 500 ml).

Fifth or regular (25.4 fluid ounces or 750 ml).

Quart or large (33.8 fluid ounces or 1.0 liter [1,000 ml].

Half gallon or extra large (59.2 fluid ounces or 1.75 liters).

Tennessee whiskey is a distinctive type of American whiskey because of its unique production methods, and it is recognized as such by law. After distillation, the spirits of Tennessee whiskey are filtered through maple charcoal before aging. It is claimed that this filtering process eliminates the unwanted harsher elements of the spirit and imparts its own unique character to the whiskey. The two legal distilleries in Tennessee are Jack Daniel's and Geo. A. Dickel, and each produces Tennessee sour mash whiskey.

Blended whiskey (by federal standard of identity) is "a mixture which contains at least 20 percent by volume of 100 proof straight whiskey and . . . whiskey or neutral spirits." Some major brands are Seagram's 7 Crown, Kessler's, Calvert, Fleishman's Preferred, and Imperial.

Canadian whiskey is "a distinctive product of Canada in compliance with the laws of Canada regulating the manufacture of whiskey for consumption in Canada." Canadian whiskey is light whiskey, as it is taken off the still at or above 160 proof, and cannot be called "straight"; therefore it is called "blended Canadian whiskey." Some major brands are Canadian Club, Seagram's V.O., Black Velvet, Wiser's Deluxe, and O.F.C.

Irish whiskey is generally taken off the still at a high proof and is therefore a light spirit. It is a distinctive product of Ireland and contains no distilled spirits less than three years old, although it is aged seven years before bottling. It also must be designated "blended Irish whiskey" and cannot be called "straight." Some major commercial brands of Irish whiskey are Old Bushmills, Dunphy's, Jamesons', and Paddy Irish.

Scotch whiskey is a distinctive product of Scotland and carries with it the same identity as that of Irish whiskey. But Scotch carries the characteristic "peat reek" or smoky flavor, which is developed from the drying of the sprouted barley over peat fires. Single-malt Scotch whiskey has become a popular drink; it differs slightly from the blended Scotch whiskeys, but still has the characteristic smoky flavor. Single-malt Scotches as distinct from blended Scotch whiskey include the well-recognized brands Glenlivet and Glenfiddich, as well as other limited edition boutique brands. Some popular blended Scotch whiskeys are Teacher's, Dewar's, Lauder's, Cutty Sark, Chivas Regal, J & B Rare, Johnny Walker (Red and Black), Haig & Haig Pinch and Five Star, Black & White, Usher's, Ballantines, Highland Queen, Grand Old Parr, Vat 69, Usher's Green Stripe, Ambassador Deluxe, and Highland Cream. Scotch drinkers are traditionally and typically very loyal to their brand.

Vodka

Vodka is "neutral spirits distilled from any material at or above 190 proof, reduced to not more than 110 proof, and not less than 80 proof, and after such reduction in proof, so treated as to be without distinctive character, aroma, or taste." In other words, vodka is not supposed to taste like anything! Different distillers have their own techniques for producing even a more tasteless spirit. Perhaps this characteristic has given rise to the great sales boom that vodka and the other white goods are enjoying. Some major commercial brands are Smirnoff, Gilbey's, Stolichnaya, Absolut, Romanoff, Gordon's, Popov, Wolfschmidt, and Hiram Walker. Flavored vodkas scented with lemon and other botanicals have become popular alternatives to standard vodka.

Gin

Gin (dry gin) is a redistillation of neutral spirits (in the United States distilled at or above 190 proof) which are flavored with juniper berries (required by law) and other botanicals (cocoa, Cassia bark, anise, calamus, lemon and orange peel, licorice, coriander, caraway, orris root, etc.). English gin makers typically use a spirit distilled at a lower proof in their processes (180° to 188°), resulting in a finished product with a more pronounced flavor than its American counterpart.[3] The Dutch gins, Genever, Holland, or Schiedam, are consumed ice cold or on the rocks and have a more pronounced, full-flavored, and full-bodied taste in contrast to the flavor of the dry gins from England and the United States. Some major commercial brands are Bols Genever, Booth's, Beefeater, Gilbey's, Walker's, Old Mr. Boston, Seagram's, Tanqueray, Gordon's, and Calvert. Gin drinkers are considered the fussiest of the drinking public.

Rum

The federal standards of identity states: Rum is any alcoholic distillate from the fermented juice of sugar cane, sugar cane syrup, sugar cane molasses, or other sugar cane products distilled at less than 190 degrees, in such a manner that the distillate possesses the taste, aroma, and characteristics generally attributed to rum; and includes mixtures solely of such distillates. In other words, rum tastes like rum! Rum does not have to be mashed, as the sugars are fermentable and can be consumed by the yeast, thereby producing CO_2 and alcohol. There are two types of rum on the market: the light rums from Puerto Rico, Mexico, the Virgin Islands, and other Spanish-speaking Caribbean Islands; and the dark (molasses flavored) rums from Jamaica, Barbados, and other English-speaking areas. Light rum mixes well with anything and, except for vodka, leads all other distilled spirits in sales volume. There are some amber-colored rums (called Añejo) that should not be confused with the dark rums of Jamaica or Barbados. These rums have been aged in wooden casks and take on an amber color (i.e., similar to bourbon). They are mellow in flavor and are usually used for sipping rather than mixing, although many are used for mixing. Some major commercial brands of light rums are Bacardi, Ron Rico, and Don Q. The dark Jamaican type rums include Lemon Hart, Myer's, and Appleton brands.

Tequila

"Tequila is an alcoholic distillate from a fermented mash derived principally from the *Agave tequilana Weber* ("blue" variety), with or without additional fermentable substances, distilled in such a manner that the distillate possesses the taste, aroma, and characteristics generally attributed to tequila and bottled at not less than 80 proof; it also includes mixtures soley of such distillates."[4] While most tequila is not aged, *añejo* (aged) is gold-colored, aged in used, charred-oak barrels (obtained from used Bourbon barrels), and imparts a more mellow flavor. This is distinct from the fiery taste of the white, un-aged product. Popular brands include Two Fingers, Jose Cuervo, Montezuma, and Sauza.

Brandy

Brandy is a potable spirit obtained from the distillation of wine or a fermented mash of fruit, which usually has been suitably aged in wood.[5] Fermentable sugars are available naturally from the grape as with wine; and after distillation, brandy is aged "usually three to seven years." Cognac is brandy that is distilled in the Cognac region in France. In other words, all Cognac is brandy, but not all brandy is Cognac. Cognac is labeled or otherwise marked with stars (3 star, 5 star, etc.) with coded letters (V.S.O.P.) or with the words "Fine Champagne" or "Grande Fine Champagne." The "champagne" designations are related to quality and the grapes to produce the product must come from the Grand Champagne or Petite Champagne sections of Cognac. The stars and other letters refer only to relative quality from one producer. For example, Courvoisier V.S.O.P. is a finer product than Courvoisier V.S.; it cannot, however, be compared on the basis of the lettering above to Delamain or Hennessey. Other than those listed above, some other Cognacs and brandies include The Christian Bros., Camus, Gallo, Remy Martin, Napoleon, and Martell.

Armagnac is brandy from France, but it does not come from the Cognac region. Apple Jack and Calvados are hard ciders or brandies made from apples. There are many other fruit flavored brandies (e.g., Kirsch from cherries), as well as coffee-flavored brandy (not a coffee liqueur), and other flavored brandies.

Cocktails (Mixed Drinks)

Mixed drinks or cocktails can be divided into five basic categories: **highballs**, **lowballs** or **on-the-rocks,** cocktails, cream drinks, and lemon or fruit drinks. A highball is a distilled spirit and a mixer, such as soda, ginger ale, or cola. Highballs are served appropriately in highball glasses while lowballs are served in on-the-rocks glasses. Some examples of highballs are rum and Coke, Seven and Seven, gin and tonic, while lowballs may include scotch on the rocks and other similar drinks. Cocktails are usually served in "up" or cocktail glasses and include martinis, Manhattans, gimlets, and Gibsons. Cream drinks are basically spirits, light cream, and flavorings, and are shaken. Some examples include Brandy Alexander, grasshopper, and golden cadillac. Lemon drinks or fruit drinks typically include all the sours and the collins drinks as well as daiquiris and margaritas. Lemon drinks can be further subdivided into short fruit or tall fruit drinks. Lemon drinks are almost always shaken and may be served in cocktail glasses or sour glasses (when served up), or on-the-rocks in on-the-rocks glasses. Two shakers should be used in mixing, as cream and lemon drinks both are shaken and should not be mixed. Shakers used for cream drinks must be rinsed after each use.

Abbreviated Checklists for Service Personnel

The following checklists may be given to service personnel as a supplement to an introduction to beverage service.

Mixers

Bitter lemon—Schweppe's

Bitters—Angostura, Holland House (orange)

Club soda—Canada Dry, Schweppe's

Cola—Coca-Cola, Pepsi-Cola

Cranberry juice

Cream—use light cream only, heavy cream dulls the flavor

Eggs—yolk can be used for body in a mixer, but generally only egg whites are used.

Ginger ale—Canada Dry, Schweppe's

Grapefruit—Fresca, Squirt, Wink

Grapefruit juice

Grenadine—Giroux, Wupperman's, Holland House

Hot sauce—Tabasco

Ice cream—can be substituted for light cream

Lemon lime—7-Up, Sprite, Mountain Dew

Milk

Orange juice

Simple syrup—sugar water super fine sugar—used to sweeten drinks, not as a garnish

Sweetened lime juice extract—Rose's lime juice

Tomato juice and tomato juice cocktails—Holland House, Mr. & Mrs. T, Snap-e-Tom, V-8, common tomato juice brands

Tonic (quinine water)—Schweppe's, Canada Dry

Bottled water (vichy) (Natural mineral water)—Imported, domestic

Worcestershire Sauce—Lea & Perrin's, Heinz, French's

Bar Garnishes

Carrots (stick)—Bloody Marys (occasionally).

Celery (stick)—Bloody Marys (occasionally).

Cherries—all Collins, all sours, slings, fizzes, Planter's punch, kiddie cocktails, old fashioned (sometimes), Rob Roys (sweet—sometimes).

Cocktail onions—Gibson, Bloody Caesar.

Bar Garnishes *(Concluded)*

Confectionery sugar(10x)—use as garnish only, not to sweeten.

Lemon (slice)—old fashioned (garnish or muddled).

Lemon (twist)—Martinis (extra dry or on request), all dry Manhattans, perfect Manhattans, all Rob Roys, mist, Dubonnet cocktails, campari, vermouth on rocks; ask if desire twist with aperitif.

Lime (wedge or a squeeze)—Bloody Mary, Virgin Mary, gimlet, gin and tonic, Cuba Libra, gin Ricky.

Olives (Spanish)—Martinis, occasionally dry Manhattans.

Oranges—same as cherries.

Pineapple (stick)—Planter's punch, mai-tai.

Nutmeg—Brandy Alexander.

Common Bar Terms

Aperitif—appetizer; usually appetizer beverage.

Back bar—location of call and premium brands.

Bitters—a flavoring used in mixing drinks.

Call liquor—a liquor ordered by brand name, but not a premium brand (e.g., Johnny Walker Red).

Decanter—a container into which wines or spirits are decanted from their original containers for service.

Frappe—iced. Term for service of liqueur with finely cracked ice.

Garnish—fruit, onion, olive, and so on, in a cocktail.

Highball—a drink of alcoholic liquor and water or a carbonated beverage served in a tall glass.

House liquor—liquor used by the establishment. Usually not a well-known brand.

Jigger—a jigger refers to the portion used at the particular establishment. The size of a jigger may vary from establishment to establishment.

Muddler—a wooden tool used for crushing fruit or cracking ice for cocktails.

On-the-rocks—a drink, other than a highball, that requires ice cubes in it.

Perlick—portable draft beer dispensing machine (brand name).

Premium brands/Top shelf—top-of-the-line brands (e.g., Johnny Walker Black).

Up—any drink that is served without ice cubes.

Shaker—the glass and stainless steel container used for thorough blending of drinks.

Shot—refers to a standard established by the restaurant or lounge.

Stirrer or **swizzle stick**—used in any cocktail or mixed drink with ice in the drink.

Strainer—used to pour a drink out of a shaker glass, but not allowing any ice to pour out.

Well/House well—same as house liquor.

Spirits

Aperitif—an appetizer usually a beverage. Major commercial types: Pernod, dry sherry (Widmer's, Taylor, Dry Sack) Campari, Lillet, Byrrh, White or Red Vermouth (Cora, Tribuno, Martini and Rossi, Cinzano), Dubonnet (red or white).

Apple Jack—hard cider: "Laird's"

Brandy—a potable spirit obtained from the distillation of wine or a fermented mash of fruit, which usually has been suitably aged in wood. Major commercial brands: The Christian Bros., Hiram Walker, Gallo, Cognac—courvoisier, Napoleon, Remy Martin, Hennessey, Delamain. *Note:* All Cognac is brandy, but all brandy is not Cognac (must be from Charente, France).

Gins—redistillation of pure alcohol with the juniper berry. Major commercial brands: Gordon's, Walker's, Tanqueray, Gilbey's, Beefeater's, Booth's, Calvert, Seagrams, Fleishman's.

Liqueurs or cordials—an alcoholic beverage prepared by combining a spirit (usually brandy) with certain flavorings (herbs, bitters, and spices) and then adding sugar syrup for sweetening. Major commercial brands: Galliano, Drambuie, Cointreau, crème de menthe (green or white), Tia Maria, Kahlua, crème de cacao, Grand Marnier, Triple Sec, Southern Comfort, Peter Heering, B & B, Forbidden Fruit.

Spirits *(Concluded)*

Rums—any alcoholic distillate from the fermented juice of sugar cane, sugar cane syrup, sugar cane molasses, or other sugar cane products distilled at less than 190 proof, in such manner that the distillate possesses the taste, aroma, and characteristics generally attributed to rum, and includes mixtures solely of such distillates. Major commercial brands: Barcardi, Ronrico, Myer's Don Q.

Vodka—neutral spirits distilled from any material at or above 190 proof reduced to not more than 110 and not less than 80 proof and, after such reduction in proof, so treated as to be without distinctive character, aroma, or taste. Major Commercial Brands: Smirnoff, Gordons, Popov, Wolfschmidt, Gilbey's, and Walker's.

Whiskeys—a potable beverage obtained from the distillation of grain. Bourbon—distilled from fermented mash of rye, corn, wheat, and malted barley or malted rye grain. Major commercial brands: *Bourbon*—Wild Turkey, Jim Beam, Old Grand Dad, Four Roses, I. W. Harper, Old Crow, Ten High, Early Times, Ancient Age, Jack Daniels (Black). *Rye*—Meadow Brook, Old Overholt, and Rittenhouse. *Canadian*—Canadian Club, Seagrams V.O., Black Velvet, Windsor Supreme, Canadian Mist. *Irish*—Old Bushmills, Jameson's. *Scotch*—Teacher's, Dewar's, Cutty Sark, Chivas Regal, J & B, Usher's, Johnny Walker (black or red), Haig & Haig, Black & White, Ballantines, Lauder's. *Tennessee*—Jack Daniel's (black or green), Geo A. Dickel.

Other Spirits

Akvavit (Aquavit)—made from grain or potatoes and flavored with caraway seeds. Aalborg is the only approved export from Sweden.

Bitters—distillation and infusion of aromatic seeds, herbs, barks, roots, and fruits blended on a spirit base. Major commercial brands: Campari, Cynar, Angostura

Tequila—distilled from pina or pineapple of the century plant cactus. Major commercial brands: Jose Cuervo, Ole, Tequila Sauza, Two Fingers.

Cocktails (Their Ingredients: garnishes)

Bacardi—a daiquiri with grenadine: none.

Black Russian—Kahlua and vodka: none.

Bloody Mary—tomato juice, Worcestershire, Tabasco, salt, pepper, vodka: squeeze of lime.

Bourbon—none.

Brandy Alexander—light cream, dark crème de cacao, brandy: nutmeg.

Collins—lemon mix with gin, club soda: orange and cherry.

Vodka, Bourbon, Sloe Gin, Rum, John—made with whiskey.

Daiquiri—lemon mix, light Rum: none.

Frappes—liqueur poured over crushed ice: none.

Gibson—same as martini, gin with white vermouth: pickled cocktail onion.

Gimlet—gin with Rose's lime juice: squeeze of lime vodka.

Gimlet—substitute vodka for gin.

Gin fizz—gin, lemon juice, sugar, club soda: cherry.

Golden Cadillac—Galliano, white crème de cacao, or triple sec and cream: none.

Grasshopper—light cream, green crème de menthe, light crème de Cacao: none.

Harvey Wallbanger—screwdriver with Galliano liqueur.

Kir—white wine with crème de cassis (currant).

Manhattan—bourbon or blended whiskey with sweet vermouth, bitters optional: cherry. (Dry—substitute dry for sweet vermouth: lemon twist.)

Margarita—unsweetened lemon juice, triple sec, tequila: salt rimmed edge.

Martini—gin with dry vermouth: olive or lemon twist. (Extra dry—gin with dark or dry vermouth: lemon twist .)

Vodka—vodka with dry vermouth: olive or lemon twist.

Mists—scotch or bourbon poured over crushed ice: twist of lemon.

Old fashioned—sugar, bitters, club soda or water, blended whiskey: muddled (optional), orange, lemon, cherry.

Perfect Manhattan—bourbon or blended whiskey with dry and sweet vermouth: lemon twist.

Perfect Martini—gin with sweet and dry vermouth: twist or olive.

Cocktails (Their Ingredients: garnishes) *(Concluded)*

Pink lady—cream, grenadine, sugar, gin.

Pink squirrel—light cream, crème de almond, light crème de cacao.

Rob Roy—Manhattan using scotch instead of bourbon (sweet, dry, and perfect): lemon twist.

Roy Rogers—a Shirley Temple.

Rusty Nail—drambuie and scotch: none.

Salty dog—vodka, grapefruit: salt-rimmed highball glass.

Screwdriver—vodka and orange juice.

Shirley Temple—nonalcoholic grenadine, ginger ale: cherry.

Sidecar—unsweetened lemon mix, triple sec, brandy: sugar-coated rim.

Singapore sling—gin, lemon mix, club soda, grenadine and cherry brandy (Kirsch).

Sours—whiskey and lemon mix: orange and cherry. (Can be made with bourbon, Scotch, vodka, gin, rum, apricot brandy, tequila: same garnish)

Stinger—brandy with white crème de menthe: none.

Virgin Mary—bloody Mary without vodka.

White Russian—cream, kahlua, vodka.

Liqueurs or Cordials

Liqueurs or cordials—synonymous terms—were originated by alchemists whose special elixirs were marketed as medicinal cures for diseases, to extend life, and as aphrodisiacs. The flavorings and the sugar (by law 2.5 percent by weight) were used to mask the flavor of an inferior spirit. A liqueur is a combination of spirits and flavorings and sugar syrup. Liqueurs have replaced brandy, in some areas, as an after-dinner drink. The flavorings are added by one of three methods or a combination of these methods:

Infusion or *maceration* method is similar to the making of tea, where the flavoring agents are steeped or soaked in the spirit until the spirit has extracted the color, aroma, and flavor of the fruits. Infusion or maceration is used primarily in the making of fruit-flavored liqueurs.

Percolation method is identical to the making of coffee, where the spirit is passed over and over the flavoring ingredients until almost all of the flavor and aroma is extracted. This method is used primarily for making the plant liqueurs such as Benedictine, Drambuie, crème de cacao, crème de menthe, and triple sec.

The *distillation method* is also used to produce the plant liqueurs, and this procedure is similar to the production of gin. Leaves, seeds, and other flavoring agents are placed on a tray, and the spirit picks up the flavor as it passes the flavoring agents.

There are five categories or types of liqueurs:

1. Fruits are the most popular flavoring agents used in liqueurs, and some types include strawberries, blackberries, peaches, apricots, and cherries.

2. Peels are also used extensively, and the most popular are the oranges from Curacao.

3. Seeds, such as aniseed (anisette) and apricot pits (amaretto) are also used to flavor liqueurs.

4. Herbs are used to flavor liqueurs; but with few exceptions (Chartreuse and Benedictine), the herbs do not predominate the flavor.

5. Cremes such as crème de menthe (mint leaves) and crème de cacao (cacao bean) are usually the sweetest liqueurs.

Some of the more popular liqueurs are listed alphabetically [(P) indicates proprietary brand; all others are generic liqueurs]:

Advocaat—eggnog brandy 40 proof.

Akvavit—rye and caraway 90 proof.

Amaretto—almond flavored 56 proof.

Anisette—from aniseed; tastes like licorice 50–60 proof.

Benedictine (P)—herb liqueur from secret formula 86 proof.

B & B (P)—Benedictine and brandy.

Chartreuse (P)—herb liqueur from France; secret formula; yellow 86 proof and green 110 proof.

Cherry Herring/Peter Herring (P)—cherry-flavored liqueur 50 proof.

Chocolat Suisse (P)—Chocolate liqueur 60 proof.

Cointreau (P)—a triple sec 80 proof.

Curacao—peel from green oranges of Curacao 50–60 proof.

Drambuie (P)—Highland malt scotch and heather honey 80 proof.

Forbidden Fruit (P)—grapefruit flavored 64 proof.

Galliano (P)—Italian herb liqueur.

Grand Marnier (P)—French orange Curacao liqueur 80 proof.

Grenadine—alcoholic 25 proof or nonalcoholic from pomegranates.

Irish Mist (P)—Irish whiskey and honey 80 proof.

Kahlua—Mexican coffee-flavored liqueur 53 proof.

Kummel—Caraway flavored 80–86 proof.

Ouzo—Greek aniseed flavored liqueur 92 proof.

Peppermint Schnapps—light mint liqueur 60–70 proof.

Pernod (P)—Absinthe type.

Rock and Rum—rum and rock candy.

Rock and Rye—rye whiskey and rock candy.

Sabra (P)—Israeli chocolate, orange liqueur 60 proof.

Sloe gin—from sloe berry 60 proof.

Strega (P)—famous Italian herb liqueur 80 proof.

Tia Maria (P)—Jamaican coffee-flavored liqueur 63 proof.

Triple Sec—orange-flavored liqueur 60–80 proof.

Vandermint (P)—Dutch chocolate mint liqueur 60 proof.

Cream Liqueurs (from 40°–80°)

Almond or Noyaux—fruit stones.

Ananas—pineapple.

Bananas.

Cacao—brown or white.

Cafe—coffee.

Cassis—black currant.

Fraises—strawberries.

Framboises—raspberries.

Menthe—mint.

Mandarin—tangerines.

Noisette—hazelnuts.

Noix—walnuts.

Noyaux—fruit stones .

Prunelle—plums.

Rose—rose petals and vanilla.

Vanille—vanilla.

Violette—violets.

Fruit-Flavored Liqueurs and Brandies (generic)

Apricot.

Blackberry.

Cherry.

Coffee.

Cranberry.

Ginger.

Peach.

Beer and Ale

Beer is one of the oldest beverages known. It is a standard beverage in every country. In fact in some countries, beer is the safest beverage to consume, as the water used to make it must be pure before the brewing process begins. Beer is made from barley, which is malted (sprouted) to change the starch to fermentable sugars. The wort, liquid (water) from the mashing process, is filtered and then boiled for several hours and flavored with hops. Rice or other adjunct grains may be added to lighten the brew. After the wort is filtered again, it is allowed to ferment and the carbon dioxide (CO_2) (gas) is collected (to be added back later). The beer is stored (lagered) at very cold temperatures for one to three months, and the solids are precipitated (i. e., collect at the bottom). The beer is then carbonated from the (previously) collected CO_2.

Malt liquor has a higher alcoholic content than beer. It is aged longer, higher priced, more bitter, and hoppier than beer. Ale is fermented at a higher temperature (the yeast remains on top), which gives it a full-bodied flavor. It is more bitter and slightly more expensive than beer. Bock beer is a heavy brew; darker and sweeter than beer. A dark malt (carmelized) that has been heated more. Stout is a very dark, bitter beer product with a licorice flavor.

Draught beer is unpasteurized (most beer is pasteurized at 140° F) and must be kept refrigerated or it will spoil. Canned or bottled draught beer is unpasteurized, and it is passed through a millipore filter. Some beer products are kroezened, which is the adding of yeast after fermentation has begun, and others use beechwood chips to aid the clarification process. *Premium* is an arbitrary term now since many beers are distributed nationally. Low-calorie beers (Lite, Bud Light, Amstel Light, etc.) have achieved wide acceptance among beer drinkers. For operations that sell a lot of beer, it behooves management to serve a good beer.

Micro-breweries, or brew-pub restaurants (with custom brewing operations), have become very popular. These *production and service* operations generally have several types of beers on hand, and all are available on tap or draught. The several types of brews include lighter beers, dark beers, unusually flavored beers, and dark, stout-type beer.

Critical Factors in Determining the Quality of Beer

Age (delivery) is a most important factor for beer. Demand a fresh product from your supplier. An old product (oxidized) has a cardboard taste. All beer is dated, and you should obtain a code card from your wholesaler.

- Draught—30 days at wholesaler and cannot exceed 60 days at retailer or keg must be destroyed.
- Cans and bottles may be held for 60 days. If you hold longer than this, you could be serving bad beer.

- Delivery personnel and you must rotate your stock—in storage, in the restaurant, and in the cooler where actually serving the guest. Delivery should be made in refrigerated trucks or at least insulated ones, as temperature should not rise above 50° F. Hand trolleys should be used to move beer to prevent agitation. The best storage temperature for beer is 38° F. Yet, if you are in a warm climate (e.g., Texas), perhaps 35° F would be better. Best serving temperature is approximately 40° F. Pressure in the draught lines should be at 12 to 14 pounds per square inch. Lines should be flushed regularly and always after changing kegs. Lines are flushed by running water through the lines until clear; the keg is connected and the top opened until beer begins to flow.

Beer must be served in a "beer clean glass." Use the proper and compatible detergents (chemical energy), and use the proper procedure for washing (i.e., brushes, mechanical energy). The two methods for washing are (1) three steps—detergent, rinse, disinfectant; (2) two steps—detergent, disinfectant. How can you tell if you have a "beer clean glass"? Bubbles in the head should be small, and the head should stay on top until the bottom of the glass. Bubbles should not adhere to side or bottom of glass. Dirt, grease, and so on take the CO_2 out of solution. Lacing is the foam that clings to the side of the glass when you drink, and it should be present in a "beer clean glass." Pizza operations or other operations where there may be a lot of grease in the foods require special care. If hand washing is used, tanks may need changing every two hours. Draught beer should be dispensed by getting a rolling action at bottom of glass. Be aware of the distance of glass from the faucet and of the angle of the glass to the faucet. The glass should be tilted slightly and then moved to the vertical position as the glass fills. Bottled beer should be served by pouring the beer down the center of the glass. Beer *should not* be trickled down the side of the glass.

Beer Glassware

Mugs are durable and eye appealing for certain types of operations. In certain elegant dining rooms, mugs would not complement the decor of the room. Straight shells or pilsner glasses should be used; however, straight shells (tall footed pilsner glasses) are not good for draught beer. Stemware looks nice, but breakage may be excessive.

Abbreviated Review for Service Personnel

Beer and Ale Definitions: Beer is a generic name embracing all malt beverages. Specifically, it is a brewed and fermented beverage made from malted barley and other starchy cereals, flavored with hops. *Ale* is an aromatic malt or cereal brew, usually fuller-bodied and more bitter than beer. *Stout* is a very dark ale with a strong malt flavor, a sweet taste, and a strong hop character.

Serving Beer and Cocktails

Standard service for cocktails and beer requires the use of a cocktail or hand-held tray. Guests should be served from the right side with the server's right hand, and in the center of the cover. The tray should be carried in the left hand (see Operational Procedures in Chapter 9). A cocktail napkin should be placed in front of the guest just prior to serving the cocktail. The practice of leaning over the guests' table and placing cocktail napkins around when the guests first order is not recommended for formal dining environments. However, this practice is popular in casual-theme environments as a nonverbal indicator to all dining staff that the seated guests have been greeted by their server and that the beverage order has been taken.

Decanter Service for Cocktails

When decanters are used for cocktails, the spirit should be poured into the glass (with or without ice already in the proper glass), and the mixer added to the guest's desires. This should be accomplished on the tray while the server holds the tray with his left hand and performs this operation with his right hand. The highball or cocktail is then served in the center of the cover on a cocktail napkin. Some operations use supreme dishes with ice to serve cocktails from a decanter. The cocktail glass and a small, four- or six-ounce decanter is placed on ice in a supreme dish and carried to the guest's table on a cocktail tray. A cocktail napkin should be placed in the center of the cover (with the crest, if any, facing the guest) and the proper glass should be centered on the napkin. The supreme dish, with the decanter in it, should be placed to the right and slightly above the cover. The server may remove the decanter from the supreme dish, circle the bottom of the decanter on the rim of the supreme dish (for show and also to remove water), and pour the spirit, appetizer, or dessert wine for the guest.

Banquet Service

It is difficult to determine whether portable bars are necessary for servicing banquet operations without knowledge of the particular facilities. Certain advantages become apparent however. First, any room may become a cocktail lounge. Second, several outlets (bars) may be available in a large room (advantageous for cash bar). Anytime one is served, rather than serving himself, the caliber of service is improved. Additionally, whenever preparation (cocktails) is performed away from the guest's view, the caliber of service is also superior. With these two thoughts in mind, an elegant banquet would have no bars visible, and each guest would be served by a server. Yet service bars may be some distance from the party and a temporary setup may be required. This practice is not productive or efficient however.

Questions

1. How are wines classified?
2. What are the five major categories of wines? List three examples of each.
3. How are wines named?
4. Recall the procedure for serving red wine, white wine, and sparkling wine.
5. How should you decant a madeirized wine? Why take the foil completely off?
6. How does pouring a sparkling wine differ from pouring a still wine?
7. Why is Scotch not considered "straight" whiskey?
8. What are bourbon, vodka, rum? Why are these products so different?
9. Distinguish between beer and stout.
10. What are the ways that flavorings are added to cordials?
11. What five major ingredients (categories) are used to flavor cordials?
12. What are the five categories of mixed drinks?

Endnotes

1. R. A. Lipinski and K. A. Lipinski, Professional *Guide to Alcoholic Beverages* (New York: Van Nostrand Reinhold, 1989), p. 31.
2. R. S. Alonzo, *Owning and Managing a Bar or Tavern* (Dover, NH: Upstart Publishing Company, Inc., 1995), p.158; and D. A. Bell, *Wine and Beverage Standards* (New York: Van Nostrand Reinhold, 1989), p.185.
3. D. A. Bell, p. 221.
4. D. A. Bell, p. 215.
5. D. A. Bell, p. 200.

Additional Readings

Adams, L. *The Wines of America*. New York: McGraw-Hill, 3rd ed., 1985.

Alonzo, R. S. *Owning and Managing a Bar or Tavern*. Dover, NH: Upstart Publishing Company, Inc., 1995.

Amerine, M. A., and V. L. Singleton. *Wine: An Introduction*. Berkeley, CA: University of California Press, 2d ed., 1977.

Balzer, R. L. *Wines of California*. New York: Harry N. Abrams, 1978.

Bell, D. A. *Wine and Beverage Standards*. New York: Van Nostrand Reinhold, 1989.

Berberoglu, H. *The World of Wines, Spirits, and Beers*, 2d ed., Dubuque, IA: Kendall/Hunt, 1984.

Coombs, J. H. *Bar Service*. 2d ed. London: Barrie & Jenkins, 1975.

Dallas, P. *Italian Wines*. London: Faber and Faber, 2d ed., 1983.

Grossman, H. J. *Grossman's Guide to Wines, Beers and Spirits*, 7th ed. by Harriet Lembeck. New York: Scribners, 1983.

Johnson, F. *The Professional Wine Reference*. 3d ed., New York: Harper and Row, 1983.

Johnson, H. *Modern Encyclopedia of Wine*. New York: Simon and Schuster, 1983.

Katsigris, C., and M. Porter. *The Bar and Beverage Book*. New York: John Wiley & Sons, 1983.

Lichine, A. *Alexis Lichine's Guide to Wines and Vineyards of France*. New York: Alfred A. Knopf, 1982.

Lichine, A. *New Encyclopedia of Wines and Spirits*. New York: Alfred A. Knopf, 1981.

Lipinski, R. A., and K. A. Lipinski. *Professional Guide to Alcoholic Beverages*. New York: Van Nostrand Reinhold, 1989.

Osterland, E. *Wine and the Bottom Line*. Washington, DC: The National Restaurant Association, 1980.

Robards, T. *Terry Robard's New Book of Wine*. 2d ed. New York: Putnam, 1984.

Sutcliffe, S. *Andre Simon's Wines of the World*. 2d ed. New York: McGraw-Hill, 1981.

APPENDIX A · Pronunciation Guide

Menu Terminology

Agneau (ahn-yó)—Lamb

Aigre (áy-grr)—Sour

À la Carte—Food prepared to order; each dish priced separately.

À la King—Served in cream sauce containing mushrooms, green peppers, pimentos

À la Mode—Usually refers to ice cream on top of pie, but may refer to other dishes served in a special way, such as beef à la mode, which calls for a scoop of mashed potatoes

Amande (ah-maẃnd)—Almond

Amandine (ah-maun-deén)—With almonds

Americaine (ah-mair-ee-kén)—American style

Ananas (ah-nah-nah)—Pineapple

Anchois (awn-schwáh)—Anchovy

Andalouse (awn-dah-loos)—With tomatoes and peppers

Antipasto—Italian name for hors d'oeurves; assortment of appetizers such as salted or pickled fish, olives, anchovies, peppers, etc.

Artichaut (ahr-ti-shów)—Artichoke

Asperges (ah-spaýrge)—Asparagus

Aspic (ah-spéek)—Decorated jellied piece

Aubergines (oh-bare-zhéen)—Eggplant

Au Buerre (o-búrr)—With butter

Au Gratin (oh-grah-tán)—Food covered with a sauce, usually cheese, sprinkled with crumbs and baked

Au Jus (oh-jóo)—With natural gravy

Au Lait (oh-láy)—With milk

Bake—To cook by dry heat, usually in oven

Baked Alaska—Brick ice cream on cake

Baste—To moisten a roast with water, drippings, or seasoned sauce while it is roasting to prevent drying out

Bearnaise (bair-nez)—In America, a sauce similar to Hollandaise, fortified with meat glaze, and with tarragon flavor predominating

Bechamal (báy-shaw-mel)—Cream sauce

Beurre (burr)—Butter

Beurre Noir (burr nwáh)—Browned butter

Bien Cuit (be-en-kẃi)—Well-done (meats)

Bifteck (bíf-teck)—Beefsteak

267

Bisque (beesk)—Thick, rich soup

Blanc (blawnk)—White

Blanchi (Blahn-shée)—Blanched

Blanquette (blawn-két)—Stew with white wine

Blintzes—Thin pancakes rolled around a filling of cream cheese, chopped meat, or fruit

Boeuf (böff)—Beef

Bombe (bomb)—Ice cream molded in globular form

Bonne Femme (bon fém)—Literally menas good *wife*. Term used to indicate simple family-style or home-style.

Bouillabaisse (bwée-yuh-baze)—Fish stew

Bouilli (bu-yée)—Boiled; to cook with moist heat, with liquid (at its boiling point) as a surrounding medium

Bouillon (bwee-yawn)—Broth

Bouquetiere (boo-ket-yér)—With mixed vegetables

Bourguignonne (boor-geen-yawn)—With onions and red burgundy wine

Braise—To cook slowly in a small amount of liquid

Brochettes (broshetté)—Meat broiled on skewers

Broil—To cook by exposing food to direct intense heat

Brouille (bru-eé)—Scrambled

Brunoise (broon-wáz)—Small diced or shredded vegetables sauteed in butter or fat

Café (kah-fáy)—Coffee

Canard (kah-nahŕ)—Duck

Canape (kah-nah-páy)—Sliced bread used as the base for foods to make small open-faced sandwiches

Caneton (kah-nuh-tawń)—Duckling

Carre (káh-ray)—Rack

Carte du Jour (cárt-du-zhur)—Menu of the day

Celeri (se-le-rée)—Celery

Cepe (sep)—A variety of mushroom

Cervelle (sir-vél)—Brain

Cerises (sir-rée-say)—Cherries

Champignon (shaw-peen-yawn)—Mushroom

Chantilly Cream—Dessert of vanilla whipped cream

Chapon (shah-pawń)—Capon

Chardonnay (shar-doh-nay)—The noble white grape of Burgundy

Chasseur (sha-súr)—Sauteed with mushrooms, shallots, and white wine

Chateaubriand (sha-tó-bree-yawń)—Thick filet mignon

Chaud (show)—Warm, hot

Chou-Fleur (shoo-fluŕe)—Cauliflower

Choux de Bruxelles (shoo-duh-breśael)—Brussel sprouts

Chowder—Thick soup usually made of clams, oysters, or fish; New England style: with milk, cream; Manhattan style: with tomatoes

Chutney—Relish, sweet and highly seasoned, made of chopped vegetables and/or fruit

Cochon (ko-shawń)—Suckling pig

Compote (kawn-pawt́)—Stewed fruit

Consomme (kawn-saw-máy)—Clear soup

Coquille (ko-kée)—Shell for baking

Crème (krem)—Cream

Creme Fouettee (krem-fo-et-táy)—Whipped cream

Crepe (krep)—Pancake

Crevette (kruh-vét)—Shrimp

Crisson (kree-sawń)—Watercress

Croquette (kro-két)—Patty of meat

Croutons (kroo-tawńs)—Diced, fried bread floated on top of soup or used in salads

Cuisine (kwe-zeén)—Kitchen

Deep Fry—To cook in fat as a surrounding medium

Déjeuner (day-zhoo-náy)—Breakfast, lunch

De Jour (du-zhúr)—Of the day

Demi (deh me)—Half or small

Démitasse (day-me-tás)—A small cup or spoon; black coffee Du served in small cup

Diable (dee-abl)—Deviled

Duchesse (du-chéss)—Potatoes mixed with egg and forced through a pastry tube

Echalotes (esh-a-lót)—Shallots

Eclairs (ek-lares)—French choux paste filled with cream and iced

Ecrevisse (ay-kruh-veéce)—Crayfish

Encasserole—Baked or served in an individual dish

En Papillote (en páh-pee-yote)—Baked in an oil papered bag

Entree (én-tray)—Originally, food served between heavy courses; now, generally, the main dish

Entremets (awn-truh-méh)—Sweet; desserts

Epinard (ay-pee-nahr)—Spinach

Escargots (es-kahr-go)—Snails

Faisan (fay-zawn)—Pheasant

Farce (fahrce)—Ground meat

Farci (fahr-sée)—Stuffed

Filet (fee-láy)—Boneless ribbon

Filet Mignon (fee-lay me-nyon)—Tenderloin of beef, choicest cut

Fillet (fill-it)—a cut of fish, sliced lengthwise without the bone

Flambe (flawn-báy)—Flamed

Florentine (flaw-ren-teén)—With spinach

Foie (fwa)—Liver

Foie de Veau (fwa-du-vó)—Calve's liver

Foie Gras (fwa-gráh)—Goose liver

Fondue (fawn-dóo)—Melted cheese; cooked in a pot (e.g., chocolate, broth, ect.)

Fricassee (free-kah-sáy)—Chicken or veal stew

Frit (free)—Deep fat fried

Froid (frwah)—Cold

Fruit (fweet)—Fruit

Fromage (froh-mahge)—Cheese

Fume (foo-máy)—Smoked

Galantine (gäl-än-teén)—Boned meat, fish, or poultry stuffed and pressed in a symmetrical shape

Garni (gahr-née)—Garnished

Gateau (gah-tóe)—Cake

Gelee (zhuh-láy)—Jelly

Gigot (zhee-gó)—Leg of lamb

Glace (glah-sáy)—Glazed, iced, frosted

Goulash—Stewed beef or veal seasoned with paprika (Hungarian specialty)

Gratine (grah-tee-náy)—With breadcrumbs

Grill—To cook by direct heat, normally over a heavy cast steel or aluminum grill plate

Haricot (ah-ree-kó)—Bean

Haricot Vert (ah-ree-ko-ver)—String (green) bean

Hollandaise (aw-lawn-déz)—Sauce made from egg yolk, melted butter, and lemon

Homard (oh-már)—Lobster

Hors d'oeuvres (or-durvé)—Predinner tidbits

Huitre (wheatr)—Oyster

Jambon (zhahm-bawn)—Ham

Jardiniere (zhahr-dan-yér)—With vegetable

Julienne (zhool-yén)—Thin strips

Jus (zhoo)—Juice, gravy

Kabob—Pieces of meat (usually lamb or beef) broiled on a skewer

Lait (lay)—Milk

Langouste (lawn-goóst)—Sea crayfish or rock lobster

Langue (long)—Tongue

Legumes (lay-goóm)—Vegetables

Lyonnaise Potatoes—Sauteed with onions

Maître D'Hôtel (Maytr-doe-téll)—With spiced butter

Marinate—To allow food to soak or steep in a marinade so flavoring is absorbed

Marmite (mahr-méet)—Pot; stew

Meringue (meh-ráng)—Beaten egg white

Meuniere (moon-yér)—Pan fried and served with brown butter

Mignon (mee-yawn)—Dainty

Minestrone (mi-na-stŕo-ne)—Italian vegetable soup with noodles and cheese

Mornay (mornáy)—Cheese sauce

Mousse (moose)—Whipped foam

Naturel (nah-tew-rél)—Plain

Noir (nwah)—Black

Noisette (nwah-zét)—Hazelnut

Nouille (noo-ée)—Noodle

Oeuf (uf)—Egg

Oignon (awn-yawn)—Onion

Pain (pan)—Bread

Panache (pah-nash)—Mixed vegetables

Paner (paney)—Covered with bread crumbs

Pate (pah-táy)—Meat pie; sieved or mashed meat, fish, or vegetables bound with aspic

Patisserie (pah-tee-súh-ree)—Pastry

Peche (pesh)—Peach

Petit (puh-tée)—Small

Poire (pwahr)—Pear

Pois (pwah)—Peas

Poisson (pwah-sawn)—Fish

Pomme (paum)—Apple

Pomme de Terre (paum duh tér)—Potato

Potage (pah-tahǵe)—Soup

Pot au Feu (paw-toe-fóo)—Broiled beef with a variety of vegetables and broth served as a meal

Poulet (poo-láy)—Chicken

Prix fixe (prée feeks)—Complete meal at a fixed price; table d'hôte

Printaniere, a la (preen-taun-yér)—Meat dishes garnished with early spring or mixed vegetables

Prosciutto (pra-zhoóto)—Italian ham specially processed, very salty, often served with melon

Provencale, a la (pro-ven-sál)—Describes preparation characterized by tomato and garlic mixture

Puree (poo-ráy)—Sieved food

Quennelle (kuh-nél)—Forcemeat

Quiche (keesh)—Tart or piecrust filled with egg yolks, cream, and cheese, and baked (served hot)

Ragout (rah-góo)—Stew

Ris (ree)—Sweetbreads (see sweetbreads)

Riz (ree)—Rice

Roast—Originally, to cook on a spit, now the same as baking when applied to meat

Rognon (rawn-yawn)—Kidney

Rossole (rus-soúl)—Browned

Rôti (ro-tee)—Roasted

Russe (roos)—Russian

Sâlade (salahd)—Salad

Saumon (saw-moñe)—Salmon

Sauté (saw-táy)—Pan fried

Selle (sell)—Saddle

Shallots—Onion-like plant whose bulbs resemble garlic but are milder

Sorbet (sawr-báy)—Sherbet (ice)

Souffle (soo-fláy)—Whipped pudding made of egg whites and baked in the oven

Steep—To soak in a liquid below boiling point to extract flavor

Sweetbreads (ris)—The thymus gland of a young animal (calf) used for food; choice delicacy

Table d'hôte (tah-bla-dóte)—Meal served in several courses at set price

Tasse (tahce)—Cup

Tortue (tor-tóo)—Tortoise, turtle

Tournedos (toor-nuh-dó)—Two small tenderloin steaks

Tripe (tryp)—Lining of beef stomach

Truite (trew-eét)—Trout

Truffles (troof)—Fungus-like mushrooms which grow underground, chiefly in France

Veau (vo)—Veal

Vapeur (va-puŕr)—Steamed

Veloute (vuh-loo-táy)—White sauce made from fish, chicken, or veal stock

Vichyssoise (vee-shee-swah´z)—Hot or cold potato and leek soup

Vin (və)—Wine

Vinaigre (vin-ay-grr)—Vinegar

Vinaigrette (vee-nay-grét)—Dressing with oil, vinegar, and herbs

Volaille (vo-lié)—Poultry

Vol Au Vent (vole-oh-vawń)—Patty shell

Wine

Alsace (Ahl-zahss)—Region in northeastern France

Anjou (Ahn-zhóo)—Area in the Loire Valley

Appelation Contrôlee (Ah pel-ah-s'yohńg Kohn-tro-láy)—Guarantee of place and quality

Asti Spumante (Ah́-stee Spoo-mah́n-tee)—A sparkling white wine from Piedmont in Italy

Auslese (Oẃss-leh-zeh)—Select picking of fully ripened grapes

Avignon (Ah-veen-yoń)—Major city in Cotes du Rhone

Bandol (Bahn-dóhl)—A red wine from Cotes de Provence

Barbaresco (Bar-ba-réss-ko)—Red wine from Piedmont

Barbera (Bar-béh-ra)—Red wine/grape from Piedmont

Bardolino (Bar-doh-lée-no)—A Veronese red wine

Barolo (Ba-ró-lo)—A fine wine from Piedmont

Batard-Montrachet (Ba-tar-Mohńg-ra-shay)—White Grand Cru in Puligny-Montrachet

Beaujolais (Bo-sho-láy)—Major red wine region of Southern Burgundy

Beaune (Bone)—The capital of Burgundy

Beerenauslese (Beh-ren-oẃss-leh-zeh)—Individually selected overripe grapes

Bereich (Bay-rye'kh)—A smaller district within a Gebeit (Germany)

Bernkastel (Beh́rn-kas-tel)—The chief vineyard city of the Middle Moselle

Bernkasteler Doktor (Behrn-kast-ler Dohk-tór)—World-famous vineyard in Bernkastel

Blanc (Blohng)—White

Blanc Fume (Blohng Fu-may)—The Sauvignon Blanc from the Loire

Blanchot (Blawng-shó)—Grand Cru in Chablis

Bocksbeutel (Box-boy-tel)—The flat-sided squat bottle used in Franconia (similar to Mateus bottle)

Bordeaux (Bor-dóh)—Major city in Gironde

Brouilly (Broo-yée)—Largest commune in Beaujolais

Cabernet Sauvignon (Ka-behr-nay So-veen-yoh́ng)—The most important grape of Bordeaux

Campania (Kahm-pah́n-ya)—A department in southern Italy

Carbonnieux (Kar-bohn-yúh)—A classified growth in Graves (white)

Chablis (Sha-blée)—White wine region north of the Cote d'Or

Chambertin (Shawm-behr-tah́ng)—Red Grand Cru in Gevrey-Chambertin

Champagne (Shawm-pih́e)—The vineyard region northeast of Paris

Charmes (Sharm)—White Premier Cru in Meursault

Chassagne-Montrachet (Sha-sign-Mohng-ra-sháy)—White wine commune in the Cote de Beaune

Chateau (Sha-tō)—Named vineyards in Bordeaux

Chateauneuf-du-Pape (Sha-toh-nuh́f du Pahp)—Red wine area in the Cotes du Rhone

Cheval Blanc (Shuh-vah́l Blohng)—A First Great Classified Growth of St. Emilion

Chevalier-Montrachet (Shuh-vahl-yáy Mohngra-sháy)—White Grand Cru in Puligny-Montrachet

Chianti (K'yah́n-tee)—Famous red wine from Tuscany

Chianti Classico (K'yah́n-tee Kla-see-ko)—Superior Chianti

Commune (ko-muńe)—Vineyard area in the Cote d'Or

Corvo (Kor-vo)—A fine "chateau-bottled" red wine (Sicily)

Cote Chalonnais (Koht Sha-lohn-náy)—Northwestern region of Southern Burgundy

Cote de Beaune (Koht duh Bońe)—The southern region of the Cote d'Or

Cote de Beaune-Village (Koht duh Bońe-Vee-láhj)—Appellation for Cote de Beaune (red)

Cote de Brouilly (Koht duh Broo-yée)—A superior commune in Beaujolais

Cote de Nuits (Koht duh N'wee)—Northern region of the Cote d'Or

Cote de Nuits-Villages (Koht duh N'wee-Vee-láhj)—Appellation for Cote de Nuits (red)

Cote d'Or (Koht dor)—The heart of the Burgundy region

Cotes de Provence (Koht duh Pro-vawńss)—The wine region of Provence

Cote Maconnais (Koht Ma-ko-nay)—North central region of Southern Burgundy

Cotes du Rhone (Koht du Rohn)—Vineyard region in the Rhone Valley

Coutet (Koo-tay)—A classified first growth in Sauternes

Criots (Les) (Cree-yó)—White Grand Cru in Puligny-Montrachet

Dom Perignon (Dohm Pay-reen-yoh́ng)—The Benedictine monk famous in Champagne

Edelbeerenauslese (Eh-del-beh́r-en-ośss-leh-zeh)—Extraordinary individual overripe grapes

Eiswein (Iće-vine)—Perfectly ripened, partially frozen grapes

Emilia-Romagna (Ay-meél-ya Ro-mahn-ya)—A region in north central Italy

Est! Est! Est! (Est Est Est)—A delightful white wine from Montefiascone

Frascati (Fra-sḱa-tee)—A strong red wine from Latium

Fuisse (Fwee-sáy)—White wine village in the Cote Maconnais

Gamay (Ga-máy)—A red wine grape used mainly in Beaujolais

Gevrey-Chambertin (Zhev-ray-Shawn-bair-teńg)—The largest commune in the Cote de Nuits

Gewurztraminer (Guh-vurts-tra-mee-ner)—A superior quality Traminer

Gironde (Zhee-rawńd)—The major river of Bordeaux

Givry (Zhee-vrée)—A commune in the Cote Chalonnais

Goldtropfchen (Gólt-trupf-shen)—The famous vineyard in Piesport (Moselle)

Graves (Grahv)—A red and white wine district of Bordeaux

Haut-Brion (Oh-Bree-yoh́ng)—A classified first growth in Graves (red)

Hermitage (Air-mee-tah́zh)—Red wine area in the Cotes du Rhone

Himmelreich (Hiḿ-mel-rye'kh)—The most famous vineyard in Graach (Moselle)

Hipping (Hiṕ-ping)—Most famous vineyard in Nierstein (Rheinhesse)

Inferno (Een-faír-no)—A fine red wine from Valtellina (Lombardy)

Johannisberg (Yo-há-niss-bairg)—Town in the Rheingau

Kabinett (Ka-bee-nétt)—First grade of Qualitatswein Mit Pradikat

Lacryma Christi (La-kree-ma Krée-stee)—A still or sparkling white wine from Campania

Lafite-Rothschild (La-feet-Rohts-sheéld)—A classified first growth in Medoc (Pauillac)

Lambrusco (Lahm-bróo-sko)—A slightly carbonated, sweet red wine from Emilia

Lascombes (Lahs-kaẃmb)—A classified second growth in Medoc (Margaux)

La Tache (La Tahsh)—Red Grand Cru in Vosne-Romanee

Latour (La-toor)—A classified first growth in Medoc (Pauillac)

La Tour Blanche (La Toor Blawnsh)—A classified first growth in Sauternes

Lenchen (Lén-shen)—The most famous vineyard in Oestrich (Rheingau)

Leognan (Lay-oh-n'yh́ng)—A principal parish in Graves

Leoville-Barton (Lay-oh-veél Bar-toh́ng)—A classified second growth in Medoc (St. Julien)

Margaux (Mär go)—A region in Bordeau

Medoc (May dok)—A region in Bordeau

Montagny (Mohng-tahn-vée)—A commune in Cote Chalonnais

Montrachet (Le) (Mohng-ra-sháy)—White Grand Cru in Puligny-Montrachet

Monts des Milieu (Mohng day Meel-yúh)—A Premier Cru in Chablis

Moselblumchen (Mó-sel-blum-chen)—A blended wine—Liebfraumilch of the Moselle

Moulin-a-Vent (Moo-leng-ah-Veng)—The best known commune in Beaujolais

Mouton-Rothschild (Moo-tohng-Roht-sheél)—A classified second growth in Medoc (Pauillac)

Muscadet (Muss-ka-dáy)—Vineyard region of the Loire Valley

Musigny (Les) (Mu-zeen-yée)—Red Grand Cru in Chambolle-Musigny

Nebbiolo (Nebb-yó-lo)—A red wine grape of Italy

Nierstein (Néer-shtine)—A vineyard village of the Rheinhesse

Nuits St. Georges (N'wee Seng-Zhorzh)—A red wine commune in Cote de Nuits

Orvieto Abbocatto (Orv-yay-toh Ahb-bo-ká-toh)—Slightly fruity white wine from Umbria

Orvieto Secco (Orv-yáy-toh Sék-ko)—Dry white wine from Umbria

Pauillac (Pohl-yah́k)—A principal parish in the Haut-Medoc

Pavie (Pa-vée)—A first great classified growth in St. Emilion

Pessac (Pess-sah́k)—A principal parish in Graves

Petit Chablis (Puh-tee-Sha-blée)—A lesser appellation in Chablis

Petit-Village (Puh-tee Vee lahźh)—A first growth in Pomerol

Petrus (Pay-truss)—A great first growth in Pomerol

Piedmont (Peéd-mont)—A region in northeast Italy

Piesport (Peéss-port)—Vineyard village of the Middle Moselle

Pinot Noir (Pee-nó N'war)—The noble red grape of Burgundy

Pomerol (Po-may-ról)—A red wine district of Bordeaux

Pommard (Po-már)—The best known commune in Cote de Beaune

Pouilly-Fuisse (Poo-yée-Fwee-sáy)—Famous white wine from Cote Maconnais

Pouilly-Fume (Poo-yée-Fu-máy)—The important wine from the Loire Valley

Preuses (Les) (Pruhz)—A Grand Cru in Chablis

Provence (Pro-vengss)—The vineyard region of the French Riviera

Puligny-Montrachet (Pu-leen-yée Mohng-ra-shay)—White wine commune in Cote de Beaune

Qualitatswein (Kua-lee-taits-vine)—Superior German table wine (quality wine)

Rheims (Rengss)—The capital of the Champagne region

Rheingau (Rine-g'ow)—A vineyard area on the Rhine

Rheinhesse (Rine-hess-seh)—A vineyard area on the Rhine

Rheinpfalz (Palatinate) (Rine-pfahlz)—A vineyard area on the Rhine

Richebourg (Le) (Reesh-boórg)—Red Grand Cru in Vosne-Romanee

Riesling (Rees-ling)—The noble grape in Alsace and Germany

Rieussec (R'yuh-sék)—A classified first growth in Sauternes

Romanee (La) (Ro-ma-náy)—Red Grand Cru in Vosne-Romanee

Romanee-Conti (La) (Ro-ma-náy—Kohn-tée)—Red Grand Cru in Vosne-Romanee

Romanee-St. Vivant (Ro-ma-náy Seng-Vee-vaŋ́g)—Red Grand Cru in Vosne-Romanee

Rose d'Anjou (Ro-zay dahn-zhóo)—A Vin Rose from Anjou (Loire)

Rudesheimer Berg (Róo-dess-him-er Bairg)—Finest vineyards in Rudesheim (Rheingau)

Rugiens (Les) (Ru-zhéng)—Red Premier Cru in Pommard

Ruwer (Ru-ver)—A vineyard area of the Upper Moselle

Saar (Zar)—A vineyard area of the Upper Moselle

Saint-Amour (Seng Ta-moór)—The northernmost commune in Beaujolais

Saint-Marc (Sahng-már)—A classified great growth in Barsac (Sauternes)

Santenay (Sahng-tuh-náy)—Southernmost commune in the Cote de Beaune

Santenots (Les) (Sahn-tuh-nó)—Red Premier Cru in Volnay

Sassella (Sahs-sél-la)—A fine red wine from Valtellina (Lombardy)

Saumer (So-mur)—An important white wine of the Loire

Sauternes (So-taírn)—White wine region of Bordeaux

Sauvignon Blanc (so-vee-yoh́ng Blahng)—Major white wine grape of the Graves

Scharzhof (Shárts-hohf)—A famous estate in Wiltingen (Saar)

Schloss Johannisberg (Shlohss Yó-ha-nis-bairg)—Most famous vineyard of Johannisberg (Rheingau)

Schloss Vollrads (Shlohss Fóhl-rahts)—Most famous vineyard of Winkel (Rheingau)

Sekt (Sekt)—Sparkling wine from Germany

Semillon (Say-meel-yoh́ng)—Major grape of the Sauternes

Sicily (Siś-sil-ly)—Island region at southern tip of Italy

Soave (So-áh-vay)—A Veronese white wine

Sonnenuhr (Zoh-nen-oor)—Most famous vineyard in Wehlen (Moselle)

Spatlese (Shpáyt-leh-seh)—Late-picked fully ripened grapes

Steinberg (Shtíine-bairg)—Most famous vineyard in Hattenheim (Rheingau)

Steinwein (Shtíine-vine)—The generic name for Franconian wines

St. Emilion (Seng-tay-meel-yohŋ́g)—Red wine district of Bordeaux

St. Estephe (Seng-tes-téff)—A principal parish in the Haut-Medoc

St. Julien (Seng-zhul-yeńg)—A principal parish in the Haut-Medoc

Strasbourg (Strahss-boórg)—The capital of Alsace

Sylvaner (Sil-vá-ner)—White wine grape used in Alsace and Germany

Syrah (See-rá)—Red wine grape of the Cotes Du Rhone

Tafelwein (Táh-fel-vine)—Ordinary German table wine (table wine)

Tavel (Ta-vél)—Vin Rose commune in the Cotes du Rhone

Teurons (Les) (Toor-ohŋ́g)—Red Premier Cru in Beaune

Tiergarten (Teér-gar-ten)—An important vineyard in Trier (Ruwer)

Traminer (Trá-min-ner)—White wine grape used mainly in Alsace

Trier (Trée-yer)—An important city on the Moselle

Trockenbeeren (Tró-ken-be-ren)—Semi-dried or shriveled grapes

Trockenbeerenauslese (Owśs-leh-zeh)—Select picking of shriveled grapes

Tuscany (Tuśs-ca-nee)—A region in central Italy

Valmur (Vahl-mur)—A Grand Cru in Chablis

Valpolicella (Vahl-po-lee-chél-la)—Veronese red wine

Vaudesir (Voday-zeér)—A Grand Cru in Chablis

Verdicchio (Vair-deék-yo)—A pale white wine

Verona (Veh-ró-na)—A region in Northern Italy

*Vieux-Chateau-Certan (V'yuh-Sha-tóh-Sair-tahńg)—A great first growth in Pomerol

Villefranche (Veel-frawńsh)—Main city of Beaujolais

———————

* Denotes Chateau

Vin Rose (Ve Ro-záy)—A light rose-colored wine

Vin Santo (Veen Sahn-toh)—A white dessert wine from Tuscany

Volnay (Vohl-náy)—Red wine commune in Cote de Beaune

Volnay-Santenots (Vohl-nay Sahn-tuh-nó)—Red Premier Cru in Volnay

Vosne-Romanee (Vone Ro-ma-náy)—Red wine commune in the Cote de Nuits

Vougeot (Voo-zhóh)—Red wine commune in the Cote de Nuits

Vouvray (Voov-ráy)—Important white wine in the Coteaux de Touraine (Loire)

Wurzburg (Vúrts-boorg)—The main city of Franconia

Yquem (d') (Dĭ-keèm)—The classified superior first growth (Sauternes)

Zeller Schwarze Katz (Tséll-er Shvar-tseh Kahtz)—The "black cat" wine from Zell (Moselle)

Table Arrangements

Any number of arrangements can be made with standard size tables available on the market: rectangular, round, oblong or oval, serpentine, quarter-round, half-round, trapezoid. When tables are to be used as display tables (e.g., buffet or gift tables), they should be draped (i.e., a ruffled or straight cloth should be attached from the edge of the table and this should extend to the floor). The front side of a head table should also be draped.

Tables used for eating, discussion, conference, etc., or where guests will be seated should not be draped, and the tablecloth should extend a minimum of 10 inches beyond the table's edge. The tablecloth should not touch the floor. For large banquets tables may also be placed on elevated platforms. This will break up the monotony of the room and will provide those guests at the rear of the room with a better view of the head table and speaker.

For conferences or meetings, tables should be set with water glasses and water pitchers as well as ashtrays and matches. It would be foolish to specify the number of ashtrays required as different groups will have different habits, and the total time the participants will spend in the room without breaks must be taken into consideration. Additionally the number of staff servicing the meeting will determine the number of ashtrays and amount of water that should be preset. For large functions, tables with water or other refreshments may be set at strategic locations around the room.

The author recommends that a plan be drawn (to scale) for each function room and each banquet room, which includes obstructions (e.g., columns, permanent fixtures, etc.). The sketch should also show dimensions, entrances (for guests and staff), or any other pertinent information. A template may be cut out (to the *same* scale as the plan drawing) that depicts each table style owned or used by the property. It is much easier to arrange tables on paper than it is to have set up and then have to move a banquet round because it does not fit.

As with dining room setup, a minimum space of two feet or 24 inches by 15 inches deep should be allowed for each person for any function, and the space between the backs of two chairs must also not be less than two feet.

The following table arrangements depict standard tables and can be selected for buffets, gift tables, head tables, small banquets, conferences, dinner meetings, or just meetings. Endless combinations can be sketched, and those depicted below may be increased in size by the symmetric addition of more tables.

Table arrangements for buffet tables, gift tables, head tables, small banquets, conferences, dinner meetings, meetings

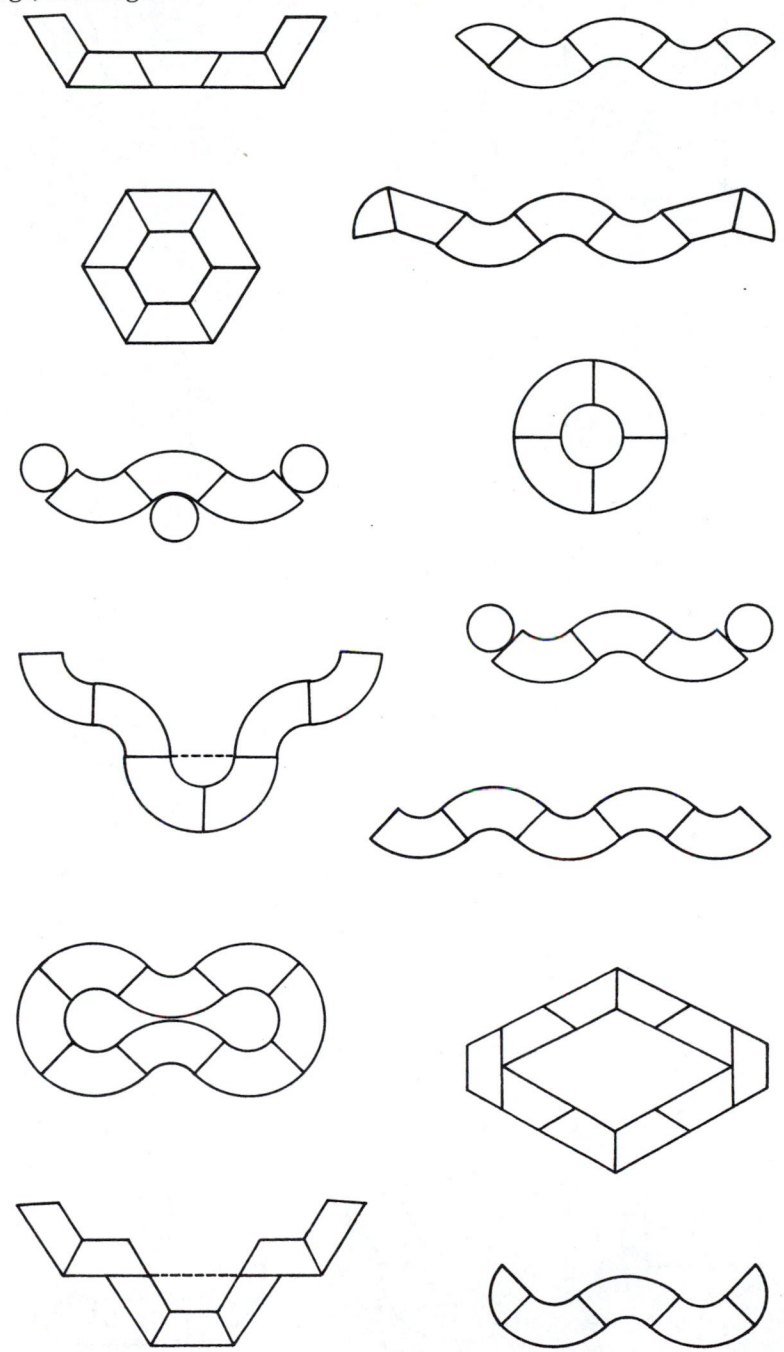

FIGURE B.1 *(Continued)*

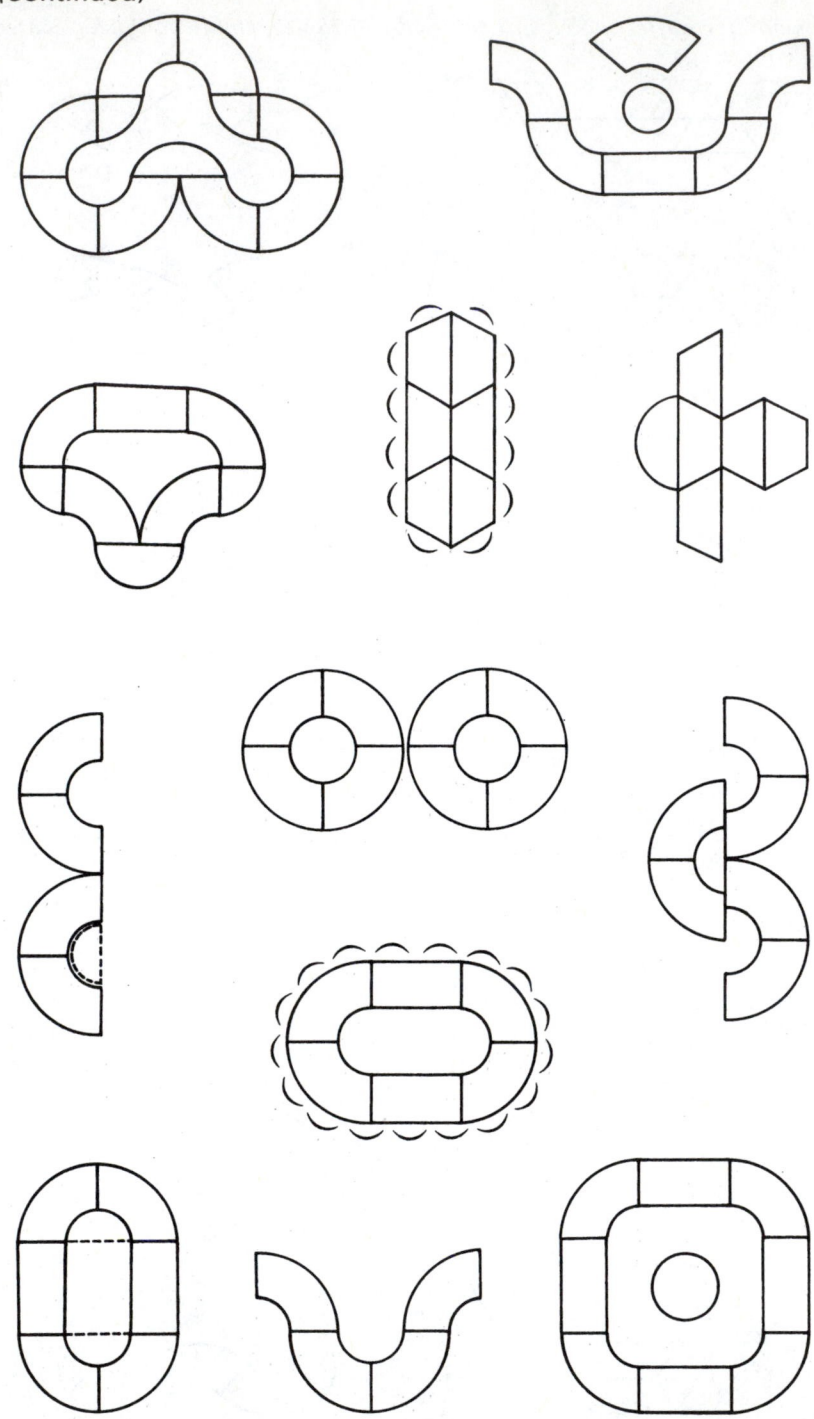

FIGURE B.1 *(Concluded)*

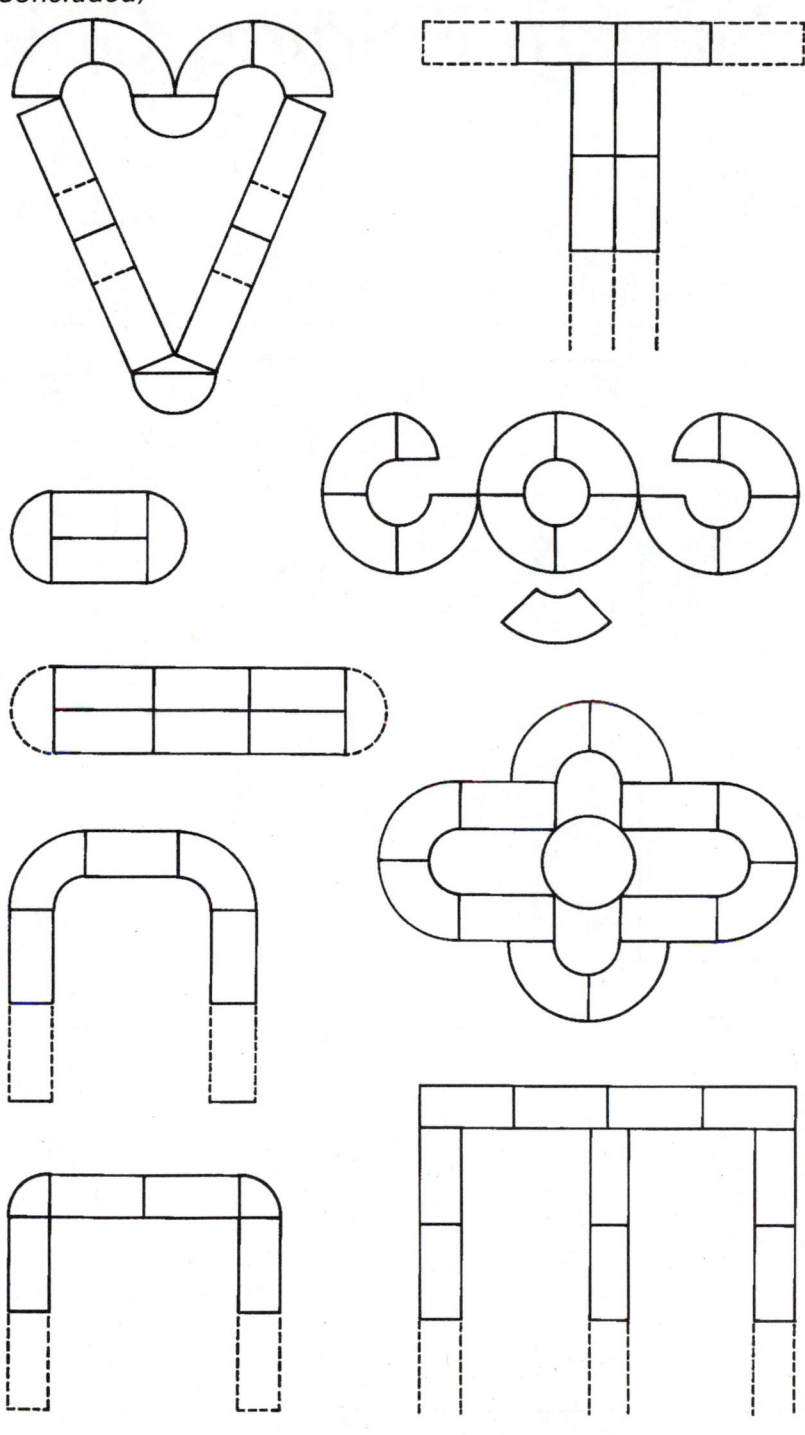

Napkin Folding Guide

FIGURE C.1

The Cumberbund

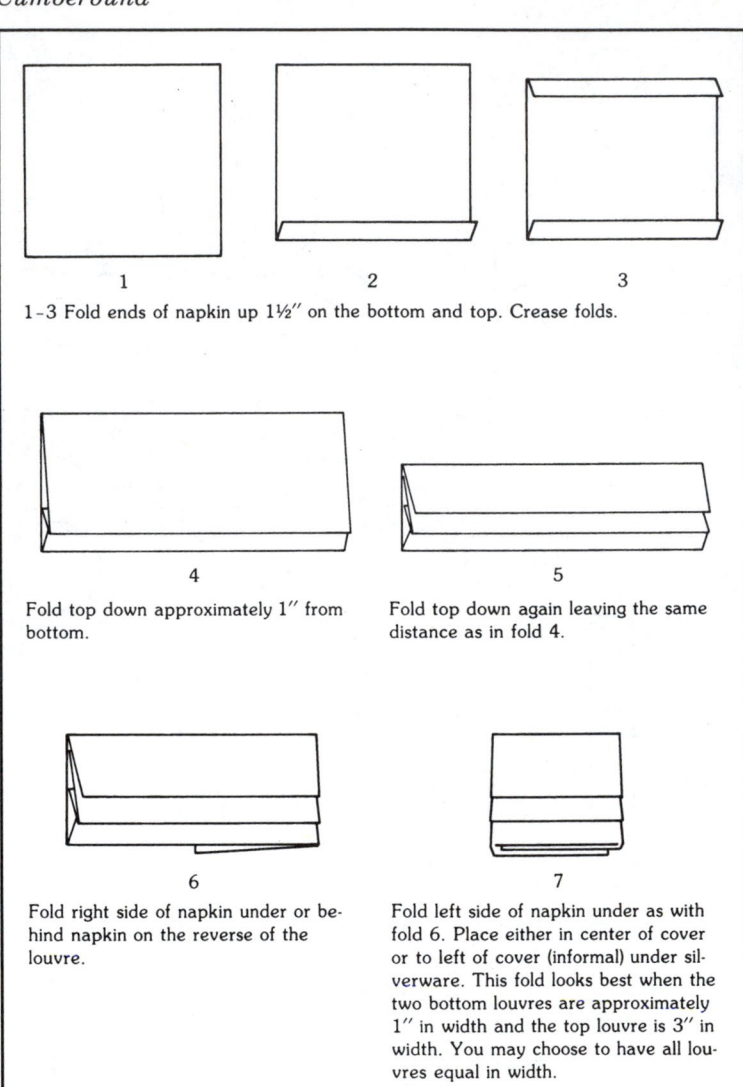

1
2
3

1–3 Fold ends of napkin up 1½″ on the bottom and top. Crease folds.

4

Fold top down approximately 1″ from bottom.

5

Fold top down again leaving the same distance as in fold 4.

6

Fold right side of napkin under or behind napkin on the reverse of the louvre.

7

Fold left side of napkin under as with fold 6. Place either in center of cover or to left of cover (informal) under silverware. This fold looks best when the two bottom louvres are approximately 1″ in width and the top louvre is 3″ in width. You may choose to have all louvres equal in width.

FIGURE C.2

The Escutcheon

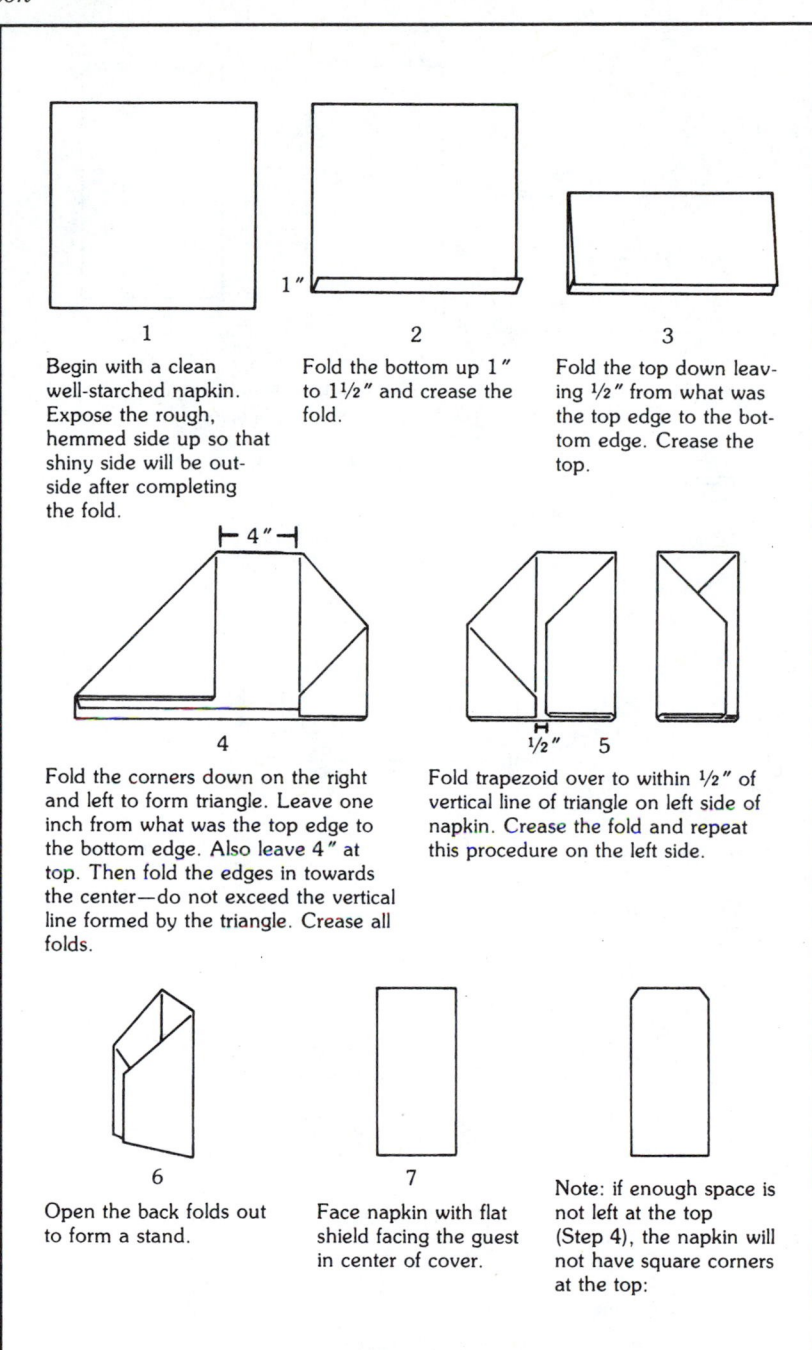

1

Begin with a clean well-starched napkin. Expose the rough, hemmed side up so that shiny side will be outside after completing the fold.

2

Fold the bottom up 1″ to 1½″ and crease the fold.

3

Fold the top down leaving ½″ from what was the top edge to the bottom edge. Crease the top.

4

Fold the corners down on the right and left to form triangle. Leave one inch from what was the top edge to the bottom edge. Also leave 4″ at top. Then fold the edges in towards the center—do not exceed the vertical line formed by the triangle. Crease all folds.

5

Fold trapezoid over to within ½″ of vertical line of triangle on left side of napkin. Crease the fold and repeat this procedure on the left side.

6

Open the back folds out to form a stand.

7

Face napkin with flat shield facing the guest in center of cover.

Note: if enough space is not left at the top (Step 4), the napkin will not have square corners at the top:

FIGURE C.3
Single Fan

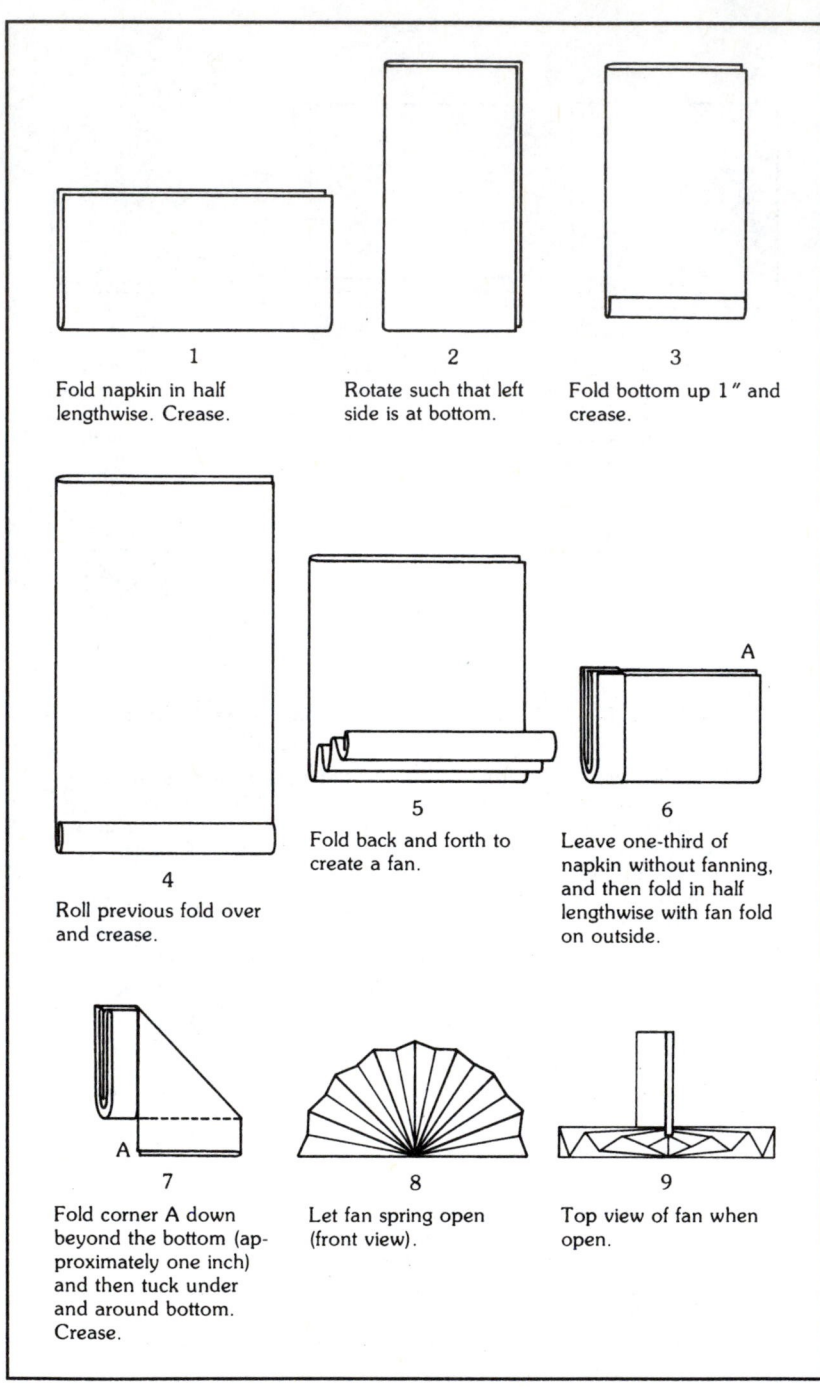

1
Fold napkin in half lengthwise. Crease.

2
Rotate such that left side is at bottom.

3
Fold bottom up 1″ and crease.

4
Roll previous fold over and crease.

5
Fold back and forth to create a fan.

6
Leave one-third of napkin without fanning, and then fold in half lengthwise with fan fold on outside.

7
Fold corner A down beyond the bottom (approximately one inch) and then tuck under and around bottom. Crease.

8
Let fan spring open (front view).

9
Top view of fan when open.

FIGURE C.4

The Double Fan

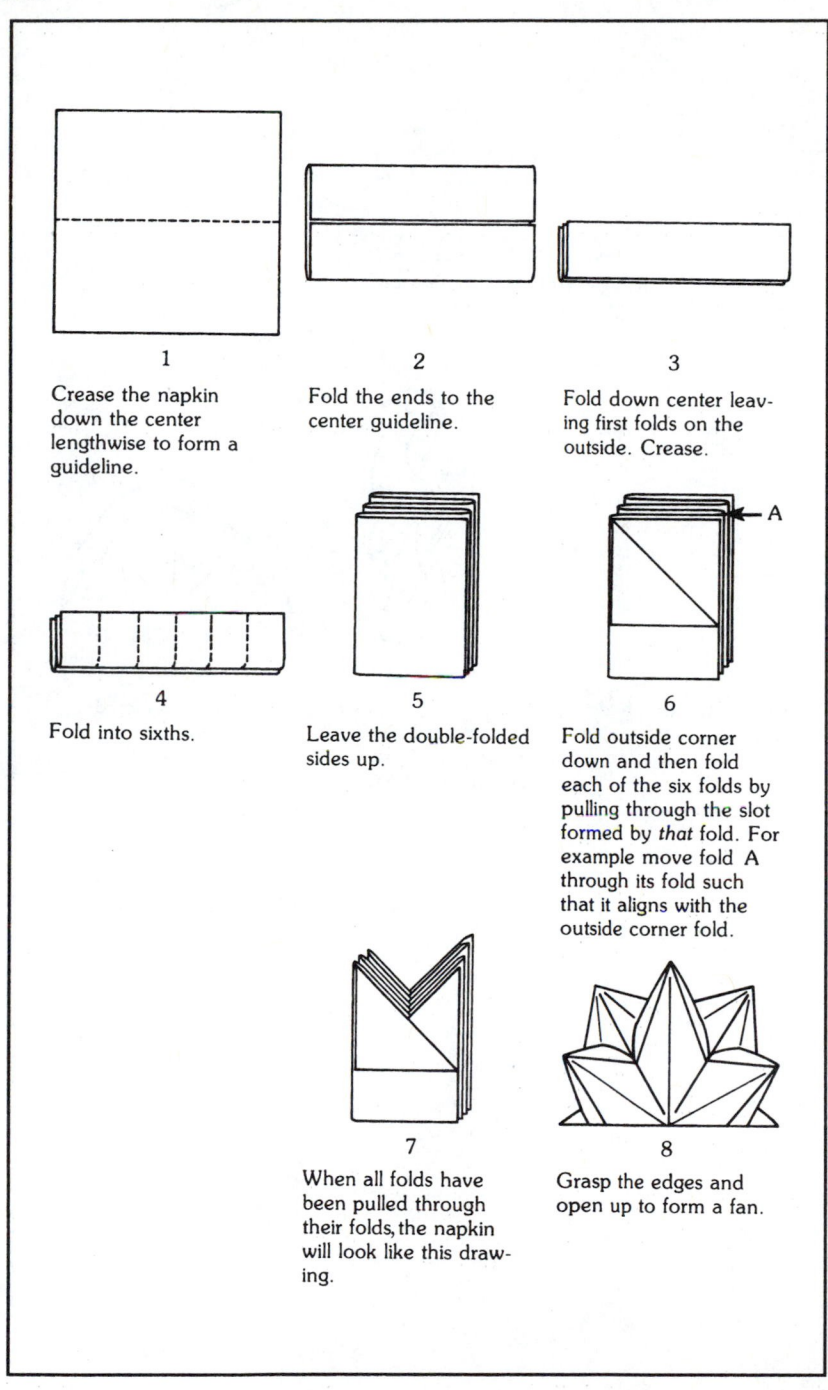

1

Crease the napkin down the center lengthwise to form a guideline.

2

Fold the ends to the center guideline.

3

Fold down center leaving first folds on the outside. Crease.

4

Fold into sixths.

5

Leave the double-folded sides up.

6

Fold outside corner down and then fold each of the six folds by pulling through the slot formed by *that* fold. For example move fold A through its fold such that it aligns with the outside corner fold.

7

When all folds have been pulled through their folds, the napkin will look like this drawing.

8

Grasp the edges and open up to form a fan.

FIGURE C.5

The Ruffled Double Fan

1-4. Follow steps as listed for the double fan.

Top View

Front View

5	6	7
Leave the single folded sides up (opposite side from the double fan).	Pull the *single folds* out to form a ruffle on either side of the straight center fold.	Spread fan centered in the cover.

FIGURE C.6

The Sailboat

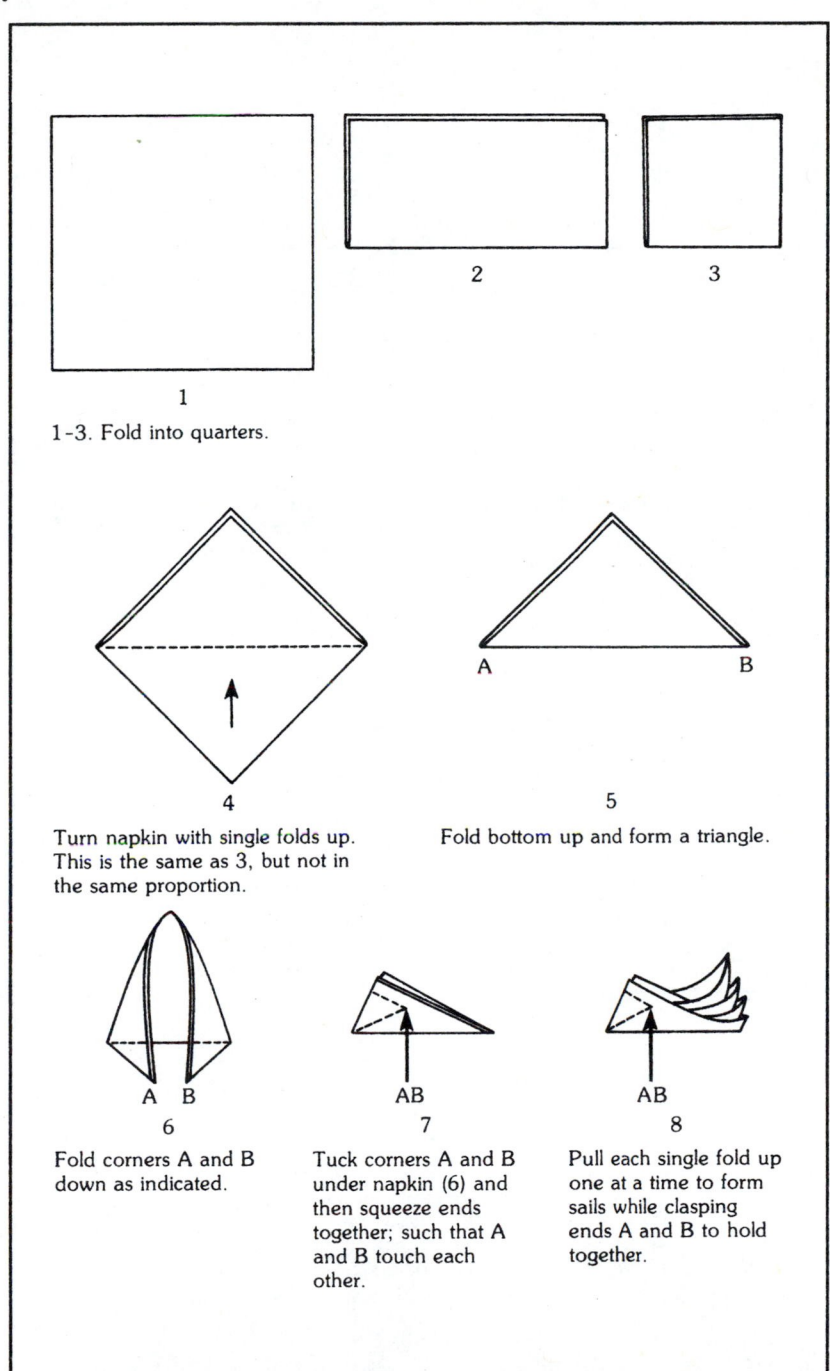

1

2

3

1–3. Fold into quarters.

4

Turn napkin with single folds up. This is the same as 3, but not in the same proportion.

5

Fold bottom up and form a triangle.

A   B

A   B

6

Fold corners A and B down as indicated.

AB

7

Tuck corners A and B under napkin (6) and then squeeze ends together; such that A and B touch each other.

AB

8

Pull each single fold up one at a time to form sails while clasping ends A and B to hold together.

FIGURE C.7
Robin Hood's Hat

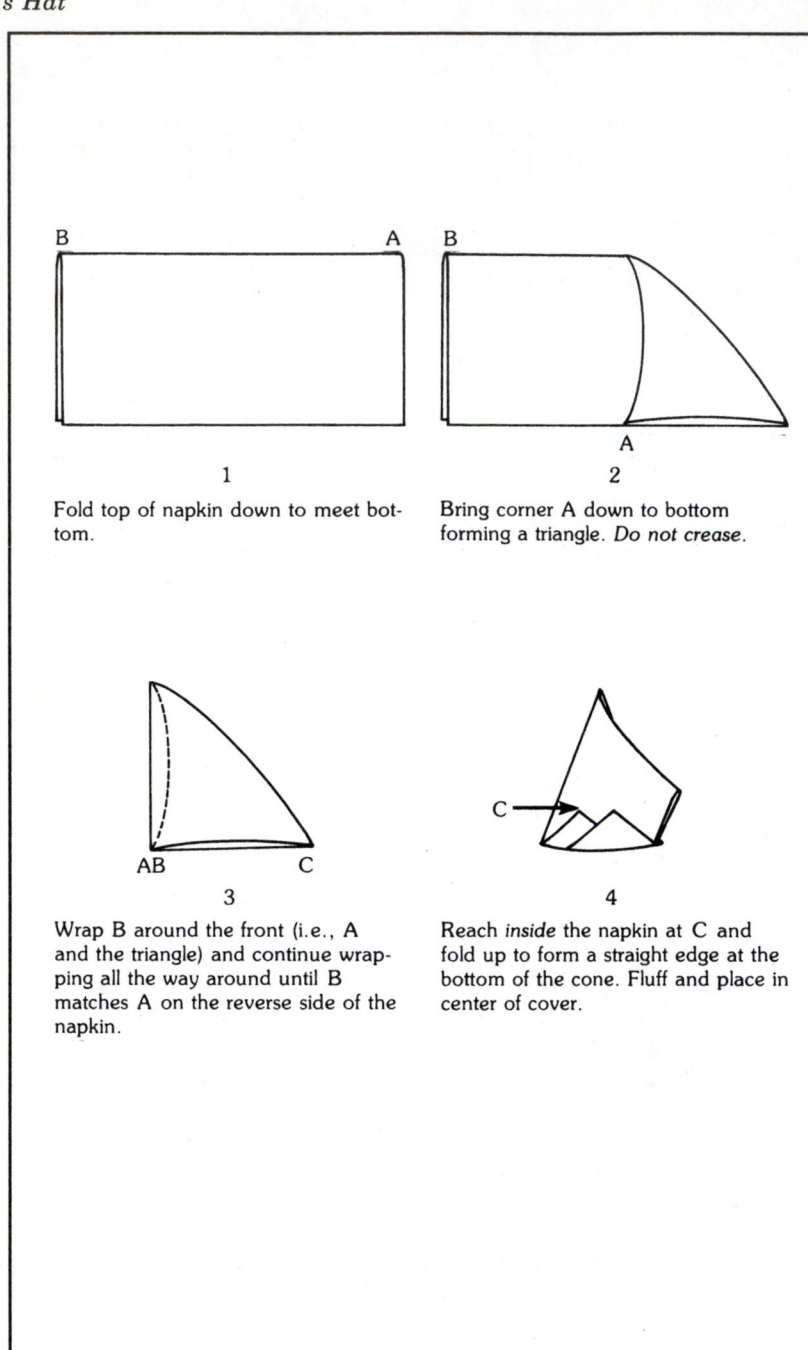

1

Fold top of napkin down to meet bottom.

2

Bring corner A down to bottom forming a triangle. *Do not crease.*

3

Wrap B around the front (i.e., A and the triangle) and continue wrapping all the way around until B matches A on the reverse side of the napkin.

4

Reach *inside* the napkin at C and fold up to form a straight edge at the bottom of the cone. Fluff and place in center of cover.

FIGURE C.8

Fleur De Lis

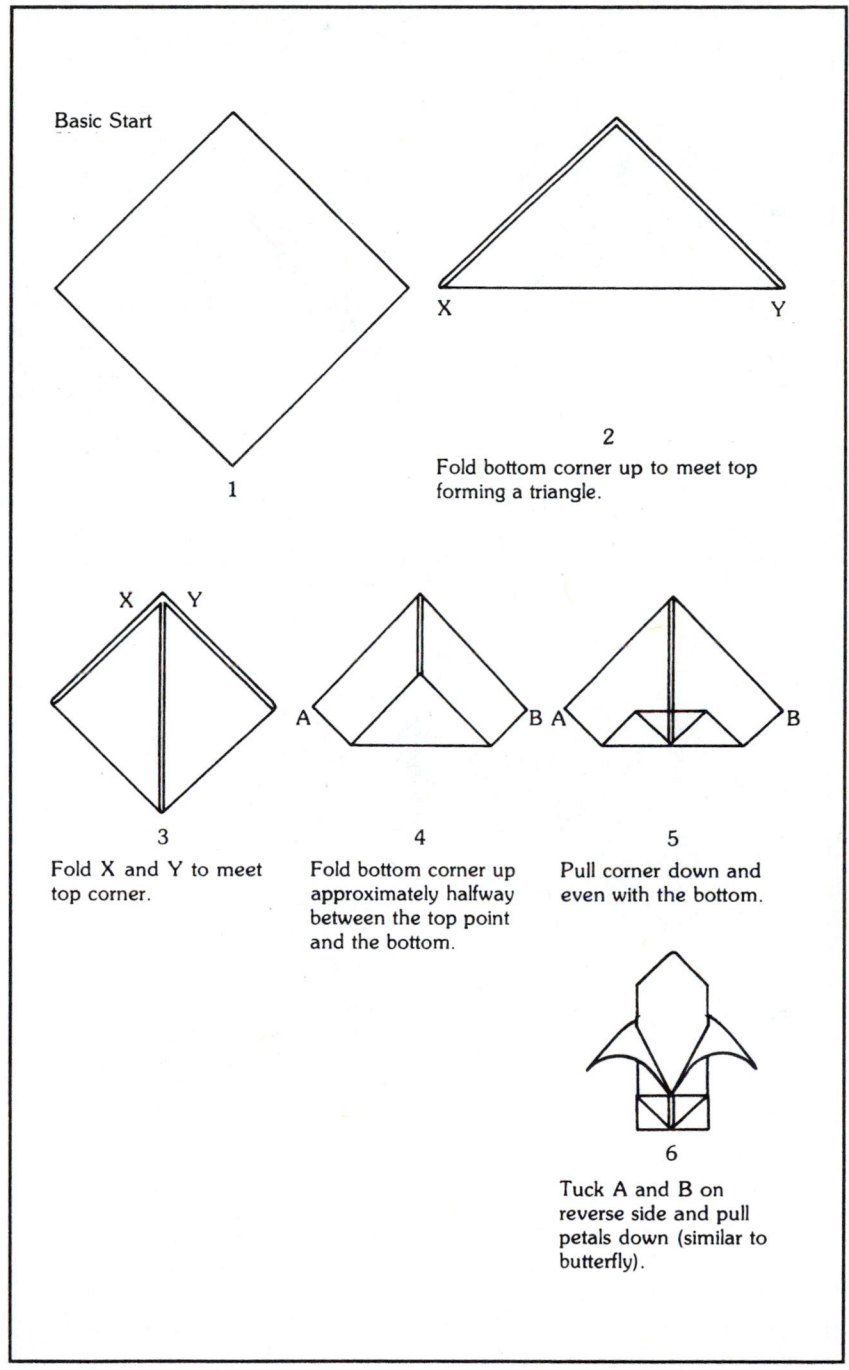

Basic Start

1

2
Fold bottom corner up to meet top forming a triangle.

3
Fold X and Y to meet top corner.

4
Fold bottom corner up approximately halfway between the top point and the bottom.

5
Pull corner down and even with the bottom.

6
Tuck A and B on reverse side and pull petals down (similar to butterfly).

FIGURE C.9

Luncheon Fold

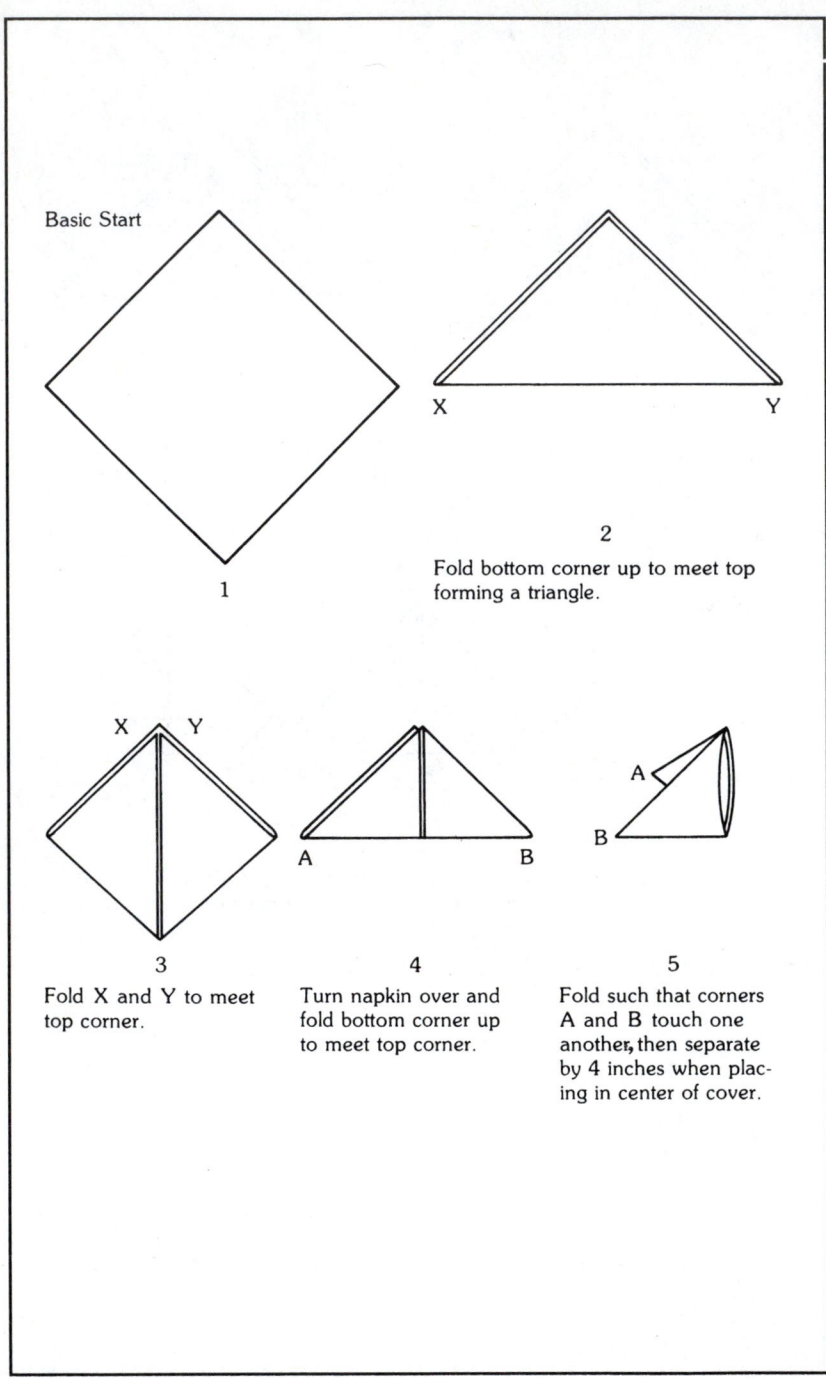

Basic Start

1

2
Fold bottom corner up to meet top forming a triangle.

3
Fold X and Y to meet top corner.

4
Turn napkin over and fold bottom corner up to meet top corner.

5
Fold such that corners A and B touch one another, then separate by 4 inches when placing in center of cover.

FIGURE C.10

Bishop's Hat

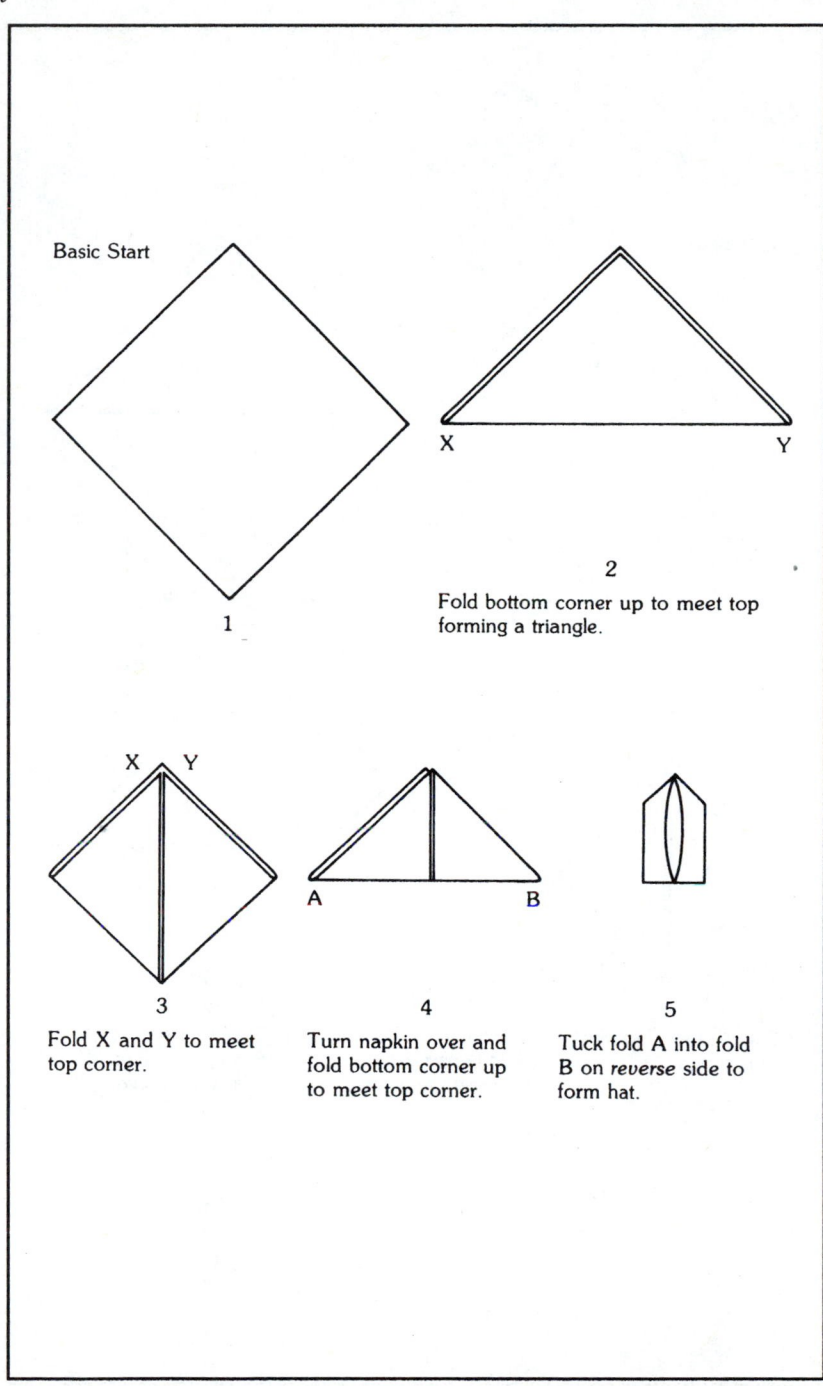

Basic Start

X   Y

1

2
Fold bottom corner up to meet top forming a triangle.

X   Y

A   B

3
Fold X and Y to meet top corner.

4
Turn napkin over and fold bottom corner up to meet top corner.

5
Tuck fold A into fold B on *reverse* side to form hat.

Figure C.11
Butterfly

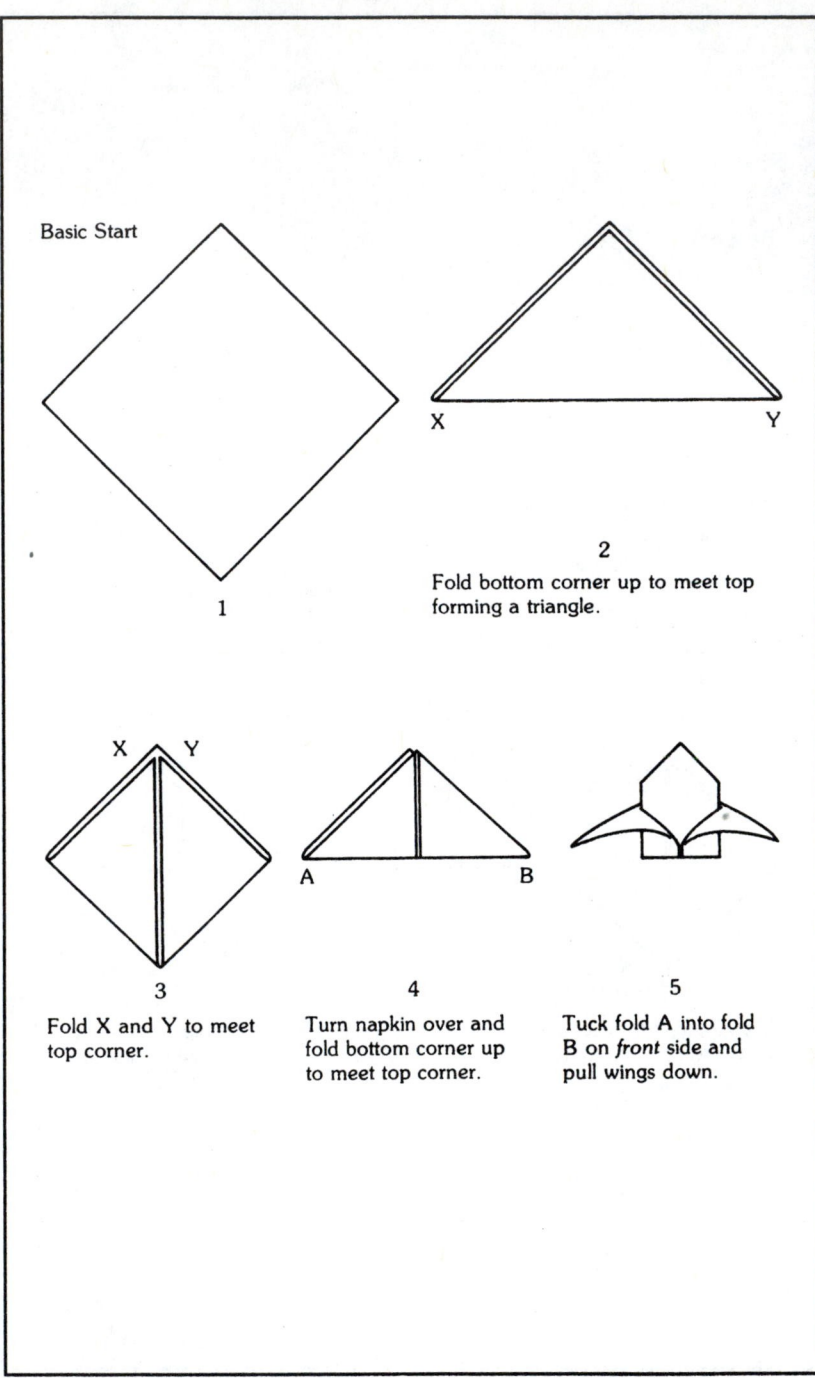

Basic Start

1

2
Fold bottom corner up to meet top forming a triangle.

3
Fold X and Y to meet top corner.

4
Turn napkin over and fold bottom corner up to meet top corner.

5
Tuck fold A into fold B on *front* side and pull wings down.

Metric Conversions for Weights and Measures in the United States and England

Weights and Measures in the United States and Great Britain and Metric Systems

For most purposes the modern units used for measures and weights in the United States are the same as those in Great Britain. The major exception is in the measurement of capacity. In the following tables, therefore, there are three systems for liquid capacity—U.S., British, and metric—instead of the two major systems—U.S.-British combined and metric.

The S.I. system (*Systeme Internationale*) is a refinement of the long-used metric system.

Length

United States Great Britain		Metric or S.I.	
		10 millimeters	= 1 centimeter
12 inches	= 1 foot	10 centimeters	= 1 decimeter
3 feet	= 1 yard	10 decimeters	= 1 meter
1,760 yards	= 1 mile	10 meters	= 1 dekameter
5,280 feet	= 1 mile	10 dekameters	= 1 hectometer
6,080 feet	= 1 nautical mile	10 hectometers	= 1 kilometer

Area

United States Great Britain		Metric or S.I.	
144 square inches	= 1 square foot	100 square centimeters	= 1 square decimeter
9 square feet	= 1 square yard	100 square decimeters	= 1 square meter (centare)
4,840 square yards	= 1 acre	100 square meters	= 1 square dekameter (are)
43,560 square feet	= 1 acre	10,000 square meters	= 1 hectare
640 acres	= 1 square mile	100 hectares	= 1 square kilometer

Volume and Dry Capacity

United States
Great Britain		*Metric or S.I.*	
1,728 cubic inches	= 1 cubic foot	1,000 cubic centimeters	= 1 cubic decimeter
27 cubic feet	= 1 cubic yard	1,000 cubic decimeters	= 1 cubic meter
1 dry pint	= 33.6 cubic inches	1,000 cubic meters	= 1 cubic dekameter
1 dry quart (2 pints)	= 67.201 cubic inches	1,000 cubic dekameters	= 1 cubic hectometer
1 peck (8 quarts)	= 537.6 cubic inches	1,000 cubic hectometers	= 1 cubic kilometer
1 bushel (4 pecks)	= 2,150.42 cubic inches	

Weight

United States
Great Britain
(avoirdupois weight)		*Metric or S.I.*	
437.5 grains	= 1 ounce	1,000 milligrams	= 1 gram
16 ounces	= 1 pound	1,000 grams	= 1 kilogram
100 pounds	= 1 cental	100 kilograms	= 1 quintal
2,000 pounds	= 1 short ton	1,000 kilograms	= 1 metric ton
2,240 pounds	= 1 long ton	

(Also in Great Britain)

14 pounds	= 1 stone
2 stones	= 1 quarter
4 quarters	= 1 hundredweight
20 hundredweights	= 1 long ton

Liquid Capacity

United States		*Metric or S.I.*	*Great Britain*
16 fluid ounces	= 1 pint	10 milliliters	= 1 centiliter
2 pints	= 1 quart	100 centiliters	= 1 liter
4 quarts	= 1 gallon	100 liters	= 1 hectoliter
5 fifths	= 1 gallon	10 hectoliters	= 1 kiloliter
1 fluid ounce	= 1.8 cubic inches	1 milliliter	= 1 cubic centimeter
1 pint	= 28.88 cubic inches	1 liter	= 1,000 cubic centimeters
1 quart	= 57.75 cubic inches	1 hectoliter	= 100,000 cubic centimeters
1 gallon	= 231 cubic inches	

Great Britain

20 fluid ounces	= 1 imperial pint
2 imperial pints	= 1 imperial quart
4 imperial quarts	= 1 imperial gallon*
1 fluid ounce	= 1.735 cubic inches
1 imperial pint	= 34.68 cubic inches
1 imperial quart	= 69.35 cubic inches
1 imperial gallon	= 277.4 cubic inches

* 1.2 American gallons = 1 imperial gallon

APPENDIX E

Temperature Conversions

Degrees Fahrenheit (°F) to Degrees Celsius (°C)*

	°F		°C		°F		°C		°F		°C
+	0	−	17.78	+	60	+	15.56	+	120	+	48.87
	1		17.22		61		16.11		121		49.44
	2		16.67		62		16.67		122		50.00
	3		16.11		63		17.22		123		50.56
	4		15.56		64		17.78		124		51.11
+	5	−	15.00	+	65	+	18.33	+	125	+	51.67
	6		14.44		66		18.89		126		52.22
	7		13.89		67		19.44		127		52.78
	8		13.33		68		20.00		128		53.33
	9		12.78		69		20.56		129		53.89
+	10	−	12.22	+	70	+	21.11	+	130	+	54.44
	11		11.67		71		21.67		131		55.00
	12		11.11		72		22.22		132		55.56
	13		10.56		73		22.78		133		56.11
	14		10.00		74		23.33		134		56.67
+	15	−	9.44	+	75	+	23.89	+	135	+	57.22
	16		8.89		76		24.44		136		57.78
	17		8.33		77		25.00		137		58.33
	18		7.78		78		25.56		138		58.89
	19		7.22		79		26.11		139		63.44
+	20	−	6.67	+	80	+	26.67	+	140	+	60.00
	21		6.11		81		27.22		141		60.56
	22		5.56		82		27.78		142		61.11
	23		5.00		83		28.33		143		61.67
	24		4.44		84		28.89		144		62.22
+	25	−	3.89	+	85	+	29.44	+	145	+	62.78
	26		3.33		86		30.00		146		63.33
	27		2.78		87		30.56		147		63.89
	28		2.22		88		31.11		148		64.44
	29		1.67		89		31.67		149		65.00

Continues

Degrees Fahrenheit (°F) to Degrees Celsius (°C)* *(Concluded)*

Water freezes (32° F) (0° C)

	°F		°C		°F		°C		°F		°C
+	30	−	1.11	+	90	+	32.22	+	150	+	65.56
	31		0.56		91		32.78		151		68.33
	32		0.00		92		33.33		152		71.11
	33	+	0.56		93		33.89		153		73.89
	34		1.11		94		34.44		154		76.67
+	35	+	1.67	+	95	+	35.00	+	155	+	79.44
	36		2.22		96		35.56		156		82.22
	37		2.78		97		36.11		157		85.00
	38		3.33		98		36.67		158		87.78
	39		3.89		99		37.22		159		90.56
+	40	+	4.44	+	100		37.78	+	160	+	93.33
	41		5.00		101		38.33		161		96.11
	42		5.56		102		38.89		162		98.89
	43		6.11		103		39.44		163		101.67
	44		6.67		104		40.00		164		104.44
+	45	+	7.22	+	105	+	40.56	+	165	+	107.22
	46		7.78		106		41.11		166		110.00
	47		8.33		107		41.67		167		112.78
	48		8.89		108		42.22		168		115.56
	49		9.44		109		42.78		169		118.33
+	50	+	10.00	+	110	+	43.33	+	170	+	121.11
	51		10.56		111		43.89		171		123.89
	52		11.11		112		44.44		172		126.67
	53		11.67		113		45.00		173		129.44
	54		12.22		114		45.56		174		132.22
+	55	+	12.78	+	115	+	46.11	+	175		+ 135.00
	56		13.33		116		46.67		176		137.78
	57		13.89		117		47.22		177		140.56
	58		14.44		118		47.78		178		143.33
	59		15.00		119		48.33		179		146.11

Ethyl alcohol boils (173° F) (78.5° C)

Water boils (212° F) (100° C)

The formula used to derive the table is:

$$°C = 5/9 \ (°F - 32)$$

*Degrees Celsius was formerly called degrees Centigrade. The change was made to honor Anders Celsius (1701–1744) in accordance with the scientific custom of naming units of measurement after famous scientists who have contributed to that field.

Index